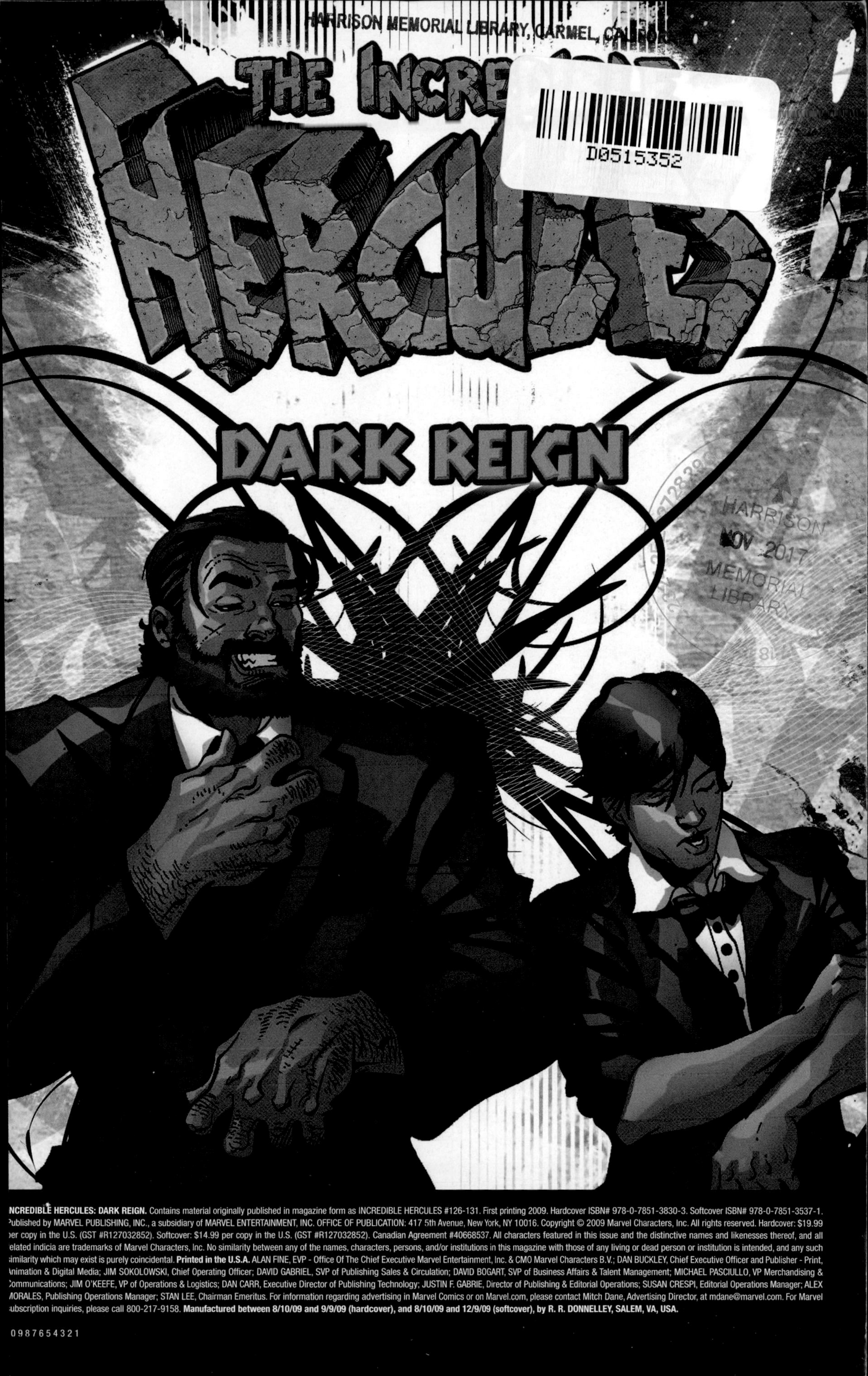
THE INCRE
HERCULES
DARK REIGN

NCREDIBLE HERCULES: DARK REIGN. Contains material originally published in magazine form as INCREDIBLE HERCULES #126-131. First printing 2009. Hardcover ISBN# 978-0-7851-3830-3. Softcover ISBN# 978-0-7851-3537-1. ublished by MARVEL PUBLISHING, INC., a subsidiary of MARVEL ENTERTAINMENT, INC. OFFICE OF PUBLICATION: 417 5th Avenue, New York, NY 10016. Hardcover: $19.99 er copy in the U.S. (GST #R127032852). Softcover: $14.99 per copy in the U.S. (GST #R127032852). Canadian Agreement #40668537. **Printed in the U.S.A.** ALAN FINE, EVP - Office Of The Chief Executive Marvel Entertainment, Inc. & CMO Marvel Characters B.V.; DAN BUCKLEY, Chief Executive Officer and Publisher - Print, nimation & Digital Media; JIM SOKOLOWSKI, Chief Operating Officer; DAVID GABRIEL, SVP of Publishing Sales & Circulation; DAVID BOGART, SVP of Business Affairs & Talent Management; MICHAEL PASCIULLO, VP Merchandising & ommunications; JIM O'KEEFE, VP of Operations & Logistics; DAN CARR, Executive Director of Publishing Technology; JUSTIN F. GABRIE, Director of Publishing & Editorial Operations; SUSAN CRESPI, Editorial Operations Manager; ALEX ORALES, Publishing Operations Manager; STAN LEE, Chairman Emeritus. For information regarding advertising in Marvel Comics or on Marvel.com, please contact Mitch Dane, Advertising Director, at mdane@marvel.com. For Marvel ubscription inquiries, please call 800-217-9158. **Manufactured between 8/10/09 and 9/9/09 (hardcover), and 8/10/09 and 12/9/09 (softcover), by R. R. DONNELLEY, SALEM, VA, USA.**

0 9 8 7 6 5 4 3 2 1

THE INCREDIBLE HERCULES

DARK REIGN

Writers: **FRED VAN LENTE** & **GREG PAK**

Pencils: **RODNEY BUCHEMI, DIETRICH SMITH** & **RYAN STEGMAN**
Inks: **GREG ADAMS, CORY HAMSCHER** & **TERRY PALLOT**
Colors: **VAL STAPLES** & **RAÚL TREVIÑO** with **CHRIS SOTOMAYOR**
Letters: **SIMON BOWLAND** & **VIRTUAL CALLIGRAPHY'S JOE CARAMAGNA**

"THE SEARCH FOR KIRBY"
Art: **TAKESHI MIYAZAWA**
Colors: **CHRISTINA STRAIN**
Letters: **VIRTUAL CALLIGRAPHY'S JOE CARAMAGNA**

Cover Artists: **ED MCGUINNESS** & **DAVID WILLIAMS** with **GURU EFX**
Assistant Editor: **JORDAN D. WHITE**
Associate Editor: **NATHAN COSBY**
Editor: **MARK PANICCIA**

Collection Editor: **CORY LEVINE**
Assistant Editors: **ALEX STARBUCK** & **JOHN DENNING**
Editors, Special Projects: **JENNIFER GRÜNWALD** & **MARK D. BEAZLEY**
Senior Editor, Special Projects: **JEFF YOUNGQUIST**
Senior Vice President of Sales: **DAVID GABRIEL**

Editor in Chief: **JOE QUESADA**
Publisher: **DAN BUCKLEY**
Executive Producer: **ALAN FINE**

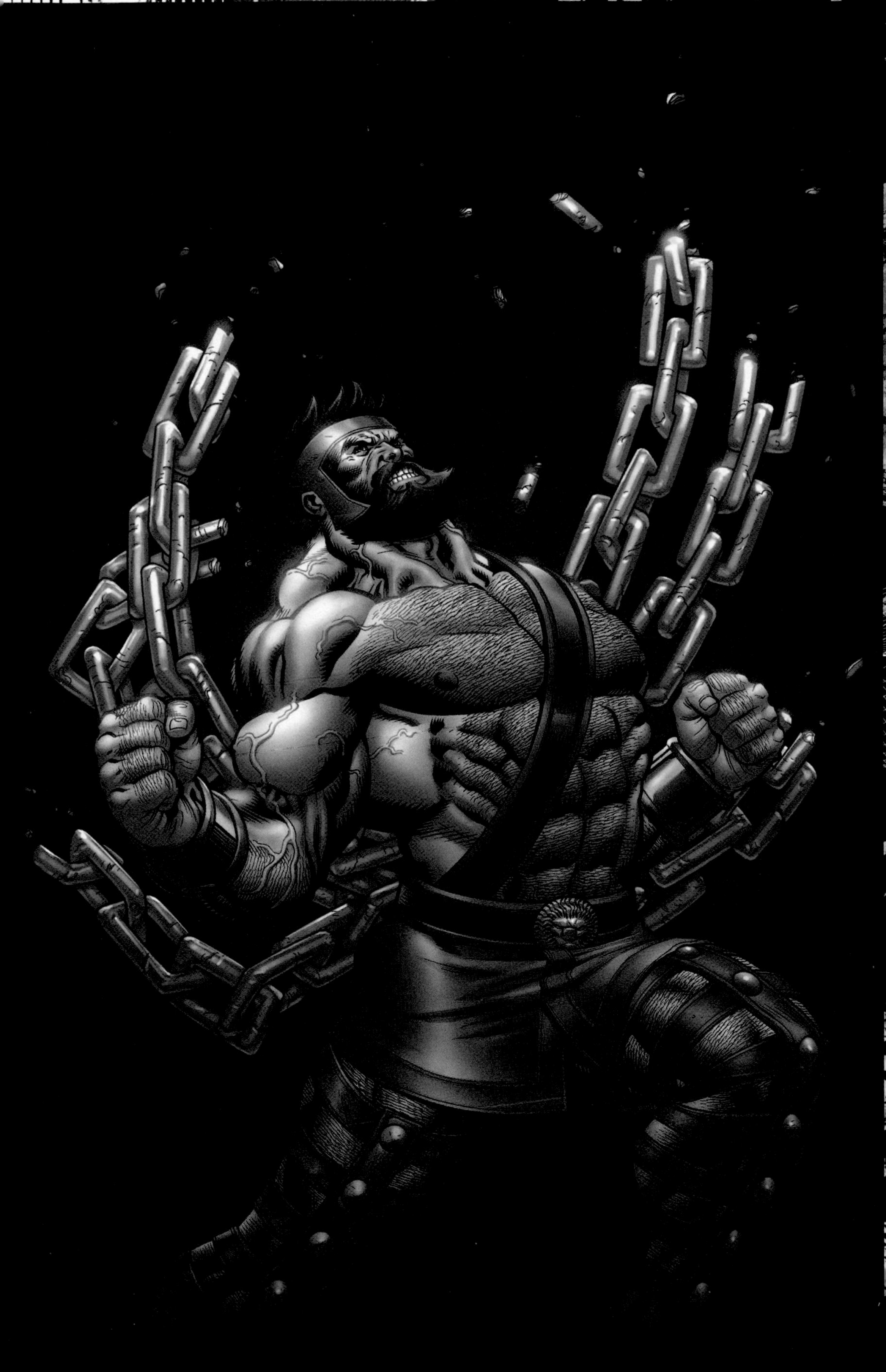

INCREDIBLE HERCULES #126

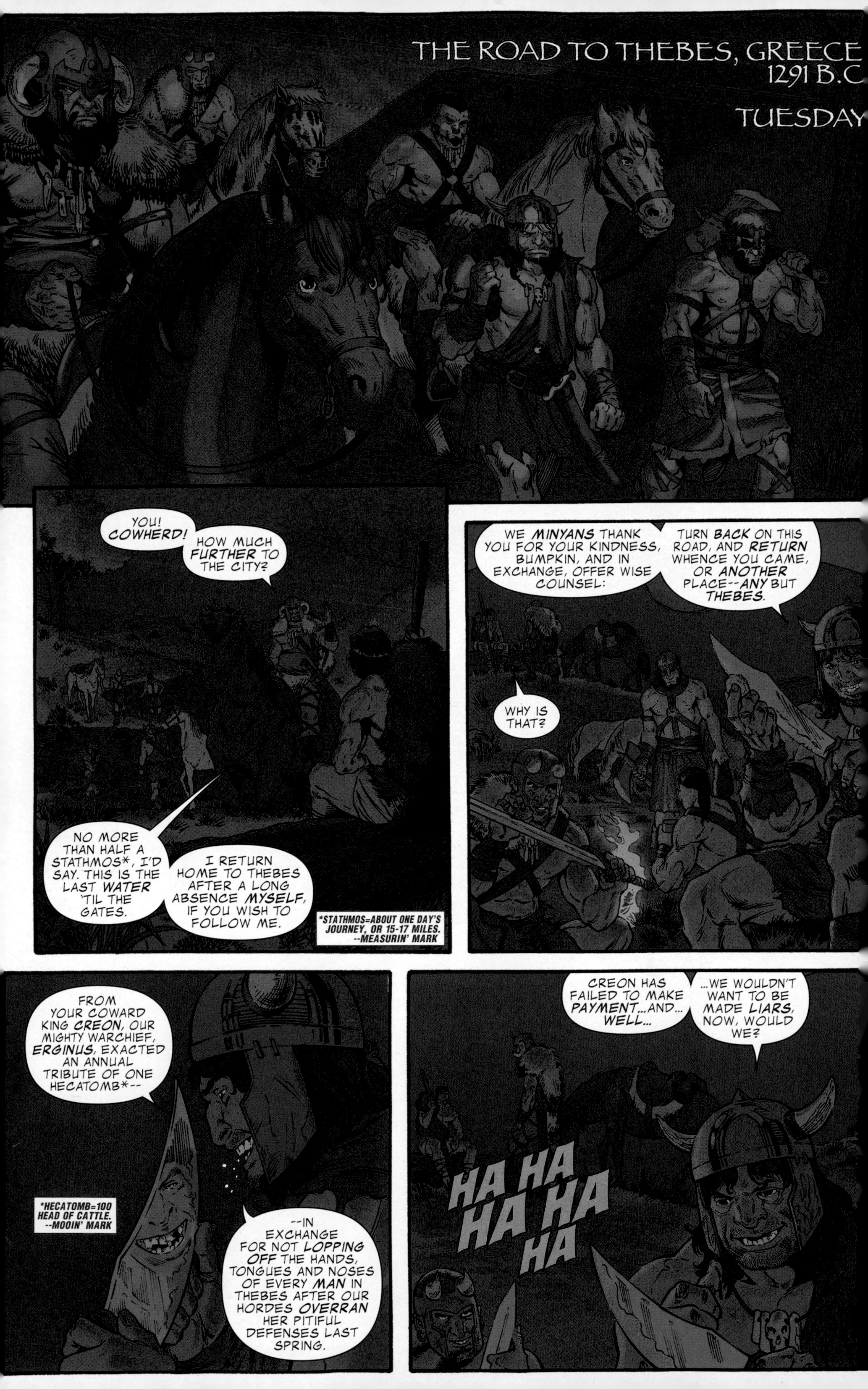
THE ROAD TO THEBES, GREECE
1291 B.C
TUESDAY
YOU! COWHERD!
HOW MUCH FURTHER TO THE CITY?
NO MORE THAN HALF A STATHMOS*, I'D SAY. THIS IS THE LAST WATER 'TIL THE GATES.
I RETURN HOME TO THEBES AFTER A LONG ABSENCE MYSELF, IF YOU WISH TO FOLLOW ME.
*STATHMOS=ABOUT ONE DAY'S JOURNEY, OR 15-17 MILES. --MEASURIN' MARK
WE MINYANS THANK YOU FOR YOUR KINDNESS, BUMPKIN, AND IN EXCHANGE, OFFER WISE COUNSEL:
TURN BACK ON THIS ROAD, AND RETURN WHENCE YOU CAME, OR ANOTHER PLACE--ANY BUT THEBES.
WHY IS THAT?
FROM YOUR COWARD KING CREON, OUR MIGHTY WARCHIEF, ERGINUS, EXACTED AN ANNUAL TRIBUTE OF ONE HECATOMB*--
*HECATOMB=100 HEAD OF CATTLE. --MOOIN' MARK
--IN EXCHANGE FOR NOT LOPPING OFF THE HANDS, TONGUES AND NOSES OF EVERY MAN IN THEBES AFTER OUR HORDES OVERRAN HER PITIFUL DEFENSES LAST SPRING.
CREON HAS FAILED TO MAKE PAYMENT...AND... WELL...
...WE WOULDN'T WANT TO BE MADE LIARS, NOW, WOULD WE?
HA HA HA HA HA

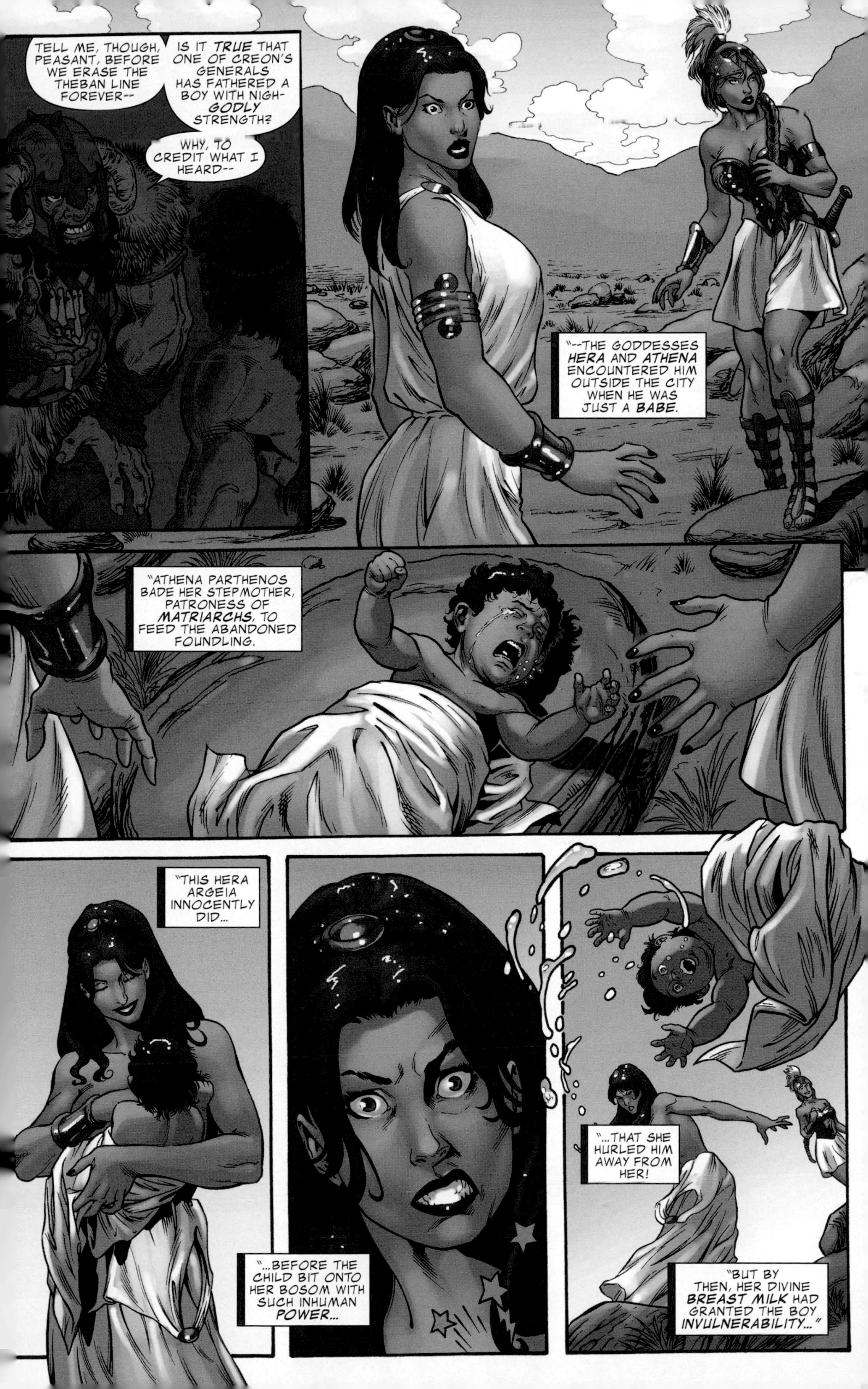
TELL ME, THOUGH, PEASANT, BEFORE WE ERASE THE THEBAN LINE FOREVER--
IS IT TRUE THAT ONE OF CREON'S GENERALS HAS FATHERED A BOY WITH NIGH-GODLY STRENGTH?
WHY, TO CREDIT WHAT I HEARD--
"--THE GODDESSES HERA AND ATHENA ENCOUNTERED HIM OUTSIDE THE CITY WHEN HE WAS JUST A BABE.
"ATHENA PARTHENOS BADE HER STEPMOTHER, PATRONESS OF MATRIARCHS, TO FEED THE ABANDONED FOUNDLING.
"THIS HERA ARGEIA INNOCENTLY DID...
"...BEFORE THE CHILD BIT ONTO HER BOSOM WITH SUCH INHUMAN POWER...
"...THAT SHE HURLED HIM AWAY FROM HER!
"BUT BY THEN, HER DIVINE BREAST MILK HAD GRANTED THE BOY INVULNERABILITY..."

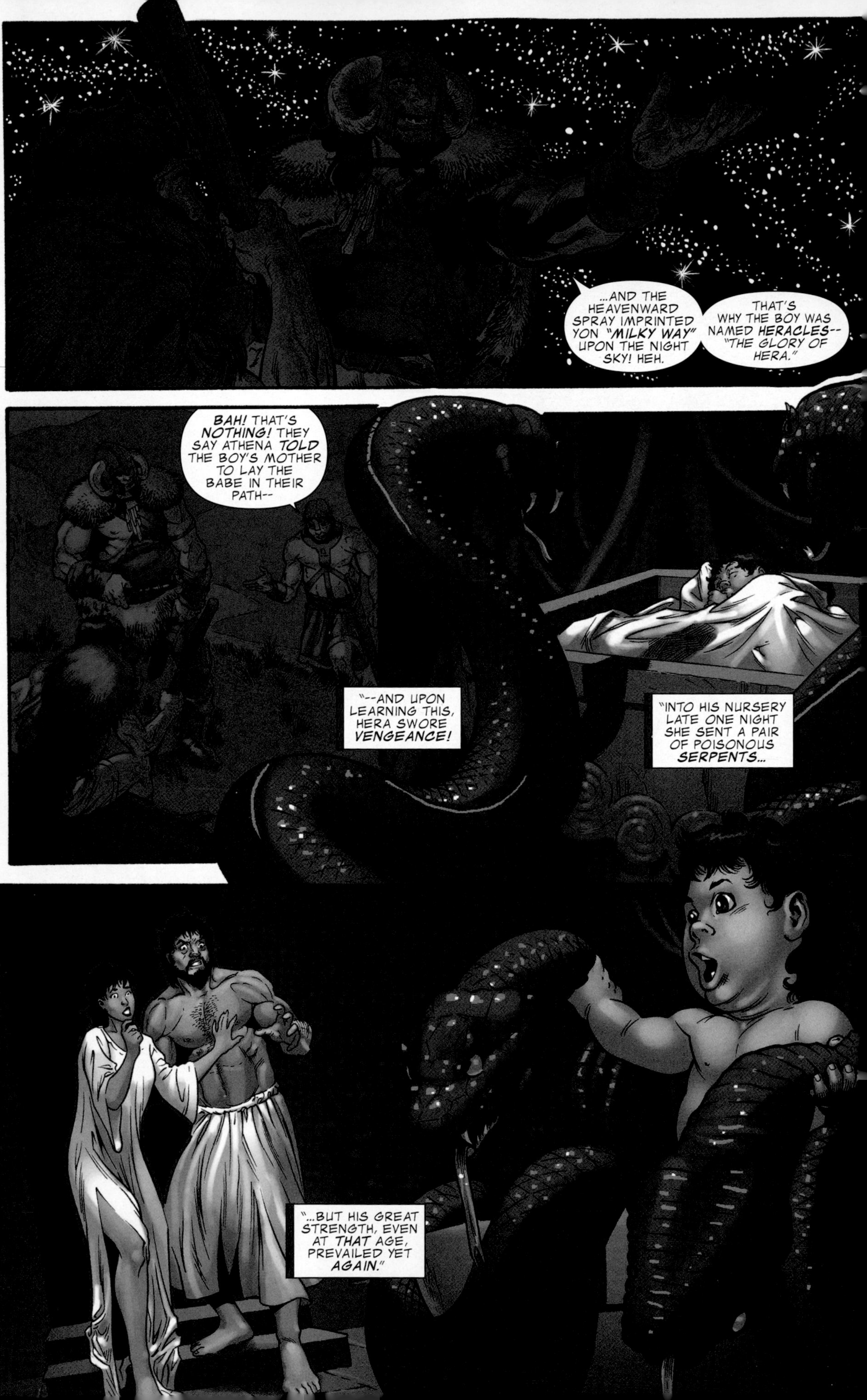
...AND THE HEAVENWARD SPRAY IMPRINTED YON "MILKY WAY" UPON THE NIGHT SKY! HEH.
THAT'S WHY THE BOY WAS NAMED HERACLES-- "THE GLORY OF HERA."
BAH! THAT'S NOTHING! THEY SAY ATHENA TOLD THE BOY'S MOTHER TO LAY THE BABE IN THEIR PATH--
"--AND UPON LEARNING THIS, HERA SWORE VENGEANCE!
"INTO HIS NURSERY LATE ONE NIGHT SHE SENT A PAIR OF POISONOUS SERPENTS...
"...BUT HIS GREAT STRENGTH, EVEN AT THAT AGE, PREVAILED YET AGAIN."

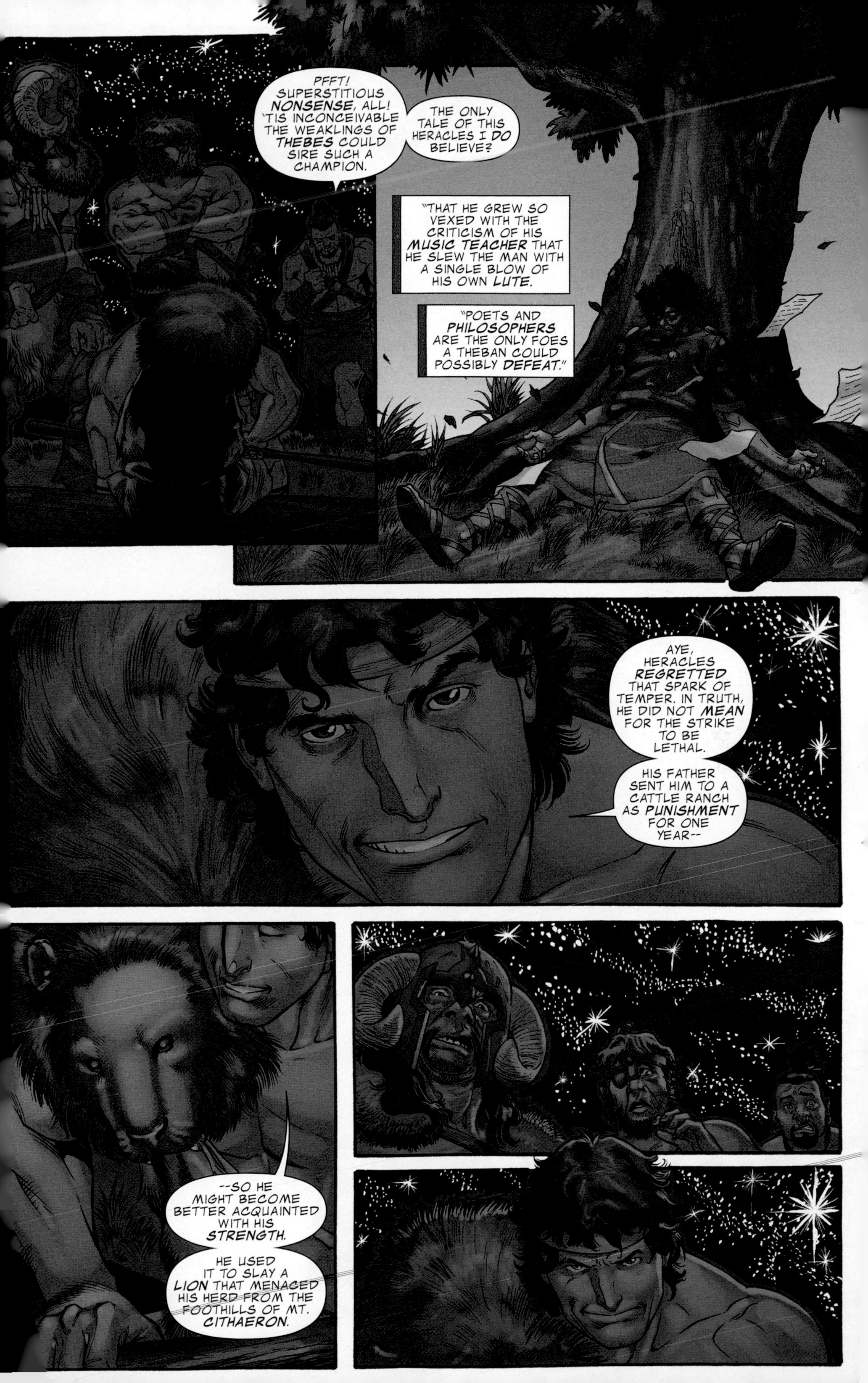
PFFT! SUPERSTITIOUS NONSENSE, ALL! 'TIS INCONCEIVABLE THE WEAKLINGS OF THEBES COULD SIRE SUCH A CHAMPION.
THE ONLY TALE OF THIS HERACLES I DO BELIEVE?
"THAT HE GREW SO VEXED WITH THE CRITICISM OF HIS MUSIC TEACHER THAT HE SLEW THE MAN WITH A SINGLE BLOW OF HIS OWN LUTE.
"POETS AND PHILOSOPHERS ARE THE ONLY FOES A THEBAN COULD POSSIBLY DEFEAT."
AYE, HERACLES REGRETTED THAT SPARK OF TEMPER. IN TRUTH, HE DID NOT MEAN FOR THE STRIKE TO BE LETHAL.
HIS FATHER SENT HIM TO A CATTLE RANCH AS PUNISHMENT FOR ONE YEAR--
--SO HE MIGHT BECOME BETTER ACQUAINTED WITH HIS STRENGTH.
HE USED IT TO SLAY A LION THAT MENACED HIS HERD FROM THE FOOTHILLS OF MT. CITHAERON.

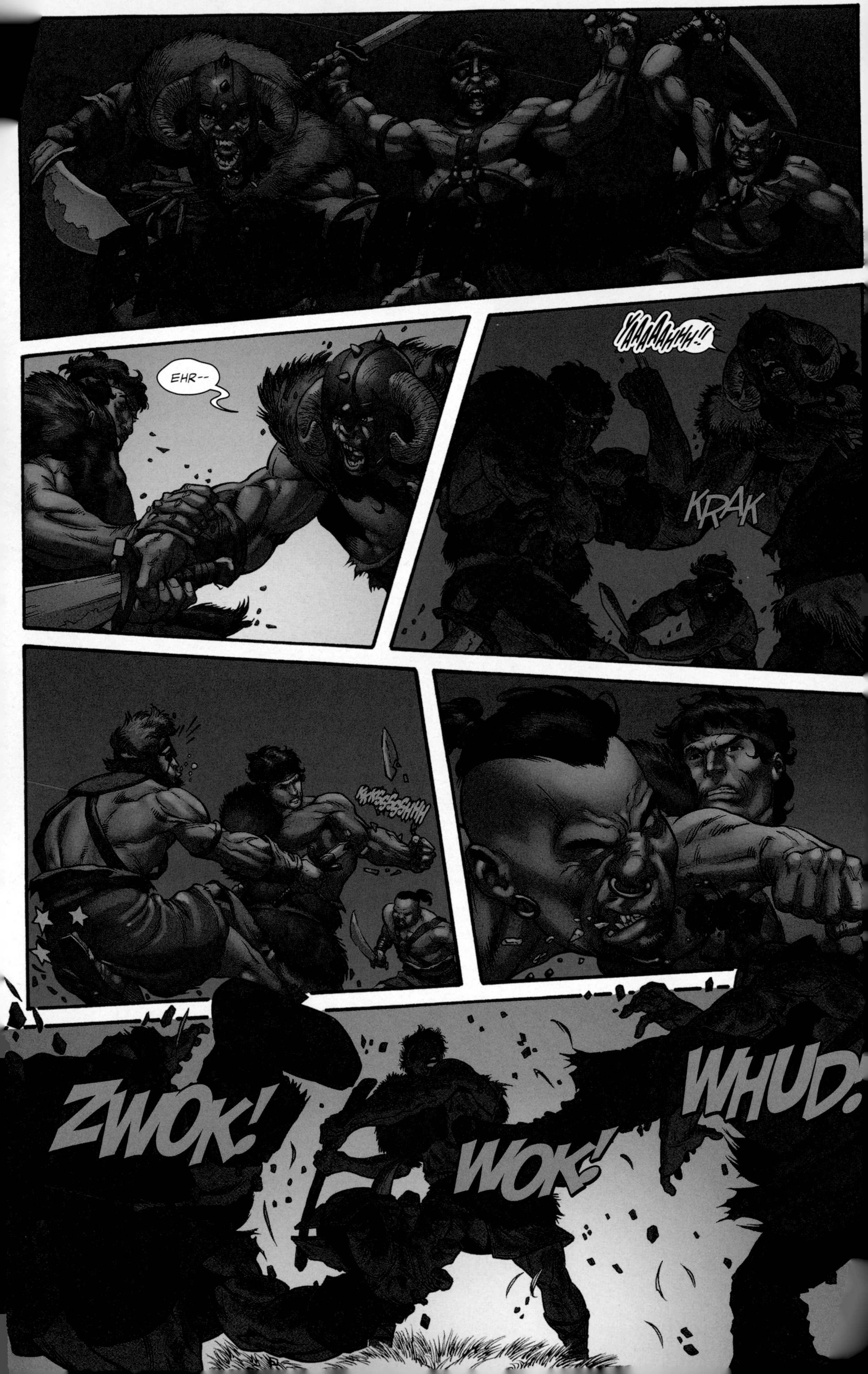
EHR--
YAAAAAHHH!!
KRAK
KKKSSSSSHHH
ZWOK!
WOK!
WHUD!

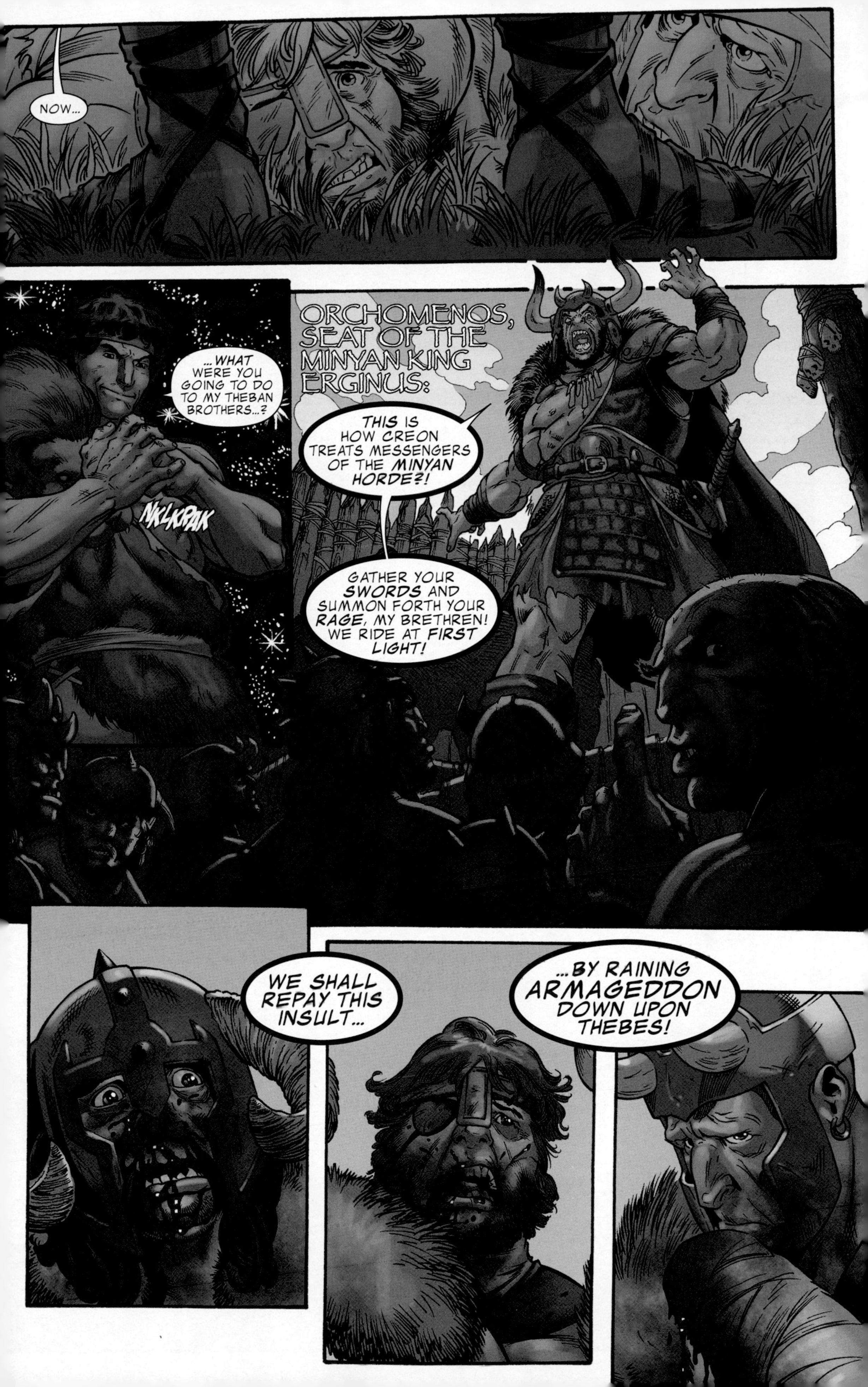
NOW...
...WHAT WERE YOU GOING TO DO TO MY THEBAN BROTHERS...?
NKLKRAK
ORCHOMENOS, SEAT OF THE MINYAN KING ERGINUS:
THIS IS HOW CREON TREATS MESSENGERS OF THE MINYAN HORDE?!
GATHER YOUR SWORDS AND SUMMON FORTH YOUR RAGE, MY BRETHREN! WE RIDE AT FIRST LIGHT!
WE SHALL REPAY THIS INSULT...
...BY RAINING ARMAGEDDON DOWN UPON THEBES!

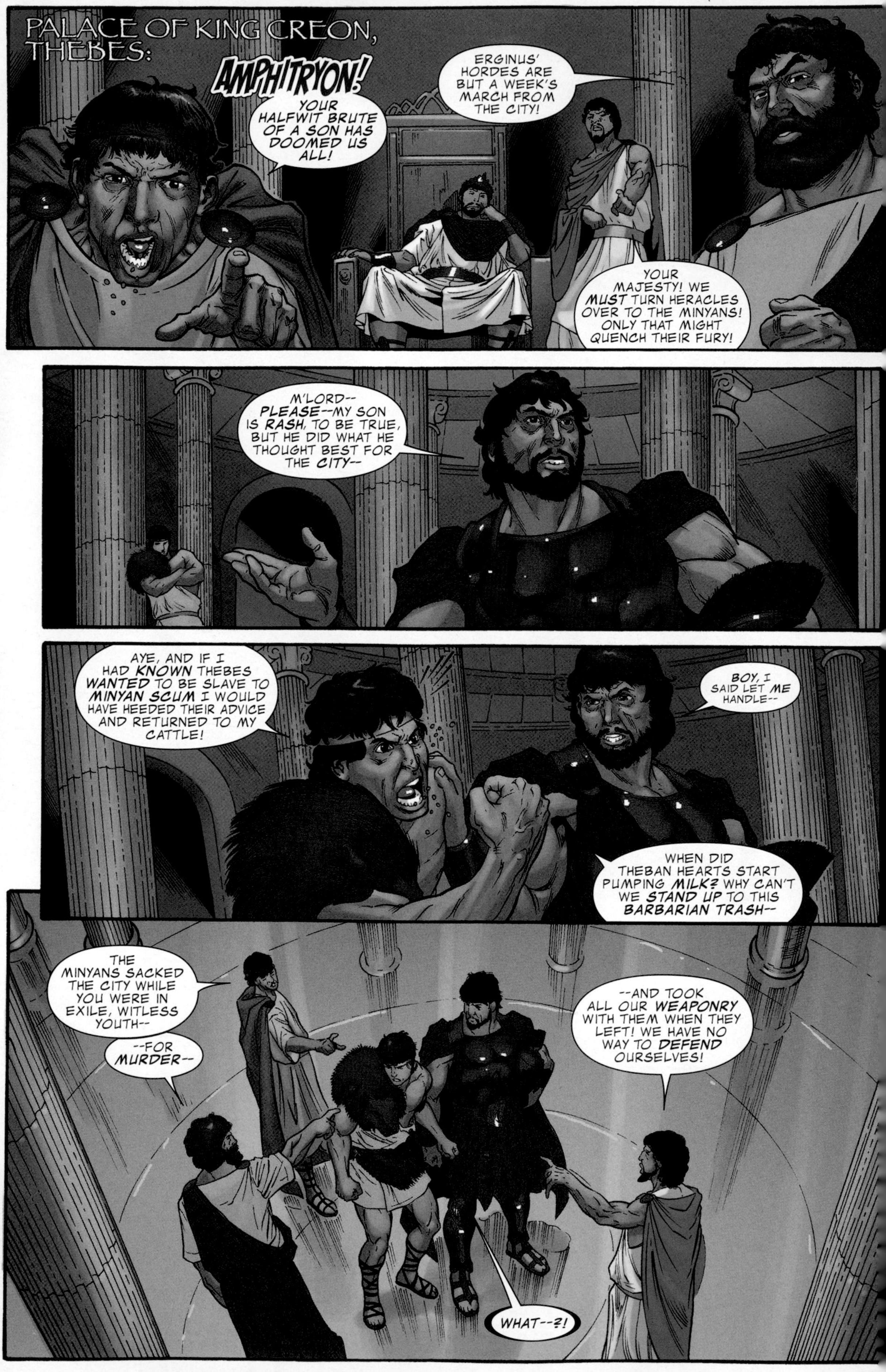
PALACE OF KING CREON, THEBES:
AMPHITRYON!
YOUR HALFWIT BRUTE OF A SON HAS DOOMED US ALL!
ERGINUS' HORDES ARE BUT A WEEK'S MARCH FROM THE CITY!
YOUR MAJESTY! WE MUST TURN HERACLES OVER TO THE MINYANS! ONLY THAT MIGHT QUENCH THEIR FURY!
M'LORD-- PLEASE--MY SON IS RASH, TO BE TRUE, BUT HE DID WHAT HE THOUGHT BEST FOR THE CITY--
AYE, AND IF I HAD KNOWN THEBES WANTED TO BE SLAVE TO MINYAN SCUM I WOULD HAVE HEEDED THEIR ADVICE AND RETURNED TO MY CATTLE!
BOY, I SAID LET ME HANDLE--
WHEN DID THEBAN HEARTS START PUMPING MILK? WHY CAN'T WE STAND UP TO THIS BARBARIAN TRASH--
THE MINYANS SACKED THE CITY WHILE YOU WERE IN EXILE, WITLESS YOUTH--
--FOR MURDER--
--AND TOOK ALL OUR WEAPONRY WITH THEM WHEN THEY LEFT! WE HAVE NO WAY TO DEFEND OURSELVES!
WHAT--?!

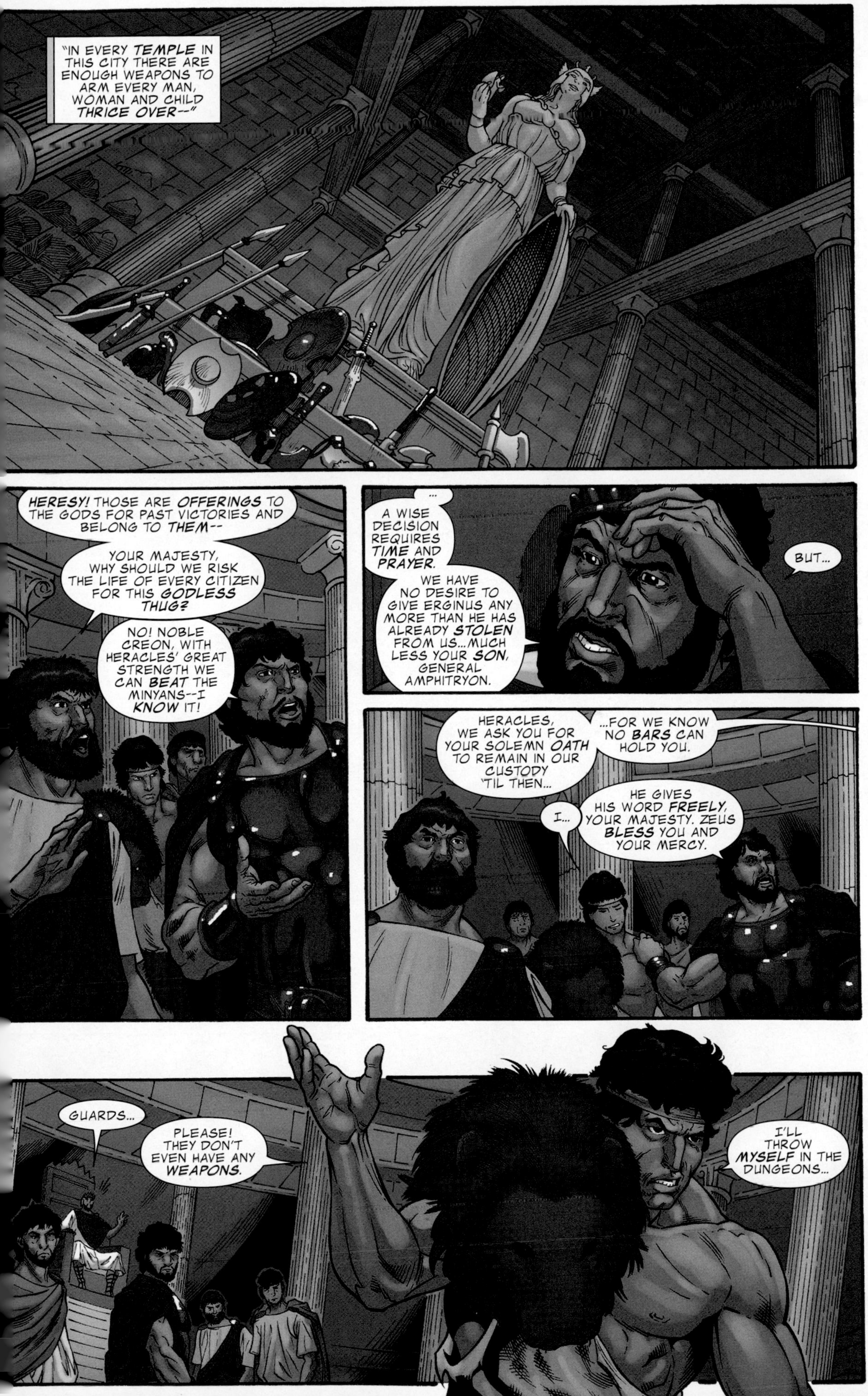
"IN EVERY TEMPLE IN THIS CITY THERE ARE ENOUGH WEAPONS TO ARM EVERY MAN, WOMAN AND CHILD THRICE OVER--"
HERESY! THOSE ARE OFFERINGS TO THE GODS FOR PAST VICTORIES AND BELONG TO THEM--
YOUR MAJESTY, WHY SHOULD WE RISK THE LIFE OF EVERY CITIZEN FOR THIS GODLESS THUG?
NO! NOBLE CREON, WITH HERACLES' GREAT STRENGTH WE CAN BEAT THE MINYANS--I KNOW IT!
...
A WISE DECISION REQUIRES TIME AND PRAYER.
WE HAVE NO DESIRE TO GIVE ERGINUS ANY MORE THAN HE HAS ALREADY STOLEN FROM US...MUCH LESS YOUR SON, GENERAL AMPHITRYON.
BUT...
HERACLES, WE ASK YOU FOR YOUR SOLEMN OATH TO REMAIN IN OUR CUSTODY 'TIL THEN...
...FOR WE KNOW NO BARS CAN HOLD YOU.
I...
HE GIVES HIS WORD FREELY, YOUR MAJESTY. ZEUS BLESS YOU AND YOUR MERCY.
GUARDS...
PLEASE! THEY DON'T EVEN HAVE ANY WEAPONS.
I'LL THROW MYSELF IN THE DUNGEONS...

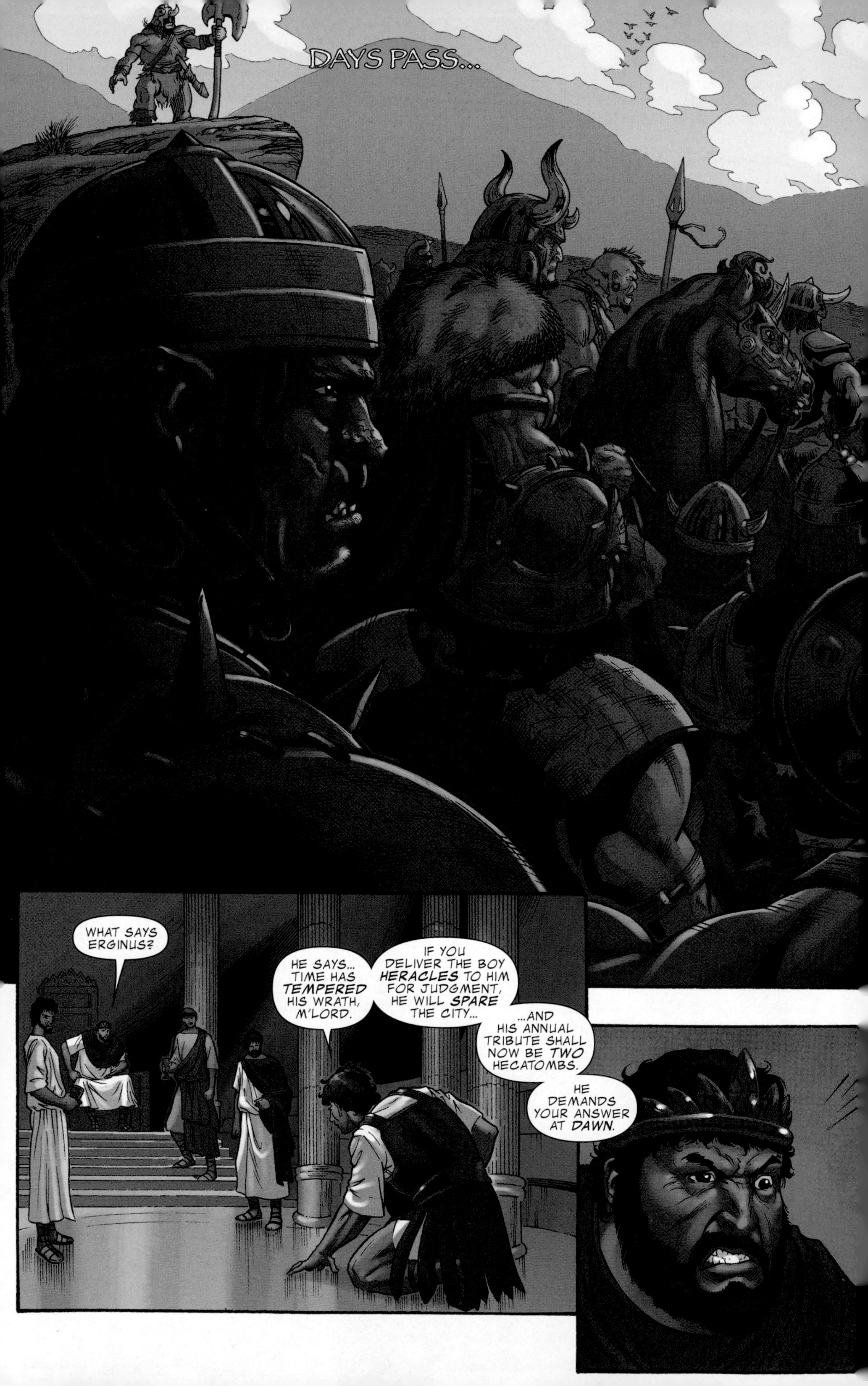
DAYS PASS...
WHAT SAYS ERGINUS?
HE SAYS... TIME HAS TEMPERED HIS WRATH, M'LORD.
IF YOU DELIVER THE BOY HERACLES TO HIM FOR JUDGMENT, HE WILL SPARE THE CITY...
...AND HIS ANNUAL TRIBUTE SHALL NOW BE TWO HECATOMBS.
HE DEMANDS YOUR ANSWER AT DAWN.

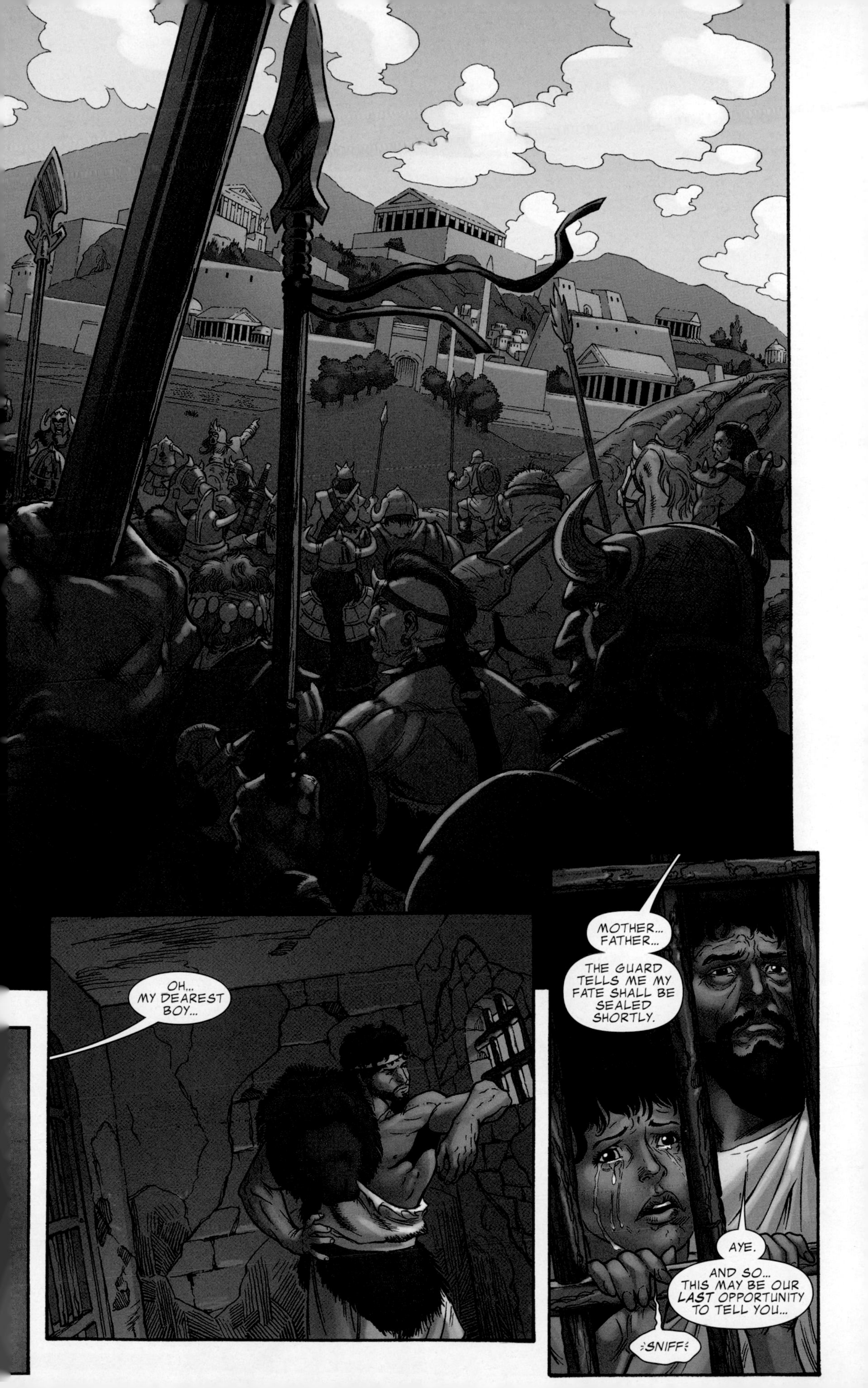
OH... MY DEAREST BOY...
MOTHER... FATHER...
THE GUARD TELLS ME MY FATE SHALL BE SEALED SHORTLY.
AYE.
AND SO... THIS MAY BE OUR *LAST* OPPORTUNITY TO TELL YOU...
SNIFF

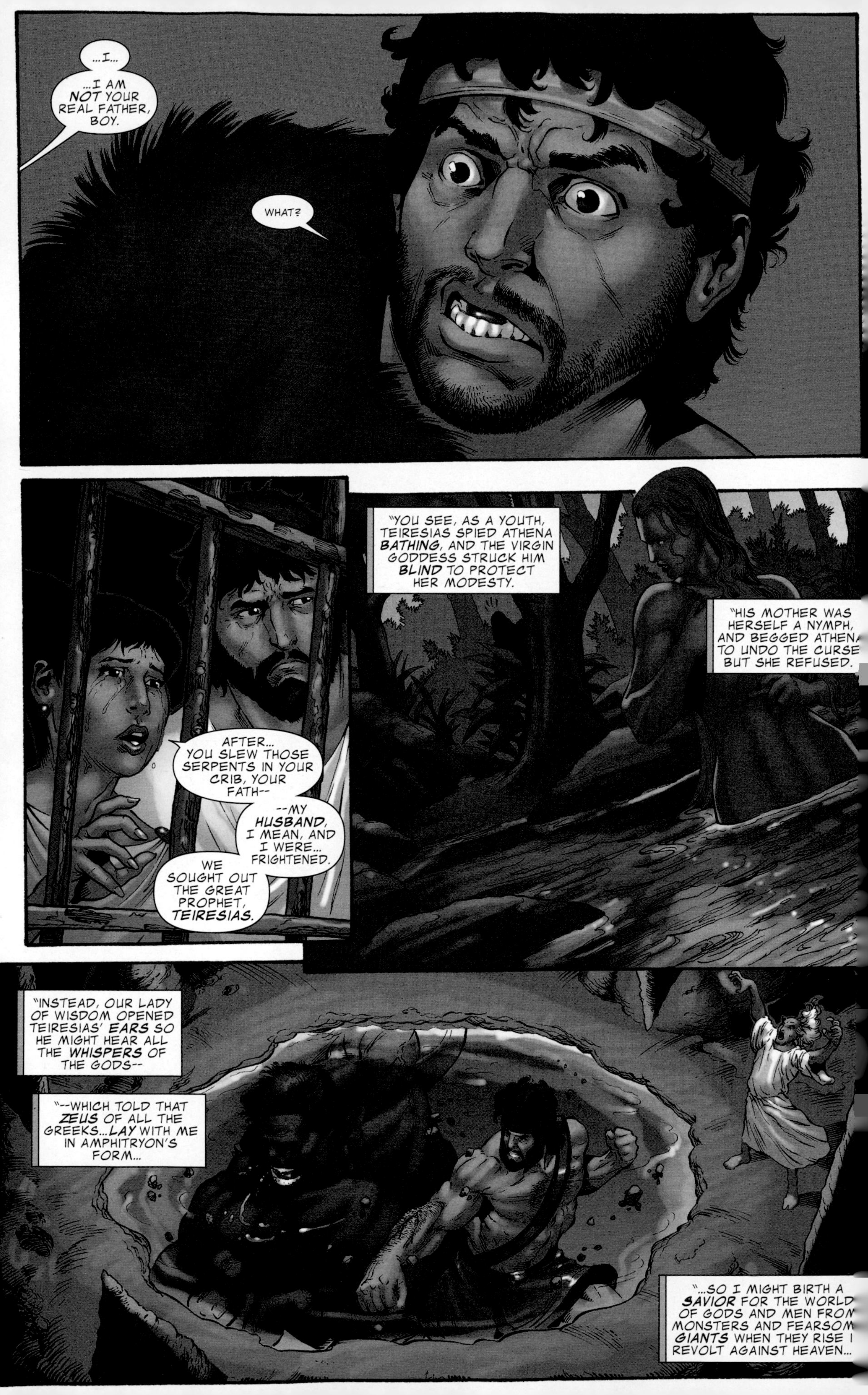
...I...
...I AM NOT YOUR REAL FATHER, BOY.
WHAT?
AFTER... YOU SLEW THOSE SERPENTS IN YOUR CRIB, YOUR FATH--
--MY HUSBAND, I MEAN, AND I WERE... FRIGHTENED.
WE SOUGHT OUT THE GREAT PROPHET, TEIRESIAS.
"YOU SEE, AS A YOUTH, TEIRESIAS SPIED ATHENA BATHING, AND THE VIRGIN GODDESS STRUCK HIM BLIND TO PROTECT HER MODESTY.
"HIS MOTHER WAS HERSELF A NYMPH, AND BEGGED ATHENA TO UNDO THE CURSE BUT SHE REFUSED.
"INSTEAD, OUR LADY OF WISDOM OPENED TEIRESIAS' EARS SO HE MIGHT HEAR ALL THE WHISPERS OF THE GODS--
"--WHICH TOLD THAT ZEUS OF ALL THE GREEKS...LAY WITH ME IN AMPHITRYON'S FORM...
"...SO I MIGHT BIRTH A SAVIOR FOR THE WORLD OF GODS AND MEN FROM MONSTERS AND FEARSOM GIANTS WHEN THEY RISE I REVOLT AGAINST HEAVEN...

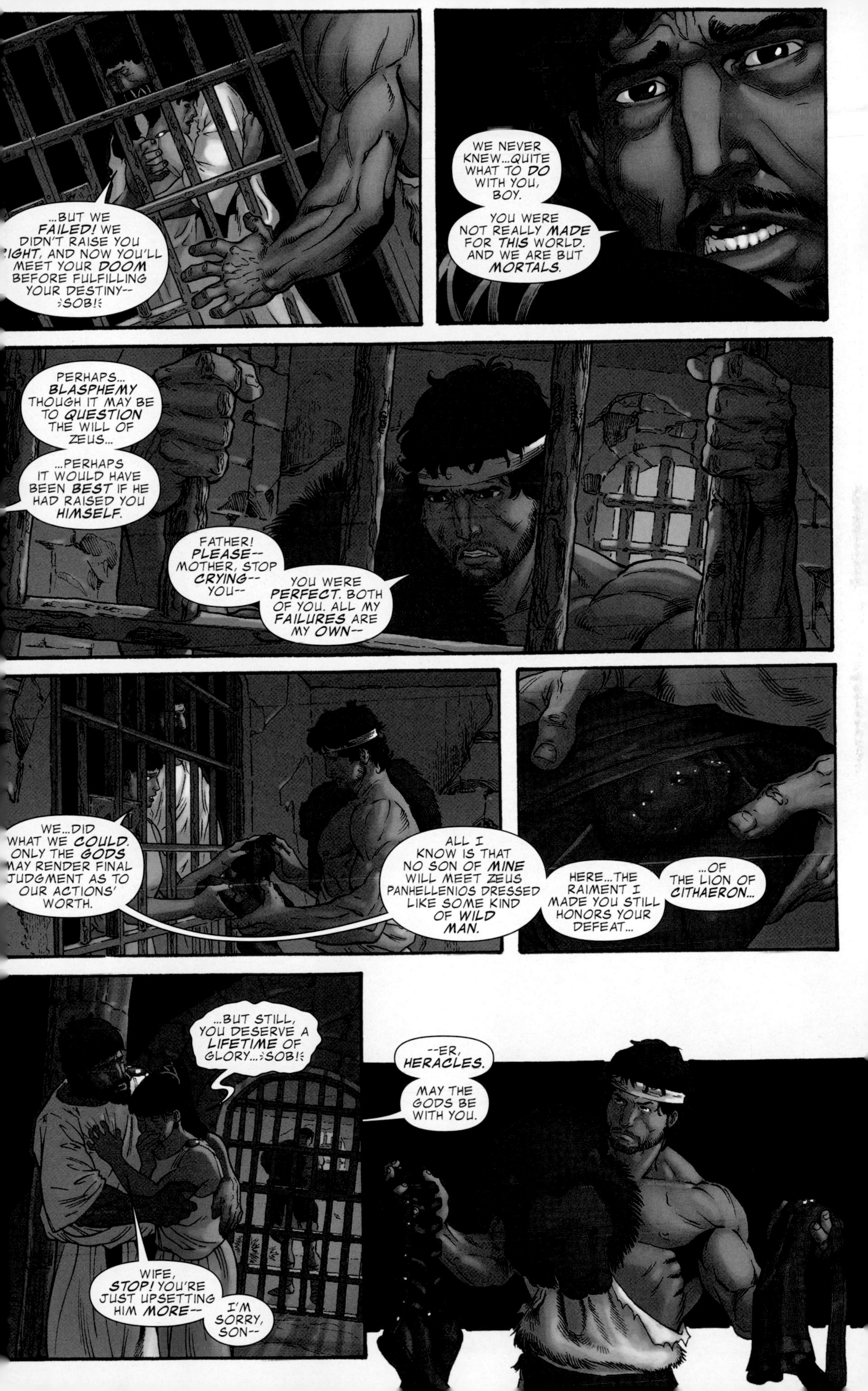
...BUT WE FAILED! WE DIDN'T RAISE YOU RIGHT, AND NOW YOU'LL MEET YOUR DOOM BEFORE FULFILLING YOUR DESTINY-- SOB!
WE NEVER KNEW...QUITE WHAT TO DO WITH YOU, BOY.
YOU WERE NOT REALLY MADE FOR THIS WORLD. AND WE ARE BUT MORTALS.
PERHAPS... BLASPHEMY THOUGH IT MAY BE TO QUESTION THE WILL OF ZEUS...
...PERHAPS IT WOULD HAVE BEEN BEST IF HE HAD RAISED YOU HIMSELF.
FATHER! PLEASE-- MOTHER, STOP CRYING-- YOU--
YOU WERE PERFECT. BOTH OF YOU. ALL MY FAILURES ARE MY OWN--
WE...DID WHAT WE COULD. ONLY THE GODS MAY RENDER FINAL JUDGMENT AS TO OUR ACTIONS' WORTH.
ALL I KNOW IS THAT NO SON OF MINE WILL MEET ZEUS PANHELLENIOS DRESSED LIKE SOME KIND OF WILD MAN.
HERE...THE RAIMENT I MADE YOU STILL HONORS YOUR DEFEAT...
...OF THE LION OF CITHAERON...
...BUT STILL, YOU DESERVE A LIFETIME OF GLORY... SOB!
--ER, HERACLES.
MAY THE GODS BE WITH YOU.
WIFE, STOP! YOU'RE JUST UPSETTING HIM MORE--
I'M SORRY, SON--

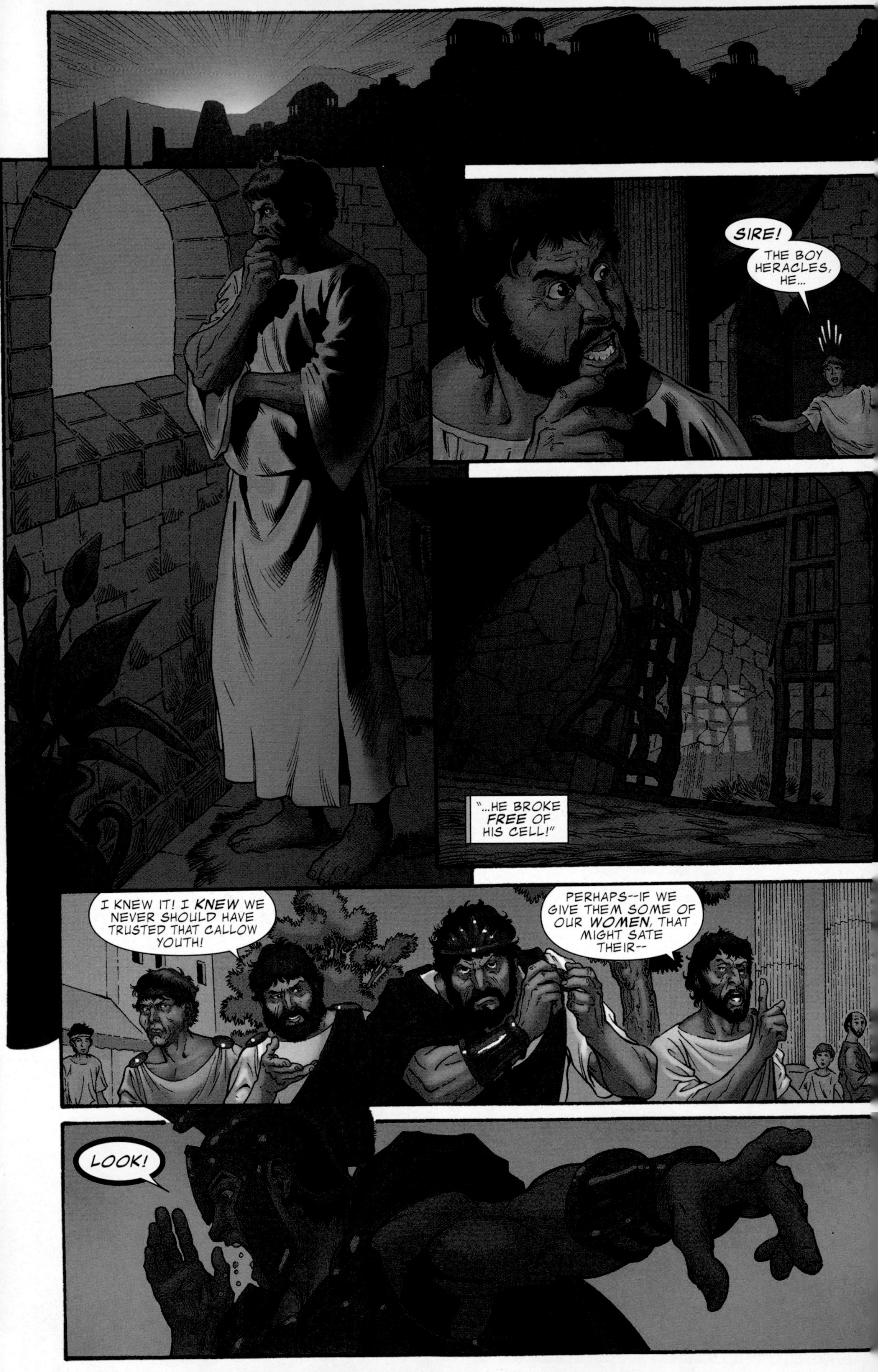
SIRE!
THE BOY HERACLES, HE...
"...HE BROKE FREE OF HIS CELL!"
I KNEW IT! I KNEW WE NEVER SHOULD HAVE TRUSTED THAT CALLOW YOUTH!
PERHAPS--IF WE GIVE THEM SOME OF OUR WOMEN, THAT MIGHT SATE THEIR--
LOOK!

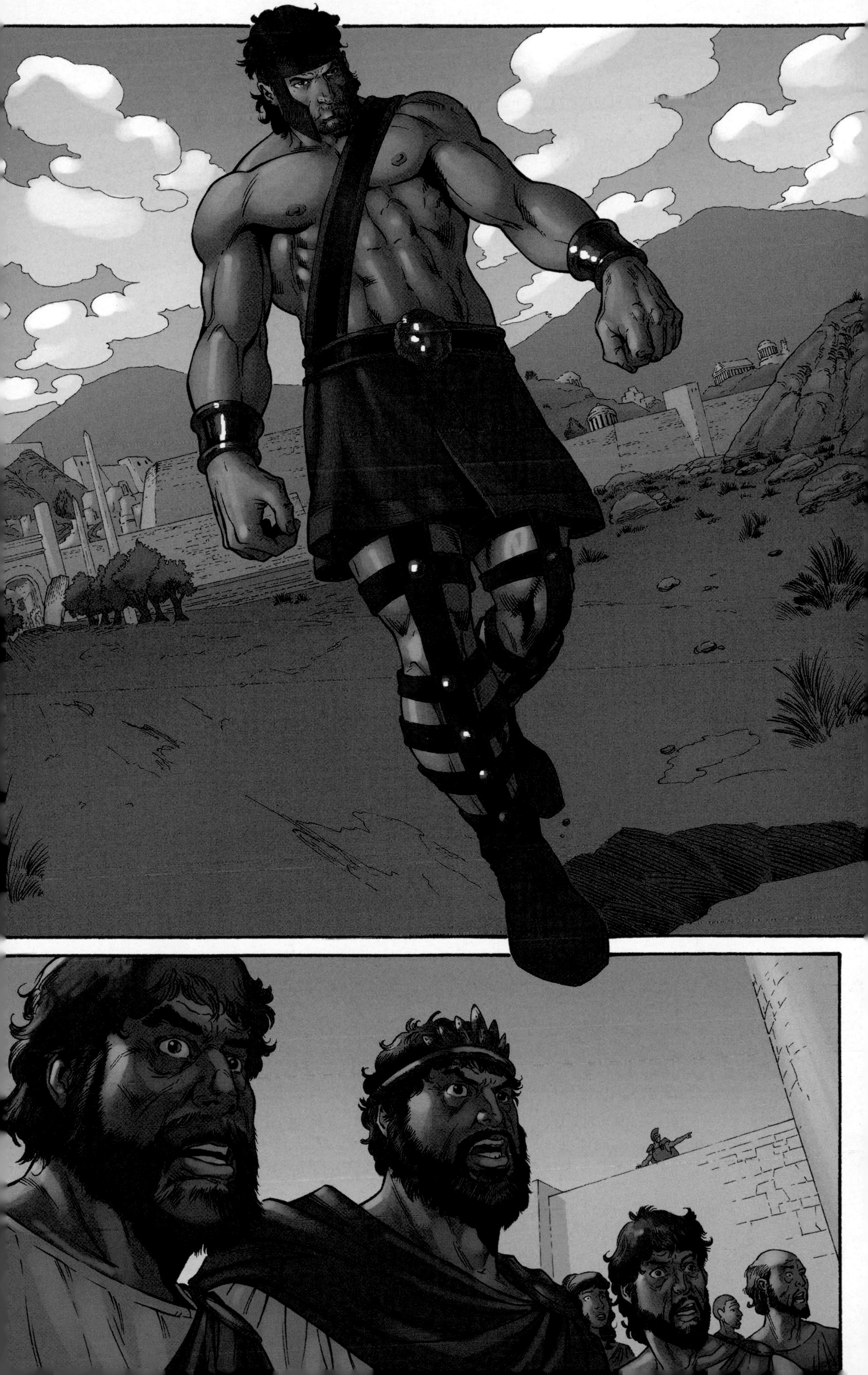

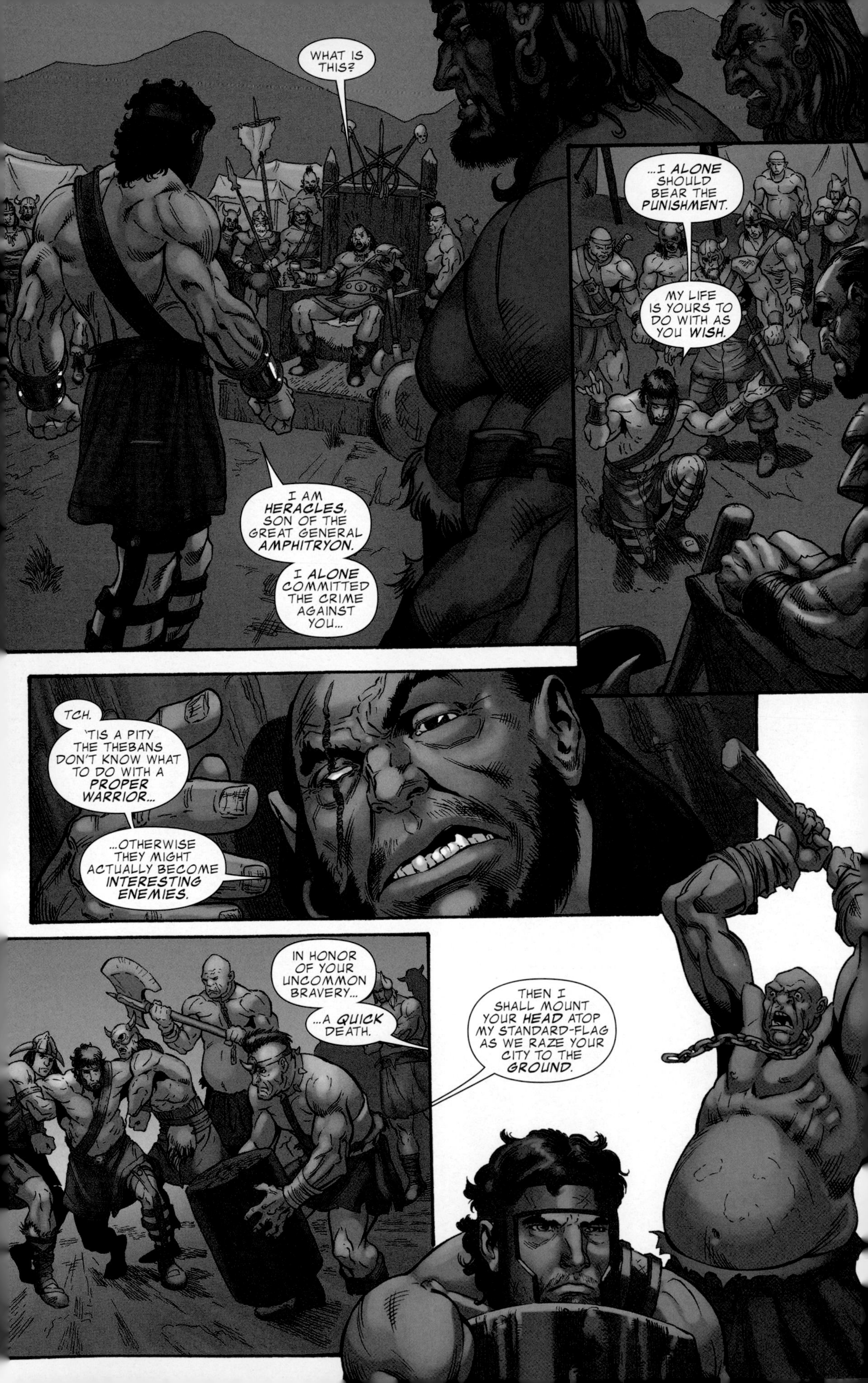
WHAT IS THIS?
I AM HERACLES, SON OF THE GREAT GENERAL AMPHITRYON.
I ALONE COMMITTED THE CRIME AGAINST YOU...
...I ALONE SHOULD BEAR THE PUNISHMENT.
MY LIFE IS YOURS TO DO WITH AS YOU WISH.
TCH.
'TIS A PITY THE THEBANS DON'T KNOW WHAT TO DO WITH A PROPER WARRIOR...
...OTHERWISE THEY MIGHT ACTUALLY BECOME INTERESTING ENEMIES.
IN HONOR OF YOUR UNCOMMON BRAVERY...
...A QUICK DEATH.
THEN I SHALL MOUNT YOUR HEAD ATOP MY STANDARD-FLAG AS WE RAZE YOUR CITY TO THE GROUND.

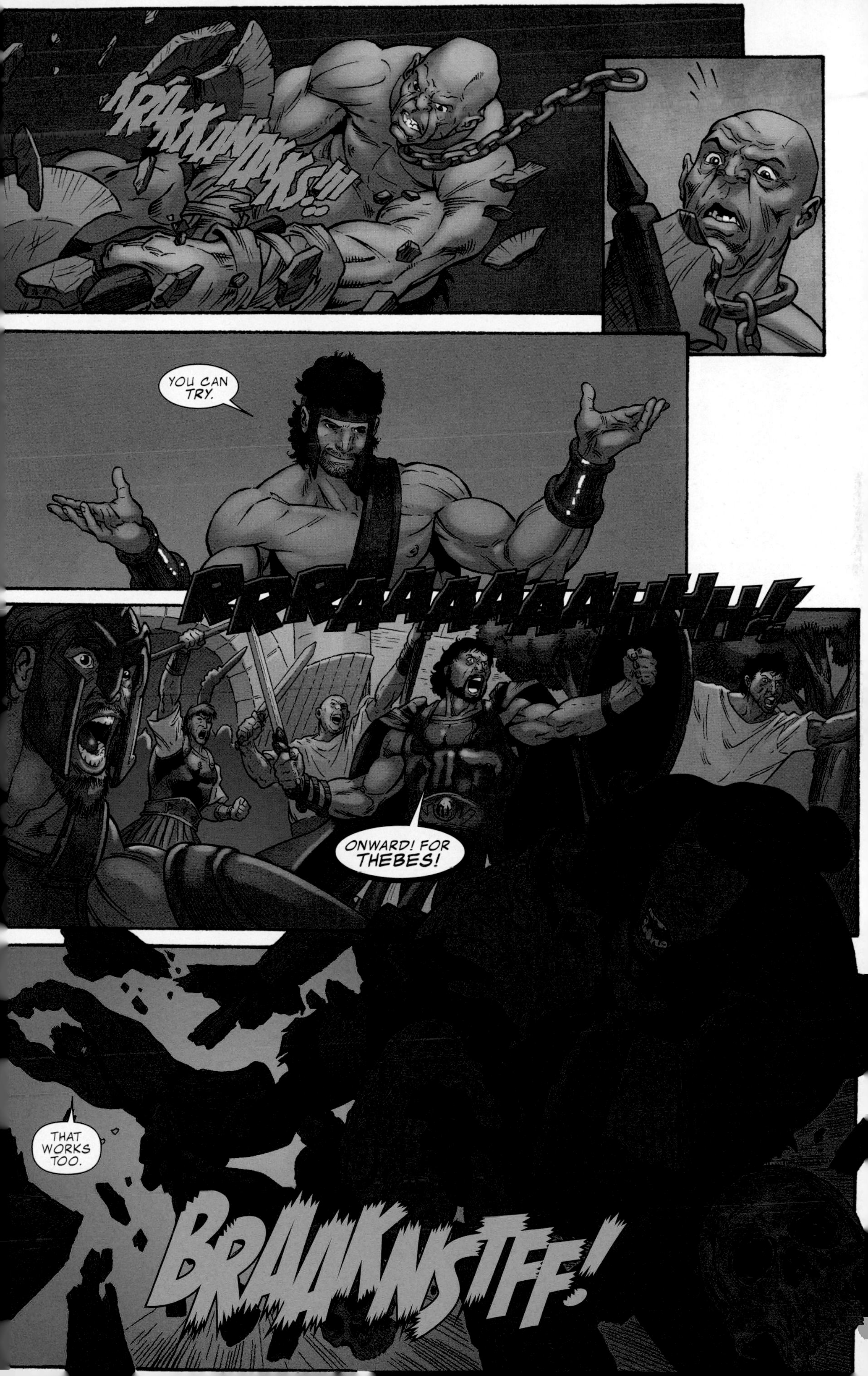
KRAKADOOKS!!!
YOU CAN TRY.
RRRAAAAAAAHHH!
ONWARD! FOR THEBES!
THAT WORKS TOO.
BRAAKASTFF!

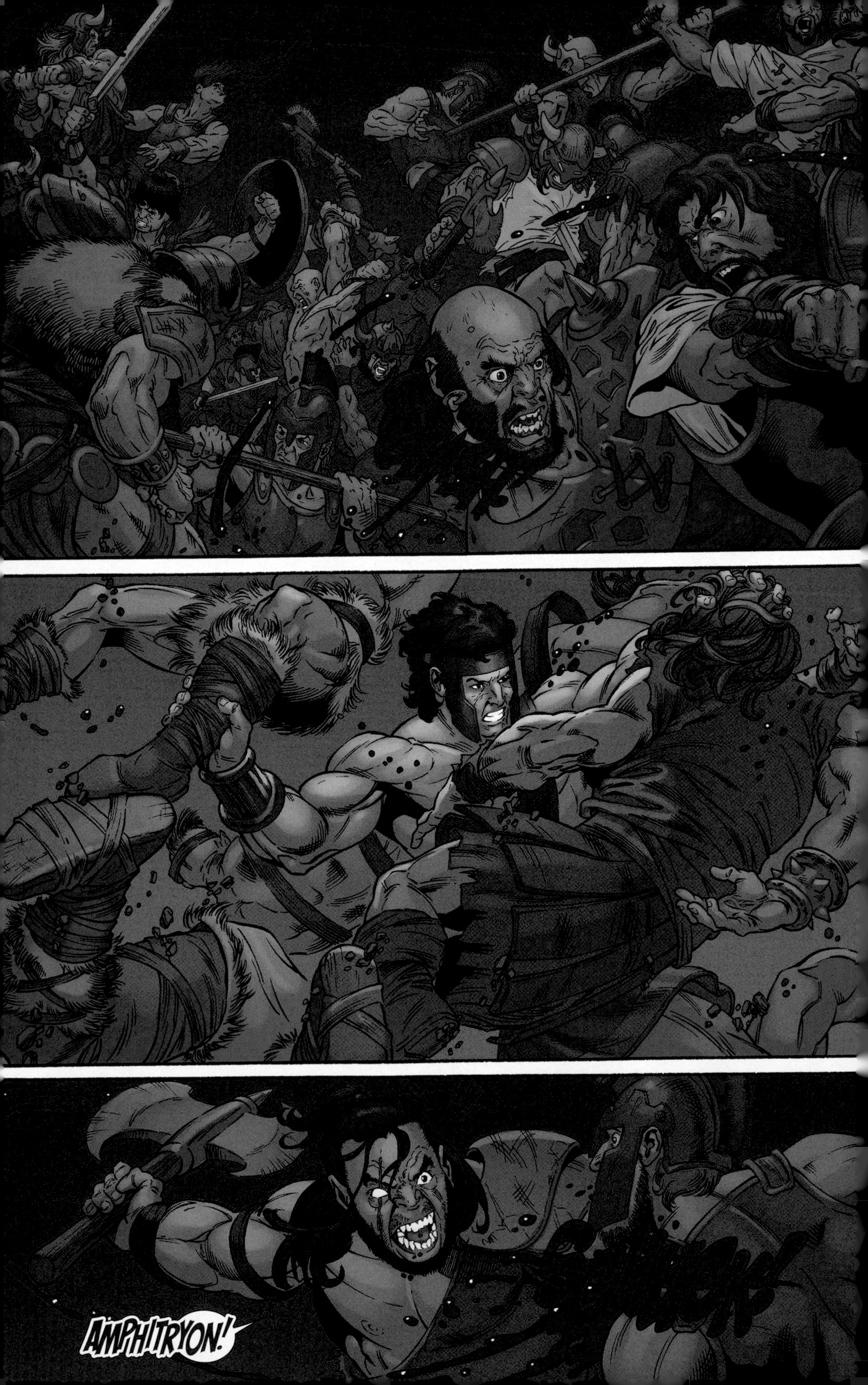
AMPHITRYON!

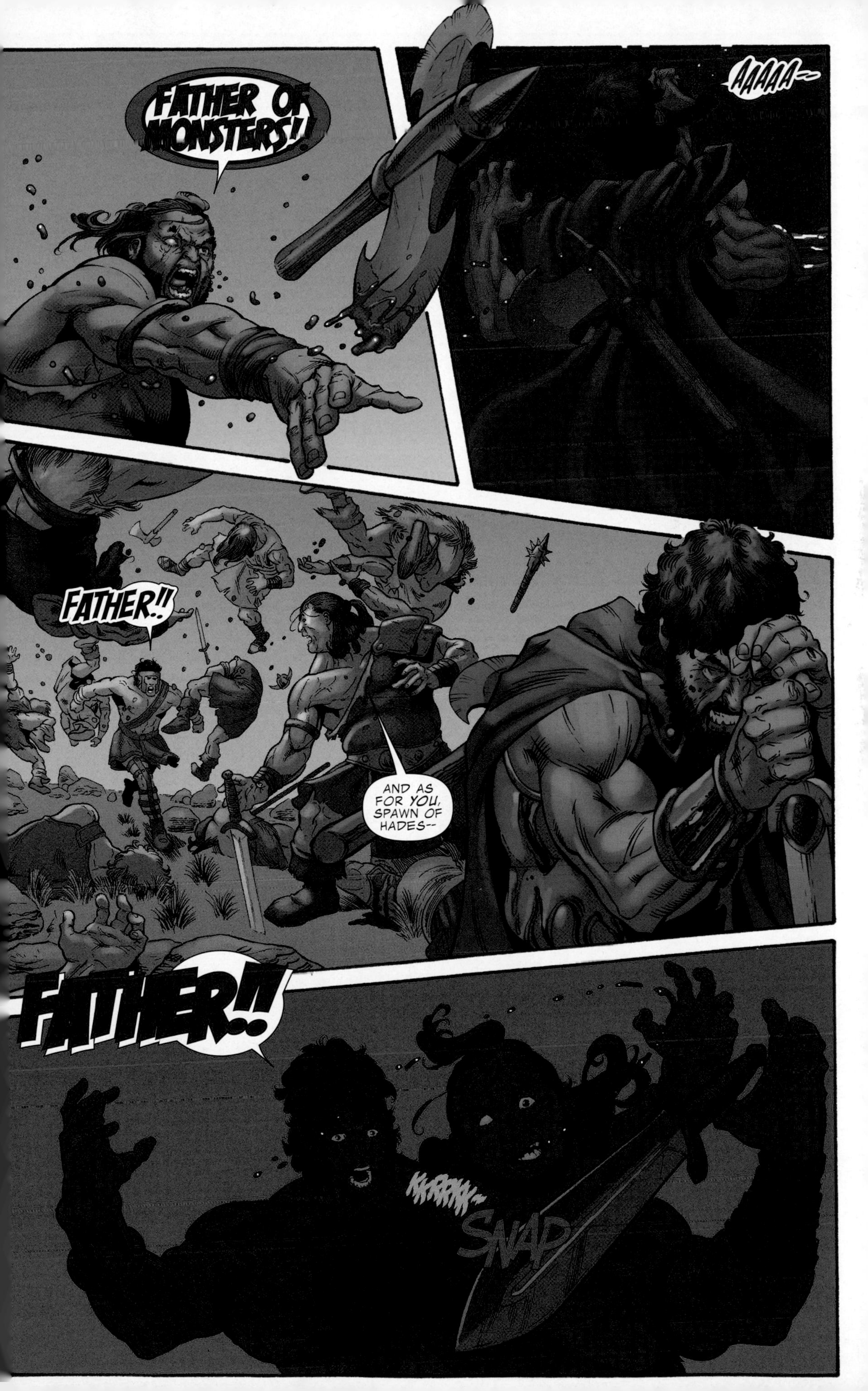
FATHER OF MONSTERS!!
AAAAA--
FATHER!!
AND AS FOR YOU, SPAWN OF HADES--
FATHER!!
KKRRKK--
SNAP

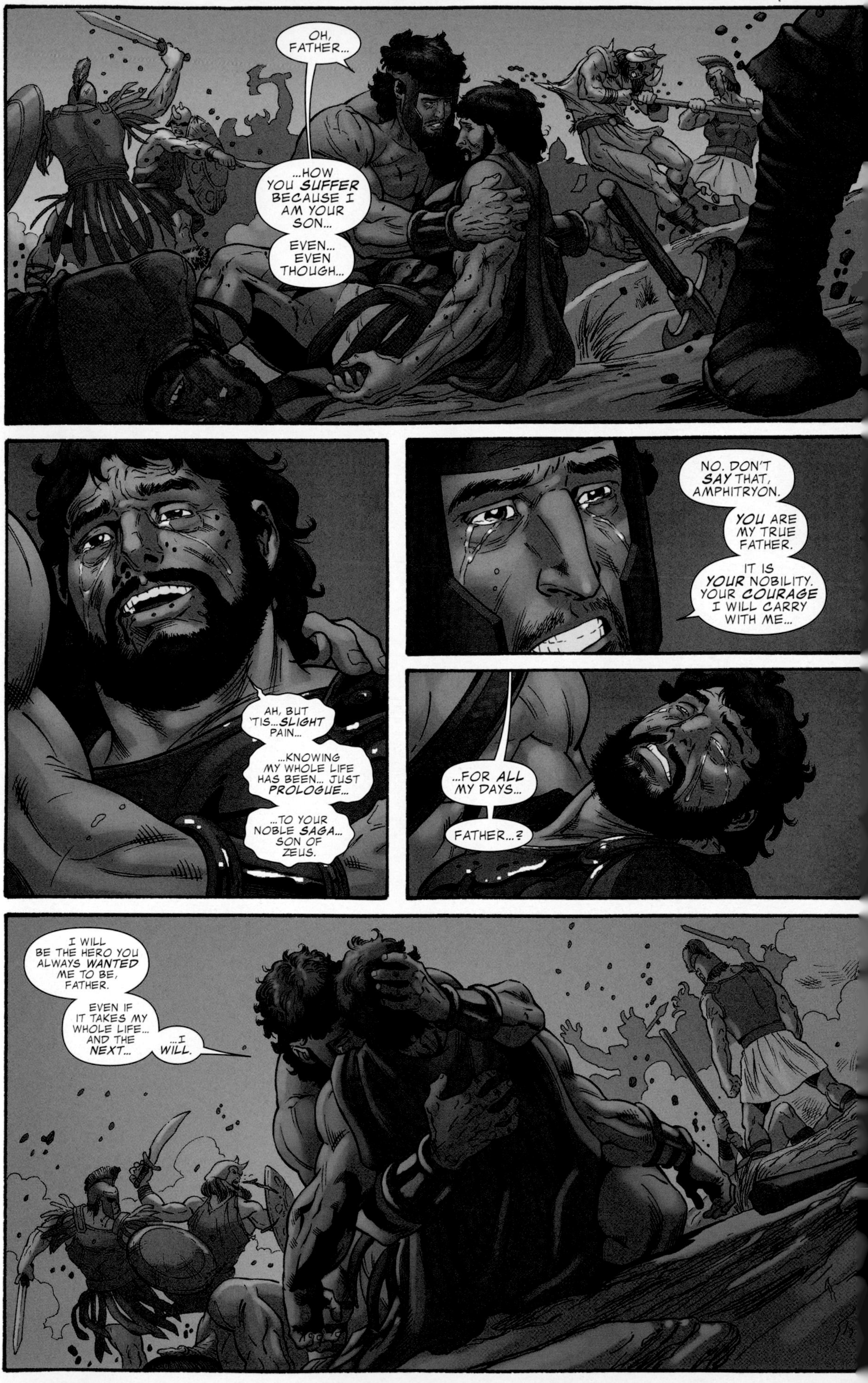
OH, FATHER...
...HOW YOU SUFFER BECAUSE I AM YOUR SON...
EVEN... EVEN THOUGH...
AH, BUT 'TIS...SLIGHT PAIN...
...KNOWING MY WHOLE LIFE HAS BEEN... JUST PROLOGUE...
...TO YOUR NOBLE SAGA... SON OF ZEUS.
NO. DON'T SAY THAT, AMPHITRYON.
YOU ARE MY TRUE FATHER.
IT IS YOUR NOBILITY. YOUR COURAGE I WILL CARRY WITH ME...
...FOR ALL MY DAYS...
FATHER...?
I WILL BE THE HERO YOU ALWAYS WANTED ME TO BE, FATHER.
EVEN IF IT TAKES MY WHOLE LIFE... AND THE NEXT...
...I WILL.

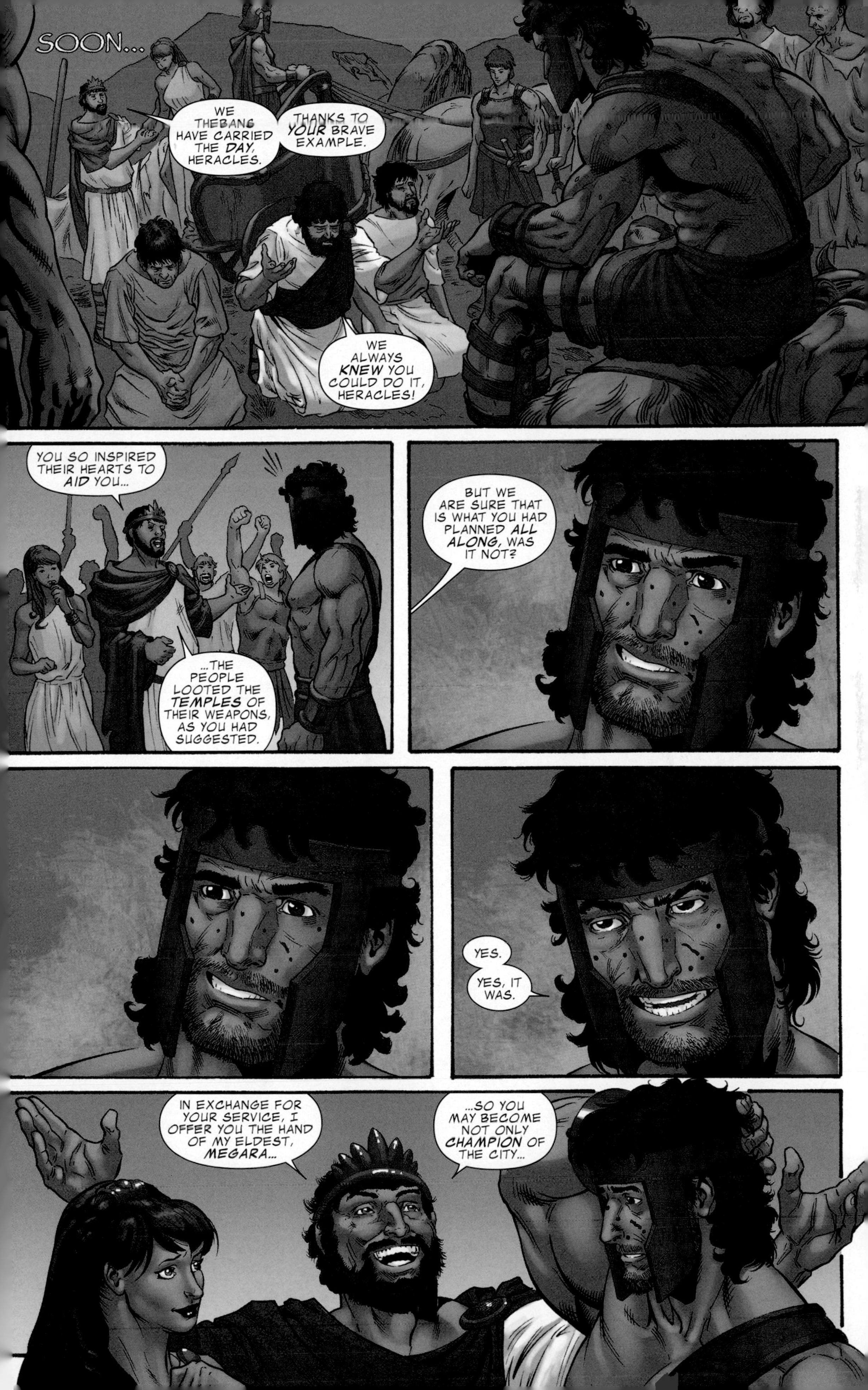
SOON...
WE THEBANS HAVE CARRIED THE DAY, HERACLES.
THANKS TO YOUR BRAVE EXAMPLE.
WE ALWAYS KNEW YOU COULD DO IT, HERACLES!
YOU SO INSPIRED THEIR HEARTS TO AID YOU...
...THE PEOPLE LOOTED THE TEMPLES OF THEIR WEAPONS, AS YOU HAD SUGGESTED.
BUT WE ARE SURE THAT IS WHAT YOU HAD PLANNED ALL ALONG, WAS IT NOT?
YES.
YES, IT WAS.
IN EXCHANGE FOR YOUR SERVICE, I OFFER YOU THE HAND OF MY ELDEST, MEGARA...
...SO YOU MAY BECOME NOT ONLY CHAMPION OF THE CITY...

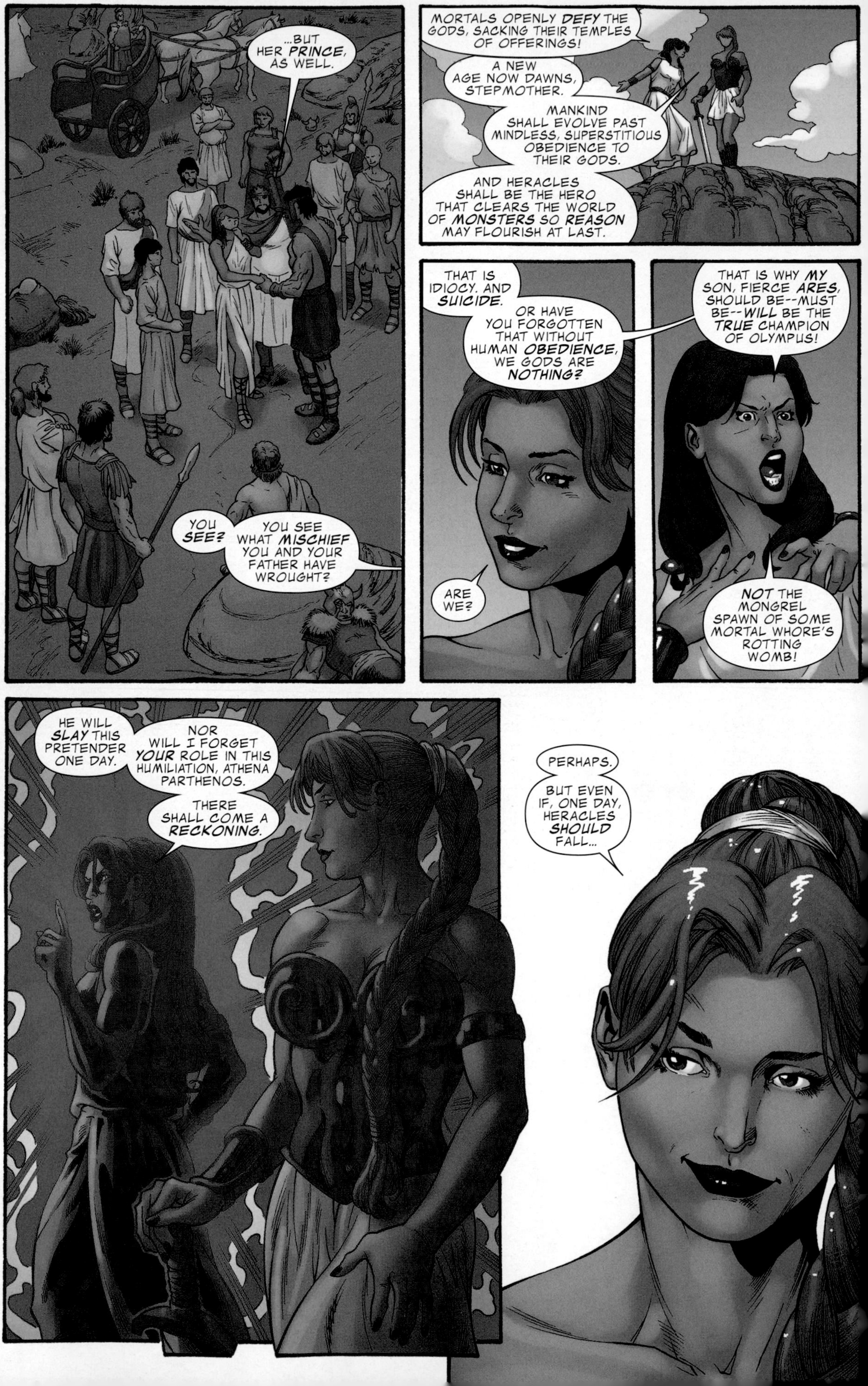
...BUT HER PRINCE, AS WELL.
YOU SEE?
YOU SEE WHAT MISCHIEF YOU AND YOUR FATHER HAVE WROUGHT?
MORTALS OPENLY DEFY THE GODS, SACKING THEIR TEMPLES OF OFFERINGS!
A NEW AGE NOW DAWNS, STEPMOTHER.
MANKIND SHALL EVOLVE PAST MINDLESS, SUPERSTITIOUS OBEDIENCE TO THEIR GODS.
AND HERACLES SHALL BE THE HERO THAT CLEARS THE WORLD OF MONSTERS SO REASON MAY FLOURISH AT LAST.
THAT IS IDIOCY. AND SUICIDE.
OR HAVE YOU FORGOTTEN THAT WITHOUT HUMAN OBEDIENCE, WE GODS ARE NOTHING?
ARE WE?
THAT IS WHY MY SON, FIERCE ARES, SHOULD BE--MUST BE--WILL BE THE TRUE CHAMPION OF OLYMPUS!
NOT THE MONGREL SPAWN OF SOME MORTAL WHORE'S ROTTING WOMB!
HE WILL SLAY THIS PRETENDER ONE DAY.
NOR WILL I FORGET YOUR ROLE IN THIS HUMILIATION, ATHENA PARTHENOS.
THERE SHALL COME A RECKONING.
PERHAPS.
BUT EVEN IF, ONE DAY, HERACLES SHOULD FALL...

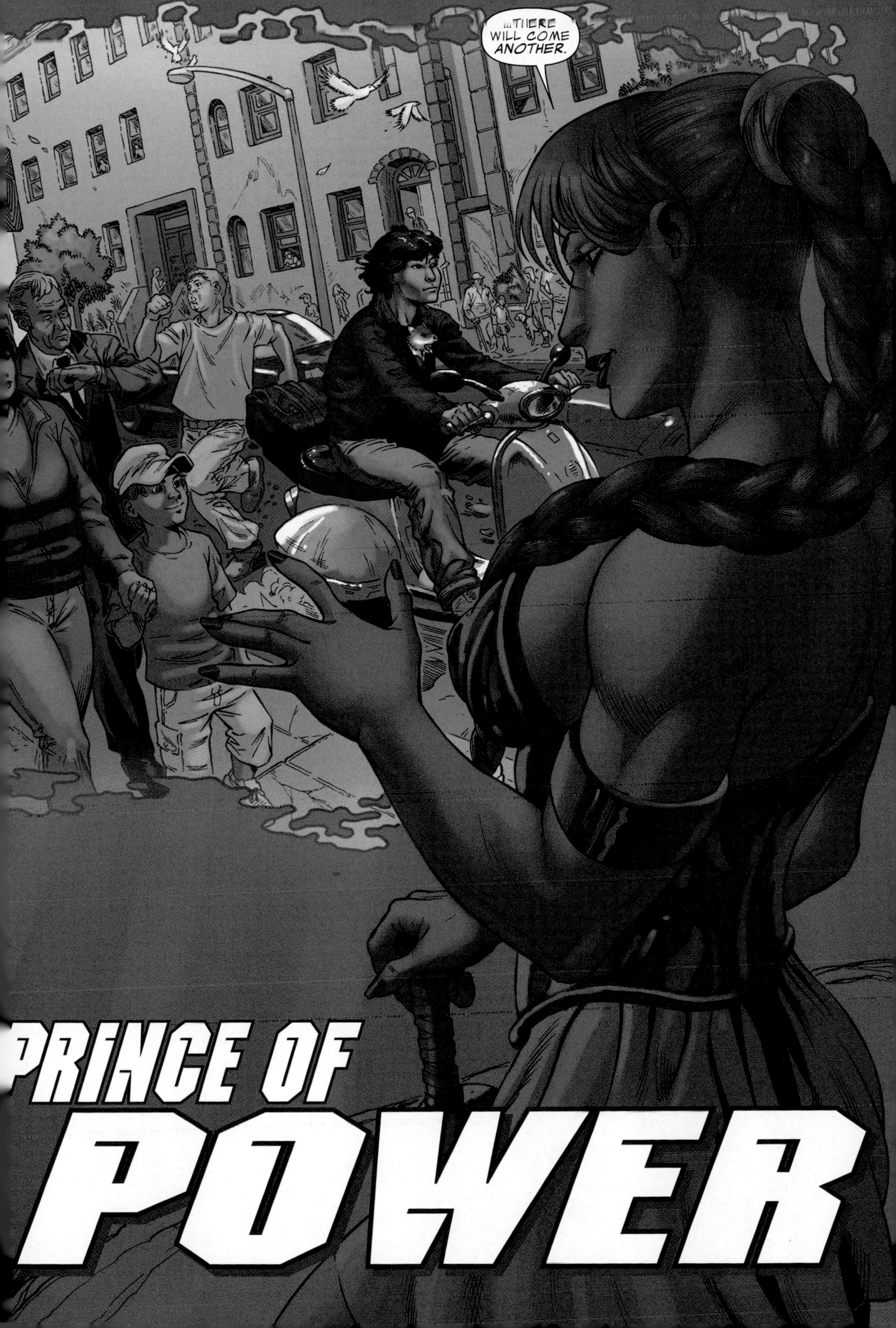
...THERE WILL COME ANOTHER.
PRINCE OF POWER

AND THUS BEGAN THE SAGA OF

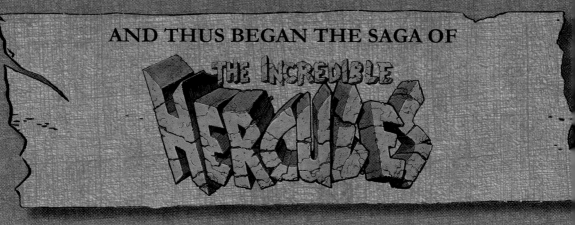

The man the Romans called "Hercules" became the great[est] of all heroes, ridding the land of the vicious beasts an[d] aberrations of the gods that had plagued it since time bega[n]. As Athena predicted, the Classical Age of Reason soo[n] began in the city named after her: Athens.

But not even Hercules' great strength could protect him from betrayal. Nessus, a centaur the hero slew for stealing away his wife, Deianira, tricked the gullible girl into putting on her husband a shirt poisoned with the blood of the Hydra, killing him in hideous agony.

BEHOLD! AN *IMAGE* HAVE I CREATED -- OF THE PLANET *EARTH!* IT IS *THERE* YOU MUST GO -- AFTER ALL THESE AGES.!!

I HEAR AND OBEY, VENERABLE LORD!

ALL THESE LONG CENTURIES -- WE THOUGHT ZEUS HAD *FORGOTTEN* EARTH! YET NOW, HE DISPATCHES *HERCULES* THERE!

HOW THE *LEGENDS*, IN AGES TO COME, SHALL SING OF THIS GLORIOUS MOMENT!

Hercules' true father, Zeus, to[ok] pity on him and raised his soul [up] to Olympus, home of the go[ds] until the Sky-Father adjudged [it] time for his great champion [to] return to Earth, during the Age [of] Marvels, for reasons that have y[et] to be fully revealed…

The Prince of Power acquitted himself well among the modern-day heroes, joining the Avengers and becoming a fast friend (and occasional sparring partner) of fellow legend of myth Thor.

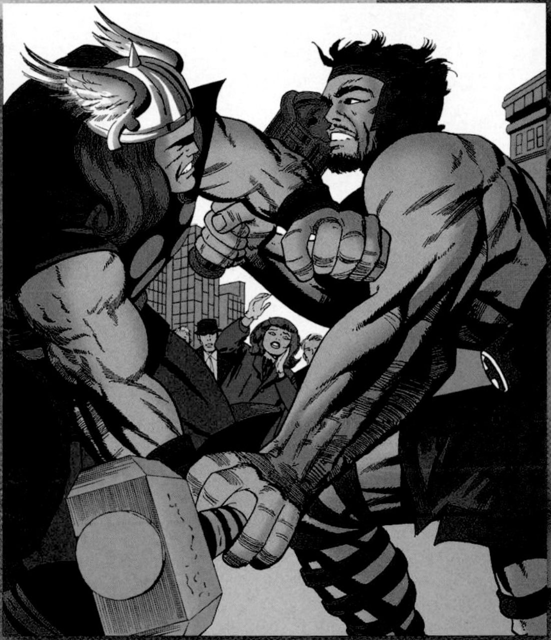

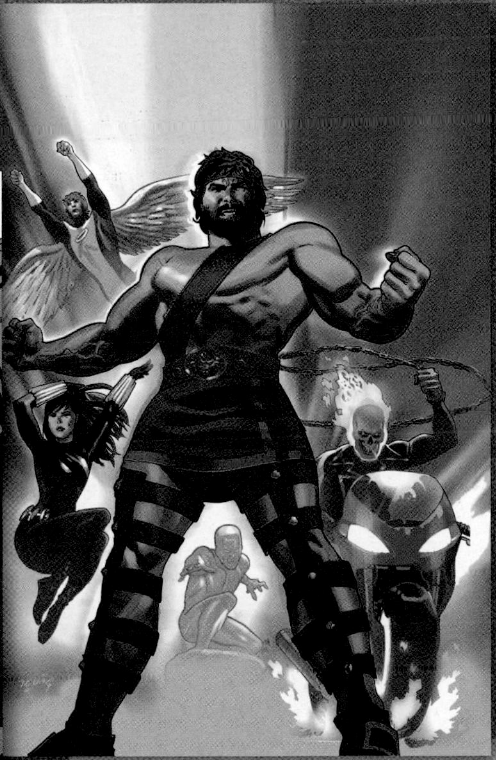

Residing for a time on America's West Coast, Hercules and a group of unaffiliated heroes formed the short-lived Champions of Los Angeles.

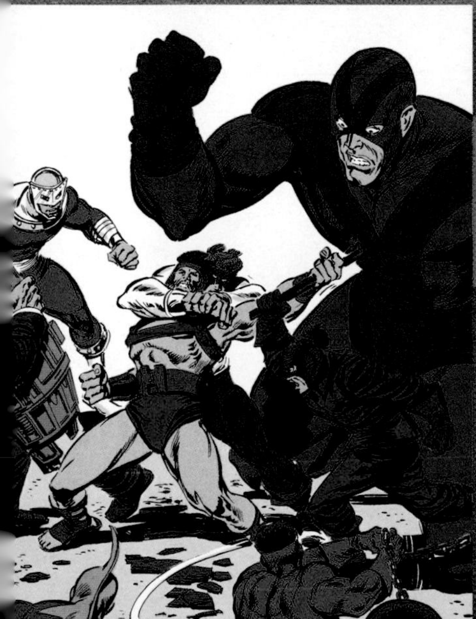

Later, the Lion of Olympus nearly suffered a second death defending Avengers Mansion from Baron Zemo's Masters of Evil army while again serving with Earth's Mightiest Heroes.

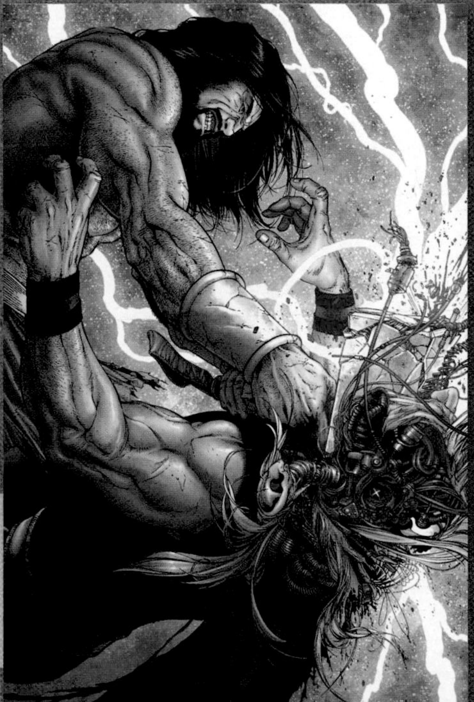

Hercules' strong belief in the nobility of heroism led him to take the side of Captain America's anti-Registration insurgency when the super hero Civil War broke out. In battle with pro-Registration forces, Herc slew the clone of his old friend Thor with the duplicate's own hammer.

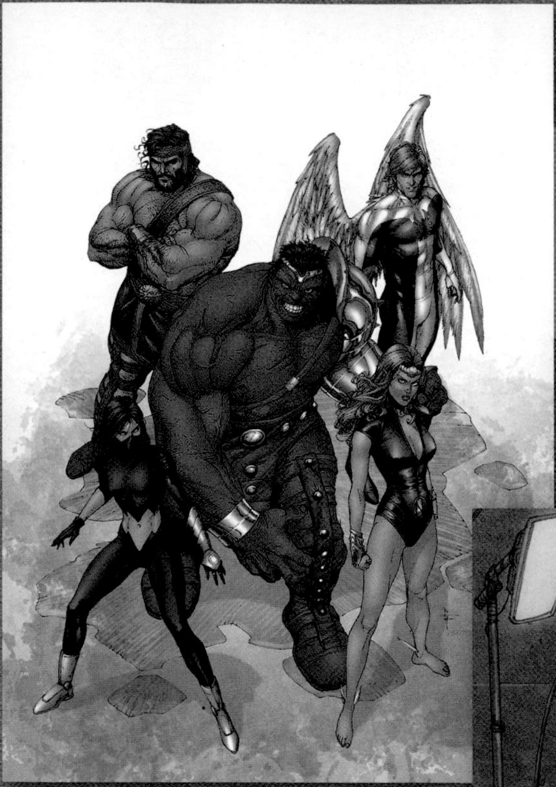

Herc continued his fierce opposition of the Superhuma
Registration Act even after Captain America surrendere
to the government. He was one of the renegade hero
boy genius Amadeus Cho, ally to the monstrous Hul
persuaded to stand with the Jade Giant in his war again
the Illuminati for exiling him into space.

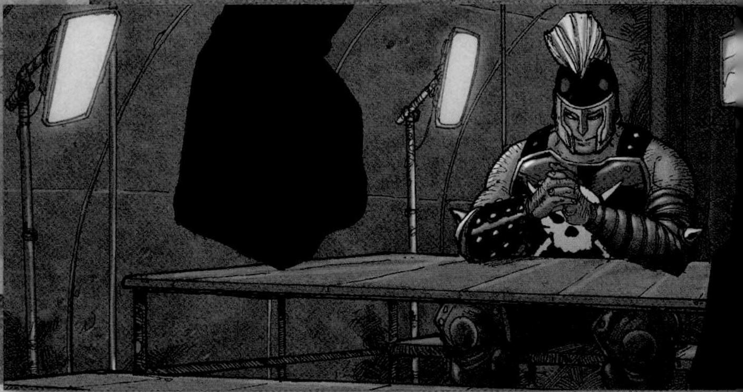

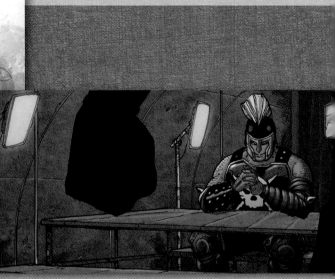

At the conclusion of World War Hulk, Hercules learned the Hulk's side ha
been duped into conflict by the treacherous alien Miek. The Prince of Pow
surrendered to S.H.I.E.L.D., but balked upon learning that meant he wou
have to serve in The Initiative with his hated half-brother Ares, God of Wa
who through a cruel twist of fate was now an Avenger himself.

And so Hercules escaped along with the unrepentant Cho…

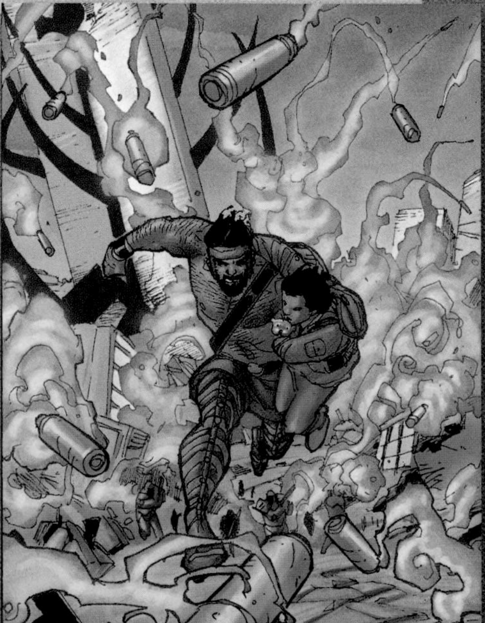

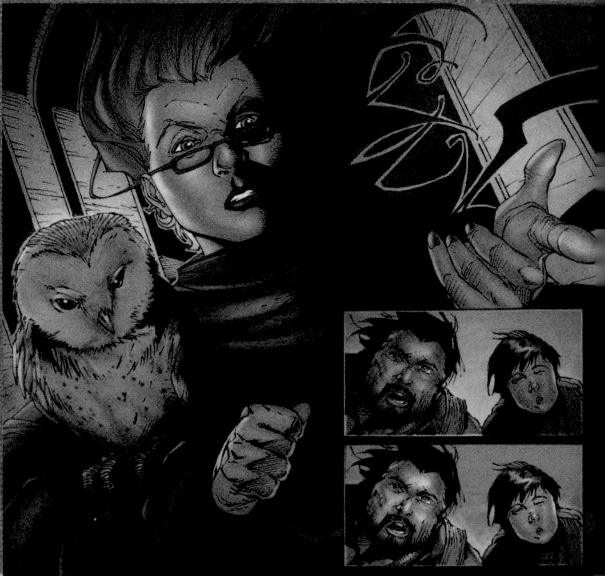

…helped by Athena, who appeared at the time to be mer
supporting her younger brother. But the Goddess of Her
Endeavor operates on a level far beyond the comprehensi
of most mortal men, and was immediately taken with t
young Cho for some inscrutable reason…

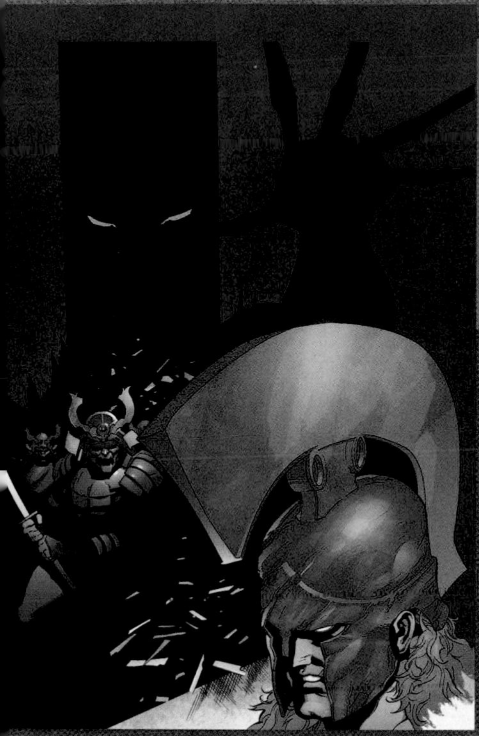

Athena now resided on Earth along with the other Olympians, for in the wake of Ragnarok, which destroyed the Asgardians, the Japanese God of Evil Amatsu-Mikaboshi set about conquering all the Earthly pantheons, beginning with the realm of the Greek gods. Hercules and Ares temporarily set aside their differences to unite against this common threat. Though Mikaboshi was ultimately defeated, once-beautiful Olympus was utterly and irrevocably destroyed…

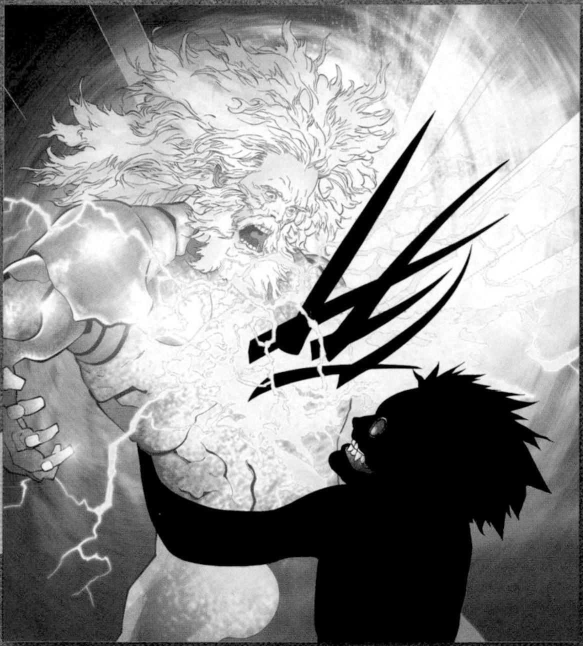

…and Zeus, Hercules' and Ares' father, was slain by the demonic god.

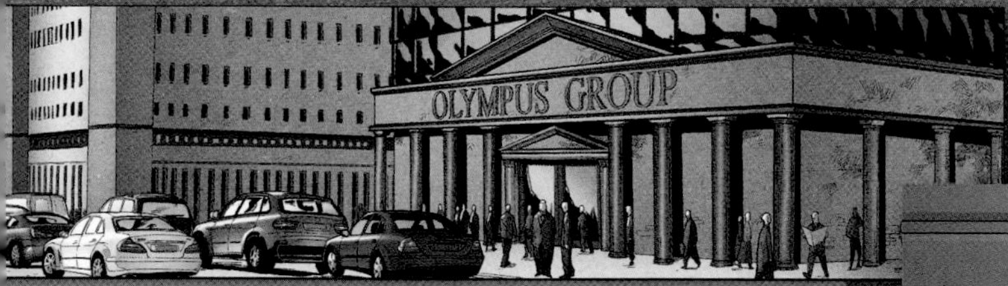
OLYMPUS GROUP

eus had anticipated the coming apocalypse, however, and nsferred the seat of the gods' power to a mortal corporation, e Olympus Group.

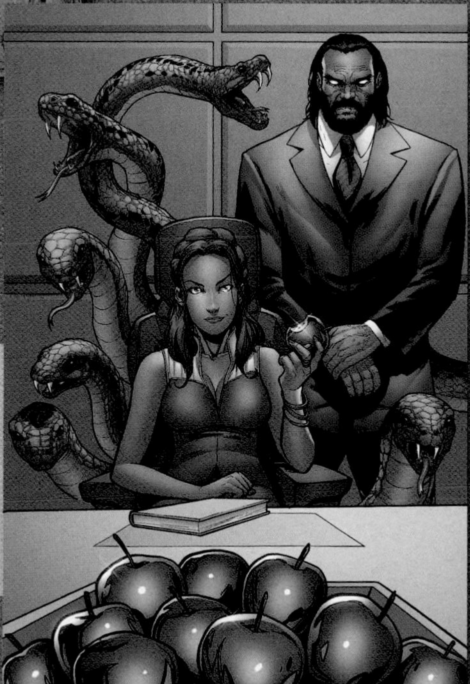

With Zeus now dead, however, Hera inherited control of the Olympus Group, along with her husband's powerful thunderbolt. Her Dark Reign has united the Olympian villains under her rule and she has declared it time to at last revenge herself against Athena and Hercules for their many crimes, real and perceived, against her – beginning immediately.

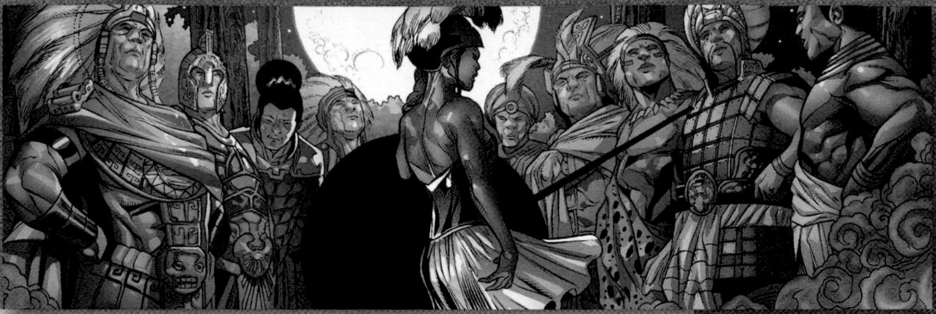

Athena continued to vex Hera by taking power into her own hands. In the wake of the Secret Invasion of Earth by the Skrulls, Athena summoned the Council Elite of Earth's pantheons together to confront the aliens' own god, Kly'bn.

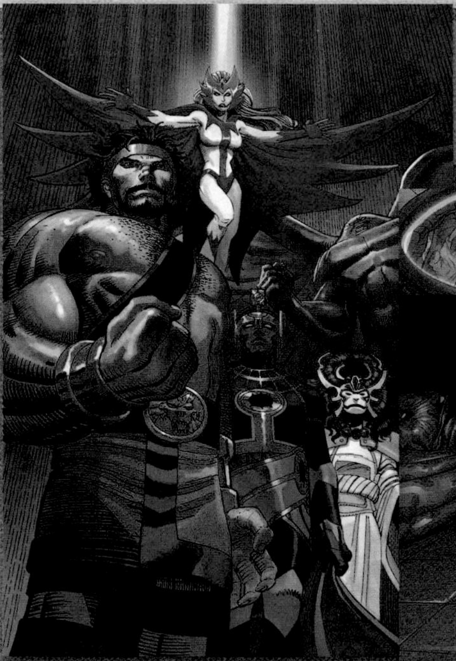

Athena conscripted Herc and Amadeus to lead a God Squa into battle against the Skrull pantheon. Over Hercules' vigorou objections, the Japanese gods sent Mikaboshi with him as the representative.

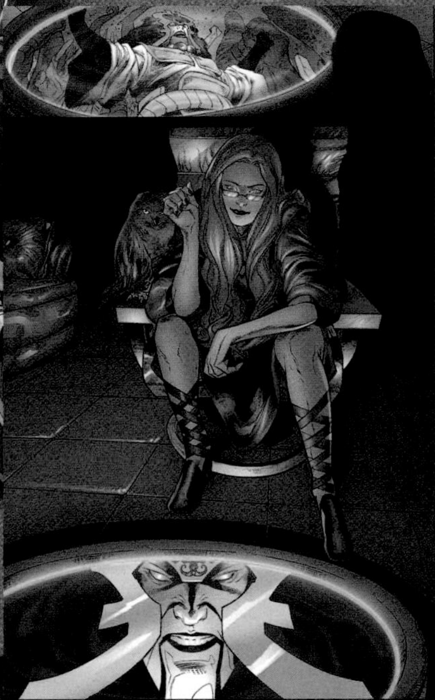

The Prince of Power's misgiving proved well-founded. Once Kly'b was slain and Herc and Cho escape back to Earth, Mikaboshi use shape-shifting deceit to assun command of the Skrulls' capti slave-gods. Yet, mysteriously, th seemed to please Athena…

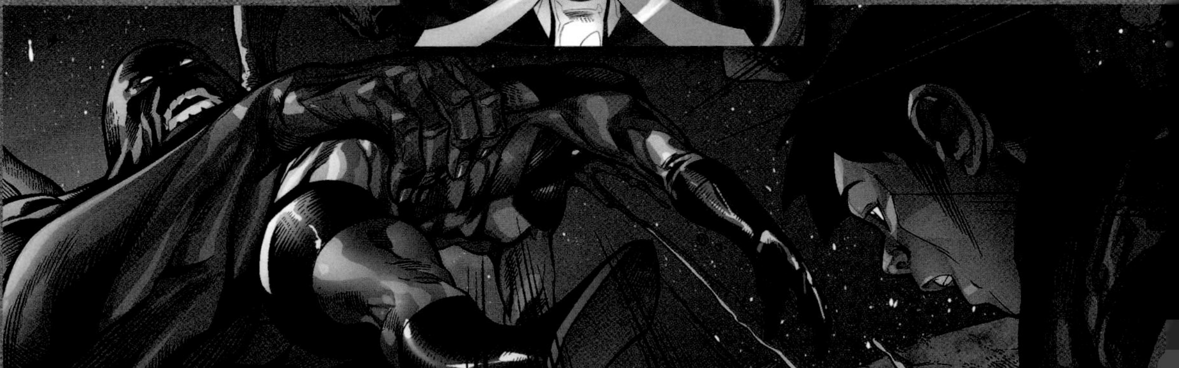

Tragically, on this adventure our heroes lost their smallest companion: Kerberos ("Kirby"), Amadeus Cho beloved coyote pup and companion throughout his wanderings, was revealed to have been replaced by Skrull to infiltrate and sabotage the God Squad.

But Amadeus Cho has proven himself a most resourceful lad, and it seemed doubtful he would allow h pet to disappear without a thorough and relentless investigation…

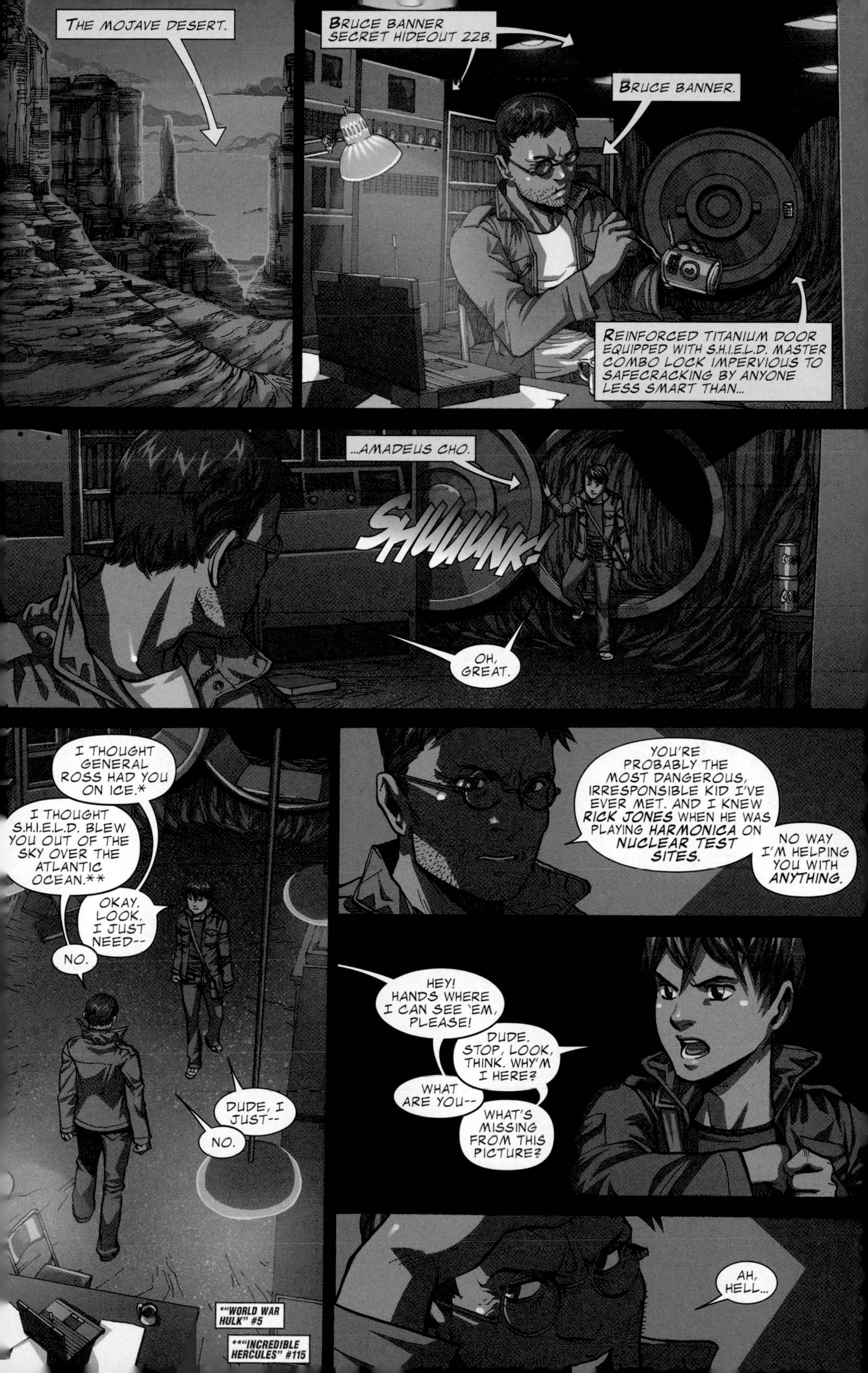
THE MOJAVE DESERT.
BRUCE BANNER SECRET HIDEOUT 22B.
BRUCE BANNER.
REINFORCED TITANIUM DOOR EQUIPPED WITH S.H.I.E.L.D. MASTER COMBO LOCK IMPERVIOUS TO SAFECRACKING BY ANYONE LESS SMART THAN...
...AMADEUS CHO.
SHUUUNK!
OH, GREAT.
I THOUGHT GENERAL ROSS HAD YOU ON ICE.*
I THOUGHT S.H.I.E.L.D. BLEW YOU OUT OF THE SKY OVER THE ATLANTIC OCEAN.**
OKAY. LOOK. I JUST NEED--
NO.
DUDE, I JUST--
NO.
*"WORLD WAR HULK" #5
**"INCREDIBLE HERCULES" #115
YOU'RE PROBABLY THE MOST DANGEROUS, IRRESPONSIBLE KID I'VE EVER MET. AND I KNEW RICK JONES WHEN HE WAS PLAYING HARMONICA ON NUCLEAR TEST SITES.
NO WAY I'M HELPING YOU WITH ANYTHING.
HEY! HANDS WHERE I CAN SEE 'EM, PLEASE!
DUDE. STOP, LOOK, THINK. WHY'M I HERE?
WHAT ARE YOU--
WHAT'S MISSING FROM THIS PICTURE?
AH, HELL...

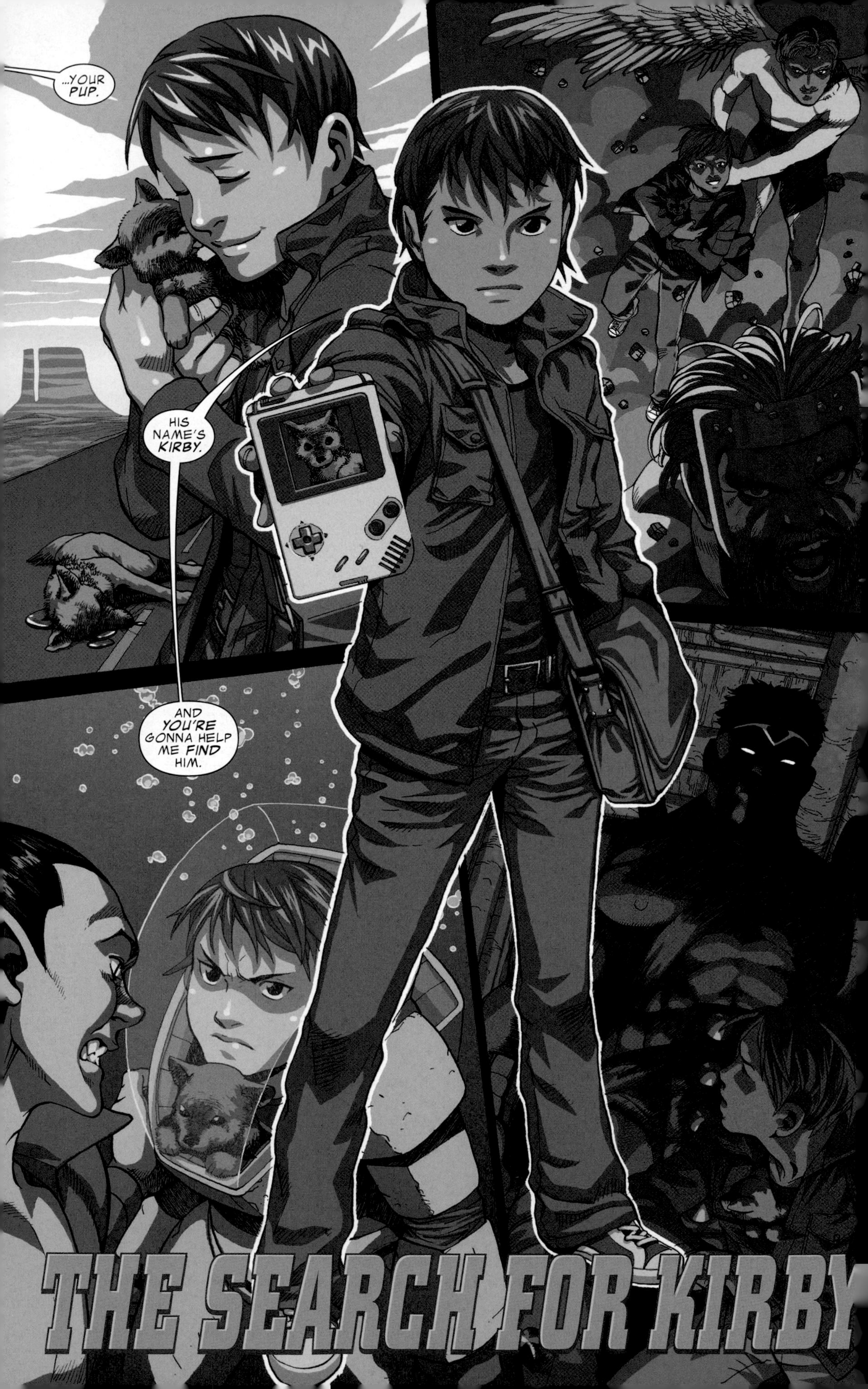
...YOUR PUP.
HIS NAME'S KIRBY.
AND YOU'RE GONNA HELP ME FIND HIM.
THE SEARCH FOR KIRBY

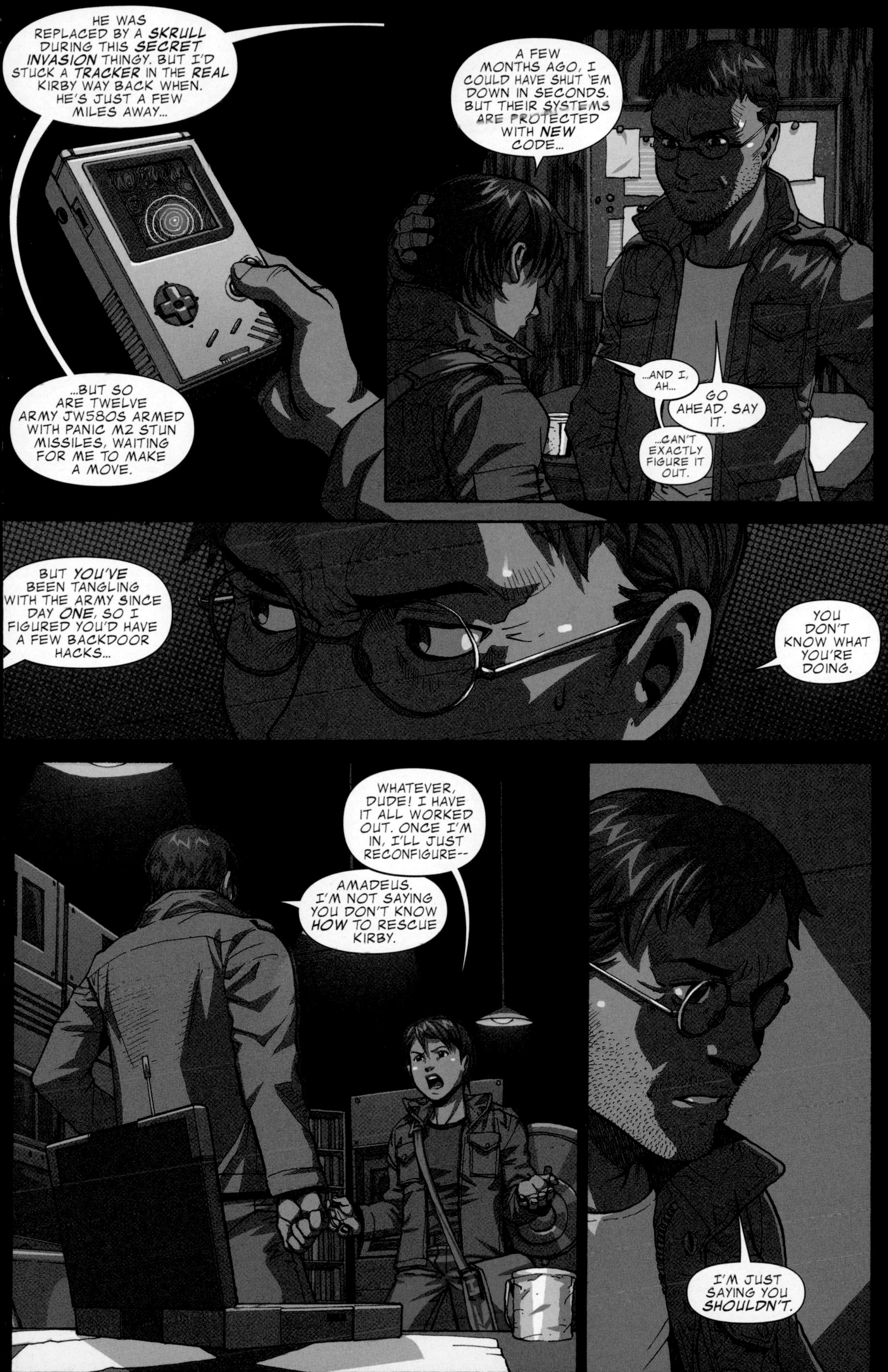
HE WAS REPLACED BY A SKRULL DURING THIS SECRET INVASION THINGY. BUT I'D STUCK A TRACKER IN THE REAL KIRBY WAY BACK WHEN. HE'S JUST A FEW MILES AWAY...
...BUT SO ARE TWELVE ARMY JW580S ARMED WITH PANIC M2 STUN MISSILES, WAITING FOR ME TO MAKE A MOVE.
A FEW MONTHS AGO, I COULD HAVE SHUT 'EM DOWN IN SECONDS. BUT THEIR SYSTEMS ARE PROTECTED WITH NEW CODE...
...AND I, AH...
GO AHEAD. SAY IT.
...CAN'T EXACTLY FIGURE IT OUT.
BUT YOU'VE BEEN TANGLING WITH THE ARMY SINCE DAY ONE, SO I FIGURED YOU'D HAVE A FEW BACKDOOR HACKS...
YOU DON'T KNOW WHAT YOU'RE DOING.
WHATEVER, DUDE! I HAVE IT ALL WORKED OUT. ONCE I'M IN, I'LL JUST RECONFIGURE--
AMADEUS. I'M NOT SAYING YOU DON'T KNOW HOW TO RESCUE KIRBY.
I'M JUST SAYING YOU SHOULDN'T.

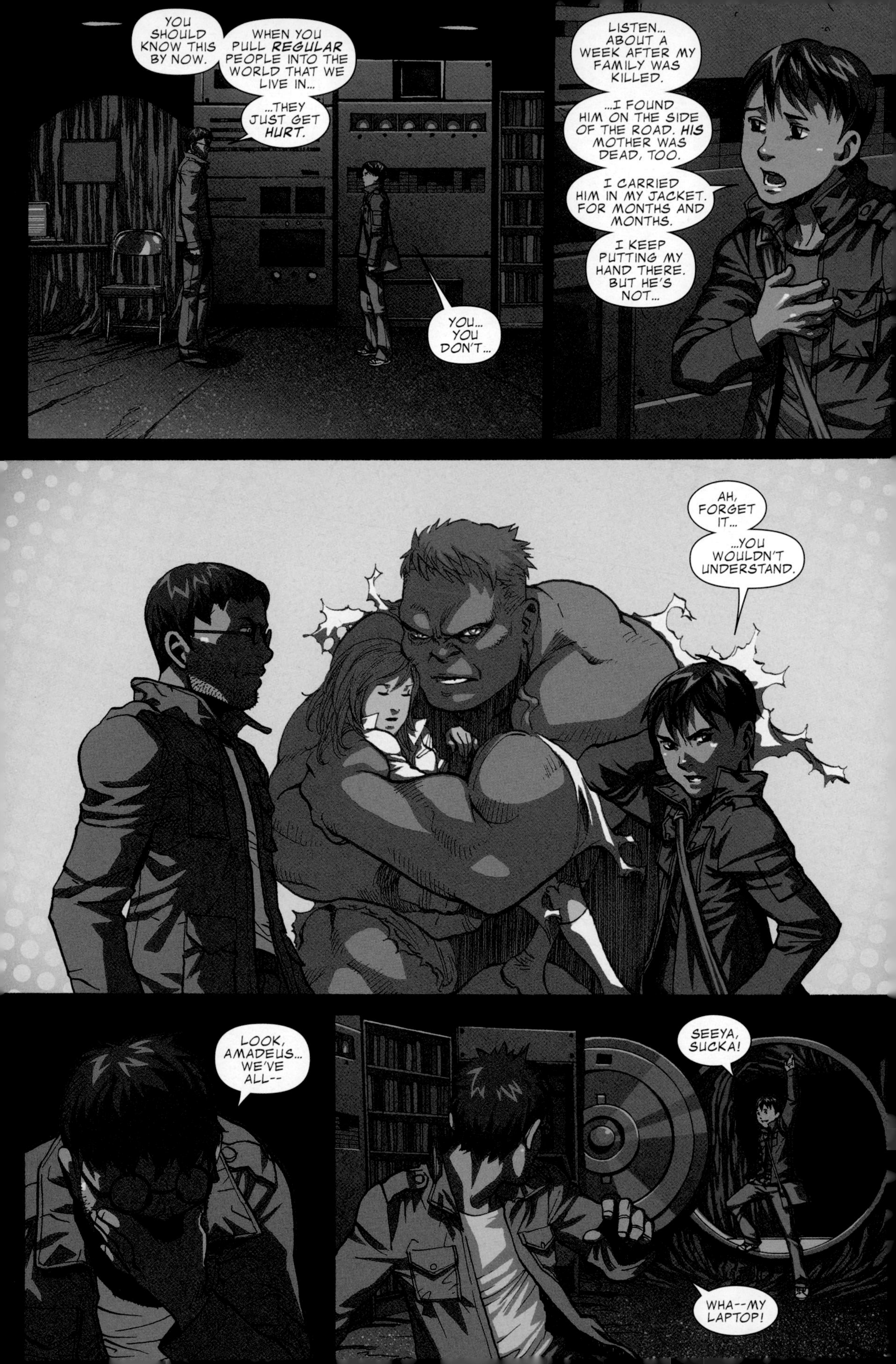
YOU SHOULD KNOW THIS BY NOW.
WHEN YOU PULL REGULAR PEOPLE INTO THE WORLD THAT WE LIVE IN...
...THEY JUST GET HURT.
YOU... YOU DON'T...
LISTEN... ABOUT A WEEK AFTER MY FAMILY WAS KILLED.
...I FOUND HIM ON THE SIDE OF THE ROAD. HIS MOTHER WAS DEAD, TOO.
I CARRIED HIM IN MY JACKET. FOR MONTHS AND MONTHS.
I KEEP PUTTING MY HAND THERE. BUT HE'S NOT...
AH, FORGET IT...
...YOU WOULDN'T UNDERSTAND.
LOOK, AMADEUS... WE'VE ALL--
SEEYA, SUCKA!
WHA--MY LAPTOP!

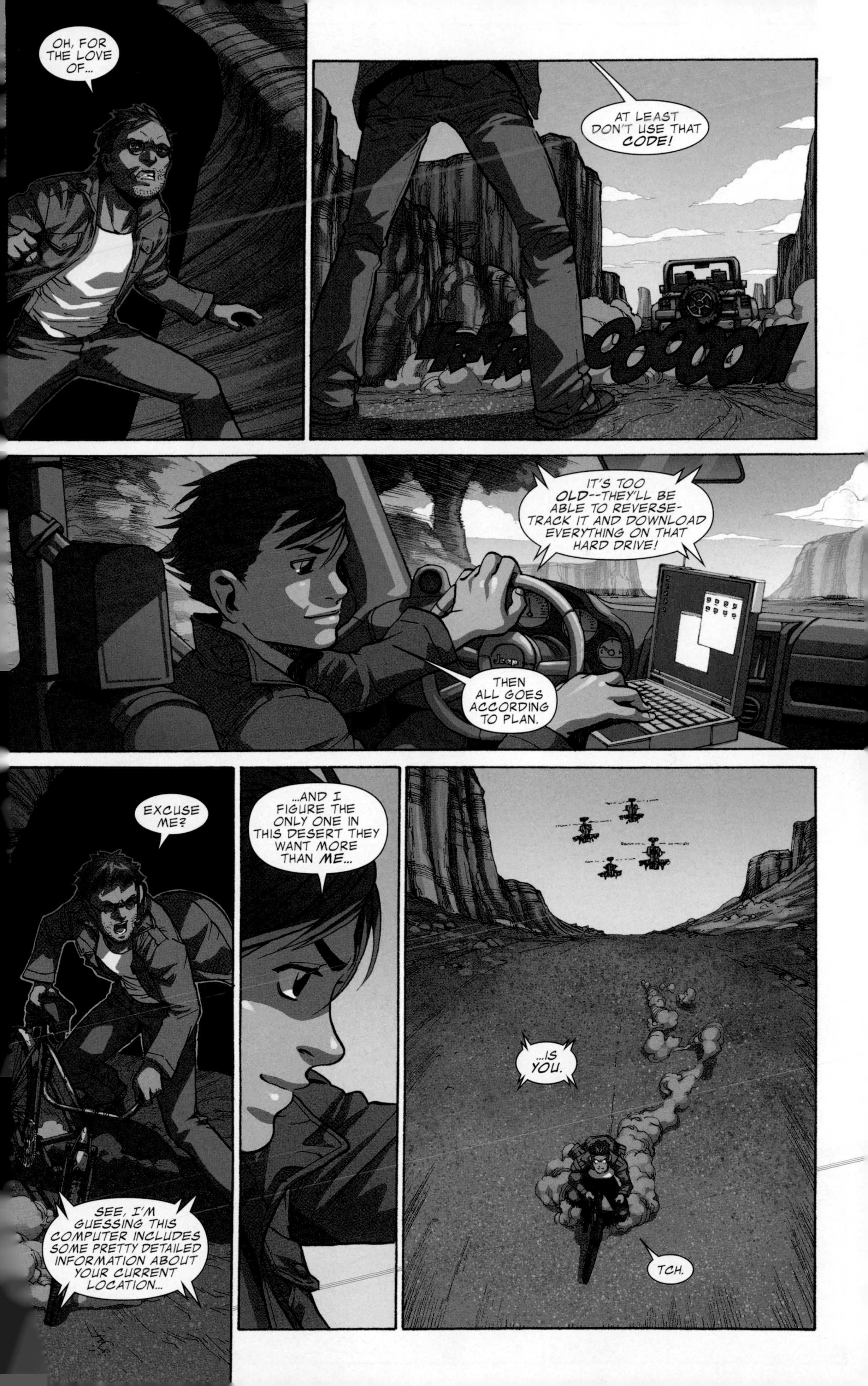
OH, FOR THE LOVE OF...
AT LEAST DON'T USE THAT CODE!
VRRROOOOOM
IT'S TOO OLD--THEY'LL BE ABLE TO REVERSE-TRACK IT AND DOWNLOAD EVERYTHING ON THAT HARD DRIVE!
THEN ALL GOES ACCORDING TO PLAN.
EXCUSE ME?
SEE, I'M GUESSING THIS COMPUTER INCLUDES SOME PRETTY DETAILED INFORMATION ABOUT YOUR CURRENT LOCATION...
...AND I FIGURE THE ONLY ONE IN THIS DESERT THEY WANT MORE THAN ME...
...IS YOU.
TCH.

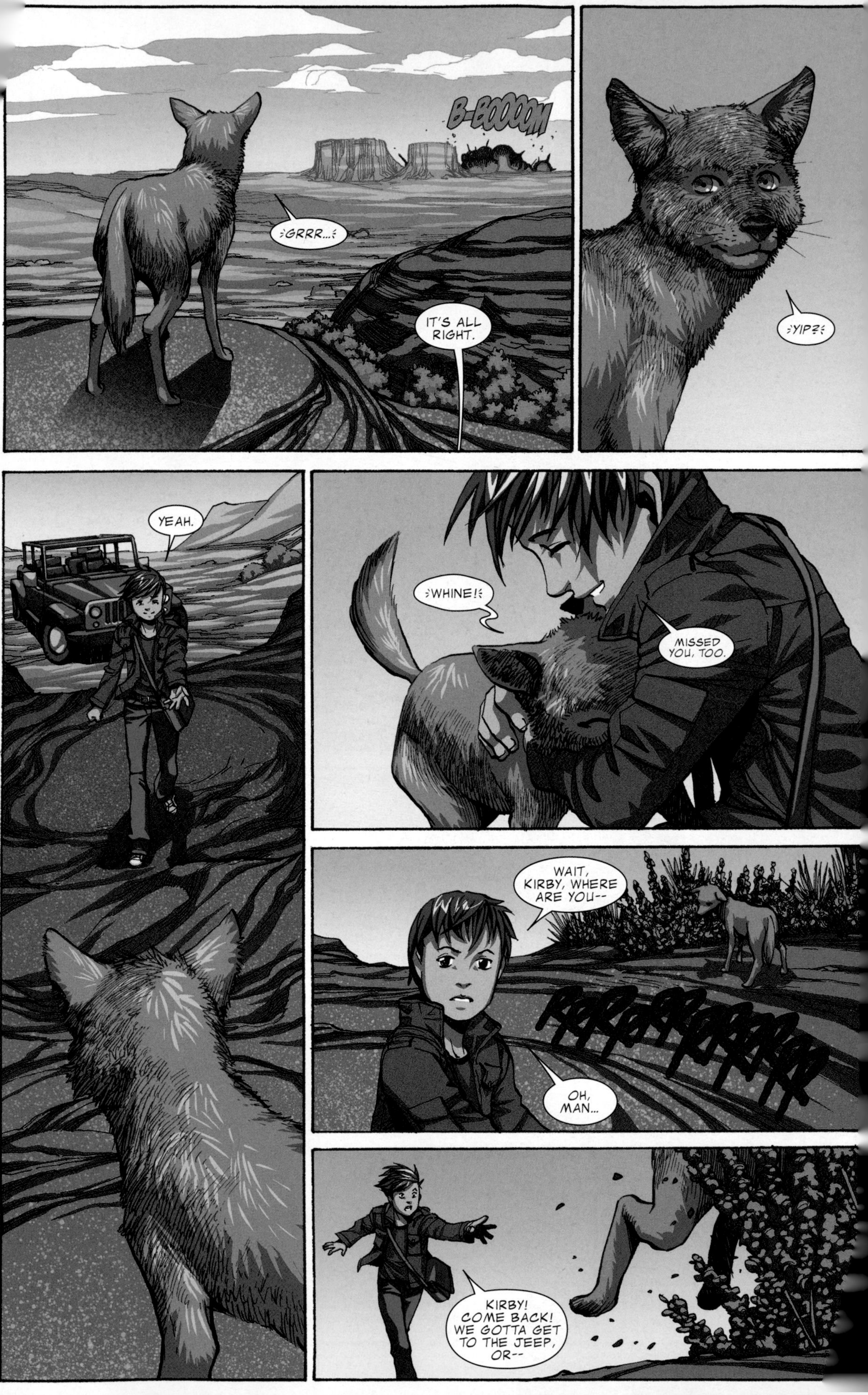
B-BOOOOM
GRRR...
IT'S ALL RIGHT.
YIP?
YEAH.
WHINE!
MISSED YOU, TOO.
WAIT, KIRBY, WHERE ARE YOU--
RRRRRRRRRRRRR
OH, MAN...
KIRBY! COME BACK! WE GOTTA GET TO THE JEEP, OR--

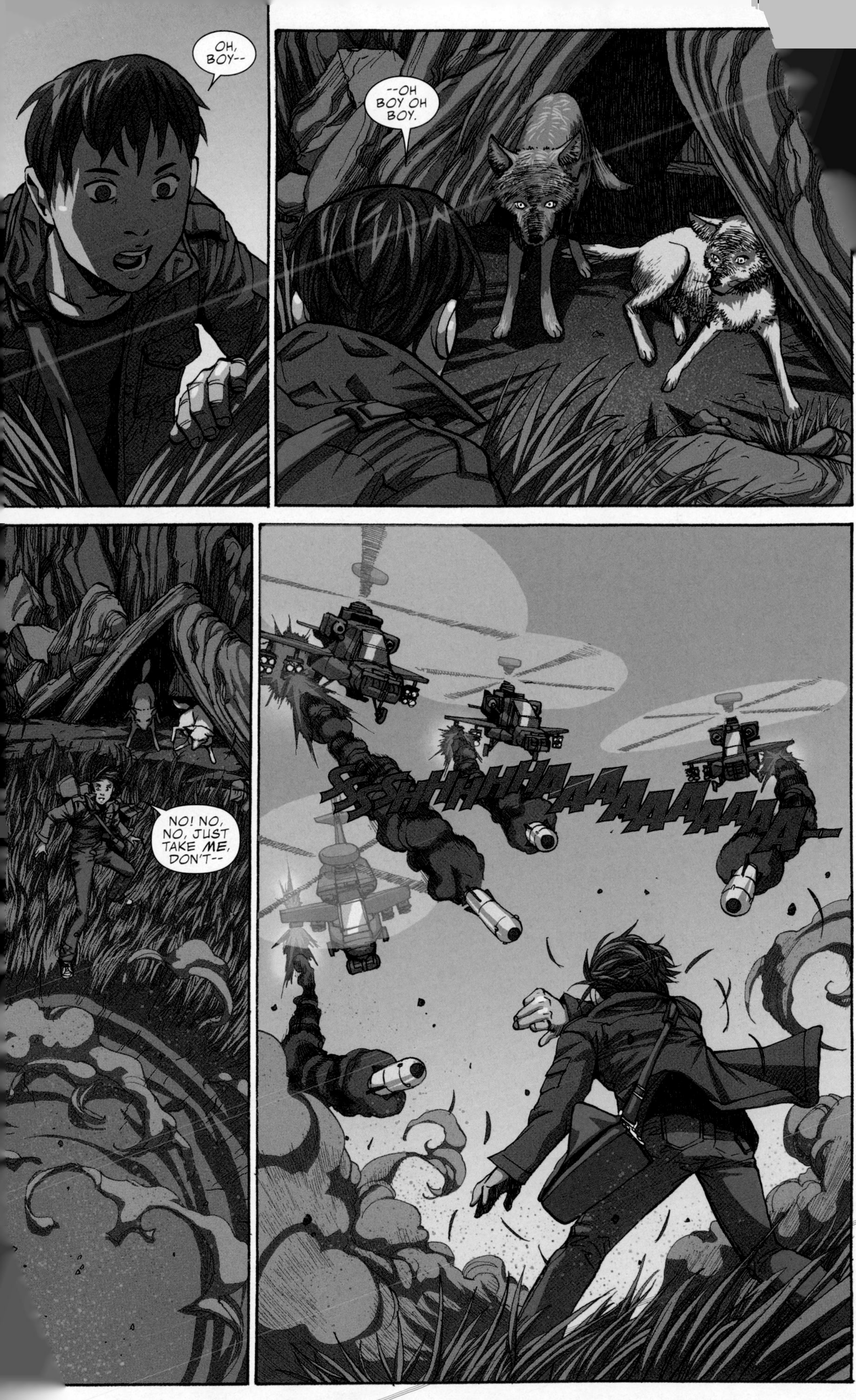
OH, BOY--
--OH BOY OH BOY.
NO! NO, NO, JUST TAKE *ME*, DON'T--
SSSHHHHHAAAAAAAAAA

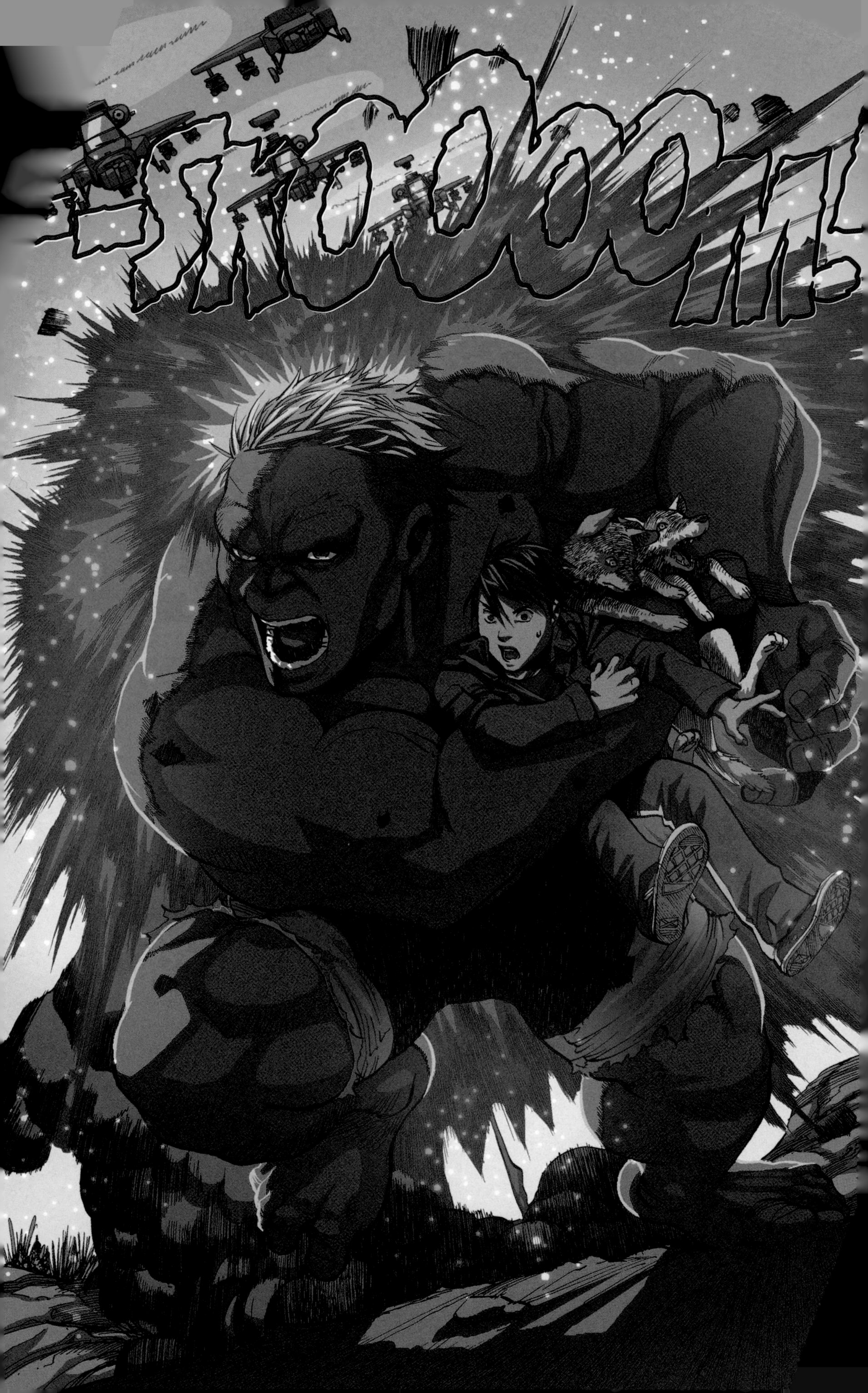

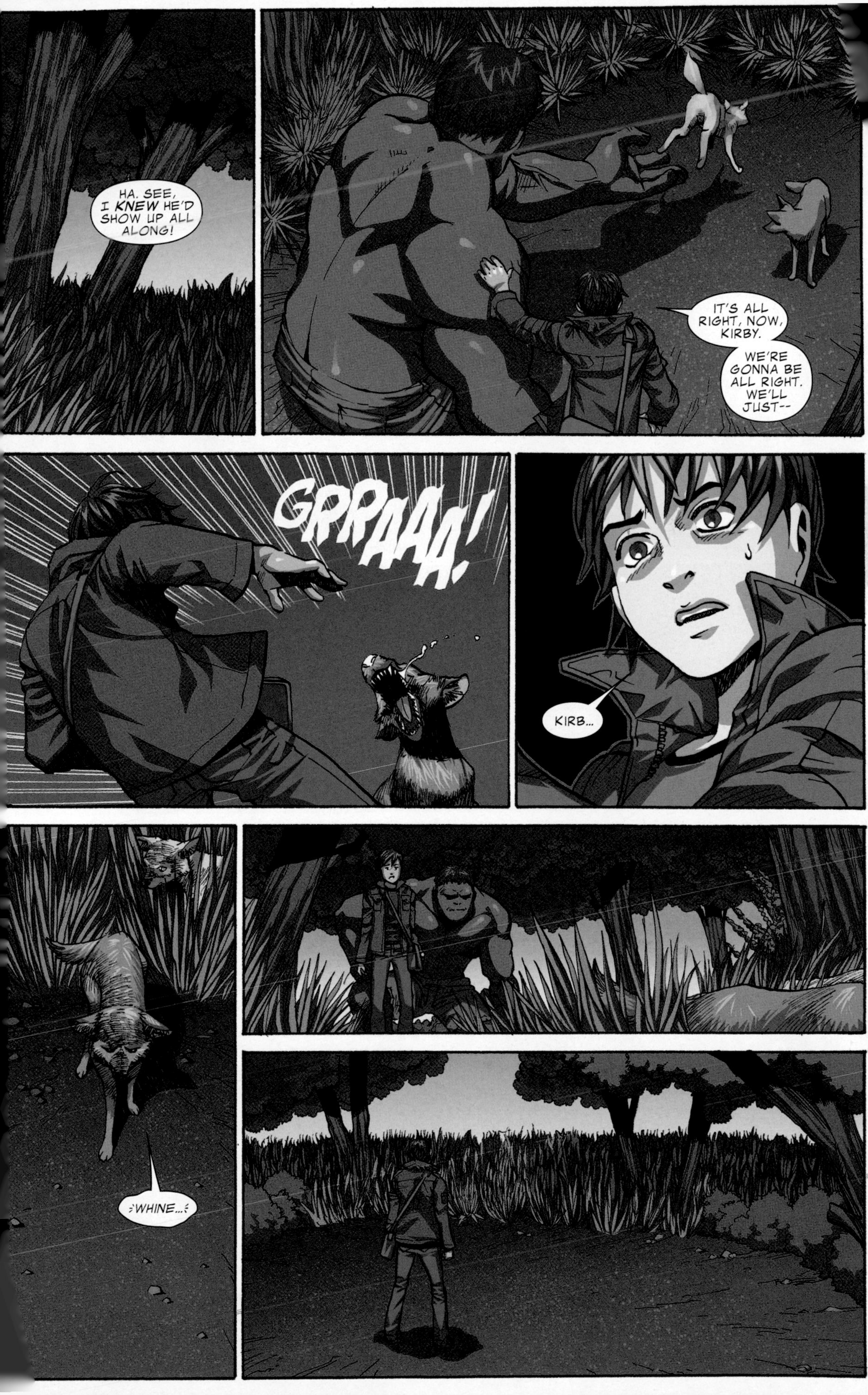
HA. SEE, I KNEW HE'D SHOW UP ALL ALONG!
IT'S ALL RIGHT, NOW, KIRBY.
WE'RE GONNA BE ALL RIGHT. WE'LL JUST--
GRRAAA!
KIRB...
WHINE...

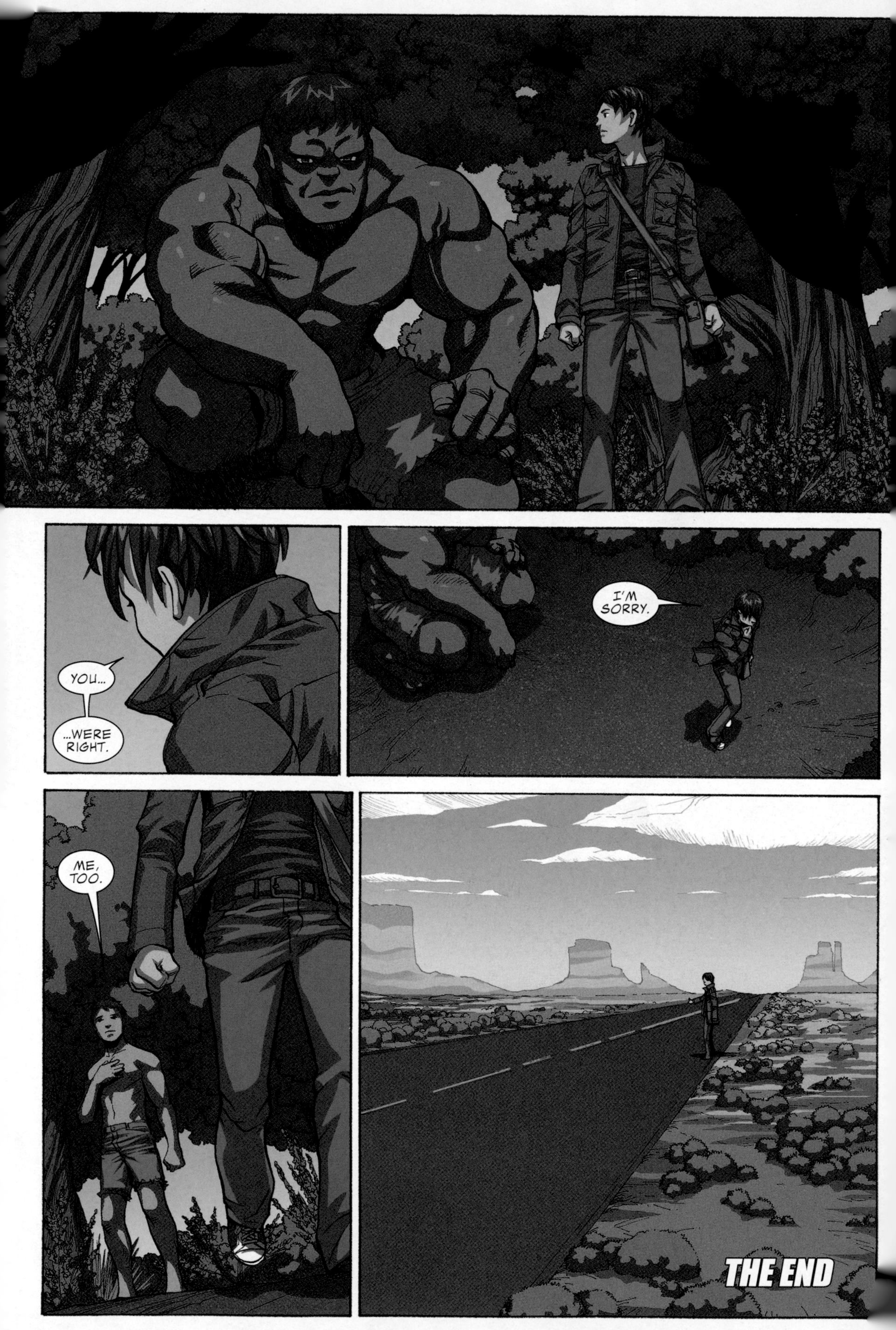
YOU...
...WERE RIGHT.
I'M SORRY.
ME, TOO.
THE END

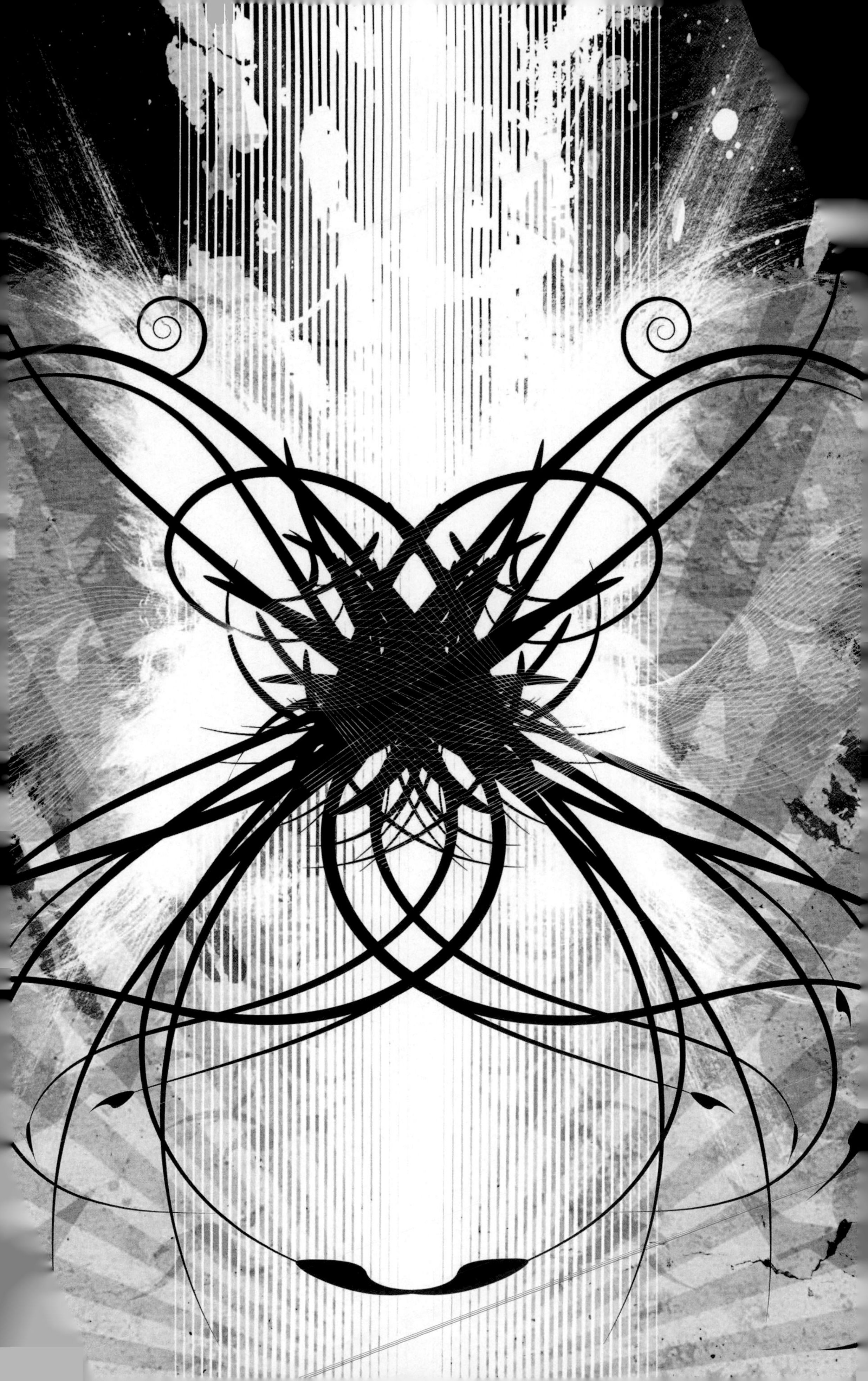

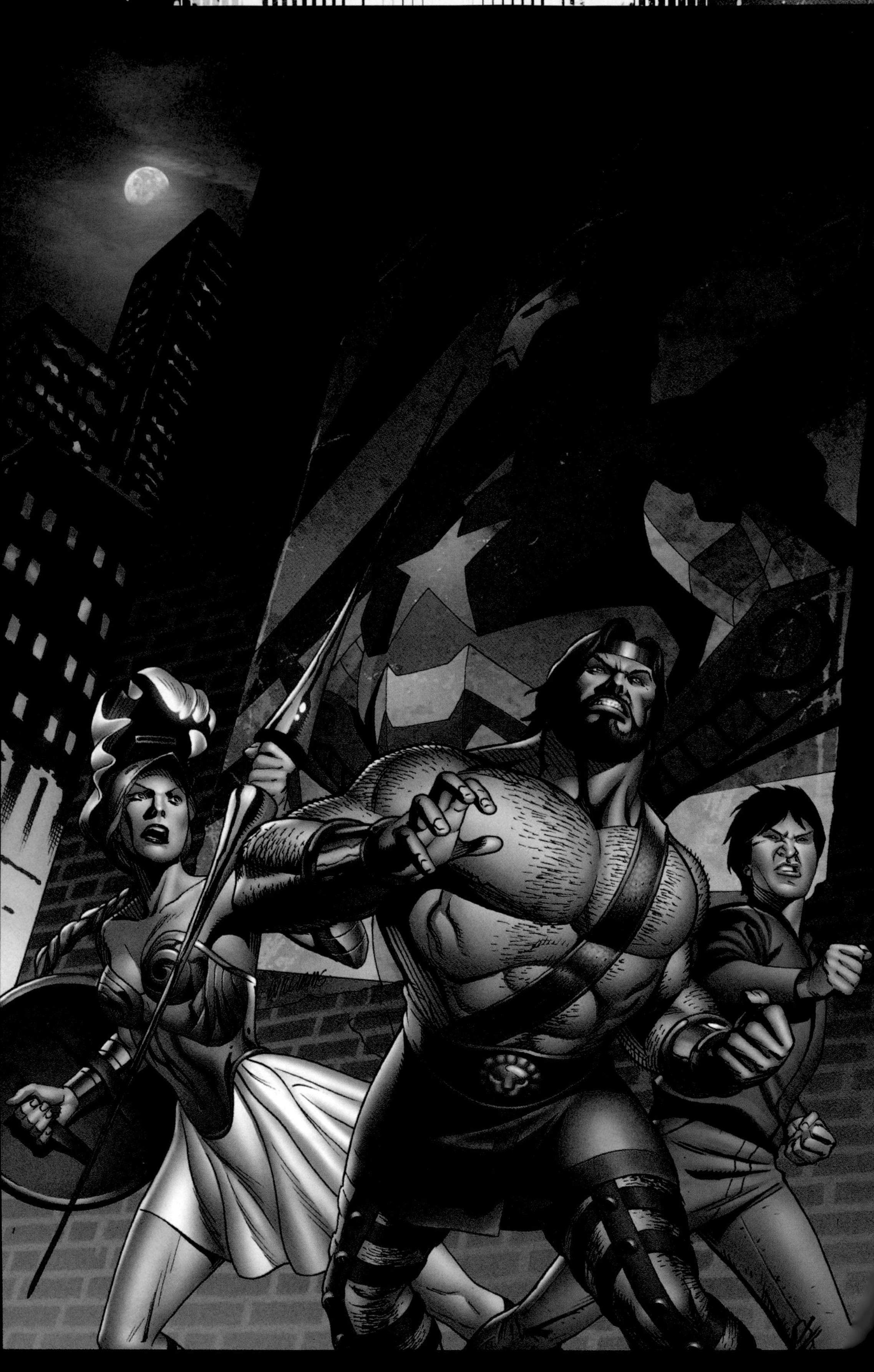

INCREDIBLE HERCULES #127

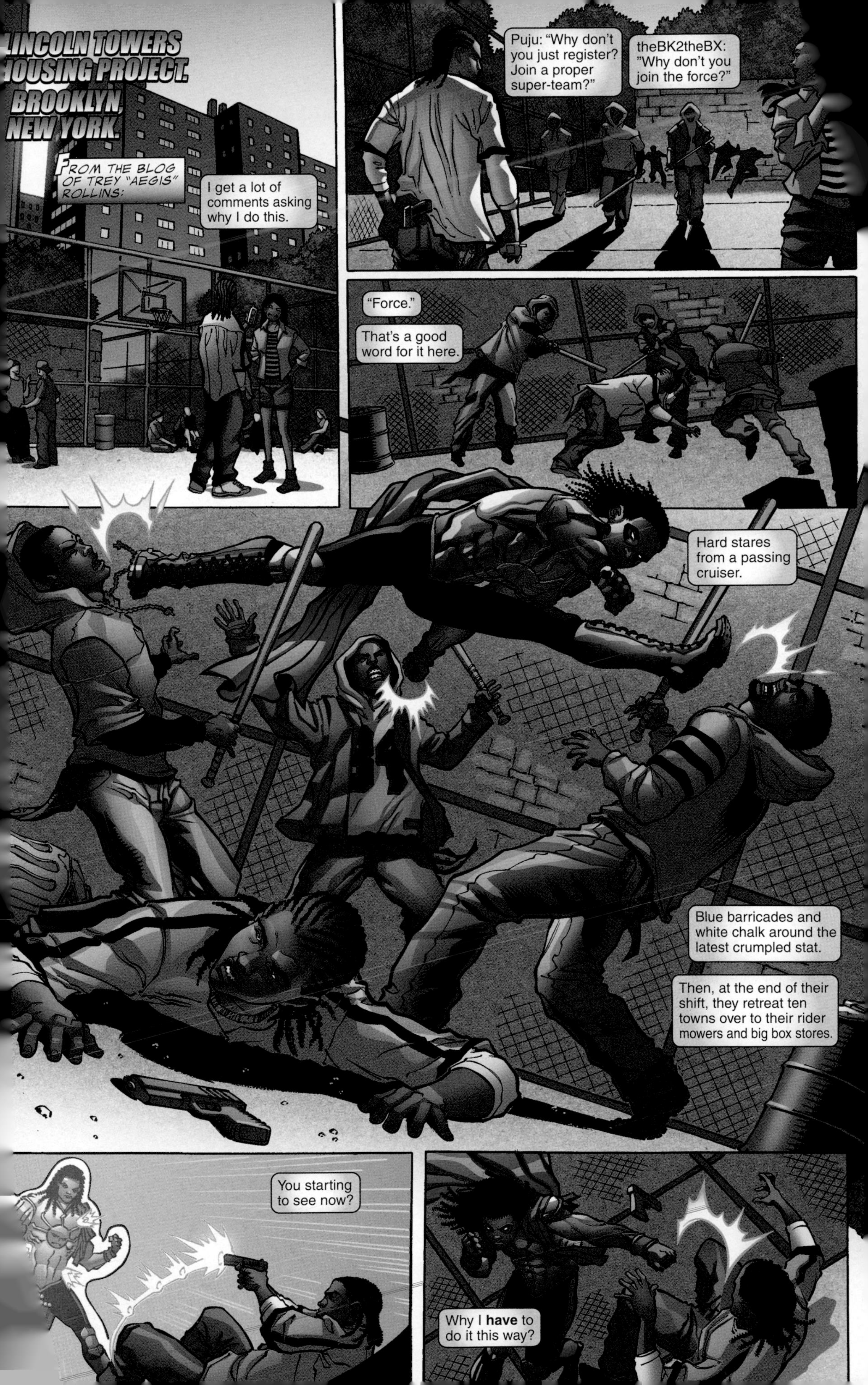
LINCOLN TOWERS HOUSING PROJECT. BROOKLYN, NEW YORK.
FROM THE BLOG OF TREY "AEGIS" ROLLINS:
I get a lot of comments asking why I do this.
Puju: "Why don't you just register? Join a proper super-team?"
theBK2theBX: "Why don't you join the force?"
"Force."
That's a good word for it here.
Hard stares from a passing cruiser.
Blue barricades and white chalk around the latest crumpled stat.
Then, at the end of their shift, they retreat ten towns over to their rider mowers and big box stores.
You starting to see now?
Why I **have** to do it this way?

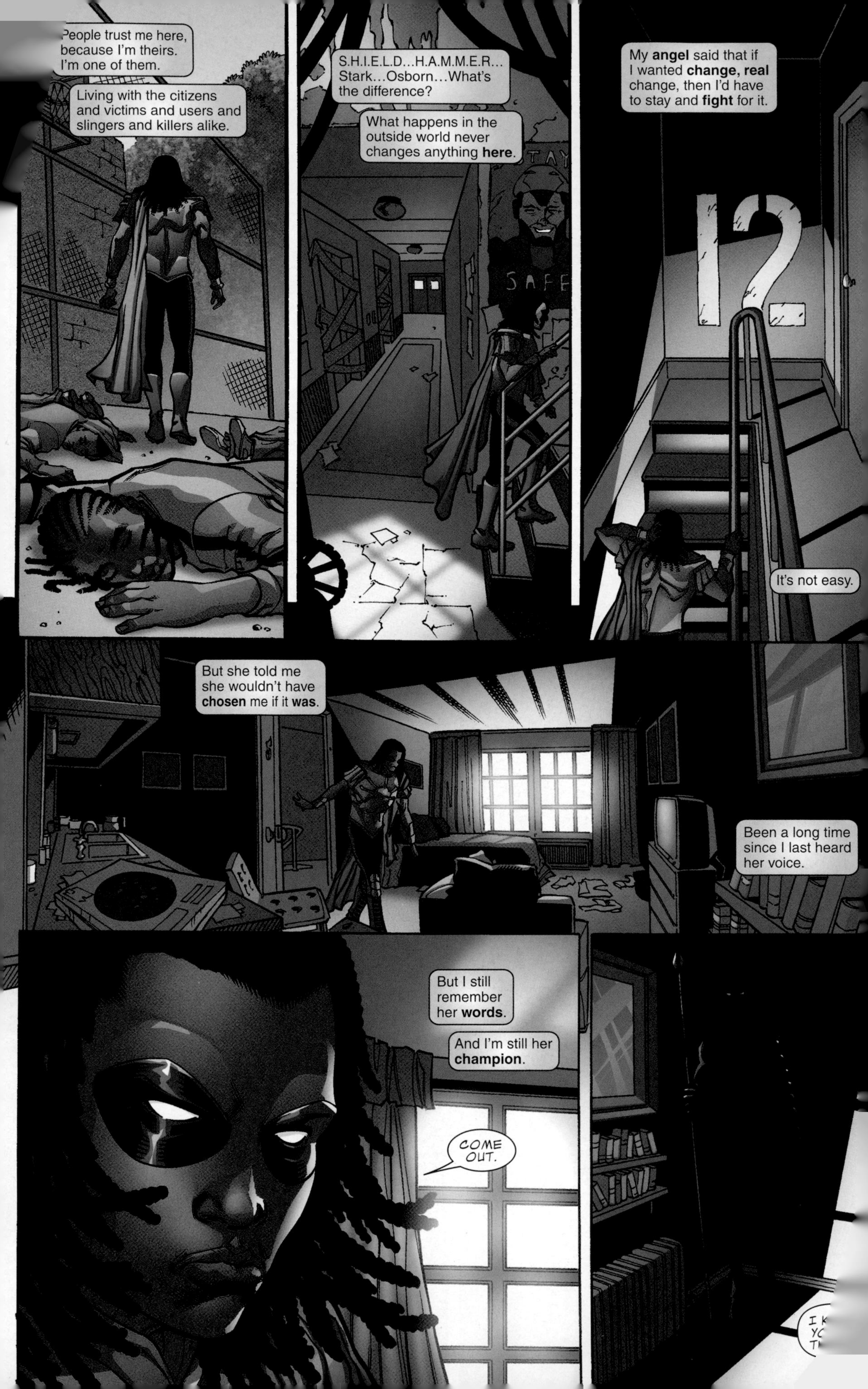
People trust me here, because I'm theirs. I'm one of them.
Living with the citizens and victims and users and slingers and killers alike.
S.H.I.E.L.D...H.A.M.M.E.R... Stark...Osborn...What's the difference?
What happens in the outside world never changes anything here.
SAFE
My angel said that if I wanted change, real change, then I'd have to stay and fight for it.
It's not easy.
But she told me she wouldn't have chosen me if it was.
Been a long time since I last heard her voice.
But I still remember her words.
And I'm still her champion.
COME OUT.

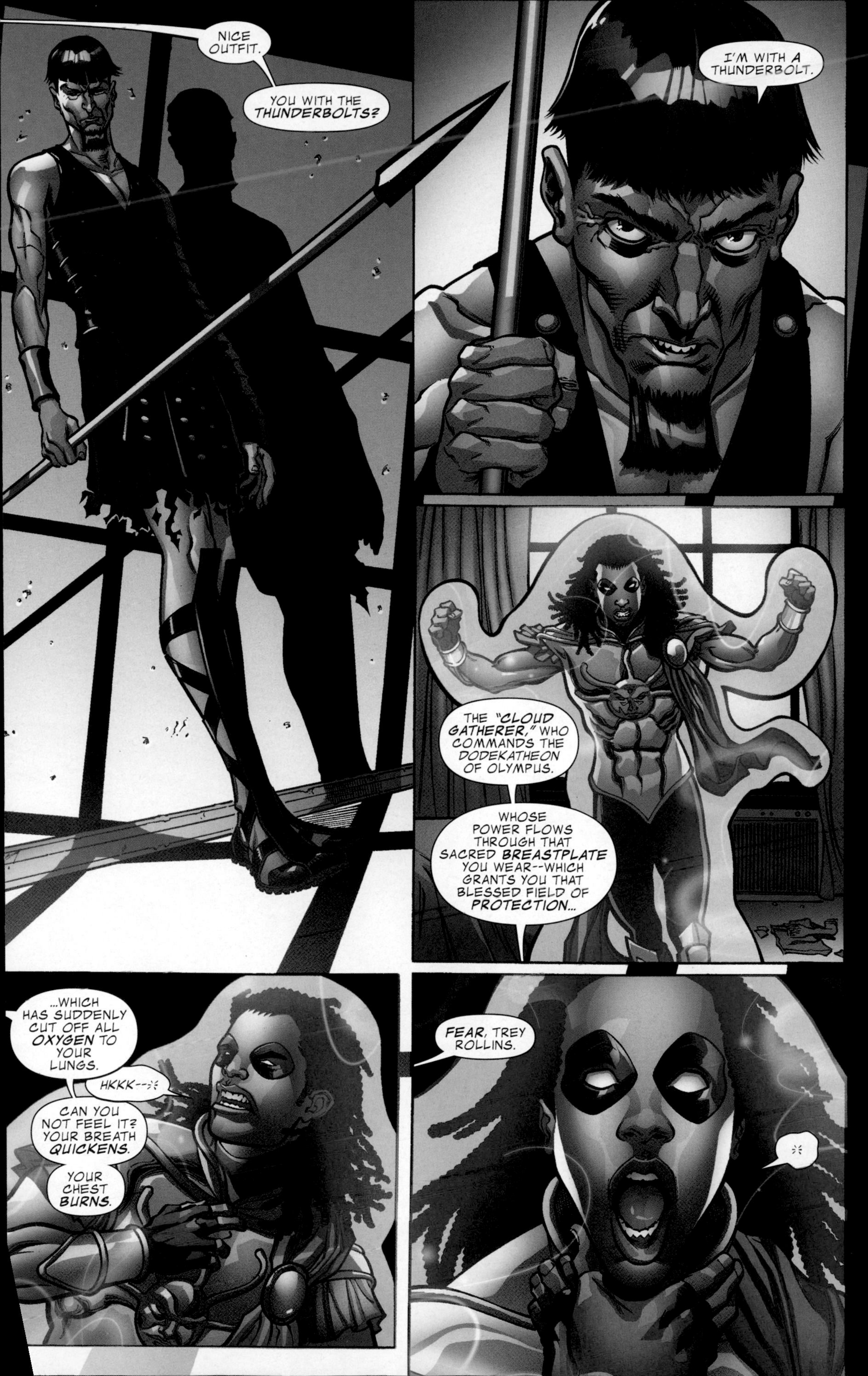

NICE OUTFIT.
YOU WITH THE THUNDERBOLTS?
I'M WITH A THUNDERBOLT.
THE "CLOUD GATHERER," WHO COMMANDS THE DODEKATHEON OF OLYMPUS.
WHOSE POWER FLOWS THROUGH THAT SACRED BREASTPLATE YOU WEAR--WHICH GRANTS YOU THAT BLESSED FIELD OF PROTECTION...
...WHICH HAS SUDDENLY CUT OFF ALL OXYGEN TO YOUR LUNGS.
HKKK--
CAN YOU NOT FEEL IT? YOUR BREATH QUICKENS.
YOUR CHEST BURNS.
FEAR, TREY ROLLINS.

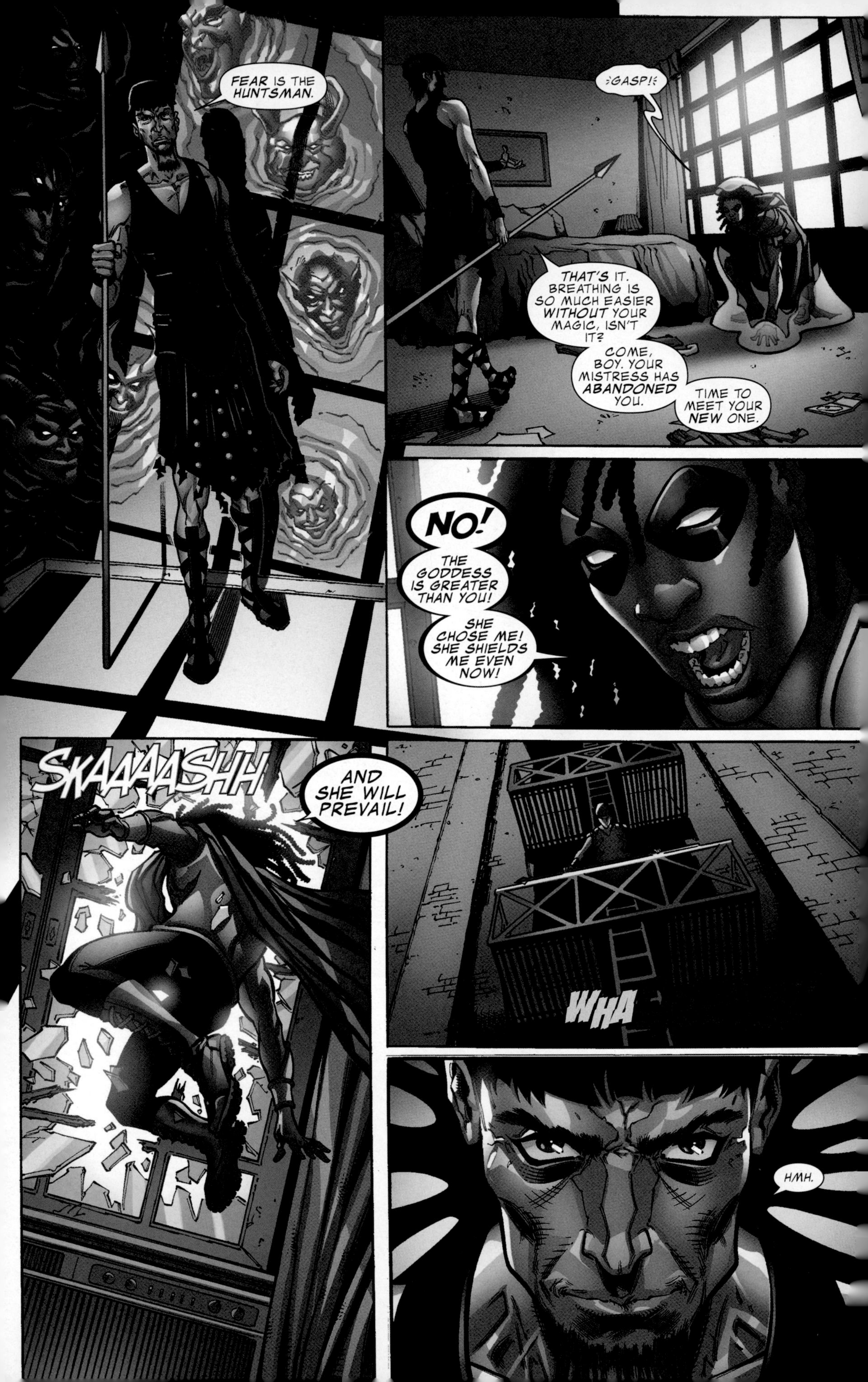
FEAR IS THE HUNTSMAN.
GASP!
THAT'S IT. BREATHING IS SO MUCH EASIER WITHOUT YOUR MAGIC, ISN'T IT?
COME, BOY. YOUR MISTRESS HAS ABANDONED YOU.
TIME TO MEET YOUR NEW ONE.
NO!
THE GODDESS IS GREATER THAN YOU!
SHE CHOSE ME! SHE SHIELDS ME EVEN NOW!
SKAAAASHH
AND SHE WILL PREVAIL!
WHA
HMH.

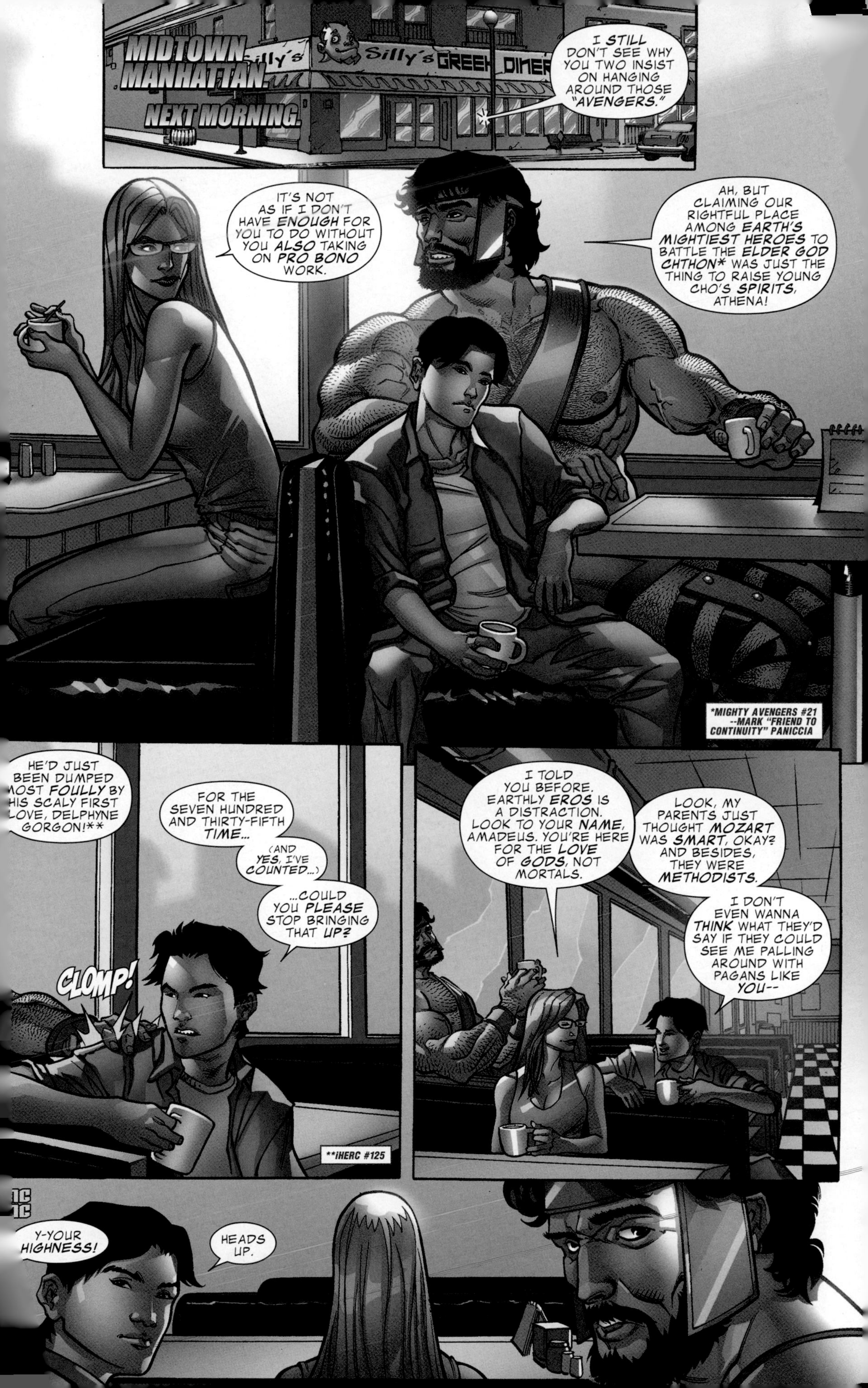
MIDTOWN MANHATTAN.
NEXT MORNING.
Silly's GREEK DINER
I STILL DON'T SEE WHY YOU TWO INSIST ON HANGING AROUND THOSE "AVENGERS."
IT'S NOT AS IF I DON'T HAVE ENOUGH FOR YOU TO DO WITHOUT YOU ALSO TAKING ON PRO BONO WORK.
AH, BUT CLAIMING OUR RIGHTFUL PLACE AMONG EARTH'S MIGHTIEST HEROES TO BATTLE THE ELDER GOD CHTHON* WAS JUST THE THING TO RAISE YOUNG CHO'S SPIRITS, ATHENA!
*MIGHTY AVENGERS #21 --MARK "FRIEND TO CONTINUITY" PANICCIA
HE'D JUST BEEN DUMPED MOST FOULLY BY HIS SCALY FIRST LOVE, DELPHYNE GORGON!**
FOR THE SEVEN HUNDRED AND THIRTY-FIFTH TIME...
(AND YES, I'VE COUNTED...)
...COULD YOU PLEASE STOP BRINGING THAT UP?
CLOMP!
**iHERC #125
I TOLD YOU BEFORE. EARTHLY EROS IS A DISTRACTION. LOOK TO YOUR NAME, AMADEUS. YOU'RE HERE FOR THE LOVE OF GODS, NOT MORTALS.
LOOK, MY PARENTS JUST THOUGHT MOZART WAS SMART, OKAY? AND BESIDES, THEY WERE METHODISTS.
I DON'T EVEN WANNA THINK WHAT THEY'D SAY IF THEY COULD SEE ME PALLING AROUND WITH PAGANS LIKE YOU--
Y-YOUR HIGHNESS!
HEADS UP.

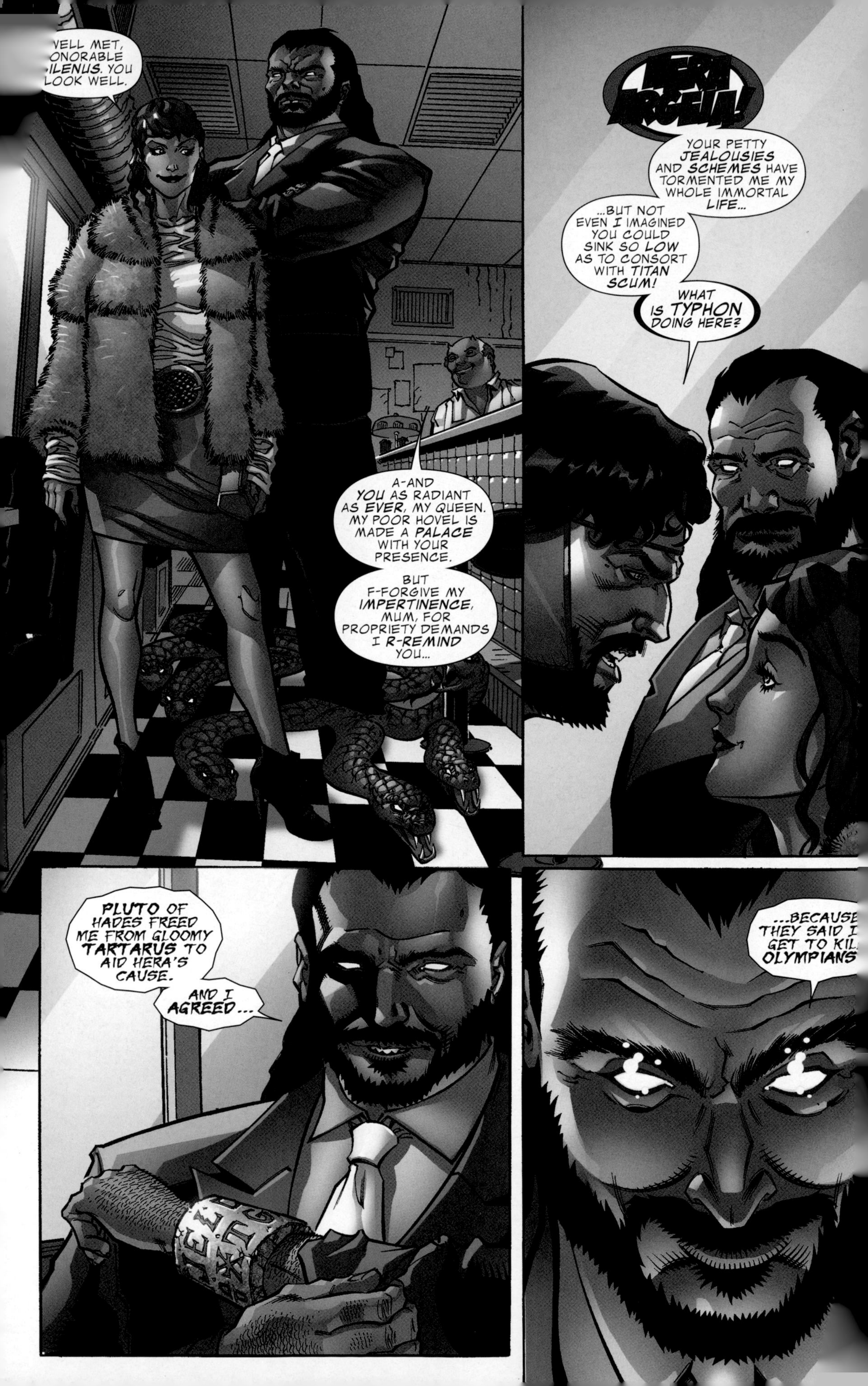
VELL MET, ONORABLE ILENUS. YOU LOOK WELL.
A-AND YOU AS RADIANT AS EVER, MY QUEEN. MY POOR HOVEL IS MADE A PALACE WITH YOUR PRESENCE.
BUT F-FORGIVE MY IMPERTINENCE, MUM, FOR PROPRIETY DEMANDS I R-REMIND YOU...
YOUR PETTY JEALOUSIES AND SCHEMES HAVE TORMENTED ME MY WHOLE IMMORTAL LIFE...
...BUT NOT EVEN I IMAGINED YOU COULD SINK SO LOW AS TO CONSORT WITH TITAN SCUM!
WHAT IS TYPHON DOING HERE?
PLUTO OF HADES FREED ME FROM GLOOMY TARTARUS TO AID HERA'S CAUSE.
AND I AGREED...
...BECAUSE THEY SAID I GET TO KIL OLYMPIANS

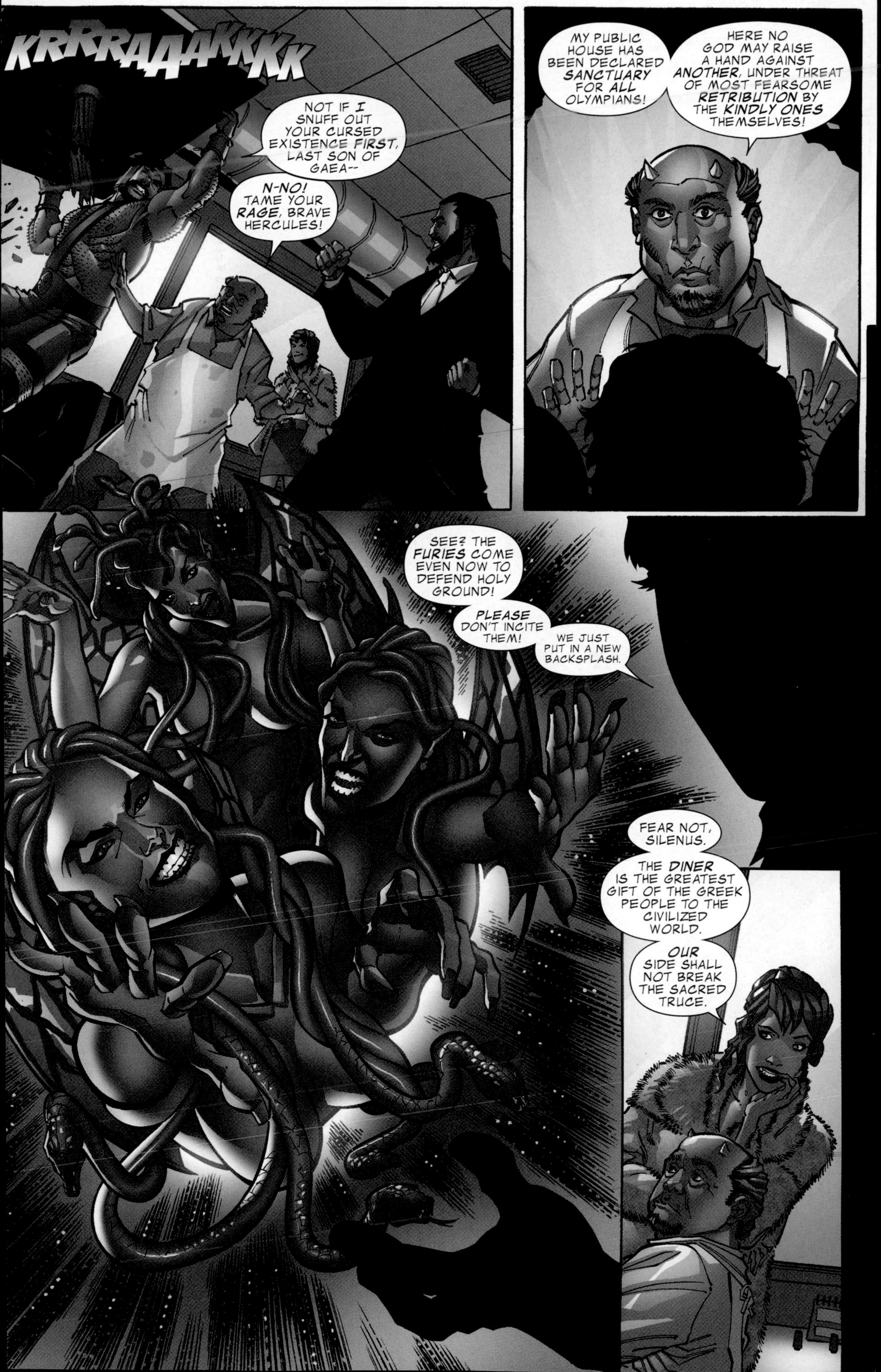
KRRRAAAKKKK
NOT IF I SNUFF OUT YOUR CURSED EXISTENCE FIRST, LAST SON OF GAEA--
N-NO! TAME YOUR RAGE, BRAVE HERCULES!
MY PUBLIC HOUSE HAS BEEN DECLARED SANCTUARY FOR ALL OLYMPIANS!
HERE NO GOD MAY RAISE A HAND AGAINST ANOTHER, UNDER THREAT OF MOST FEARSOME RETRIBUTION BY THE KINDLY ONES THEMSELVES!
SEE? THE FURIES COME EVEN NOW TO DEFEND HOLY GROUND!
PLEASE DON'T INCITE THEM!
WE JUST PUT IN A NEW BACKSPLASH.
FEAR NOT, SILENUS.
THE DINER IS THE GREATEST GIFT OF THE GREEK PEOPLE TO THE CIVILIZED WORLD.
OUR SIDE SHALL NOT BREAK THE SACRED TRUCE.

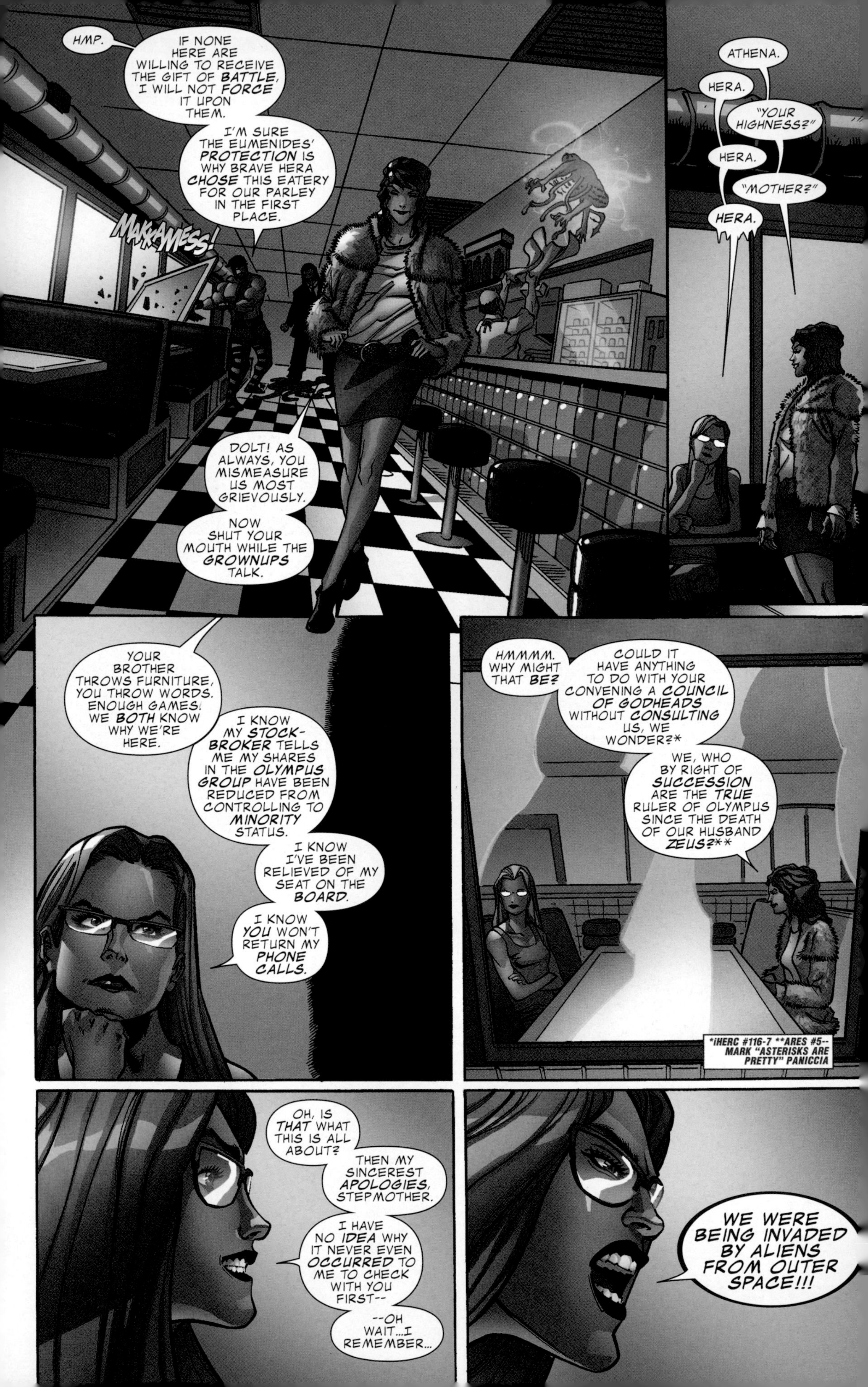
HMP.
IF NONE HERE ARE WILLING TO RECEIVE THE GIFT OF BATTLE, I WILL NOT FORCE IT UPON THEM.
I'M SURE THE EUMENIDES' PROTECTION IS WHY BRAVE HERA CHOSE THIS EATERY FOR OUR PARLEY IN THE FIRST PLACE.
MAKKAMESS!
DOLT! AS ALWAYS, YOU MISMEASURE US MOST GRIEVOUSLY.
NOW SHUT YOUR MOUTH WHILE THE GROWNUPS TALK.
ATHENA.
HERA.
"YOUR HIGHNESS?"
HERA.
"MOTHER?"
HERA.
YOUR BROTHER THROWS FURNITURE, YOU THROW WORDS. ENOUGH GAMES. WE BOTH KNOW WHY WE'RE HERE.
I KNOW MY STOCK-BROKER TELLS ME MY SHARES IN THE OLYMPUS GROUP HAVE BEEN REDUCED FROM CONTROLLING TO MINORITY STATUS.
I KNOW I'VE BEEN RELIEVED OF MY SEAT ON THE BOARD.
I KNOW YOU WON'T RETURN MY PHONE CALLS.
HMMMM. WHY MIGHT THAT BE?
COULD IT HAVE ANYTHING TO DO WITH YOUR CONVENING A COUNCIL OF GODHEADS WITHOUT CONSULTING US, WE WONDER?*
WE, WHO BY RIGHT OF SUCCESSION ARE THE TRUE RULER OF OLYMPUS SINCE THE DEATH OF OUR HUSBAND ZEUS?**
*iHERC #116-7 **ARES #5--MARK "ASTERISKS ARE PRETTY" PANICCIA
OH, IS THAT WHAT THIS IS ALL ABOUT?
THEN MY SINCEREST APOLOGIES, STEPMOTHER.
I HAVE NO IDEA WHY IT NEVER EVEN OCCURRED TO ME TO CHECK WITH YOU FIRST--
--OH WAIT...I REMEMBER...
WE WERE BEING INVADED BY ALIENS FROM OUTER SPACE!!!

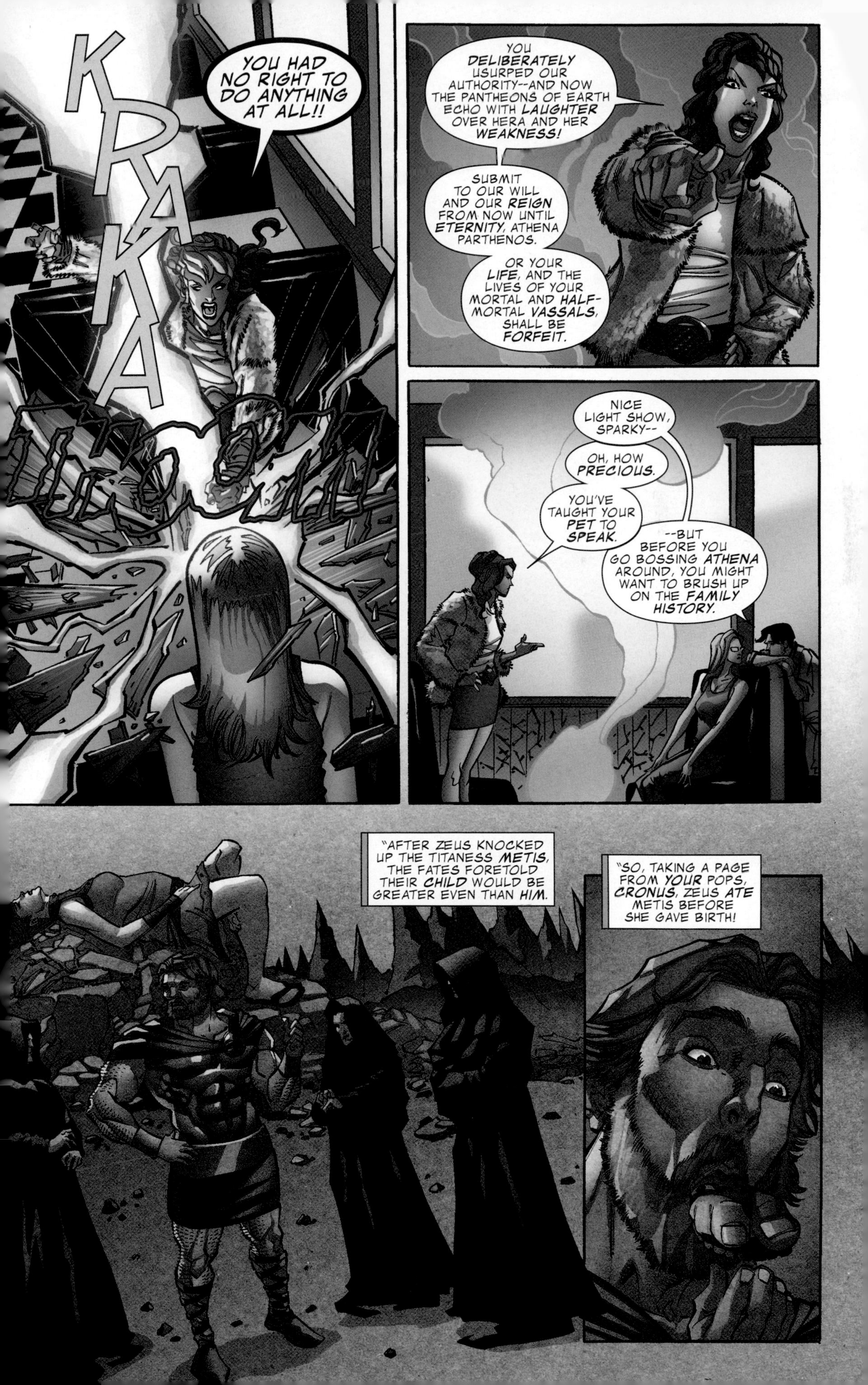
KRAKA
YOU HAD NO RIGHT TO DO ANYTHING AT ALL!!
YOU DELIBERATELY USURPED OUR AUTHORITY--AND NOW THE PANTHEONS OF EARTH ECHO WITH LAUGHTER OVER HERA AND HER WEAKNESS!
SUBMIT TO OUR WILL AND OUR REIGN FROM NOW UNTIL ETERNITY, ATHENA PARTHENOS.
OR YOUR LIFE, AND THE LIVES OF YOUR MORTAL AND HALF-MORTAL VASSALS, SHALL BE FORFEIT.
NICE LIGHT SHOW, SPARKY--
OH, HOW PRECIOUS.
YOU'VE TAUGHT YOUR PET TO SPEAK.
--BUT BEFORE YOU GO BOSSING ATHENA AROUND, YOU MIGHT WANT TO BRUSH UP ON THE FAMILY HISTORY.
"AFTER ZEUS KNOCKED UP THE TITANESS METIS, THE FATES FORETOLD THEIR CHILD WOULD BE GREATER EVEN THAN HIM.
"SO, TAKING A PAGE FROM YOUR POPS, CRONUS, ZEUS ATE METIS BEFORE SHE GAVE BIRTH!

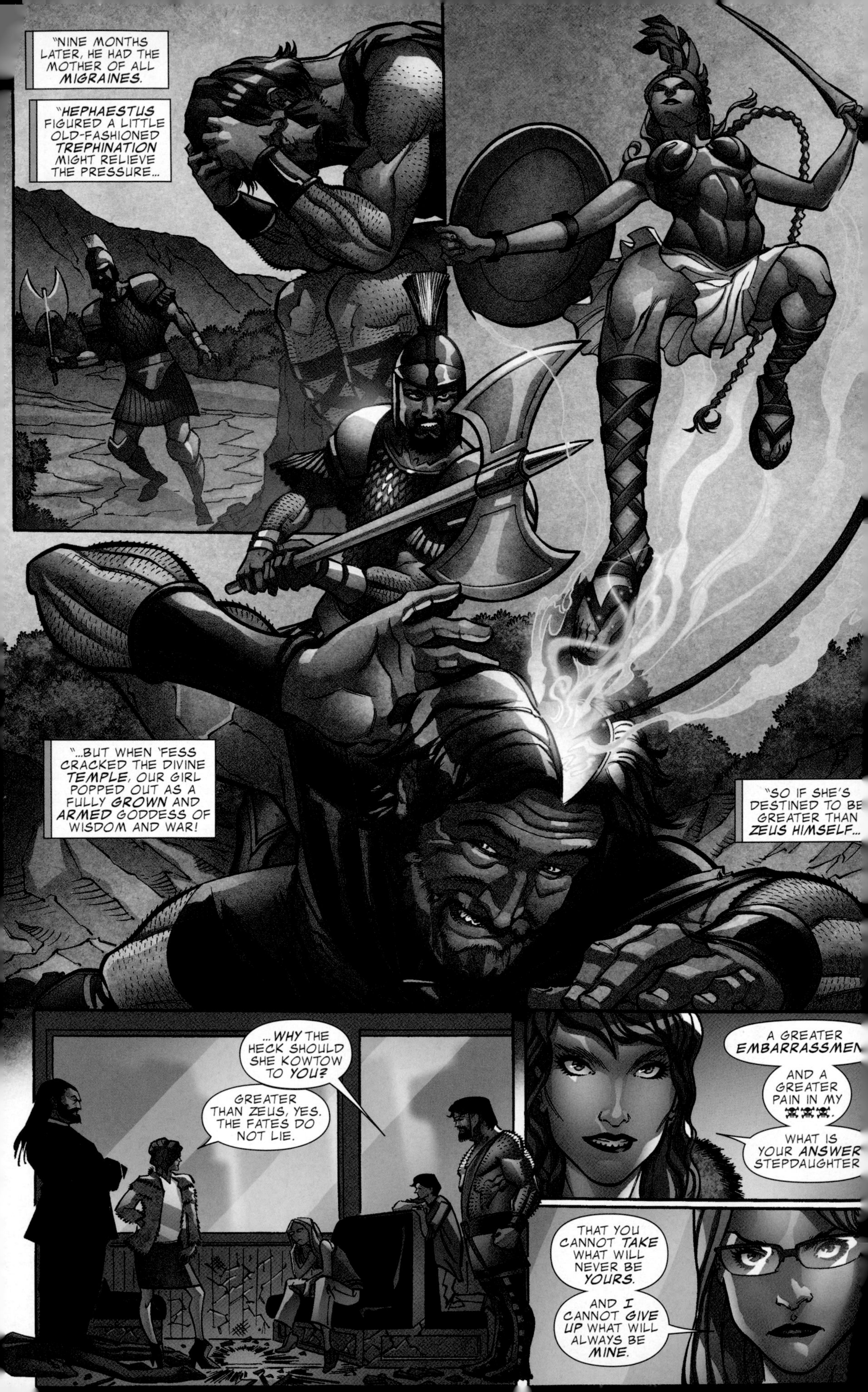
"NINE MONTHS LATER, HE HAD THE MOTHER OF ALL MIGRAINES.
"HEPHAESTUS FIGURED A LITTLE OLD-FASHIONED TREPHINATION MIGHT RELIEVE THE PRESSURE...
"...BUT WHEN 'FESS CRACKED THE DIVINE TEMPLE, OUR GIRL POPPED OUT AS A FULLY GROWN AND ARMED GODDESS OF WISDOM AND WAR!
"SO IF SHE'S DESTINED TO BE GREATER THAN ZEUS HIMSELF...
...WHY THE HECK SHOULD SHE KOWTOW TO YOU?
GREATER THAN ZEUS, YES. THE FATES DO NOT LIE.
A GREATER EMBARRASSMEN
AND A GREATER PAIN IN MY
WHAT IS YOUR ANSWER STEPDAUGHTER
THAT YOU CANNOT TAKE WHAT WILL NEVER BE YOURS.
AND I CANNOT GIVE UP WHAT WILL ALWAYS BE MINE.

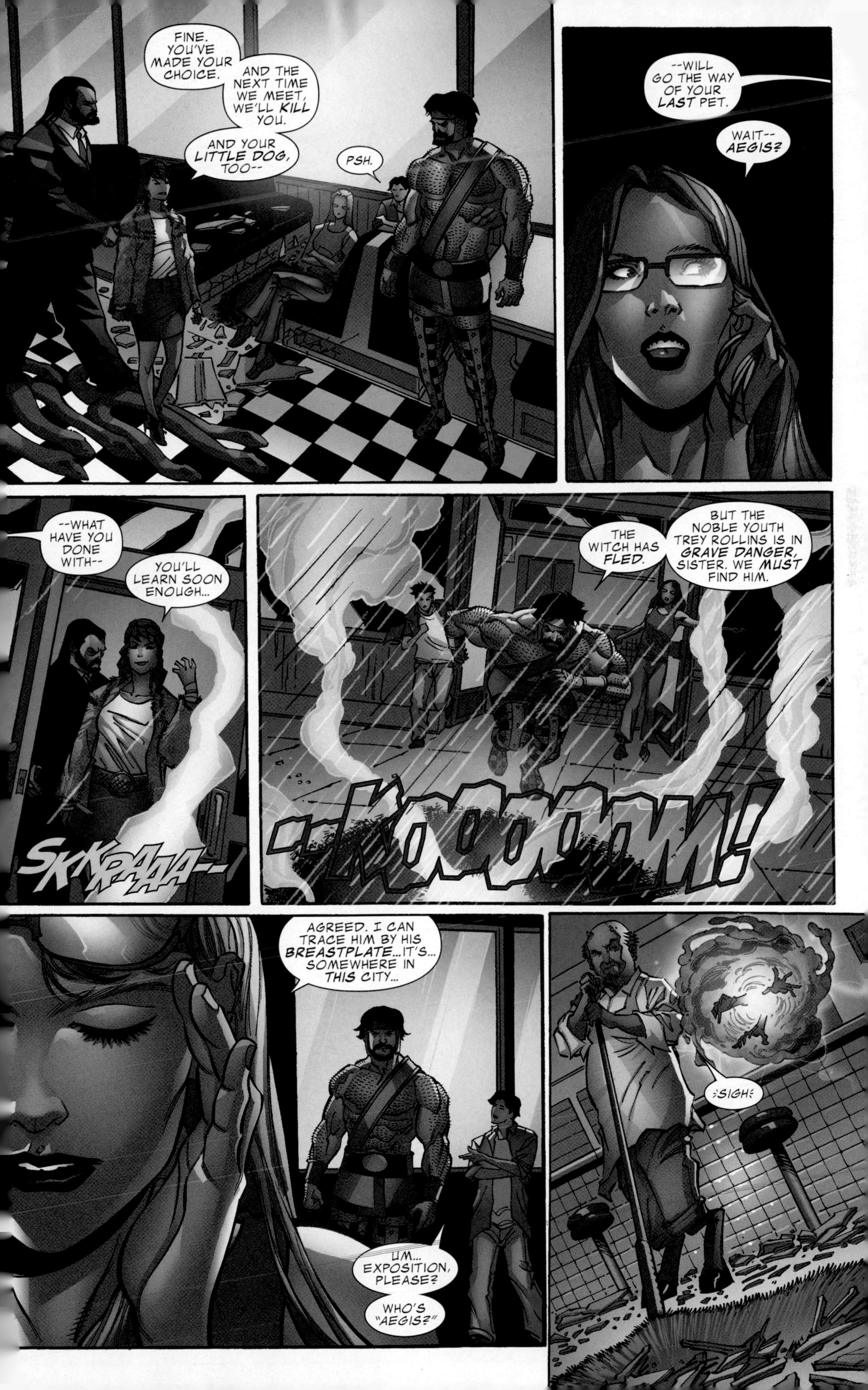
FINE. YOU'VE MADE YOUR CHOICE.
AND THE NEXT TIME WE MEET, WE'LL KILL YOU.
AND YOUR LITTLE DOG, TOO--
PSH.
--WILL GO THE WAY OF YOUR LAST PET.
WAIT-- AEGIS?
--WHAT HAVE YOU DONE WITH--
YOU'LL LEARN SOON ENOUGH...
SKKRAAA--
THE WITCH HAS FLED.
BUT THE NOBLE YOUTH TREY ROLLINS IS IN GRAVE DANGER, SISTER. WE MUST FIND HIM.
AGREED. I CAN TRACE HIM BY HIS BREASTPLATE...IT'S... SOMEWHERE IN THIS CITY...
UM... EXPOSITION, PLEASE?
WHO'S "AEGIS?"
:SIGH:

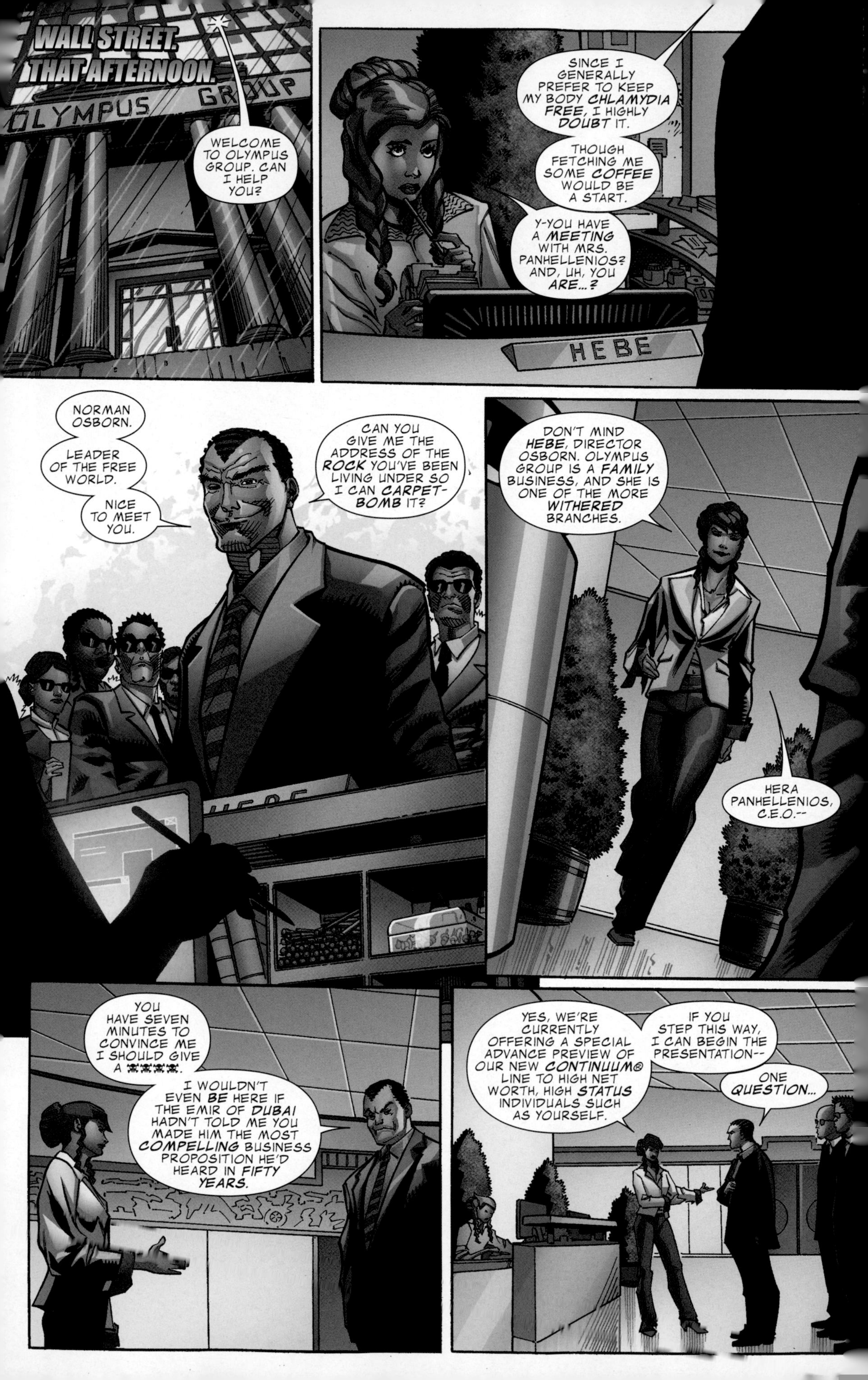
WALL STREET. THAT AFTERNOON.
OLYMPUS GROUP
WELCOME TO OLYMPUS GROUP. CAN I HELP YOU?
SINCE I GENERALLY PREFER TO KEEP MY BODY CHLAMYDIA FREE, I HIGHLY DOUBT IT.
THOUGH FETCHING ME SOME COFFEE WOULD BE A START.
Y-YOU HAVE A MEETING WITH MRS. PANHELLENIOS? AND, UH, YOU ARE...?
HEBE
NORMAN OSBORN.
LEADER OF THE FREE WORLD.
NICE TO MEET YOU.
CAN YOU GIVE ME THE ADDRESS OF THE ROCK YOU'VE BEEN LIVING UNDER SO I CAN CARPET-BOMB IT?
DON'T MIND HEBE, DIRECTOR OSBORN. OLYMPUS GROUP IS A FAMILY BUSINESS, AND SHE IS ONE OF THE MORE WITHERED BRANCHES.
HERA PANHELLENIOS, C.E.O.--
YOU HAVE SEVEN MINUTES TO CONVINCE ME I SHOULD GIVE A ☠☠☠☠.
I WOULDN'T EVEN BE HERE IF THE EMIR OF DUBAI HADN'T TOLD ME YOU MADE HIM THE MOST COMPELLING BUSINESS PROPOSITION HE'D HEARD IN FIFTY YEARS.
YES, WE'RE CURRENTLY OFFERING A SPECIAL ADVANCE PREVIEW OF OUR NEW CONTINUUM® LINE TO HIGH NET WORTH, HIGH STATUS INDIVIDUALS SUCH AS YOURSELF.
IF YOU STEP THIS WAY, I CAN BEGIN THE PRESENTATION--
ONE QUESTION...

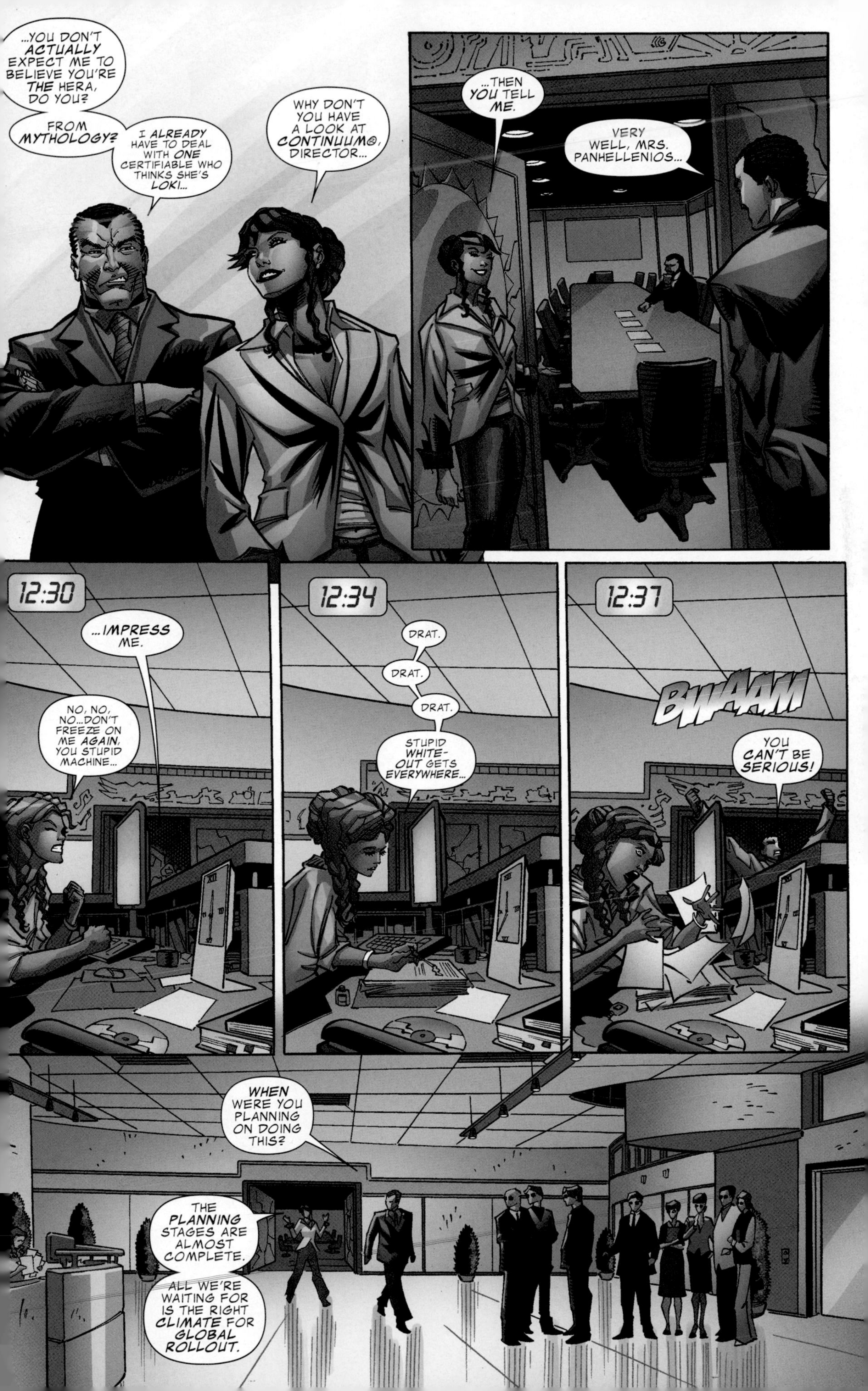
...YOU DON'T ACTUALLY EXPECT ME TO BELIEVE YOU'RE THE HERA, DO YOU?
FROM MYTHOLOGY?
I ALREADY HAVE TO DEAL WITH ONE CERTIFIABLE WHO THINKS SHE'S LOKI...
WHY DON'T YOU HAVE A LOOK AT CONTINUUM®, DIRECTOR...
...THEN YOU TELL ME.
VERY WELL, MRS. PANHELLENIOS...
12:30
...IMPRESS ME.
NO, NO, NO...DON'T FREEZE ON ME AGAIN, YOU STUPID MACHINE...
12:34
DRAT.
DRAT.
DRAT.
STUPID WHITE-OUT GETS EVERYWHERE...
12:37
BWAAM
YOU CAN'T BE SERIOUS!
WHEN WERE YOU PLANNING ON DOING THIS?
THE PLANNING STAGES ARE ALMOST COMPLETE.
ALL WE'RE WAITING FOR IS THE RIGHT CLIMATE FOR GLOBAL ROLLOUT.

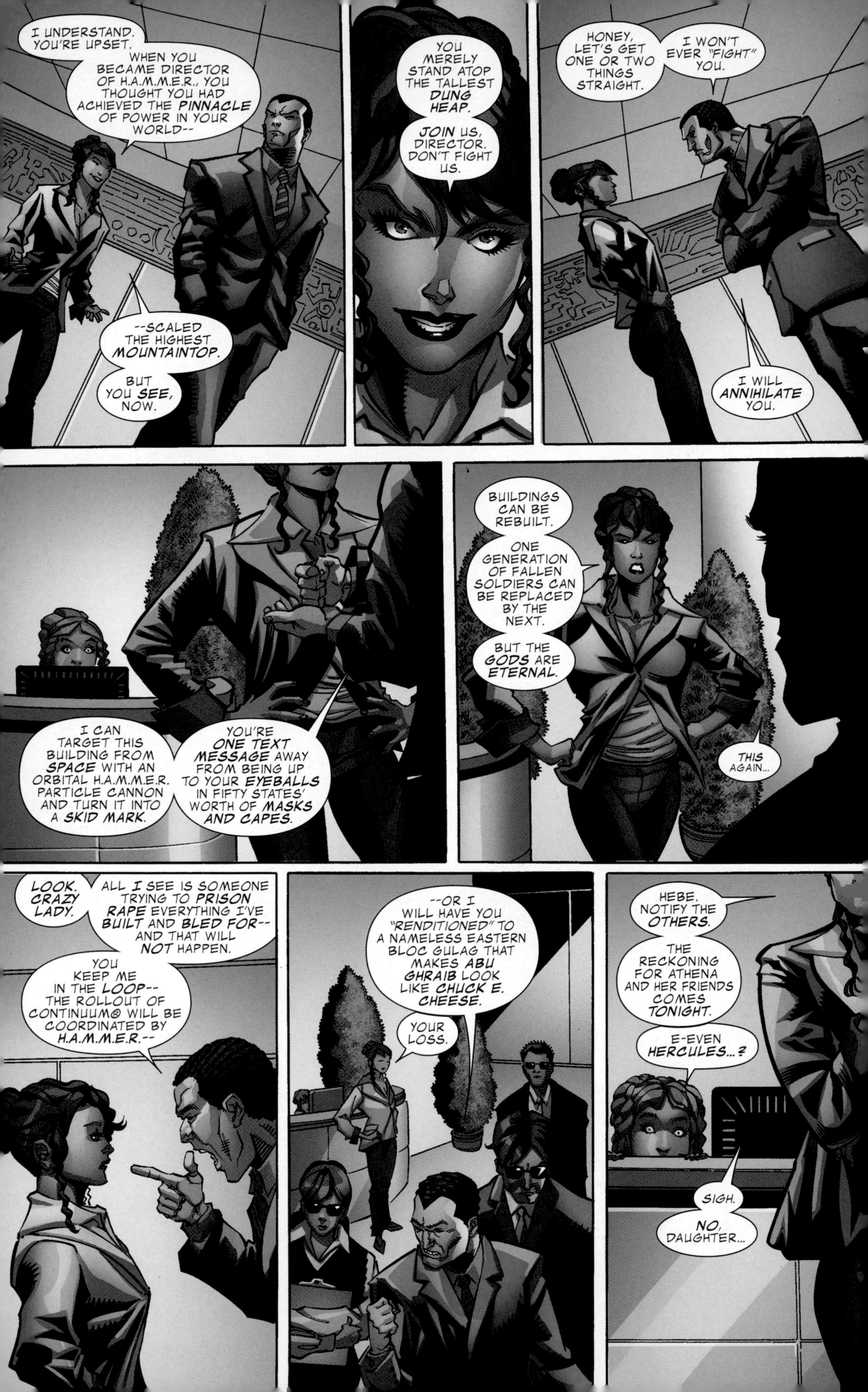
I UNDERSTAND. YOU'RE UPSET.
WHEN YOU BECAME DIRECTOR OF H.A.M.M.E.R., YOU THOUGHT YOU HAD ACHIEVED THE PINNACLE OF POWER IN YOUR WORLD--
--SCALED THE HIGHEST MOUNTAINTOP.
BUT YOU SEE, NOW.
YOU MERELY STAND ATOP THE TALLEST DUNG HEAP.
JOIN US, DIRECTOR. DON'T FIGHT US.
HONEY, LET'S GET ONE OR TWO THINGS STRAIGHT.
I WON'T EVER "FIGHT" YOU.
I WILL ANNIHILATE YOU.
I CAN TARGET THIS BUILDING FROM SPACE WITH AN ORBITAL H.A.M.M.E.R. PARTICLE CANNON AND TURN IT INTO A SKID MARK.
YOU'RE ONE TEXT MESSAGE AWAY FROM BEING UP TO YOUR EYEBALLS IN FIFTY STATES' WORTH OF MASKS AND CAPES.
BUILDINGS CAN BE REBUILT.
ONE GENERATION OF FALLEN SOLDIERS CAN BE REPLACED BY THE NEXT.
BUT THE GODS ARE ETERNAL.
THIS AGAIN...
LOOK. CRAZY LADY.
ALL I SEE IS SOMEONE TRYING TO PRISON RAPE EVERYTHING I'VE BUILT AND BLED FOR--AND THAT WILL NOT HAPPEN.
YOU KEEP ME IN THE LOOP-- THE ROLLOUT OF CONTINUUM® WILL BE COORDINATED BY H.A.M.M.E.R.--
--OR I WILL HAVE YOU "RENDITIONED" TO A NAMELESS EASTERN BLOC GULAG THAT MAKES ABU GHRAIB LOOK LIKE CHUCK E. CHEESE.
YOUR LOSS.
HEBE. NOTIFY THE OTHERS.
THE RECKONING FOR ATHENA AND HER FRIENDS COMES TONIGHT.
E-EVEN HERCULES...?
SIGH.
NO, DAUGHTER...

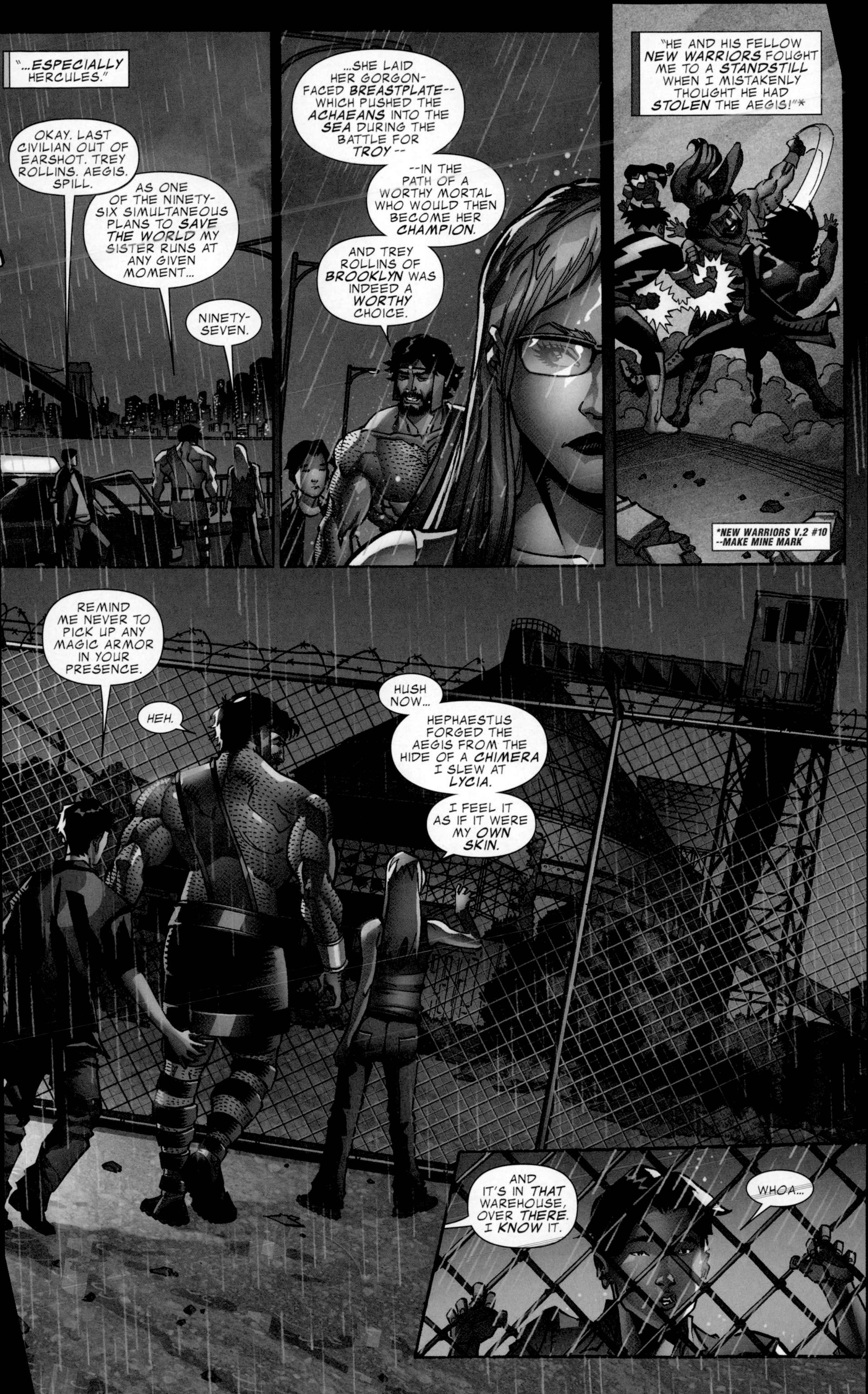
"...ESPECIALLY HERCULES."
OKAY. LAST CIVILIAN OUT OF EARSHOT. TREY ROLLINS. AEGIS. SPILL.
AS ONE OF THE NINETY-SIX SIMULTANEOUS PLANS TO SAVE THE WORLD MY SISTER RUNS AT ANY GIVEN MOMENT...
NINETY-SEVEN.
...SHE LAID HER GORGON-FACED BREASTPLATE--WHICH PUSHED THE ACHAEANS INTO THE SEA DURING THE BATTLE FOR TROY--
--IN THE PATH OF A WORTHY MORTAL WHO WOULD THEN BECOME HER CHAMPION.
AND TREY ROLLINS OF BROOKLYN WAS INDEED A WORTHY CHOICE.
"HE AND HIS FELLOW NEW WARRIORS FOUGHT ME TO A STANDSTILL WHEN I MISTAKENLY THOUGHT HE HAD STOLEN THE AEGIS!"*
*NEW WARRIORS V.2 #10 --MAKE MINE MARK
REMIND ME NEVER TO PICK UP ANY MAGIC ARMOR IN YOUR PRESENCE.
HEH.
HUSH NOW...
HEPHAESTUS FORGED THE AEGIS FROM THE HIDE OF A CHIMERA I SLEW AT LYCIA.
I FEEL IT AS IF IT WERE MY OWN SKIN.
AND IT'S IN THAT WAREHOUSE, OVER THERE. I KNOW IT.
WHOA...

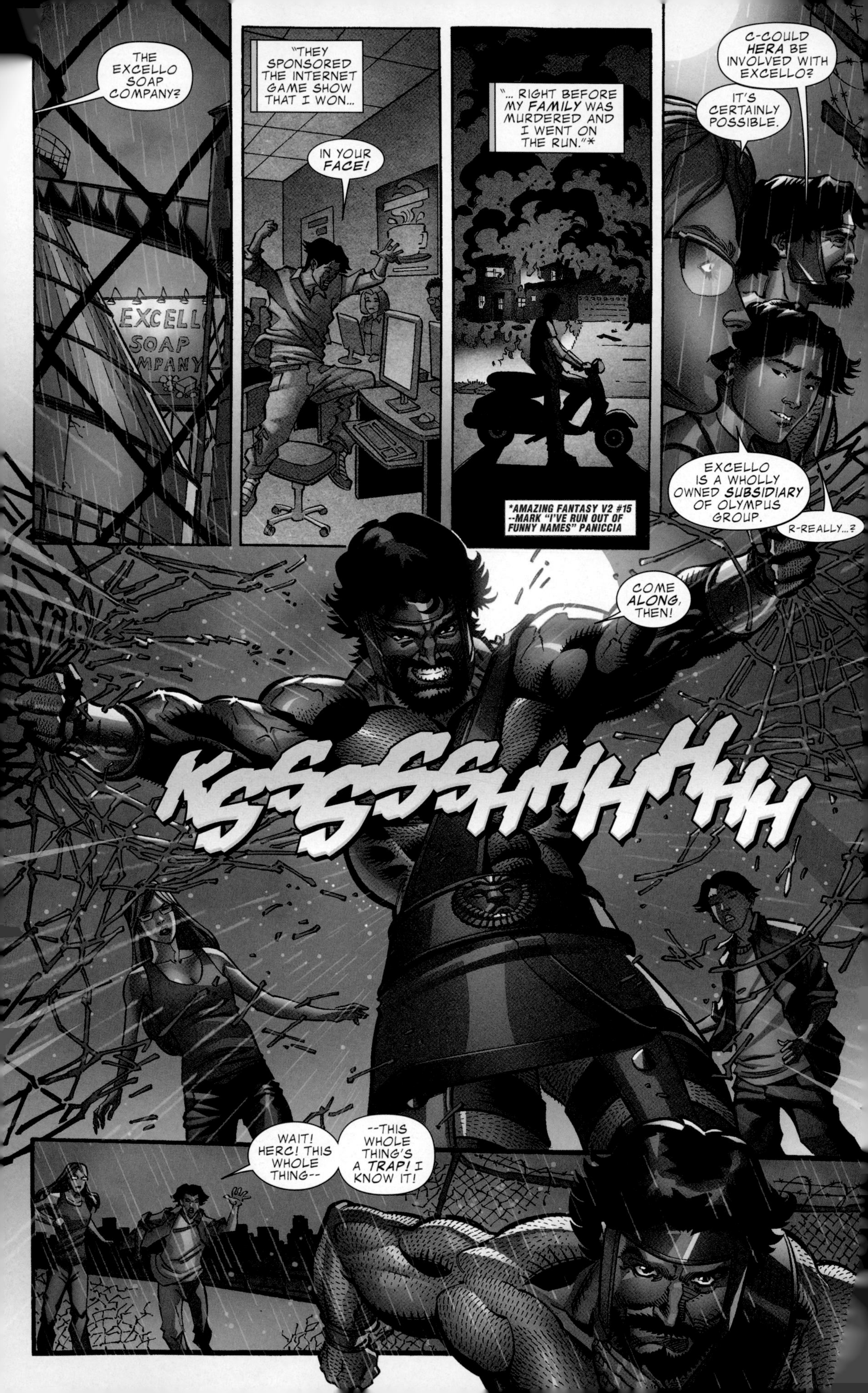
THE EXCELLO SOAP COMPANY?
EXCELLO SOAP COMPANY
"THEY SPONSORED THE INTERNET GAME SHOW THAT I WON...
IN YOUR FACE!
"... RIGHT BEFORE MY FAMILY WAS MURDERED AND I WENT ON THE RUN."*
*AMAZING FANTASY V2 #15 --MARK "I'VE RUN OUT OF FUNNY NAMES" PANICCIA
C-COULD HERA BE INVOLVED WITH EXCELLO?
IT'S CERTAINLY POSSIBLE.
EXCELLO IS A WHOLLY OWNED SUBSIDIARY OF OLYMPUS GROUP.
R-REALLY...?
COME ALONG, THEN!
KSSSSHHHHHH
WAIT! HERC! THIS WHOLE THING--
--THIS WHOLE THING'S A TRAP! I KNOW IT!

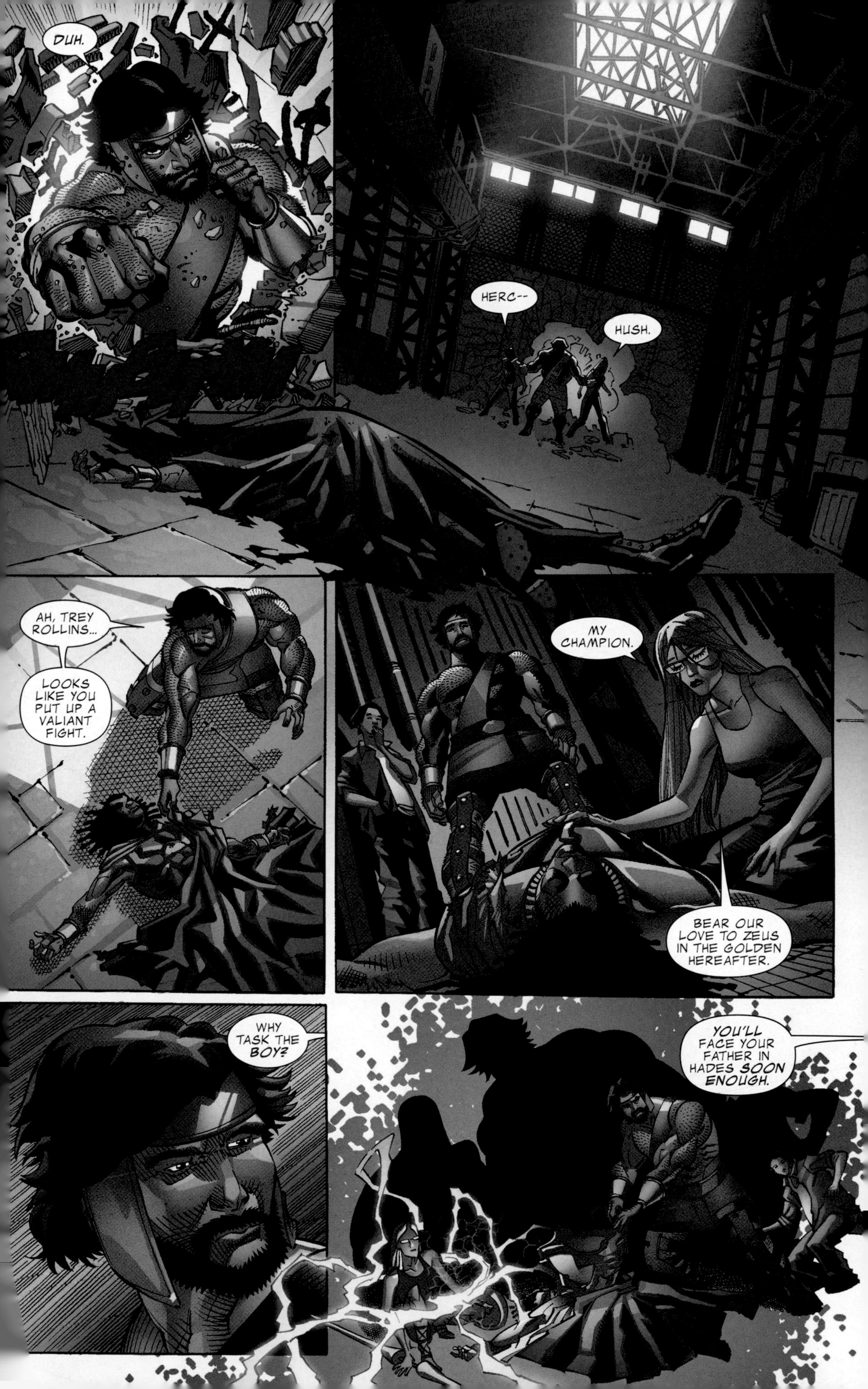
DUH.
HERC--
HUSH.
AH, TREY ROLLINS...
LOOKS LIKE YOU PUT UP A VALIANT FIGHT.
MY CHAMPION.
BEAR OUR LOVE TO ZEUS IN THE GOLDEN HEREAFTER.
WHY TASK THE BOY?
YOU'LL FACE YOUR FATHER IN HADES SOON ENOUGH.

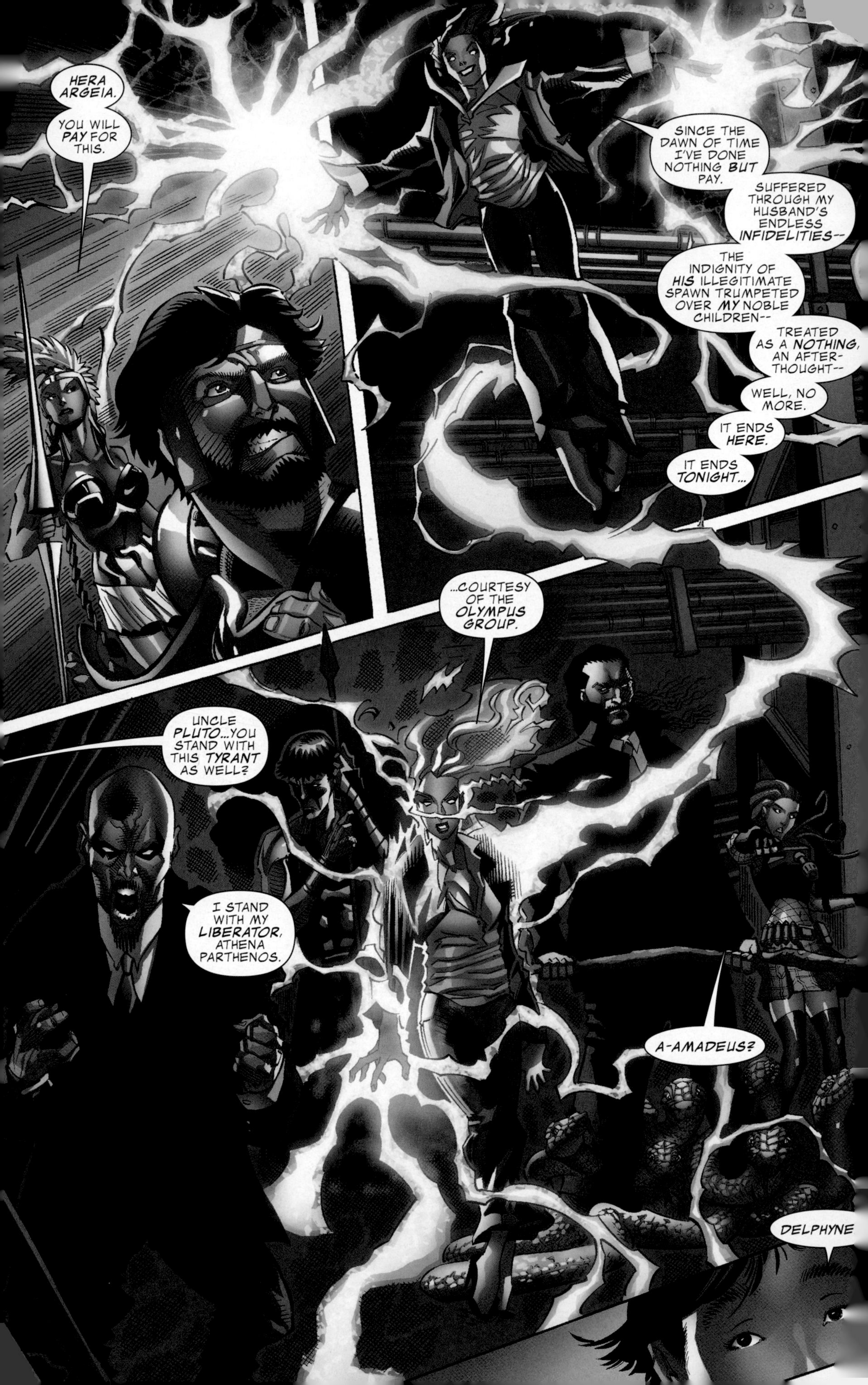
HERA ARGEIA.
YOU WILL PAY FOR THIS.
SINCE THE DAWN OF TIME I'VE DONE NOTHING BUT PAY.
SUFFERED THROUGH MY HUSBAND'S ENDLESS INFIDELITIES--
THE INDIGNITY OF HIS ILLEGITIMATE SPAWN TRUMPETED OVER MY NOBLE CHILDREN--
TREATED AS A NOTHING, AN AFTER-THOUGHT--
WELL, NO MORE.
IT ENDS HERE.
IT ENDS TONIGHT...
...COURTESY OF THE OLYMPUS GROUP.
UNCLE PLUTO...YOU STAND WITH THIS TYRANT AS WELL?
I STAND WITH MY LIBERATOR, ATHENA PARTHENOS.
A-AMADEUS?
DELPHYNE

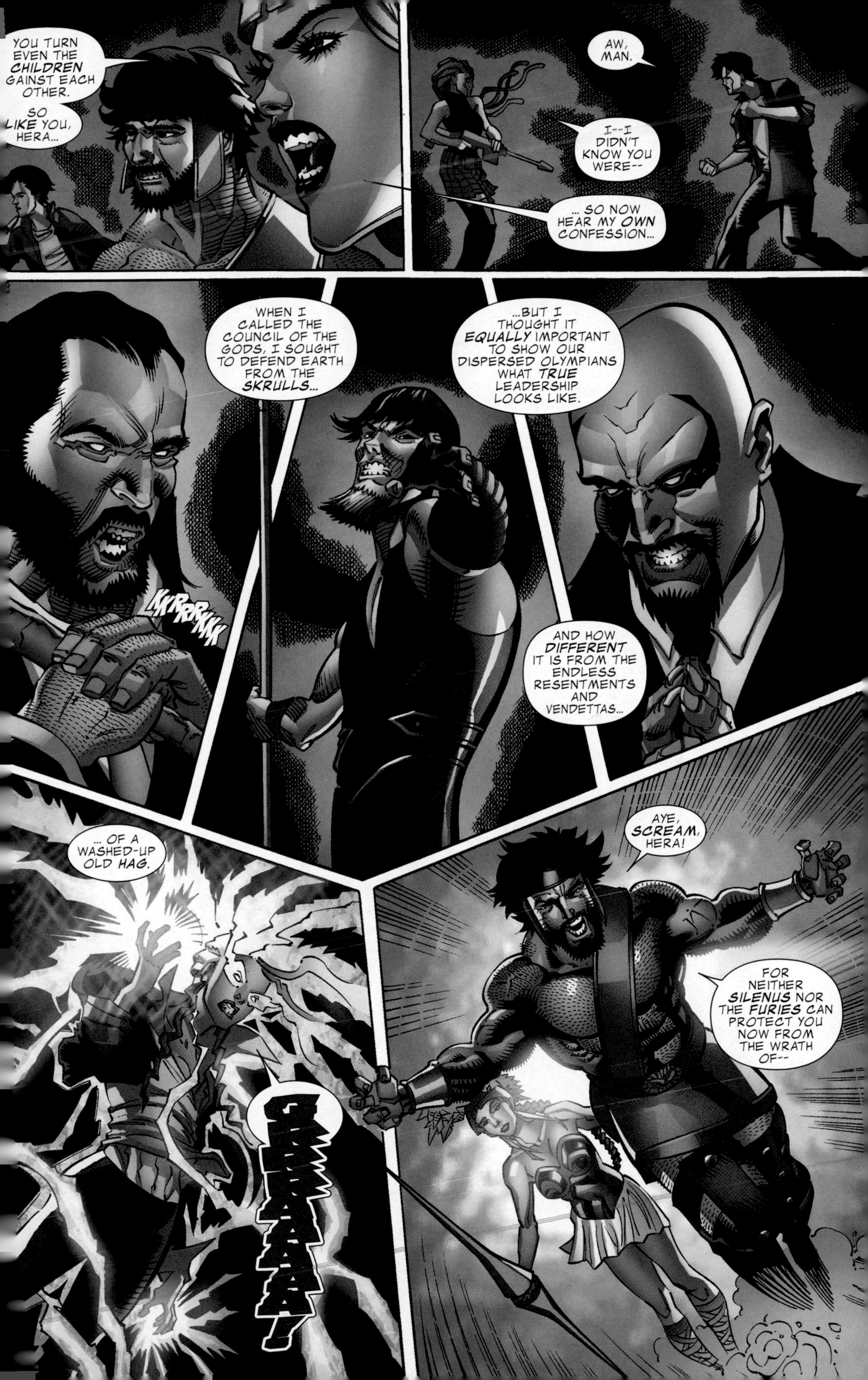
YOU TURN EVEN THE CHILDREN GAINST EACH OTHER.
SO LIKE YOU, HERA...
AW, MAN.
I--I DIDN'T KNOW YOU WERE--
... SO NOW HEAR MY OWN CONFESSION...
WHEN I CALLED THE COUNCIL OF THE GODS, I SOUGHT TO DEFEND EARTH FROM THE SKRULLS...
...BUT I THOUGHT IT EQUALLY IMPORTANT TO SHOW OUR DISPERSED OLYMPIANS WHAT TRUE LEADERSHIP LOOKS LIKE.
LKKRRRKKK
AND HOW DIFFERENT IT IS FROM THE ENDLESS RESENTMENTS AND VENDETTAS...
... OF A WASHED-UP OLD HAG.
AYE, SCREAM, HERA!
FOR NEITHER SILENUS NOR THE FURIES CAN PROTECT YOU NOW FROM THE WRATH OF--

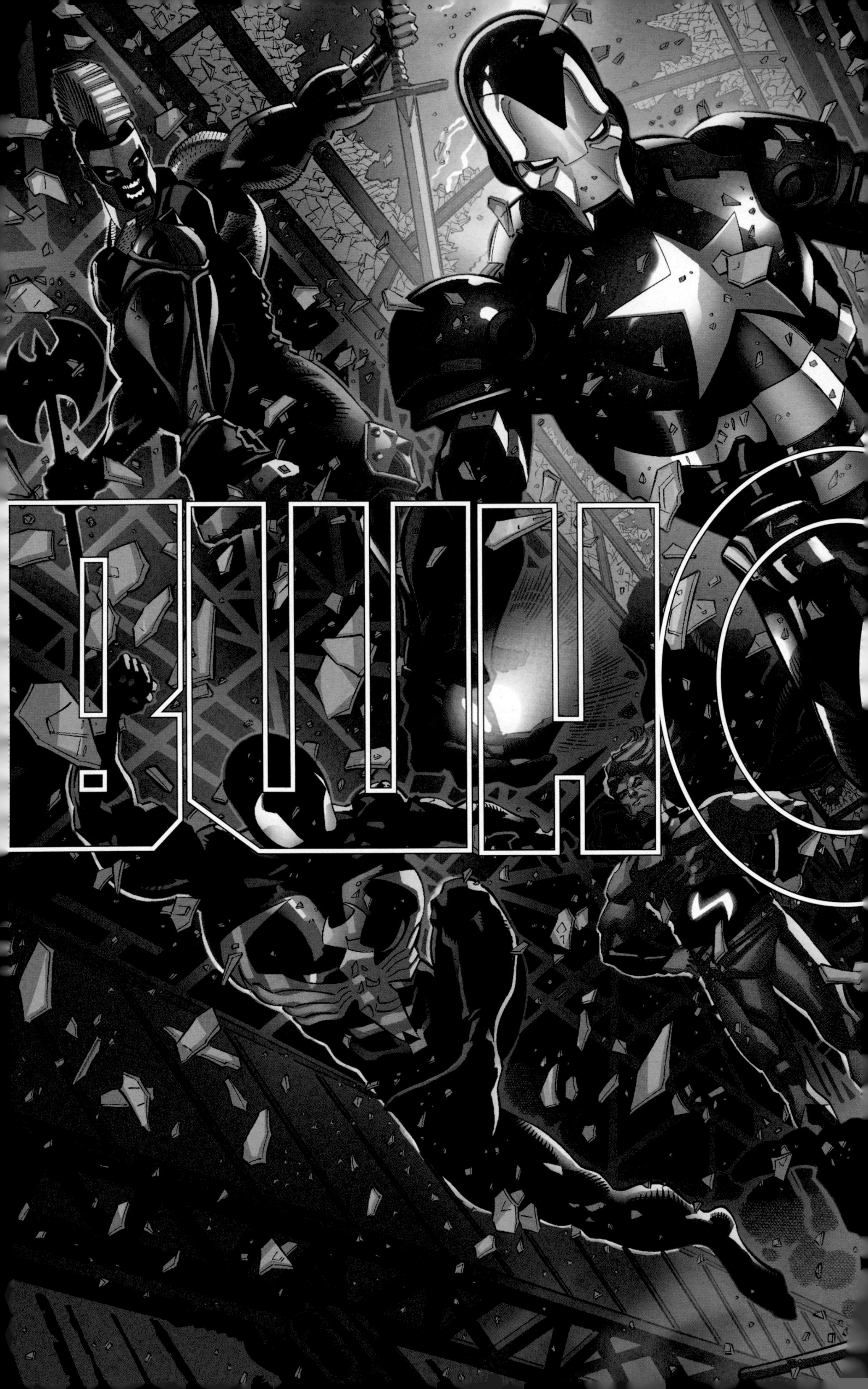

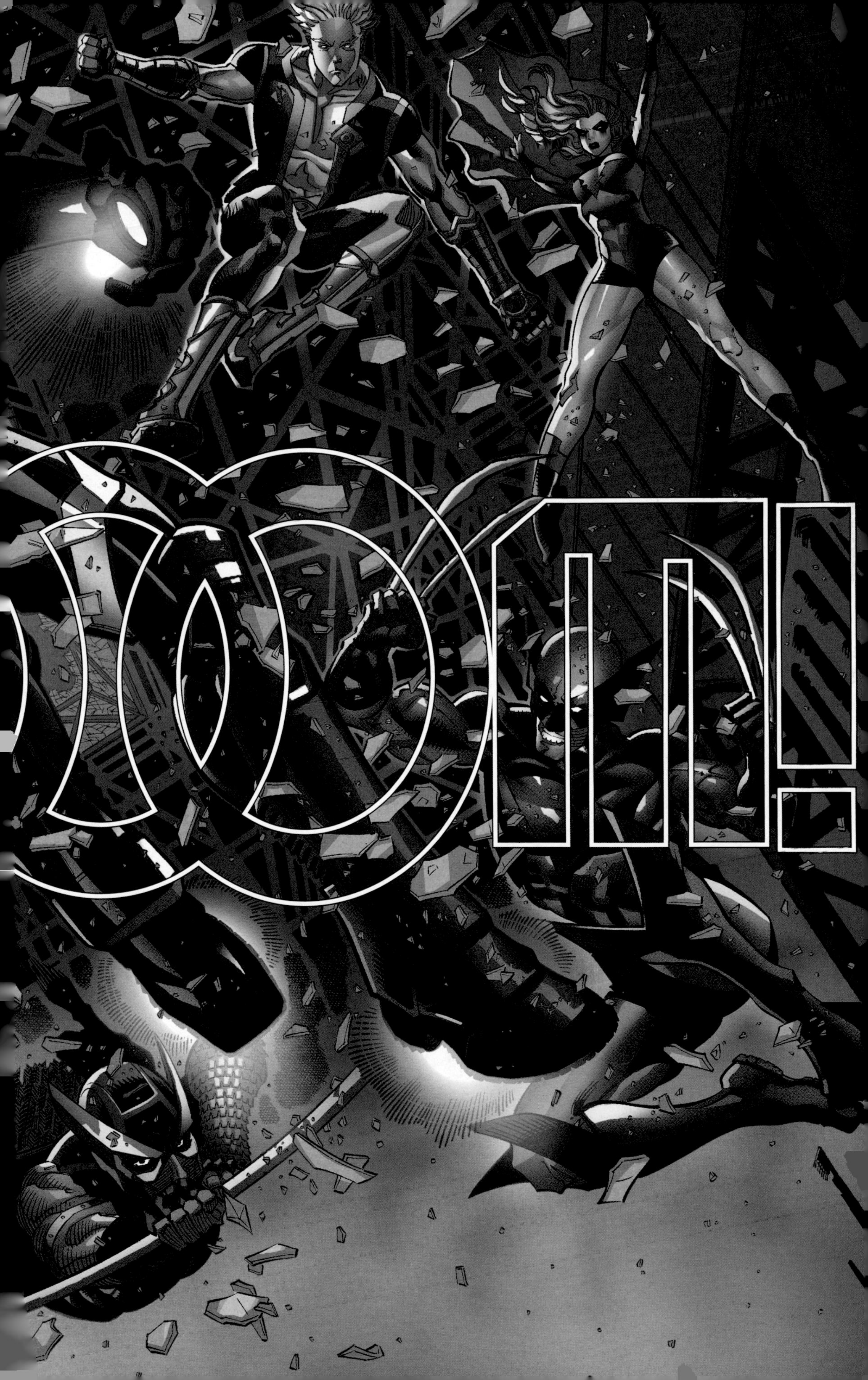
OOM!

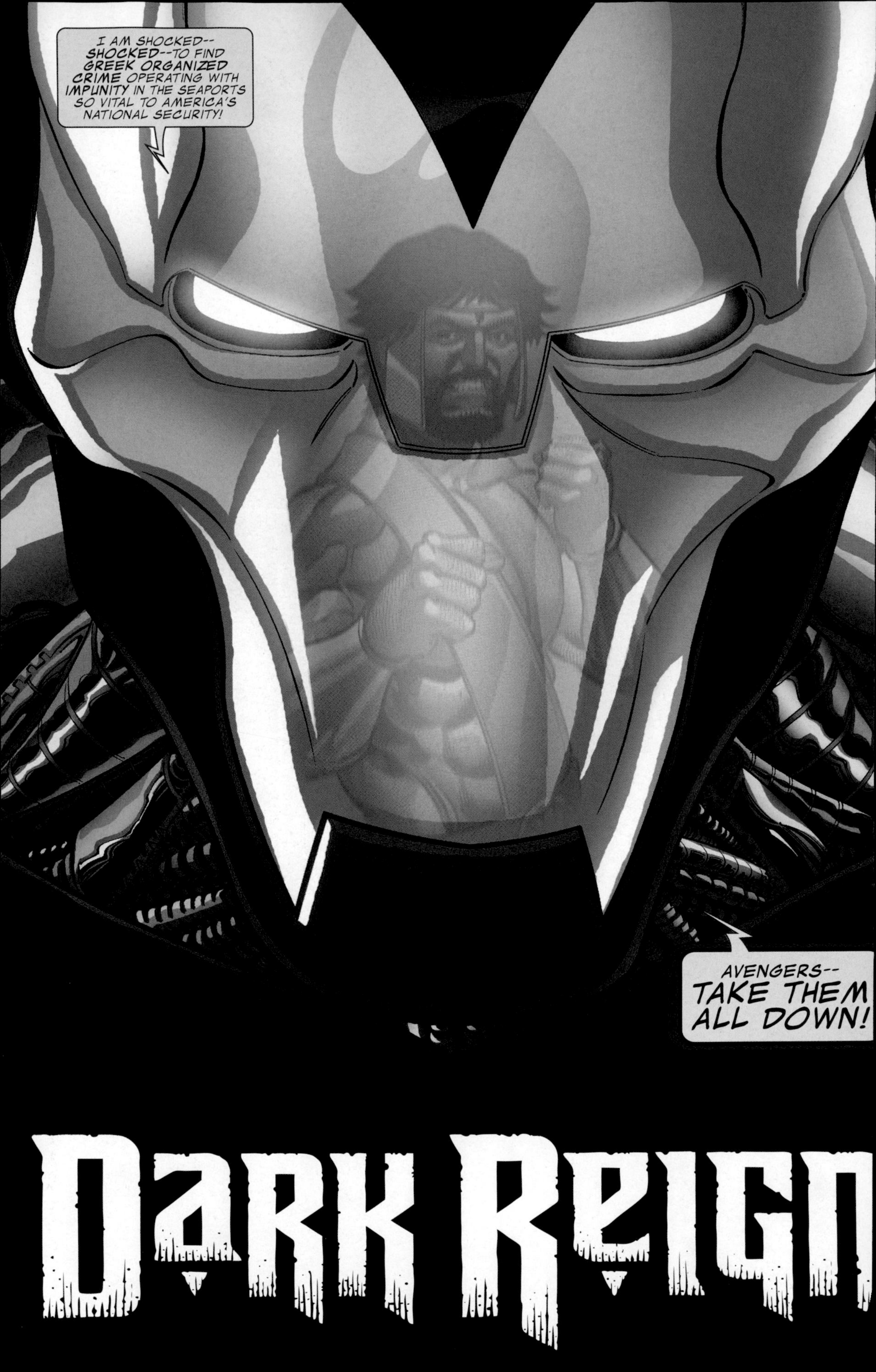
I AM SHOCKED--SHOCKED--TO FIND GREEK ORGANIZED CRIME OPERATING WITH IMPUNITY IN THE SEAPORTS SO VITAL TO AMERICA'S NATIONAL SECURITY!
AVENGERS--TAKE THEM ALL DOWN!
DARK REIGN

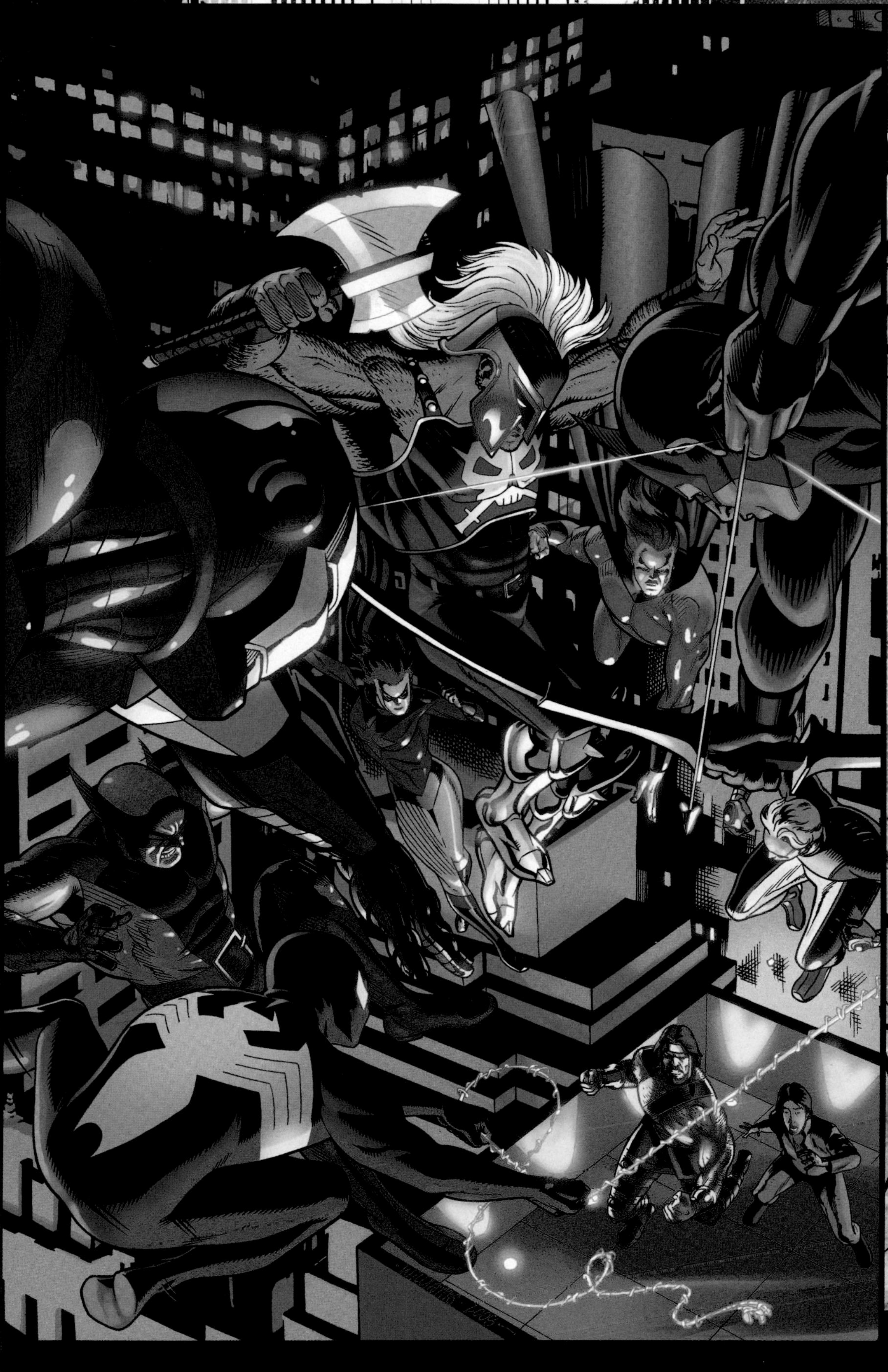

INCREDIBLE HERCULES #128

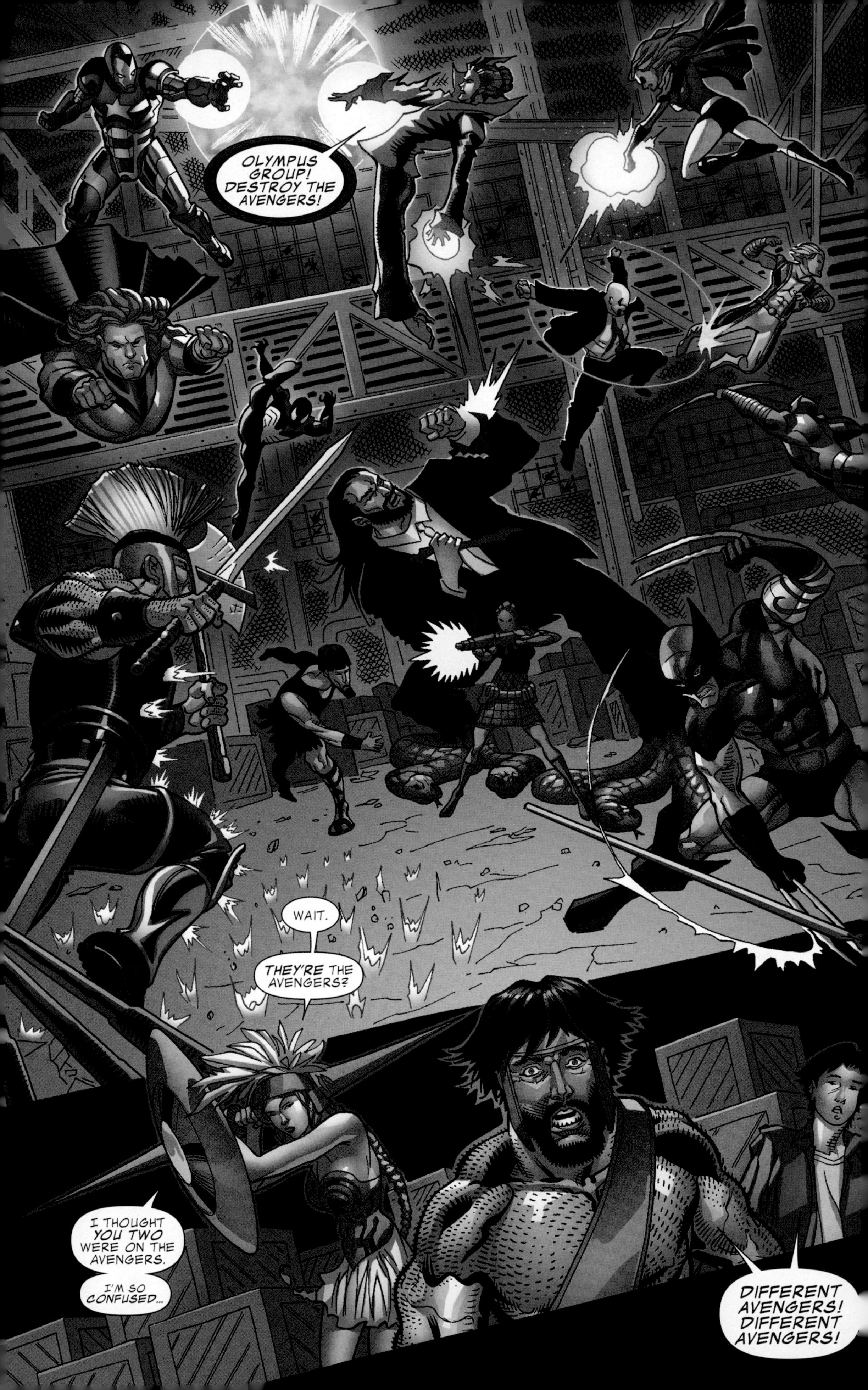
OLYMPUS GROUP! DESTROY THE AVENGERS!
WAIT.
THEY'RE THE AVENGERS?
I THOUGHT YOU TWO WERE ON THE AVENGERS.
I'M SO CONFUSED...
DIFFERENT AVENGERS! DIFFERENT AVENGERS!

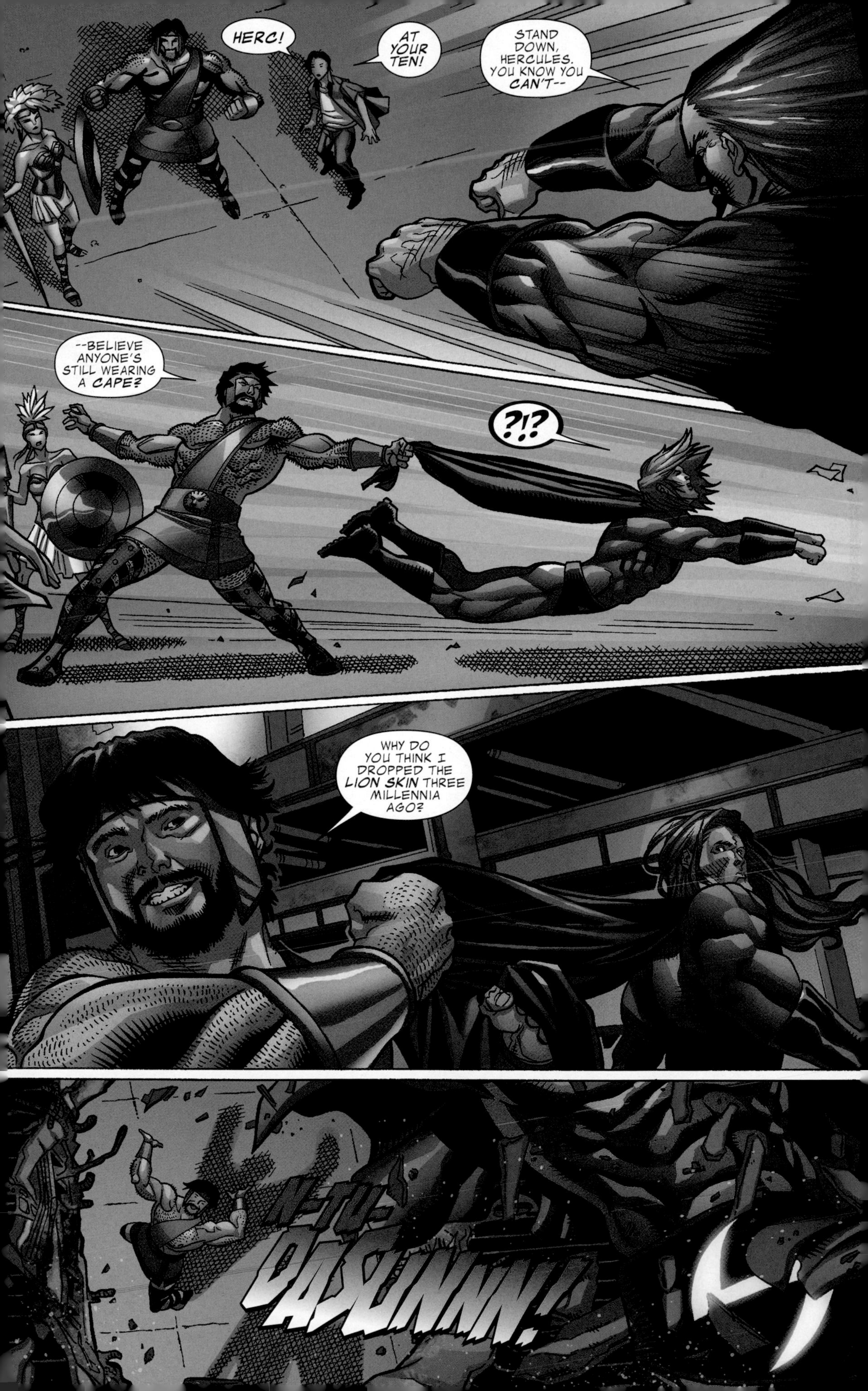
HERC!
AT YOUR TEN!
STAND DOWN, HERCULES. YOU KNOW YOU CAN'T--
--BELIEVE ANYONE'S STILL WEARING A CAPE?
?!?
WHY DO YOU THINK I DROPPED THE LION SKIN THREE MILLENNIA AGO?
N-TU-DASUNNN!

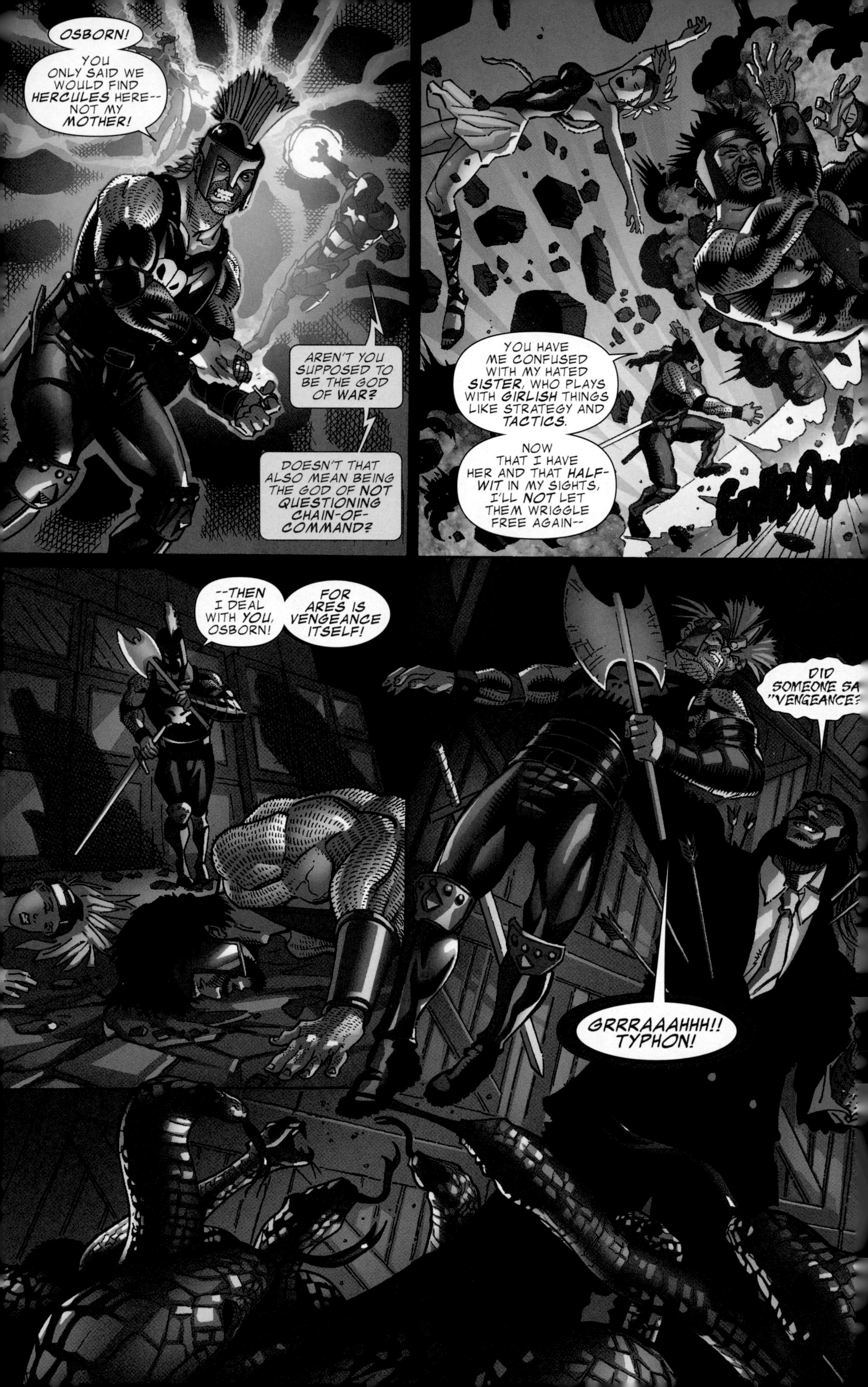

OSBORN!
YOU ONLY SAID WE WOULD FIND HERCULES HERE-- NOT MY MOTHER!
AREN'T YOU SUPPOSED TO BE THE GOD OF WAR?
DOESN'T THAT ALSO MEAN BEING THE GOD OF NOT QUESTIONING CHAIN-OF-COMMAND?
YOU HAVE ME CONFUSED WITH MY HATED SISTER, WHO PLAYS WITH GIRLISH THINGS LIKE STRATEGY AND TACTICS.
NOW THAT I HAVE HER AND THAT HALF-WIT IN MY SIGHTS, I'LL NOT LET THEM WRIGGLE FREE AGAIN--
--THEN I DEAL WITH YOU, OSBORN!
FOR ARES IS VENGEANCE ITSELF!
GRRRAAAHHH!! TYPHON!

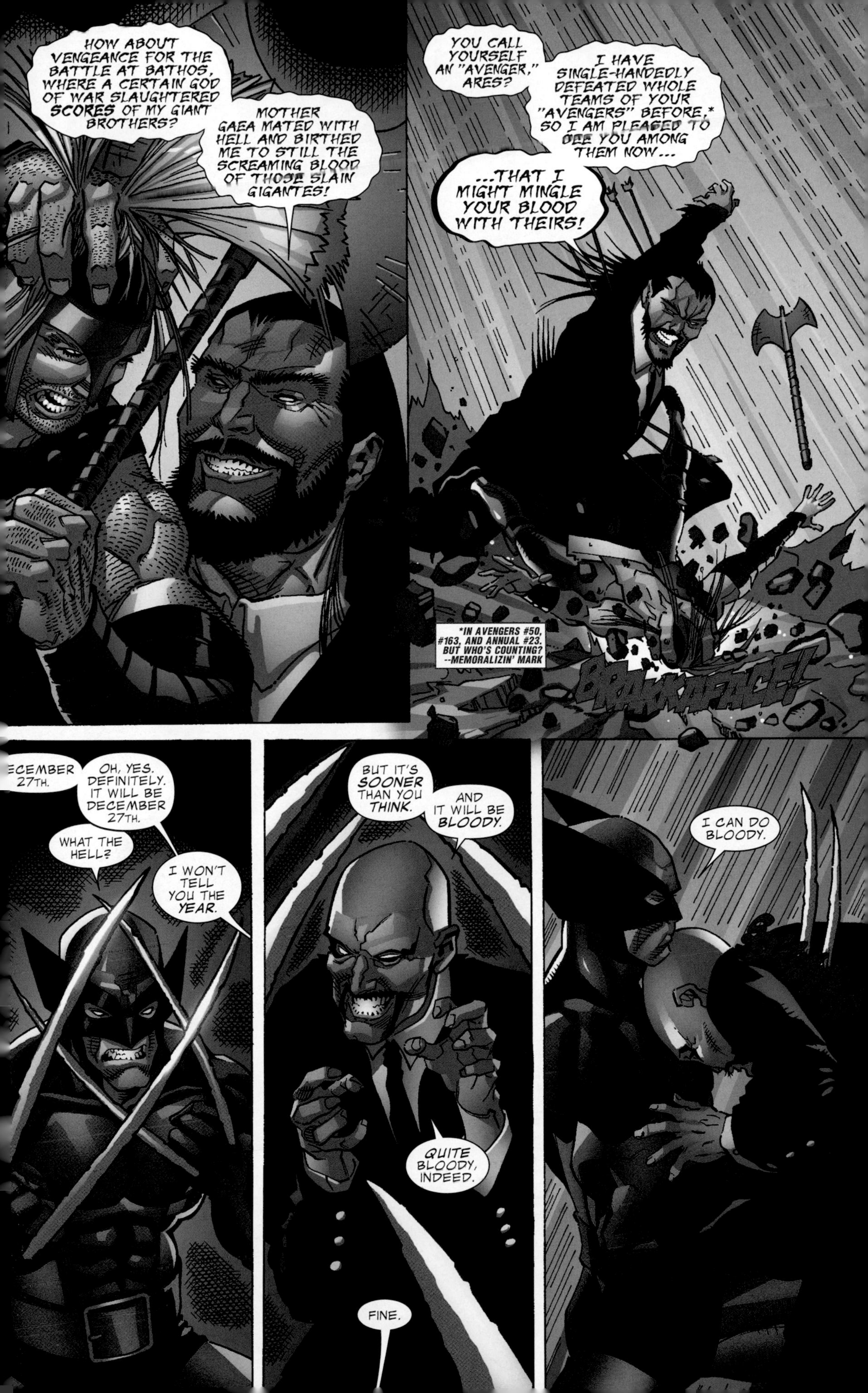
HOW ABOUT VENGEANCE FOR THE BATTLE AT BATHOS, WHERE A CERTAIN GOD OF WAR SLAUGHTERED SCORES OF MY GIANT BROTHERS?
MOTHER GAEA MATED WITH HELL AND BIRTHED ME TO STILL THE SCREAMING BLOOD OF THOSE SLAIN GIGANTES!
YOU CALL YOURSELF AN "AVENGER," ARES?
I HAVE SINGLE-HANDEDLY DEFEATED WHOLE TEAMS OF YOUR "AVENGERS" BEFORE,* SO I AM PLEASED TO SEE YOU AMONG THEM NOW...
...THAT I MIGHT MINGLE YOUR BLOOD WITH THEIRS!
*IN AVENGERS #50, #163, AND ANNUAL #23. BUT WHO'S COUNTING? --MEMORALIZIN' MARK
BRAKKAFACE!
ECEMBER 27TH.
OH, YES. DEFINITELY. IT WILL BE DECEMBER 27TH.
WHAT THE HELL?
I WON'T TELL YOU THE YEAR.
BUT IT'S SOONER THAN YOU THINK.
AND IT WILL BE BLOODY.
QUITE BLOODY, INDEED.
FINE.
I CAN DO BLOODY.

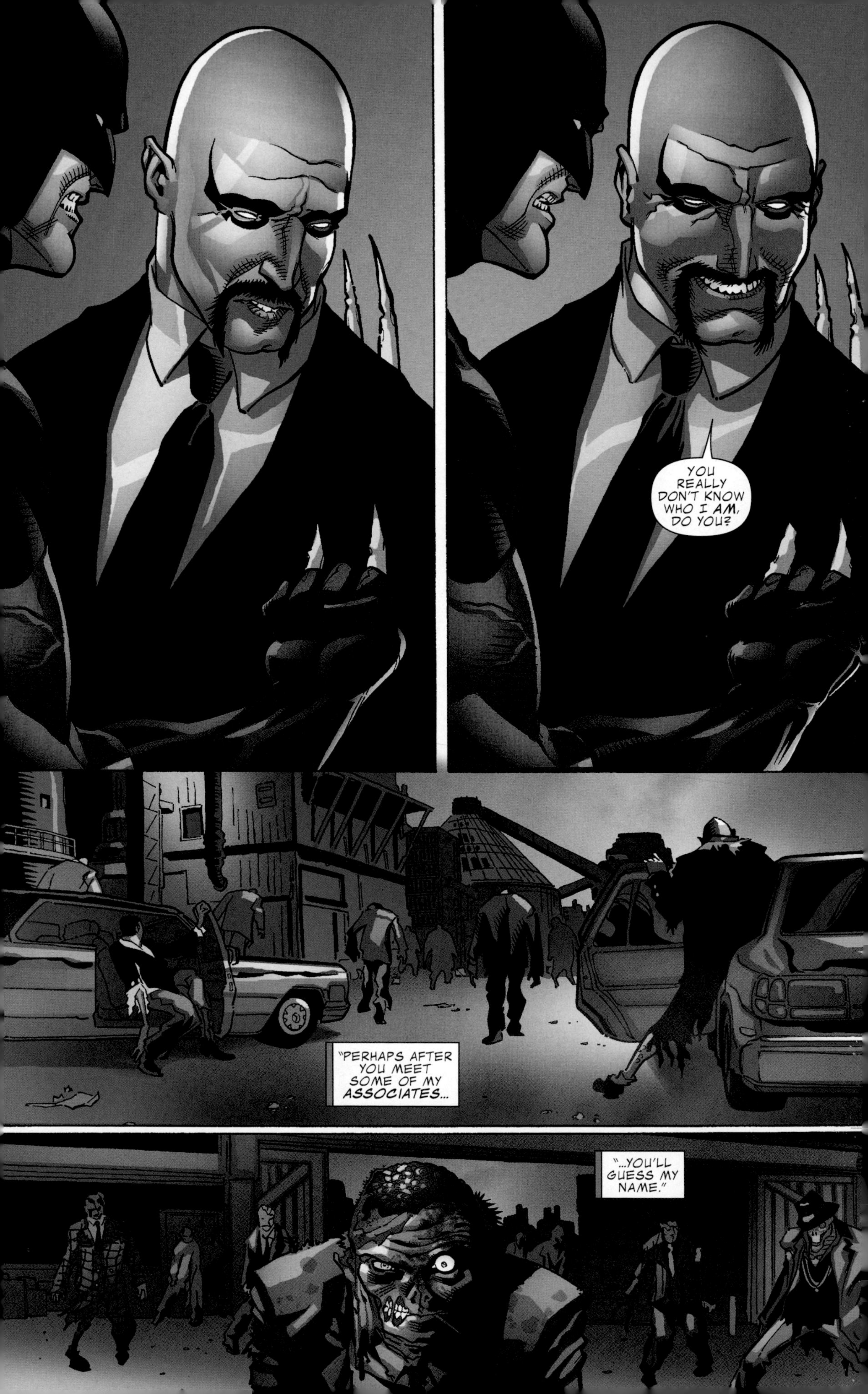
YOU REALLY DON'T KNOW WHO I *AM*, DO YOU?
"PERHAPS AFTER YOU MEET SOME OF MY *ASSOCIATES*...
"...YOU'LL GUESS MY NAME."

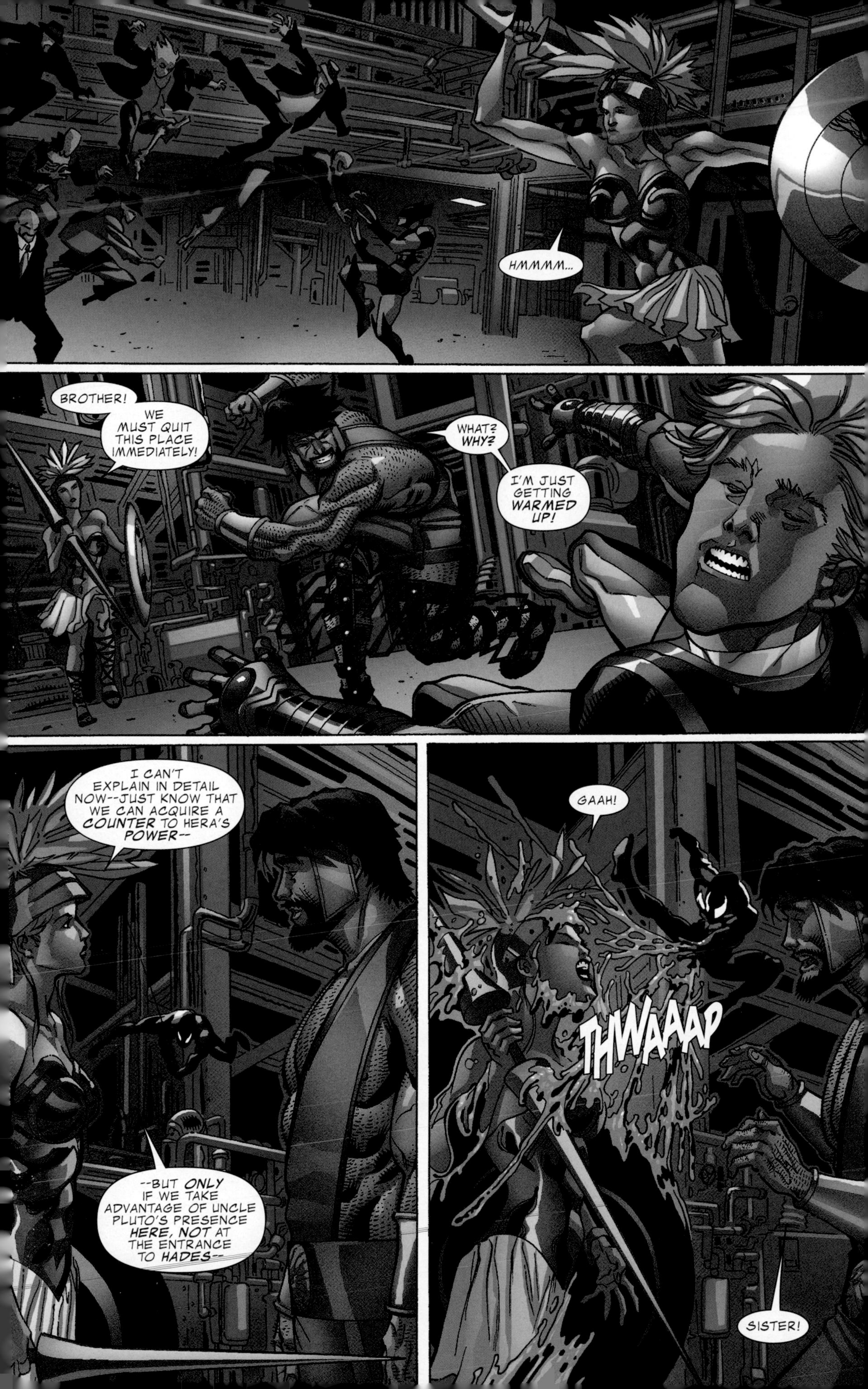
HMMMM...
BROTHER!
WE MUST QUIT THIS PLACE IMMEDIATELY!
WHAT? WHY?
I'M JUST GETTING WARMED UP!
I CAN'T EXPLAIN IN DETAIL NOW--JUST KNOW THAT WE CAN ACQUIRE A COUNTER TO HERA'S POWER--
--BUT ONLY IF WE TAKE ADVANTAGE OF UNCLE PLUTO'S PRESENCE HERE, NOT AT THE ENTRANCE TO HADES--
GAAH!
THWAAAP
SISTER!

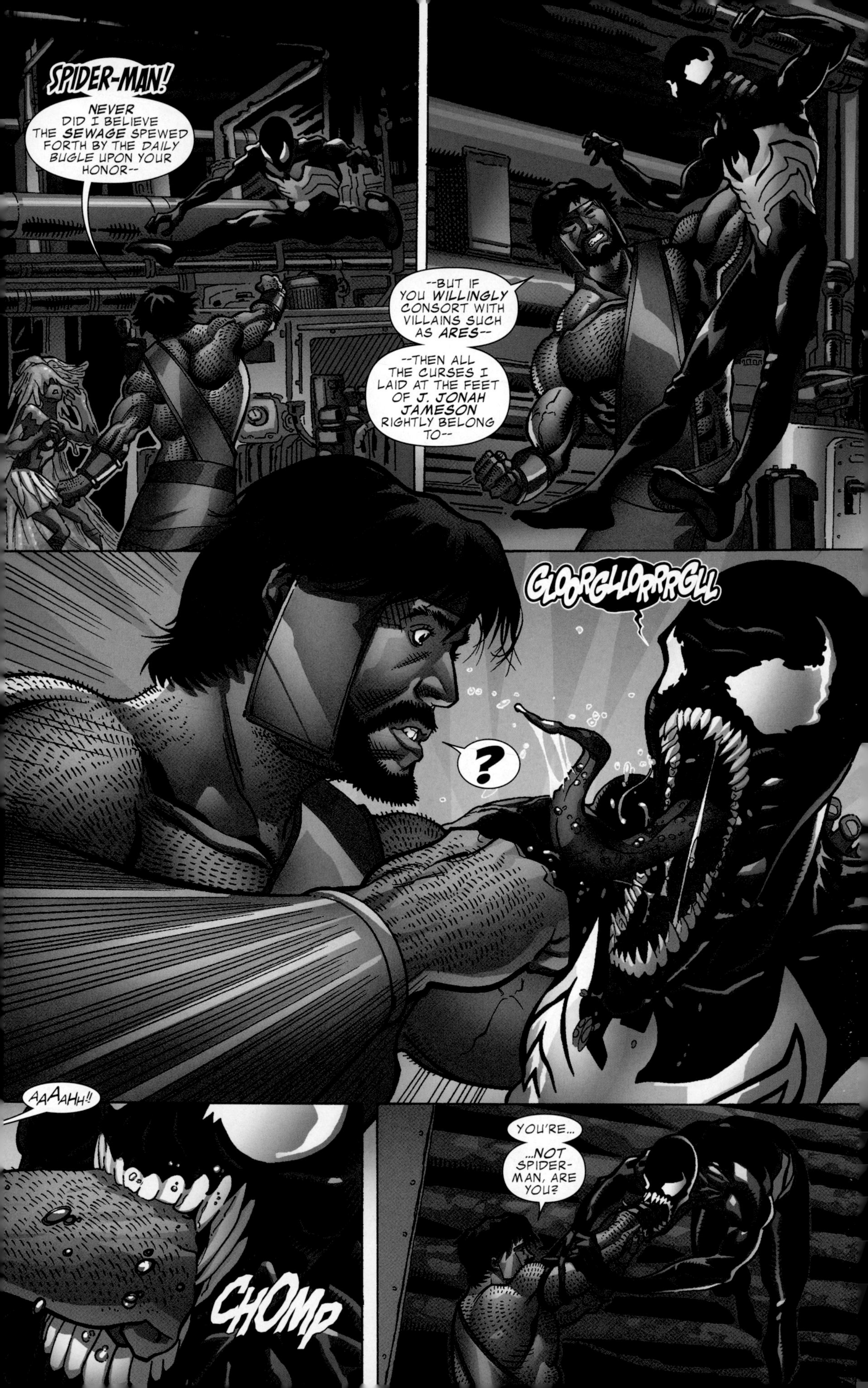
SPIDER-MAN!
NEVER DID I BELIEVE THE SEWAGE SPEWED FORTH BY THE DAILY BUGLE UPON YOUR HONOR--
--BUT IF YOU WILLINGLY CONSORT WITH VILLAINS SUCH AS ARES--
--THEN ALL THE CURSES I LAID AT THE FEET OF J. JONAH JAMESON RIGHTLY BELONG TO--
GLOORGLLORRRGLL
?
AAAAHH!!
CHOMP
YOU'RE...
...NOT SPIDER-MAN, ARE YOU?

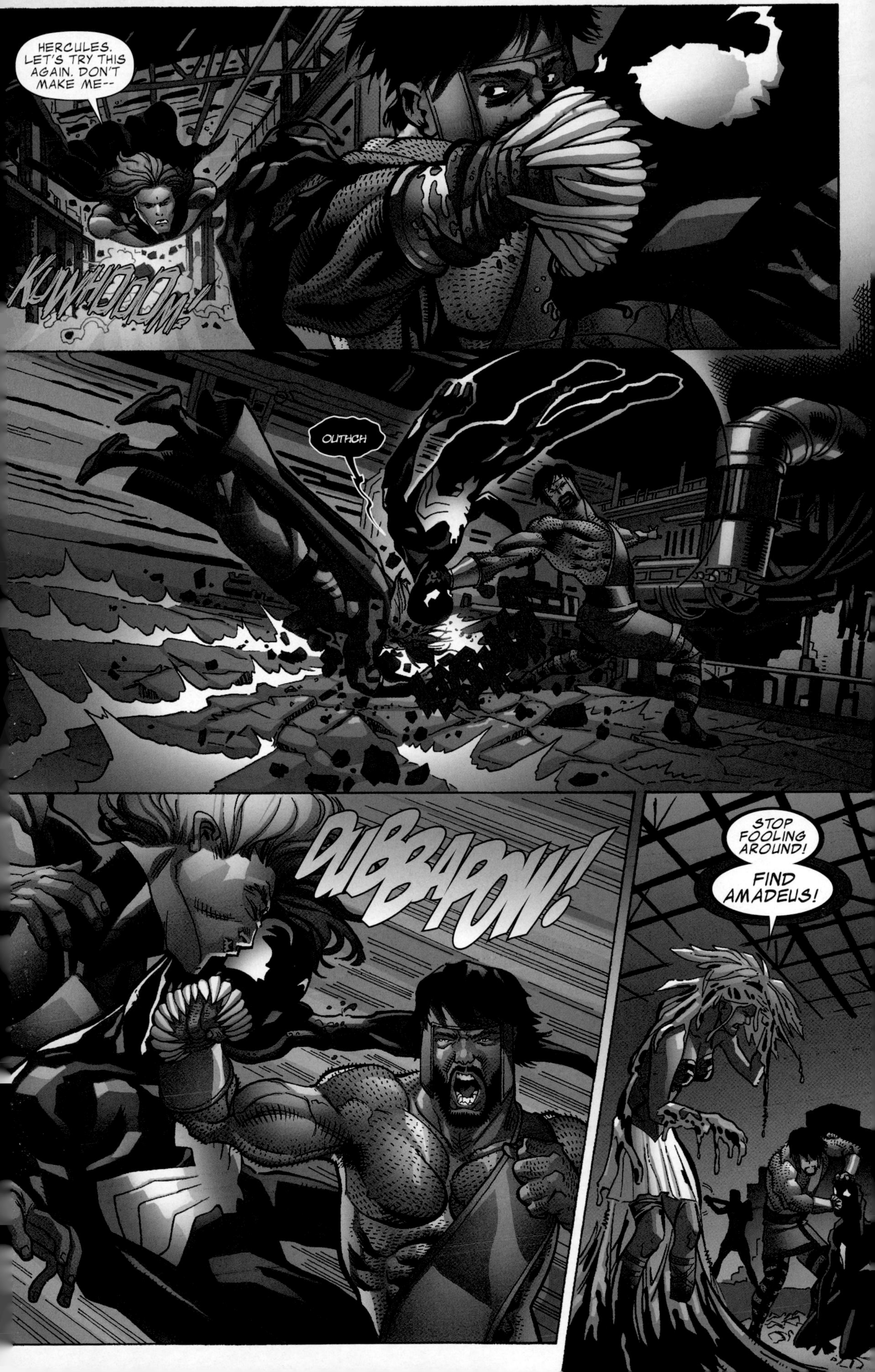
HERCULES. LET'S TRY THIS AGAIN. DON'T MAKE ME--
KUWHOOOM!
OUTHCH
DUBBAPOW!
STOP FOOLING AROUND!
FIND AMADEUS!

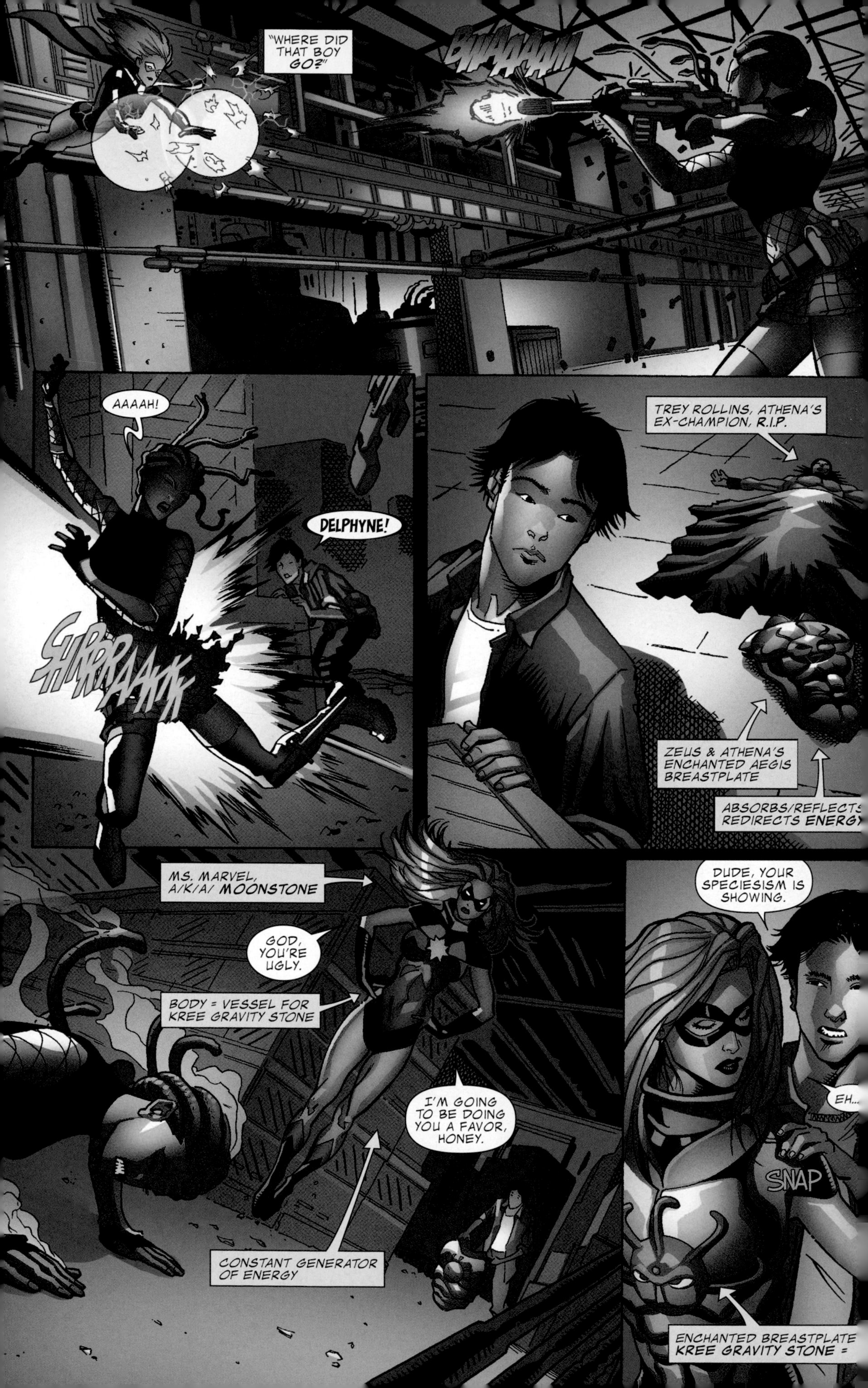
"WHERE DID THAT BOY GO?"
BWAAAAM
AAAAH!
DELPHYNE!
SHRRRAAKK
TREY ROLLINS, ATHENA'S EX-CHAMPION, R.I.P.
ZEUS & ATHENA'S ENCHANTED AEGIS BREASTPLATE
ABSORBS/REFLECTS REDIRECTS ENERGY
MS. MARVEL, A/K/A/ MOONSTONE
GOD, YOU'RE UGLY.
BODY = VESSEL FOR KREE GRAVITY STONE
I'M GOING TO BE DOING YOU A FAVOR, HONEY.
CONSTANT GENERATOR OF ENERGY
DUDE, YOUR SPECIESISM IS SHOWING.
EH...
SNAP
ENCHANTED BREASTPLATE KREE GRAVITY STONE =

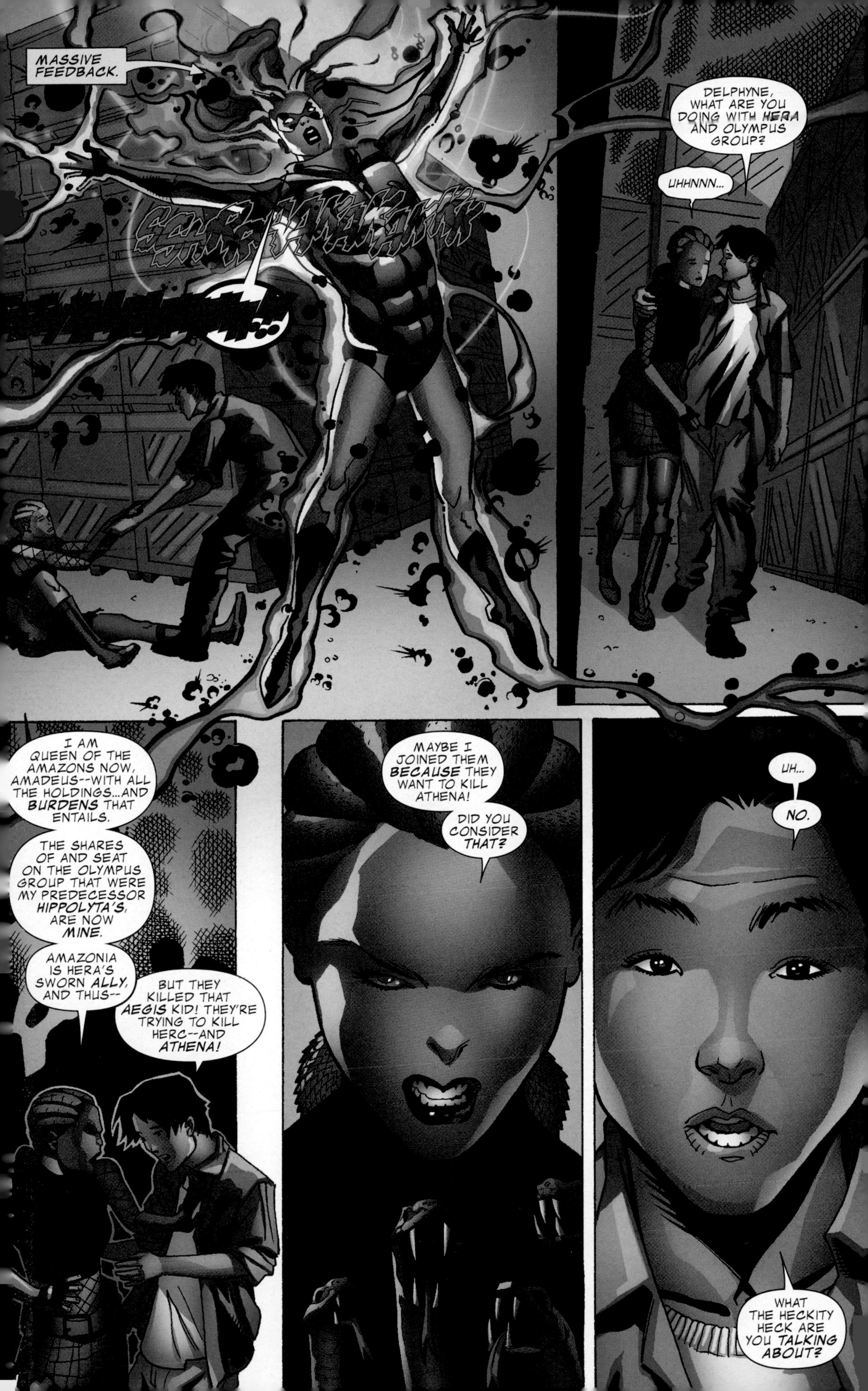
MASSIVE FEEDBACK.
DELPHYNE, WHAT ARE YOU DOING WITH HERA AND OLYMPUS GROUP?
UHHNNN...
I AM QUEEN OF THE AMAZONS NOW, AMADEUS--WITH ALL THE HOLDINGS...AND BURDENS THAT ENTAILS.
THE SHARES OF AND SEAT ON THE OLYMPUS GROUP THAT WERE MY PREDECESSOR HIPPOLYTA'S, ARE NOW MINE.
AMAZONIA IS HERA'S SWORN ALLY, AND THUS--
BUT THEY KILLED THAT AEGIS KID! THEY'RE TRYING TO KILL HERC--AND ATHENA!
MAYBE I JOINED THEM BECAUSE THEY WANT TO KILL ATHENA!
DID YOU CONSIDER THAT?
UH...
NO.
WHAT THE HECKITY HECK ARE YOU TALKING ABOUT?

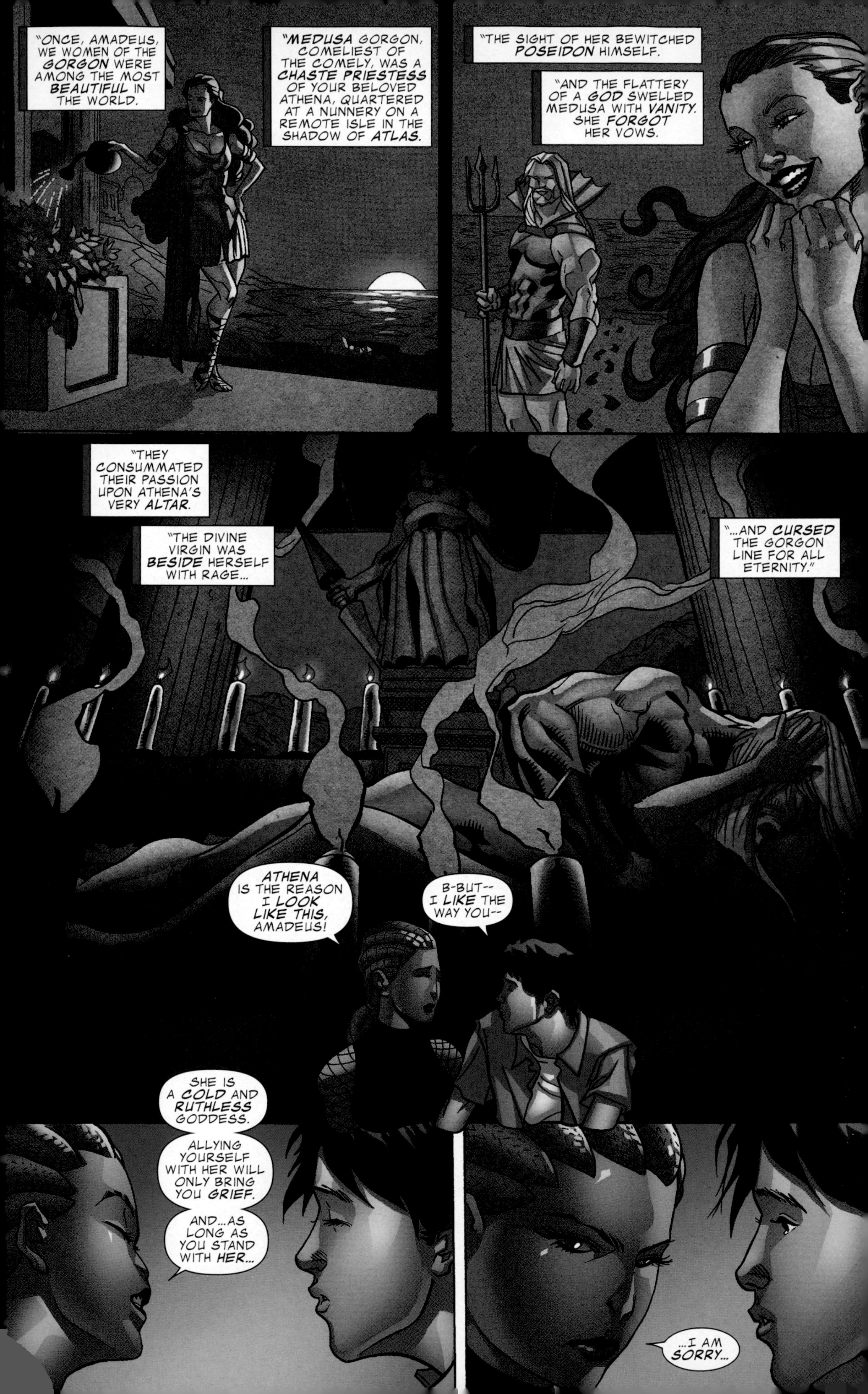
"ONCE, AMADEUS, WE WOMEN OF THE GORGON WERE AMONG THE MOST BEAUTIFUL IN THE WORLD.
"MEDUSA GORGON, COMELIEST OF THE COMELY, WAS A CHASTE PRIESTESS OF YOUR BELOVED ATHENA, QUARTERED AT A NUNNERY ON A REMOTE ISLE IN THE SHADOW OF ATLAS.
"THE SIGHT OF HER BEWITCHED POSEIDON HIMSELF.
"AND THE FLATTERY OF A GOD SWELLED MEDUSA WITH VANITY. SHE FORGOT HER VOWS.
"THEY CONSUMMATED THEIR PASSION UPON ATHENA'S VERY ALTAR.
"THE DIVINE VIRGIN WAS BESIDE HERSELF WITH RAGE...
"...AND CURSED THE GORGON LINE FOR ALL ETERNITY."
ATHENA IS THE REASON I LOOK LIKE THIS, AMADEUS!
B-BUT-- I LIKE THE WAY YOU--
SHE IS A COLD AND RUTHLESS GODDESS.
ALLYING YOURSELF WITH HER WILL ONLY BRING YOU GRIEF.
AND...AS LONG AS YOU STAND WITH HER...
...I AM SORRY...

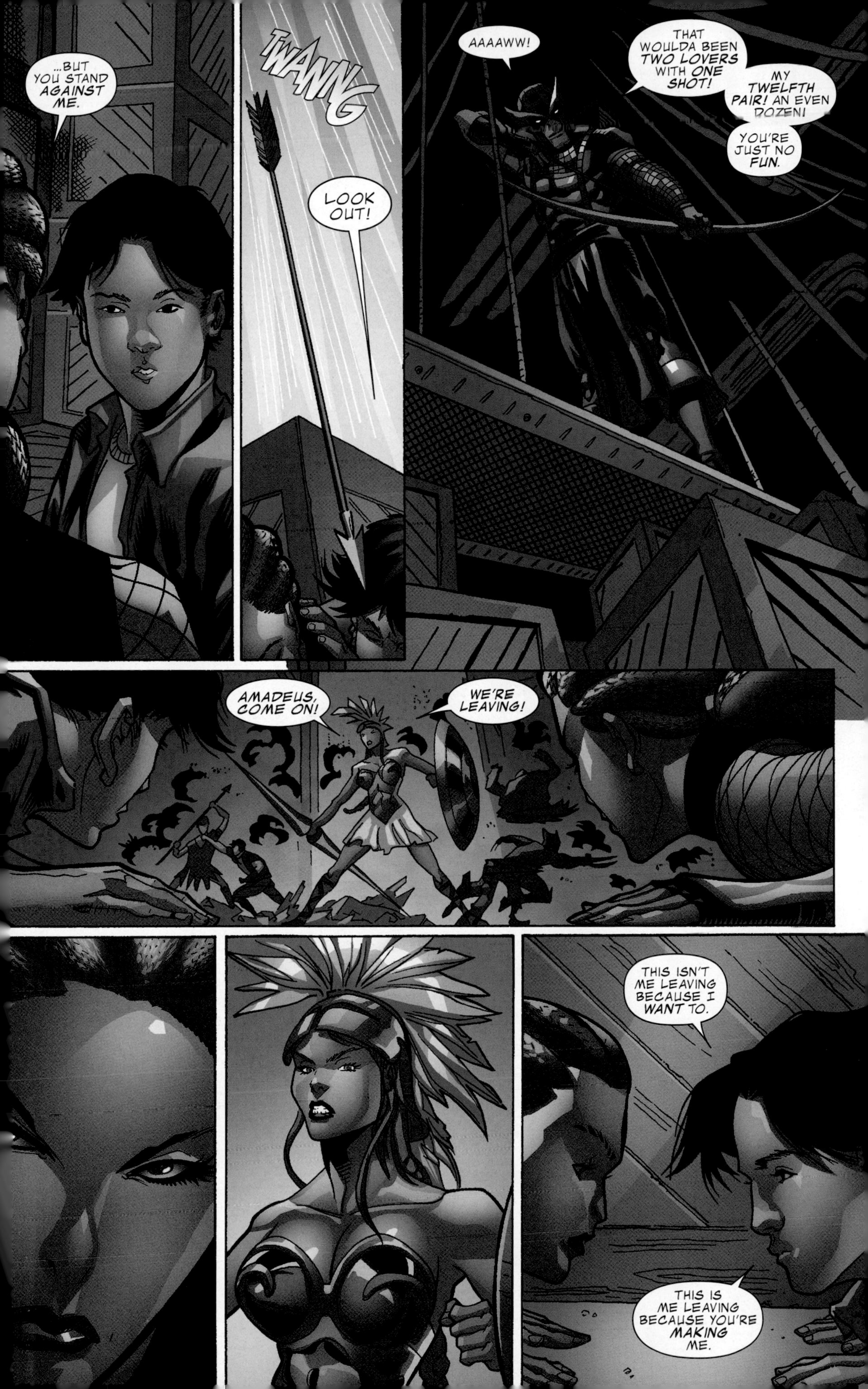
...BUT YOU STAND AGAINST ME.
TWANNG
LOOK OUT!
AAAAWW!
THAT WOULDA BEEN TWO LOVERS WITH ONE SHOT!
MY TWELFTH PAIR! AN EVEN DOZEN!
YOU'RE JUST NO FUN.
AMADEUS, COME ON!
WE'RE LEAVING!
THIS ISN'T ME LEAVING BECAUSE I WANT TO.
THIS IS ME LEAVING BECAUSE YOU'RE MAKING ME.

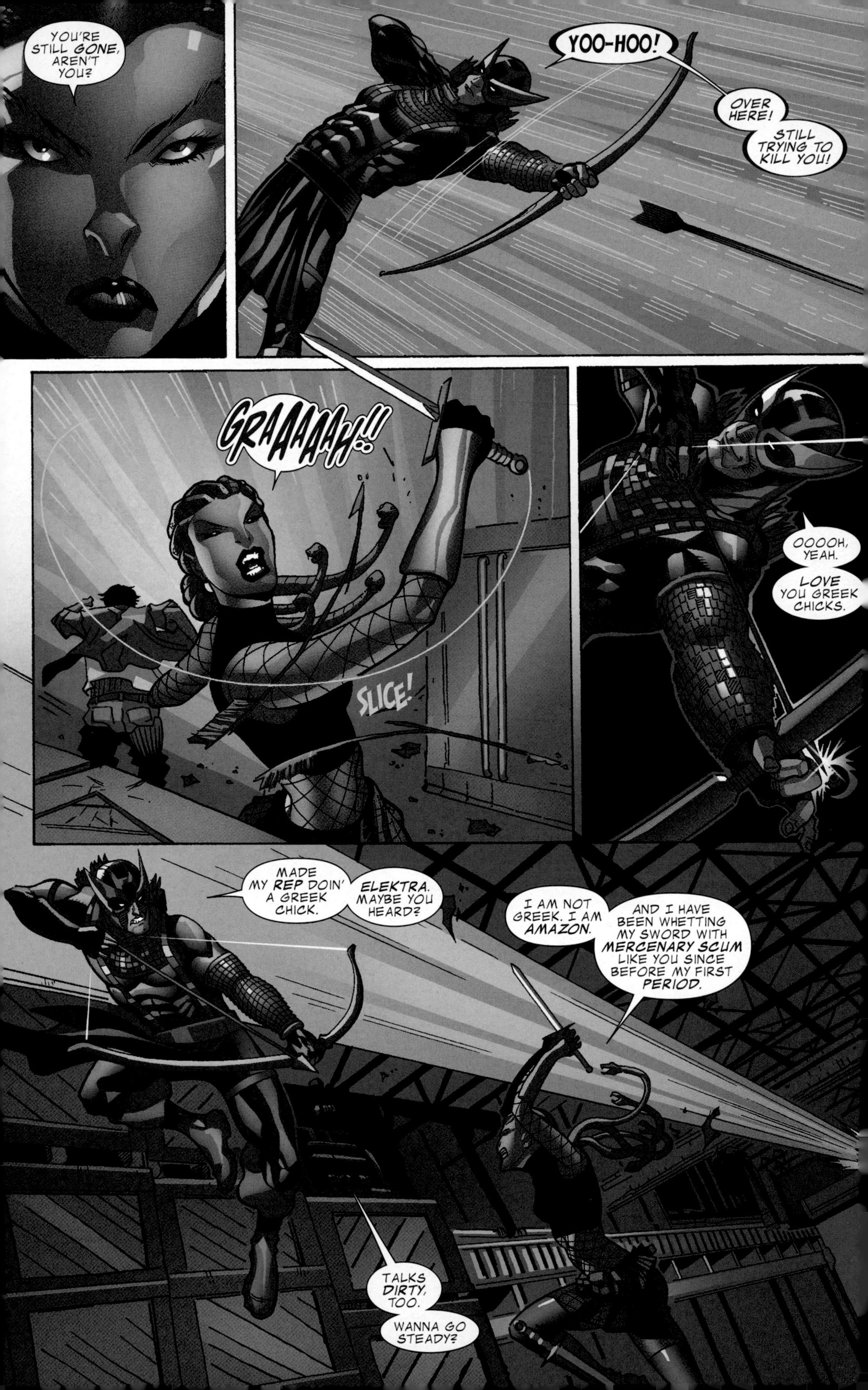
YOU'RE STILL GONE, AREN'T YOU?
YOO-HOO!
OVER HERE! STILL TRYING TO KILL YOU!
GRAAAAAH!!
SLICE!
OOOOH, YEAH. LOVE YOU GREEK CHICKS.
MADE MY REP DOIN' A GREEK CHICK.
ELEKTRA. MAYBE YOU HEARD?
I AM NOT GREEK. I AM AMAZON.
AND I HAVE BEEN WHETTING MY SWORD WITH MERCENARY SCUM LIKE YOU SINCE BEFORE MY FIRST PERIOD.
TALKS DIRTY, TOO.
WANNA GO STEADY?

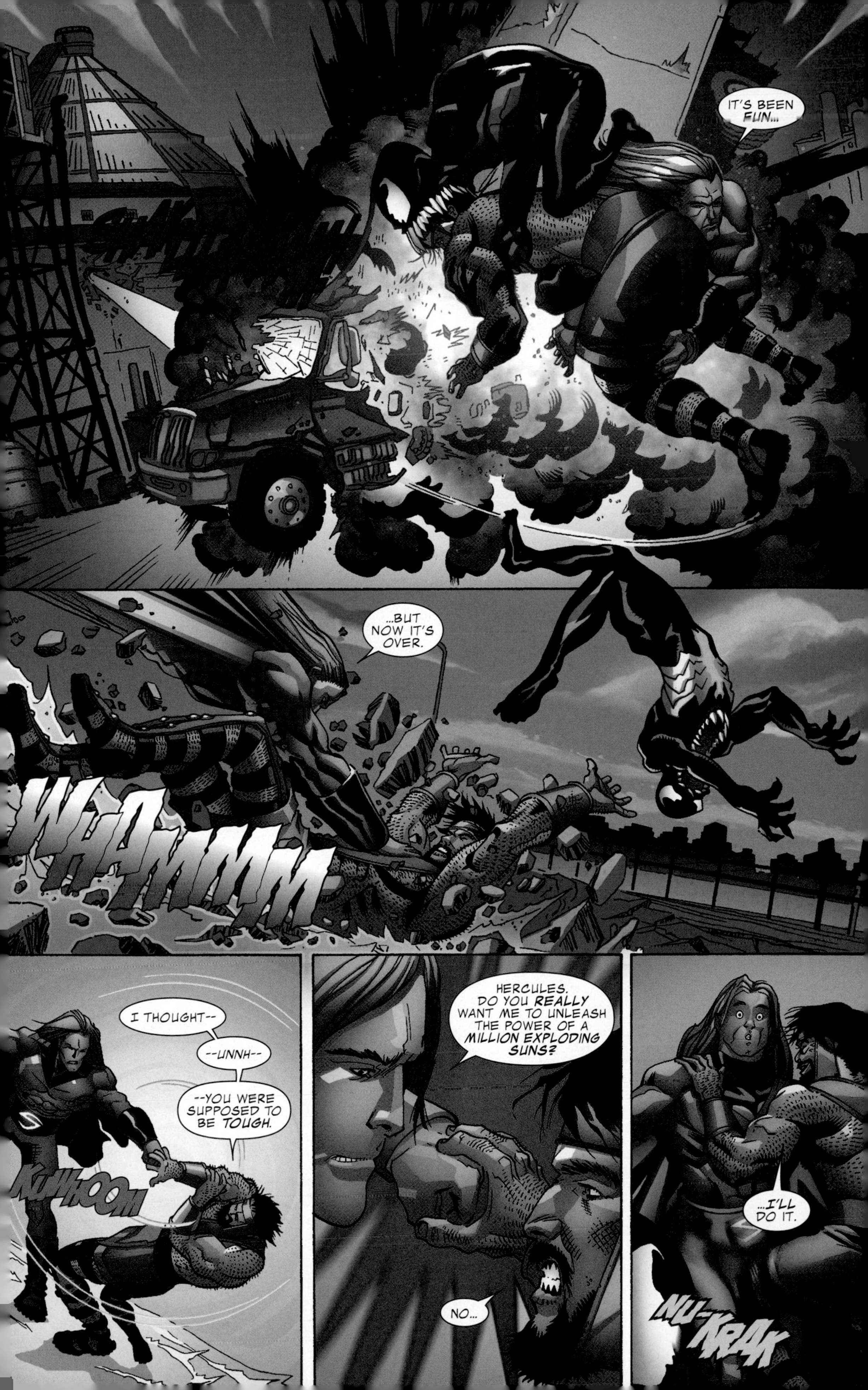
IT'S BEEN FUN...
...BUT NOW IT'S OVER.
WHAMMM
I THOUGHT--
--UNNH--
--YOU WERE SUPPOSED TO BE TOUGH.
KUHHOOM
HERCULES. DO YOU REALLY WANT ME TO UNLEASH THE POWER OF A MILLION EXPLODING SUNS?
NO...
...I'LL DO IT.
NU-KRAK

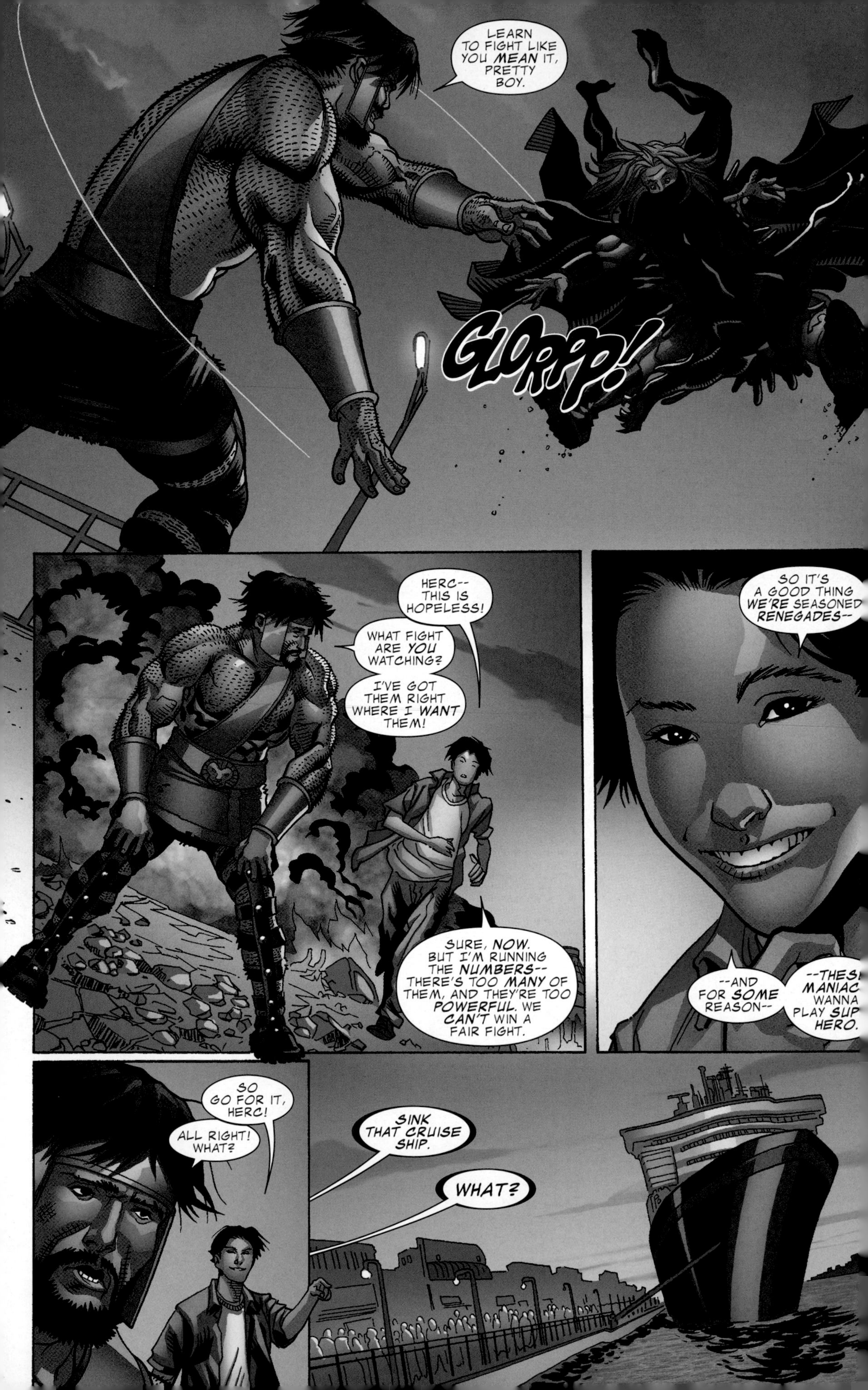

LEARN TO FIGHT LIKE YOU MEAN IT, PRETTY BOY.
GLORPP!
HERC-- THIS IS HOPELESS!
WHAT FIGHT ARE YOU WATCHING?
I'VE GOT THEM RIGHT WHERE I WANT THEM!
SURE, NOW. BUT I'M RUNNING THE NUMBERS-- THERE'S TOO MANY OF THEM, AND THEY'RE TOO POWERFUL. WE CAN'T WIN A FAIR FIGHT.
SO IT'S A GOOD THING WE'RE SEASONED RENEGADES--
--AND FOR SOME REASON--
SO GO FOR IT, HERC!
ALL RIGHT! WHAT?
SINK THAT CRUISE SHIP.
WHAT?

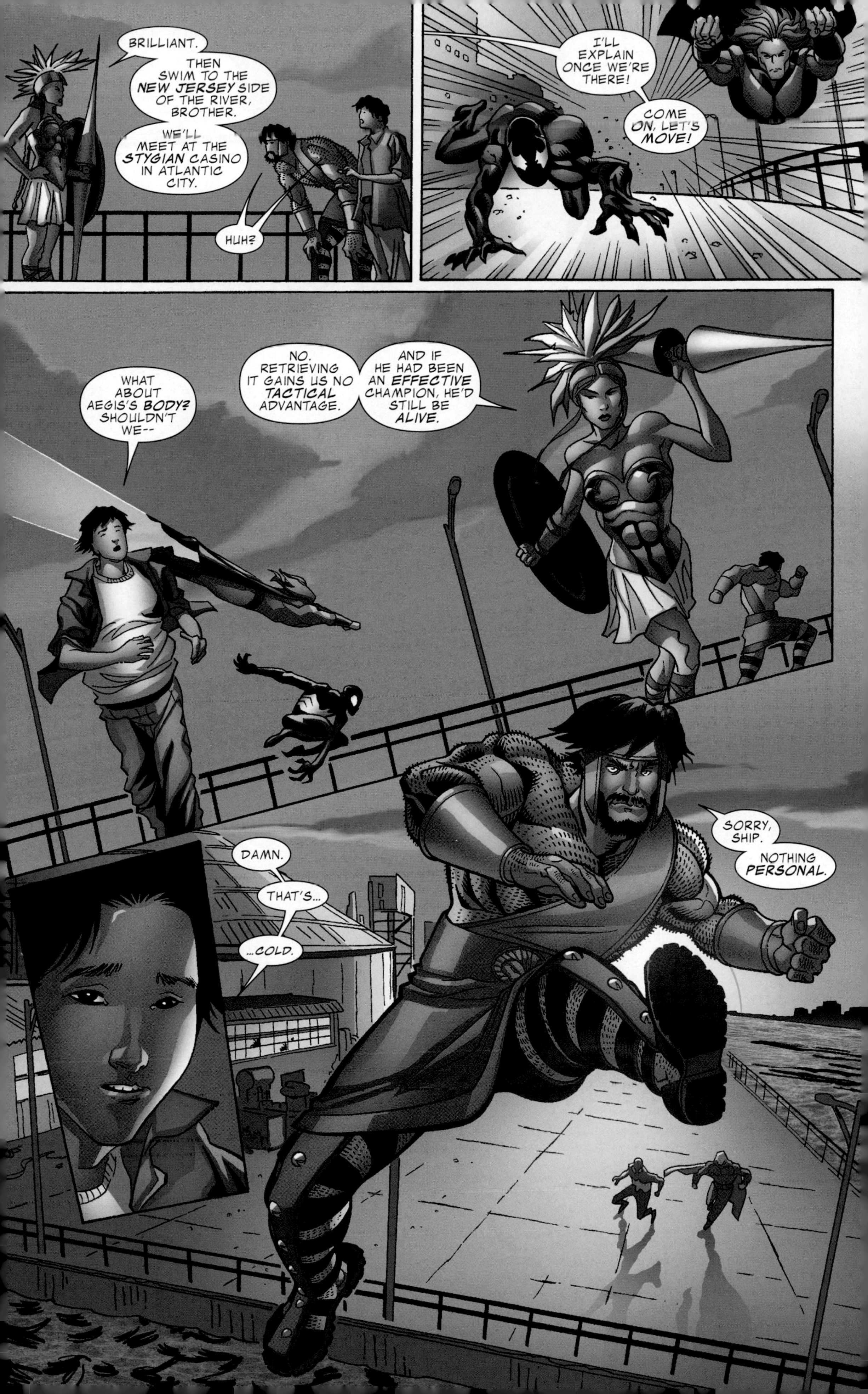
BRILLIANT.
THEN SWIM TO THE NEW JERSEY SIDE OF THE RIVER, BROTHER.
WE'LL MEET AT THE STYGIAN CASINO IN ATLANTIC CITY.
HUH?
I'LL EXPLAIN ONCE WE'RE THERE!
COME ON, LET'S MOVE!
WHAT ABOUT AEGIS'S BODY? SHOULDN'T WE--
NO. RETRIEVING IT GAINS US NO TACTICAL ADVANTAGE.
AND IF HE HAD BEEN AN EFFECTIVE CHAMPION, HE'D STILL BE ALIVE.
SORRY, SHIP.
NOTHING PERSONAL.
DAMN.
THAT'S...
...COLD.

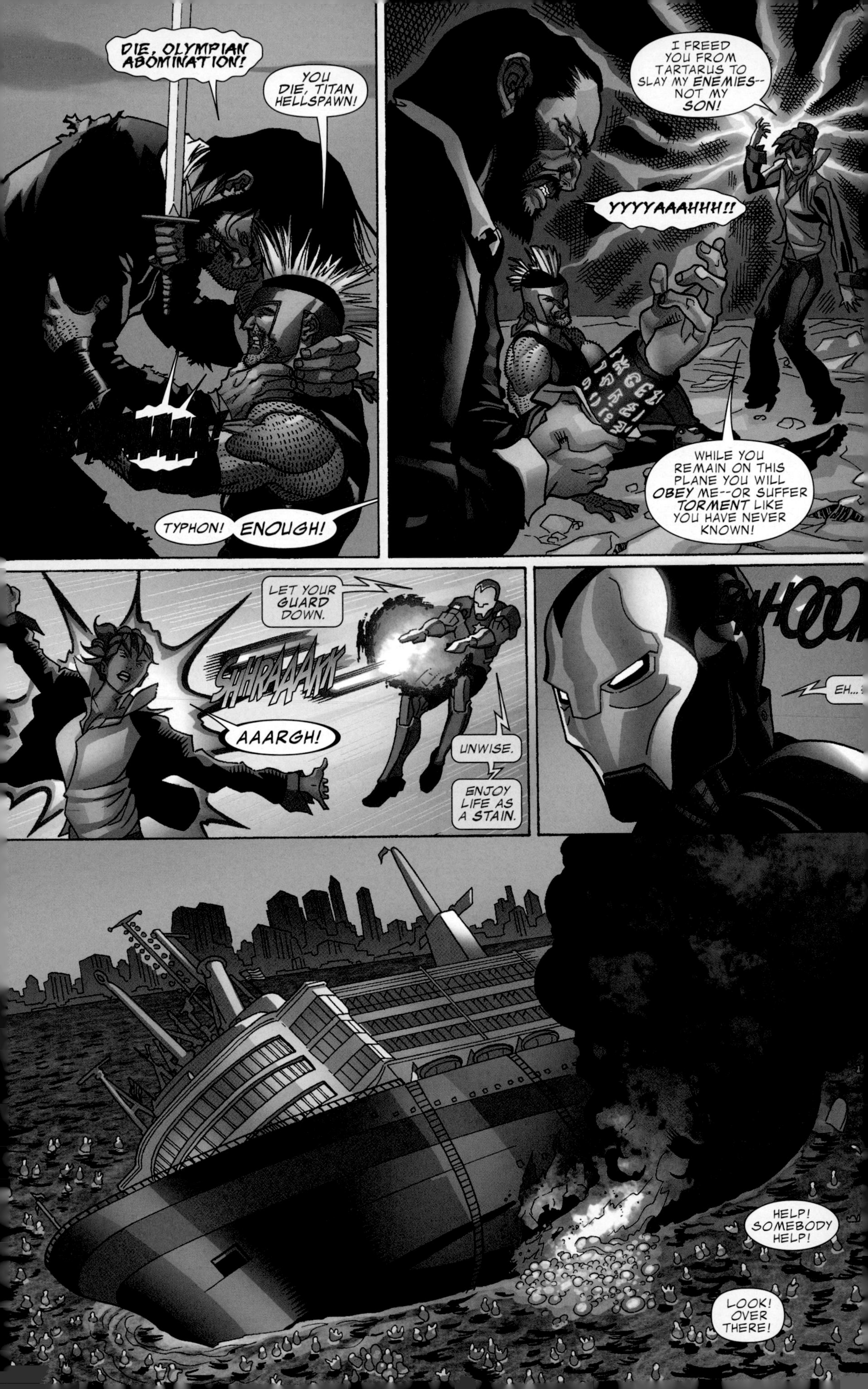
DIE, OLYMPIAN ABOMINATION!
YOU DIE, TITAN HELLSPAWN!
TYPHON!
ENOUGH!
I FREED YOU FROM TARTARUS TO SLAY MY ENEMIES--NOT MY SON!
YYYYAAAHHH!!
WHILE YOU REMAIN ON THIS PLANE YOU WILL OBEY ME--OR SUFFER TORMENT LIKE YOU HAVE NEVER KNOWN!
LET YOUR GUARD DOWN.
SHHRAAAKK
AAARGH!
UNWISE.
ENJOY LIFE AS A STAIN.
EH...?
HELP! SOMEBODY HELP!
LOOK! OVER THERE!

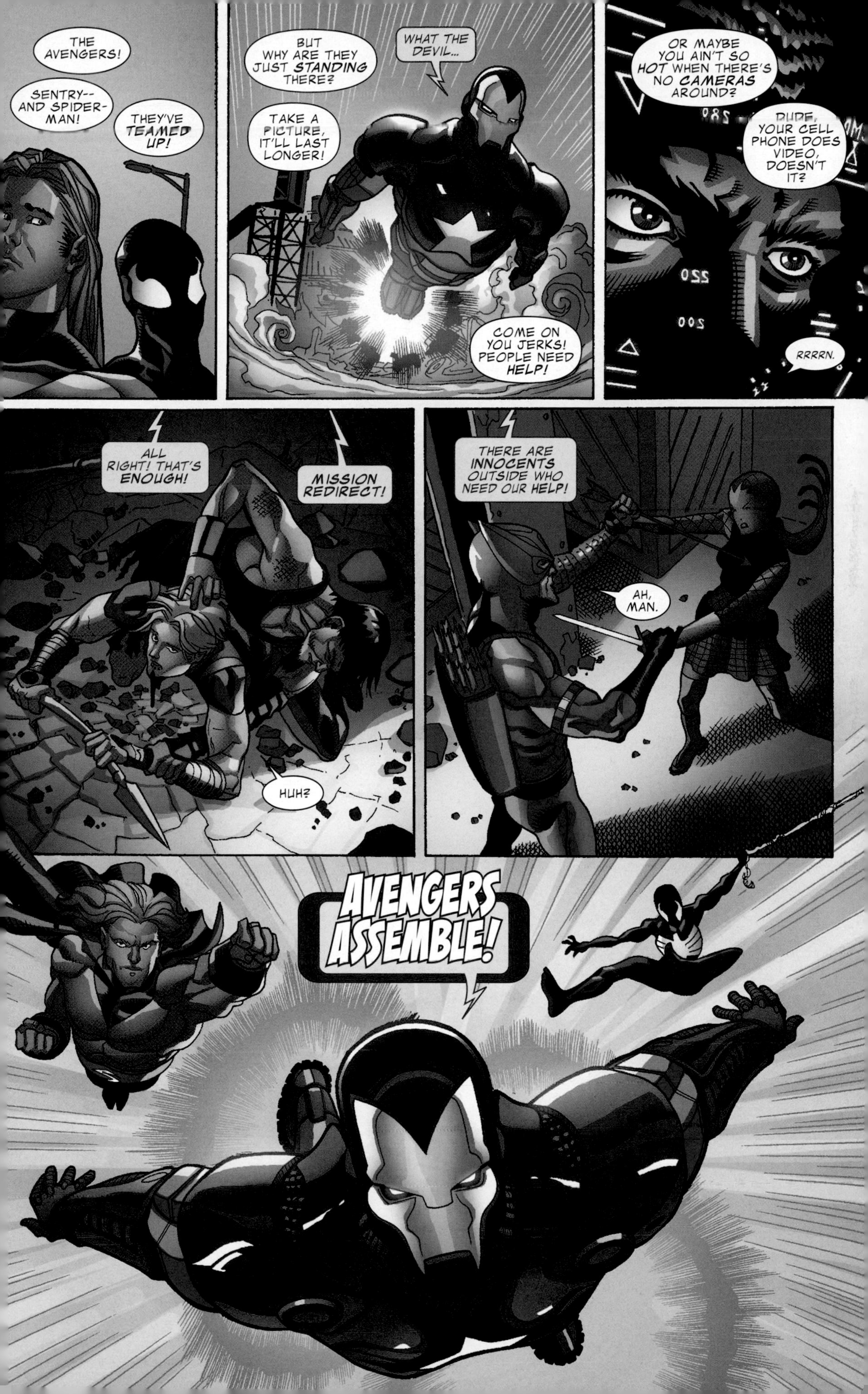
THE AVENGERS!
SENTRY-- AND SPIDER-MAN!
THEY'VE TEAMED UP!
BUT WHY ARE THEY JUST STANDING THERE?
TAKE A PICTURE, IT'LL LAST LONGER!
WHAT THE DEVIL...
COME ON YOU JERKS! PEOPLE NEED HELP!
OR MAYBE YOU AIN'T SO HOT WHEN THERE'S NO CAMERAS AROUND?
DUDE, YOUR CELL PHONE DOES VIDEO, DOESN'T IT?
RRRRN.
ALL RIGHT! THAT'S ENOUGH!
MISSION REDIRECT!
HUH?
THERE ARE INNOCENTS OUTSIDE WHO NEED OUR HELP!
AH, MAN.
AVENGERS ASSEMBLE!

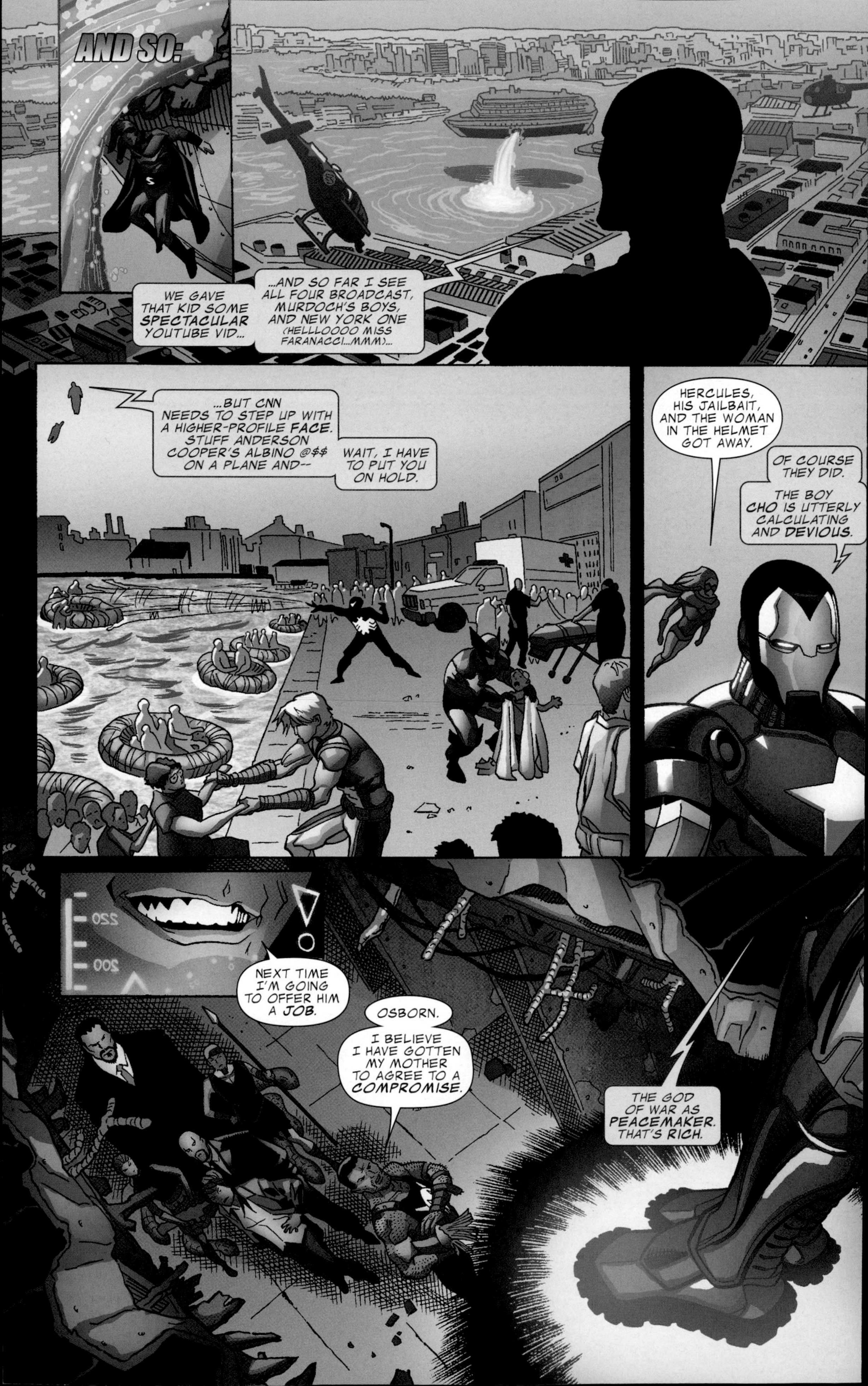
AND SO:
WE GAVE THAT KID SOME SPECTACULAR YOUTUBE VID...
...AND SO FAR I SEE ALL FOUR BROADCAST, MURDOCH'S BOYS, AND NEW YORK ONE (HELLLOOOO MISS FARANACCI...MMM)...
...BUT CNN NEEDS TO STEP UP WITH A HIGHER-PROFILE FACE. STUFF ANDERSON COOPER'S ALBINO @$$ ON A PLANE AND--
WAIT, I HAVE TO PUT YOU ON HOLD.
HERCULES, HIS JAILBAIT, AND THE WOMAN IN THE HELMET GOT AWAY.
OF COURSE THEY DID.
THE BOY CHO IS UTTERLY CALCULATING AND DEVIOUS.
NEXT TIME I'M GOING TO OFFER HIM A JOB.
OSBORN.
I BELIEVE I HAVE GOTTEN MY MOTHER TO AGREE TO A COMPROMISE.
THE GOD OF WAR AS PEACEMAKER. THAT'S RICH.

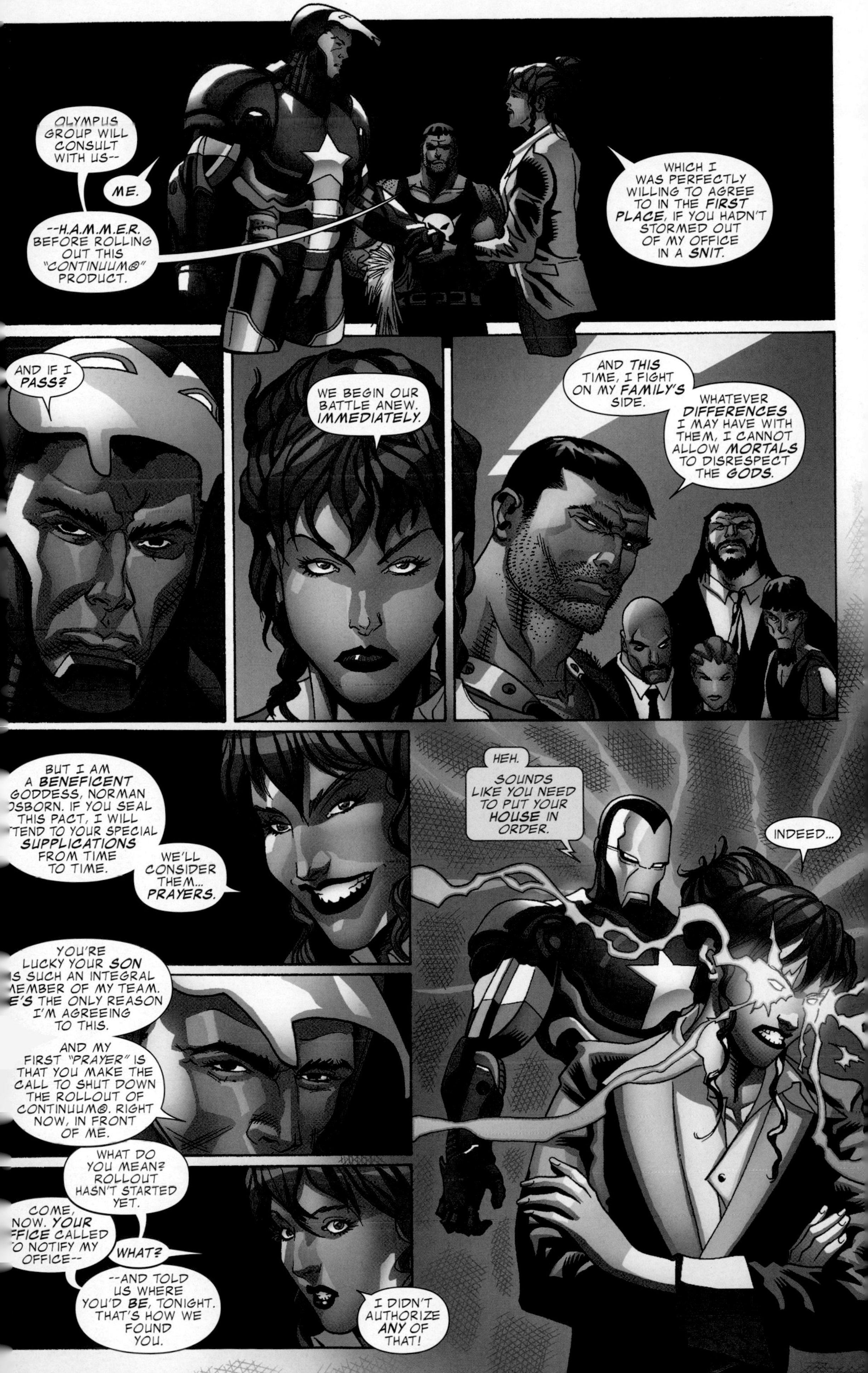
OLYMPUS GROUP WILL CONSULT WITH US--
ME.
--H.A.M.M.E.R. BEFORE ROLLING OUT THIS "CONTINUUM®" PRODUCT.
WHICH I WAS PERFECTLY WILLING TO AGREE TO IN THE FIRST PLACE, IF YOU HADN'T STORMED OUT OF MY OFFICE IN A SNIT.
AND IF I PASS?
WE BEGIN OUR BATTLE ANEW. IMMEDIATELY.
AND THIS TIME, I FIGHT ON MY FAMILY'S SIDE.
WHATEVER DIFFERENCES I MAY HAVE WITH THEM, I CANNOT ALLOW MORTALS TO DISRESPECT THE GODS.
BUT I AM A BENEFICENT GODDESS, NORMAN OSBORN. IF YOU SEAL THIS PACT, I WILL ATTEND TO YOUR SPECIAL SUPPLICATIONS FROM TIME TO TIME.
WE'LL CONSIDER THEM... PRAYERS.
YOU'RE LUCKY YOUR SON IS SUCH AN INTEGRAL MEMBER OF MY TEAM. HE'S THE ONLY REASON I'M AGREEING TO THIS.
AND MY FIRST "PRAYER" IS THAT YOU MAKE THE CALL TO SHUT DOWN THE ROLLOUT OF CONTINUUM®. RIGHT NOW, IN FRONT OF ME.
WHAT DO YOU MEAN? ROLLOUT HASN'T STARTED YET.
COME, NOW. YOUR OFFICE CALLED TO NOTIFY MY OFFICE--
WHAT?
--AND TOLD US WHERE YOU'D BE, TONIGHT. THAT'S HOW WE FOUND YOU.
I DIDN'T AUTHORIZE ANY OF THAT!
HEH. SOUNDS LIKE YOU NEED TO PUT YOUR HOUSE IN ORDER.
INDEED...

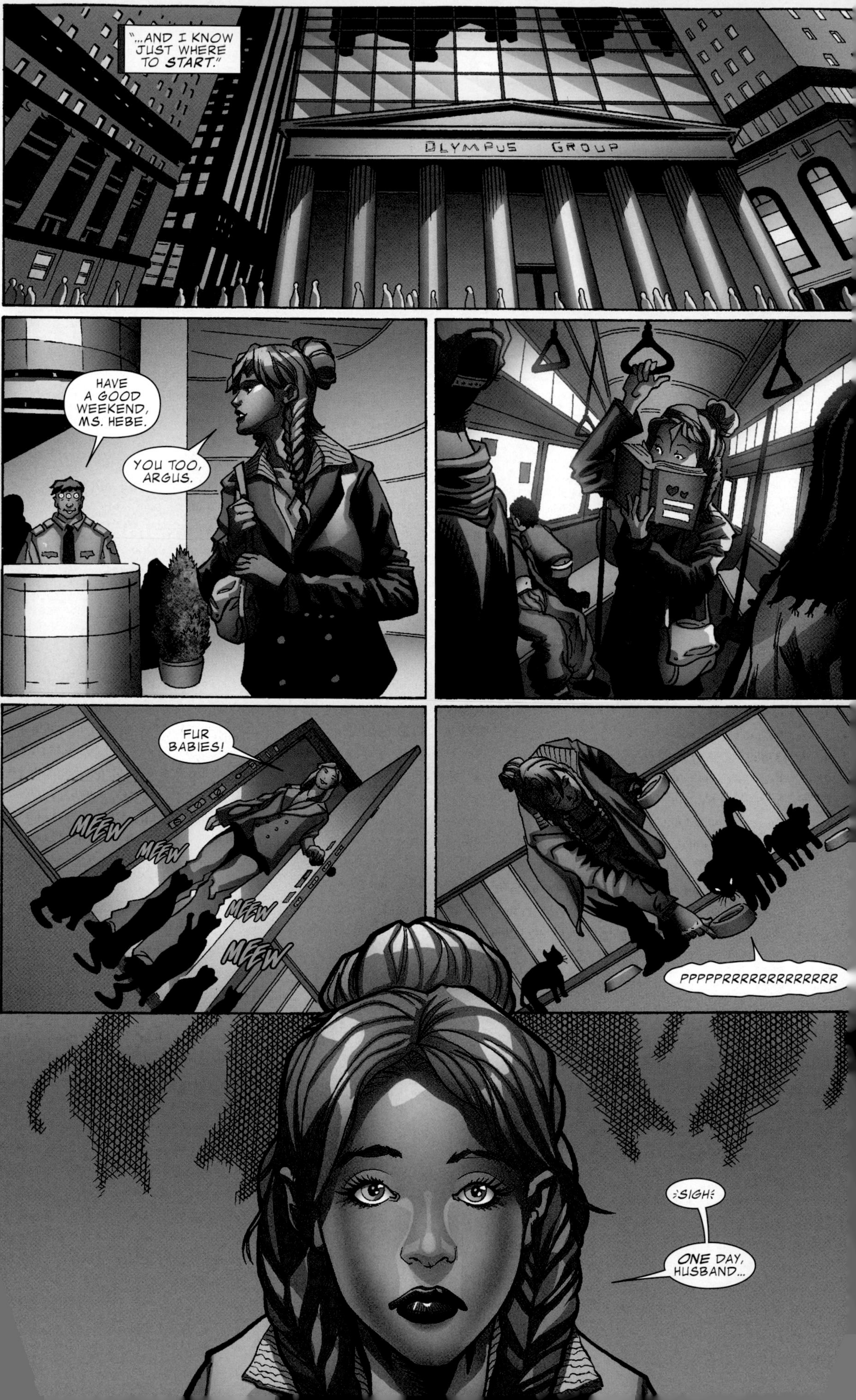
"...AND I KNOW JUST WHERE TO START."
DLYMPUS GROUP
HAVE A GOOD WEEKEND, MS. HEBE.
YOU TOO, ARGUS.
FUR BABIES!
MEEW
MEEW
MEEW
MEEW
PPPPPRRRRRRRRRRRR
SIGH
ONE DAY, HUSBAND...

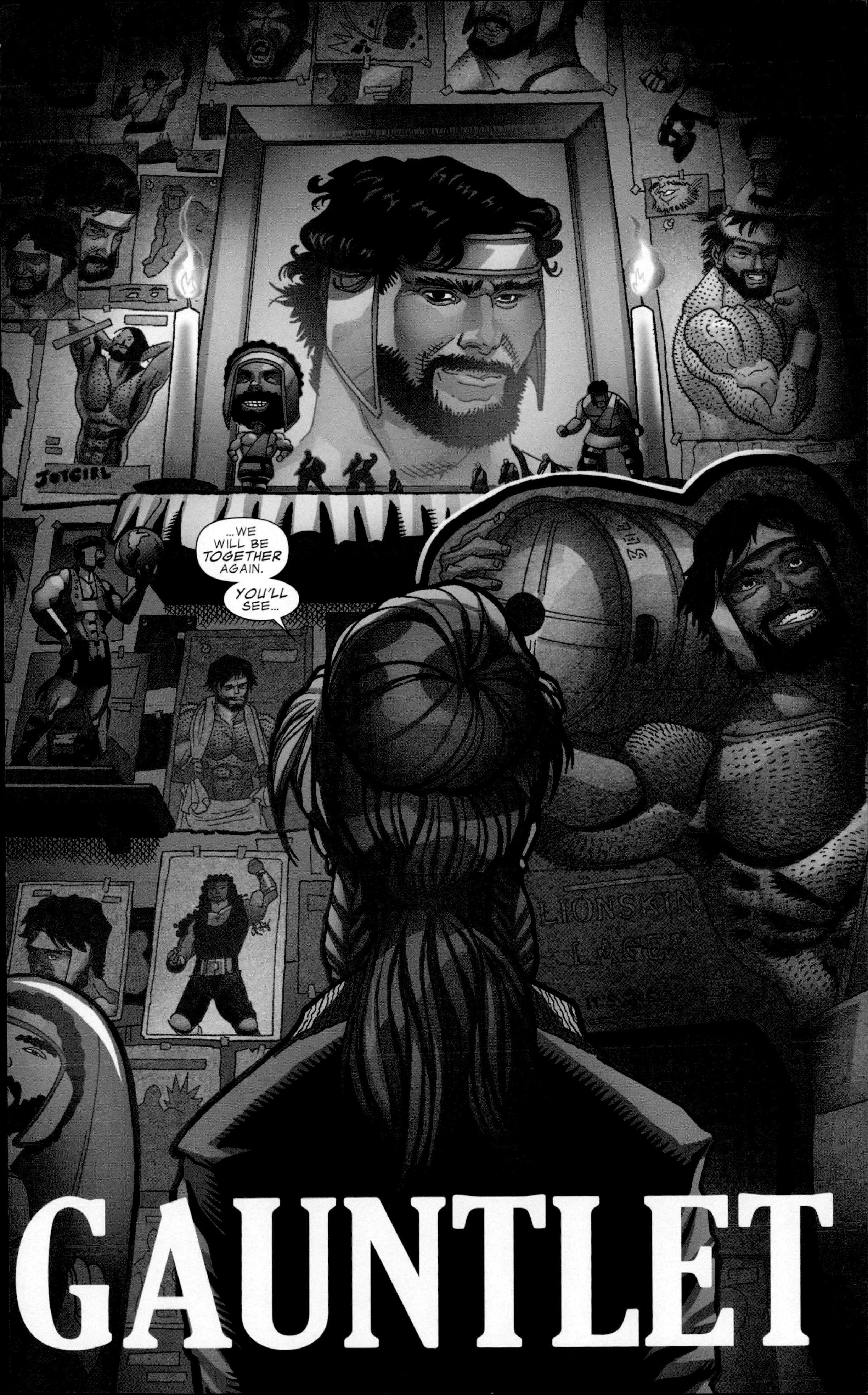
JOYGIRL
...WE WILL BE TOGETHER AGAIN.
YOU'LL SEE...
LIONSKIN LAGER
GAUNTLET

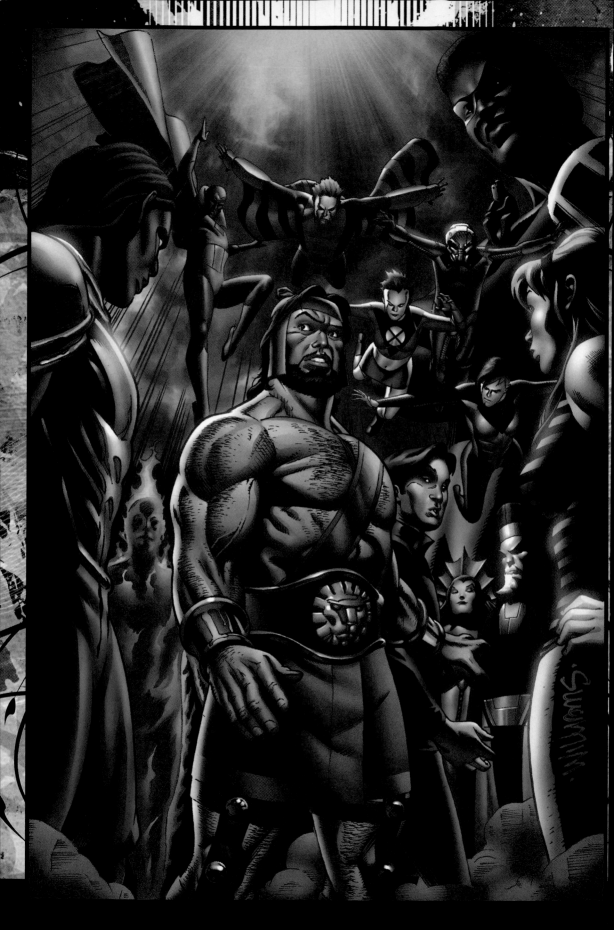

INCREDIBLE HERCULES #129

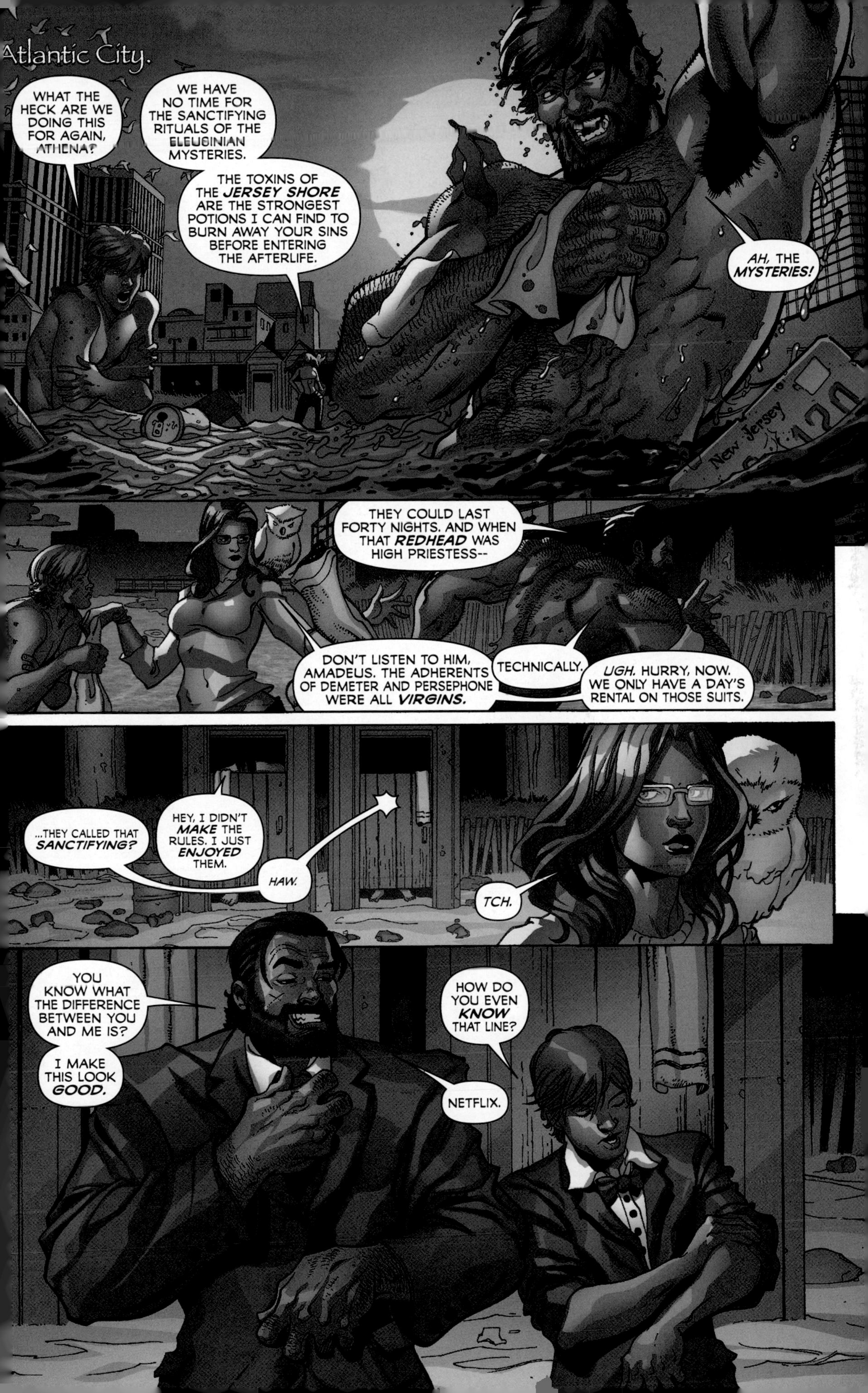
Atlantic City.
WHAT THE HECK ARE WE DOING THIS FOR AGAIN, ATHENA?
WE HAVE NO TIME FOR THE SANCTIFYING RITUALS OF THE ELEUSINIAN MYSTERIES.
THE TOXINS OF THE *JERSEY SHORE* ARE THE STRONGEST POTIONS I CAN FIND TO BURN AWAY YOUR SINS BEFORE ENTERING THE AFTERLIFE.
AH, THE *MYSTERIES!*
New Jersey
THEY COULD LAST FORTY NIGHTS. AND WHEN THAT *REDHEAD* WAS HIGH PRIESTESS--
DON'T LISTEN TO HIM, AMADEUS. THE ADHERENTS OF DEMETER AND PERSEPHONE WERE ALL *VIRGINS.*
TECHNICALLY.
UGH. HURRY, NOW. WE ONLY HAVE A DAY'S RENTAL ON THOSE SUITS.
...THEY CALLED THAT *SANCTIFYING?*
HEY, I DIDN'T *MAKE* THE RULES. I JUST *ENJOYED* THEM.
HAW.
TCH.
YOU KNOW WHAT THE DIFFERENCE BETWEEN YOU AND ME IS?
I MAKE THIS LOOK *GOOD.*
HOW DO YOU EVEN *KNOW* THAT LINE?
NETFLIX.

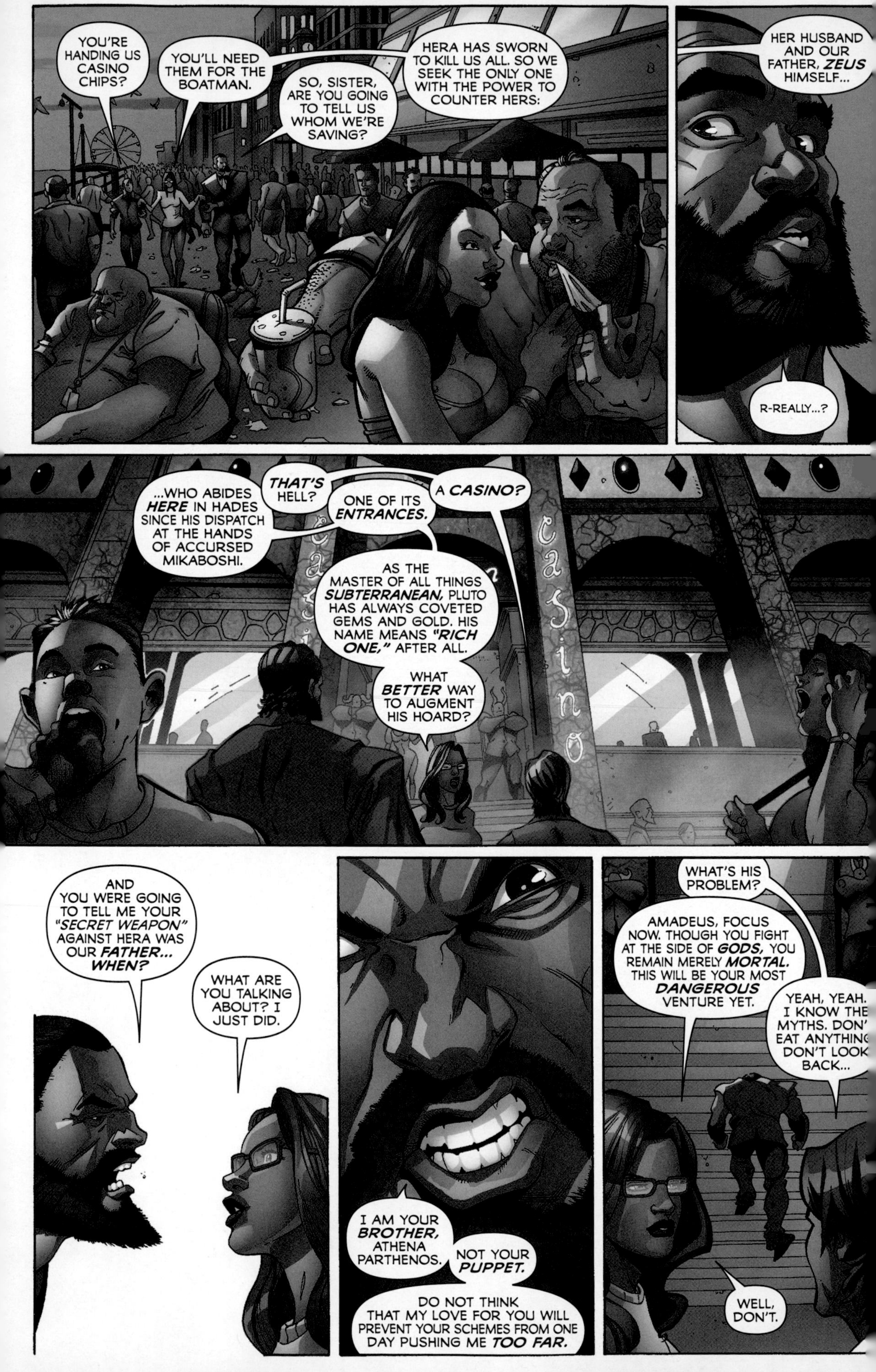
YOU'RE HANDING US CASINO CHIPS?
YOU'LL NEED THEM FOR THE BOATMAN.
SO, SISTER, ARE YOU GOING TO TELL US WHOM WE'RE SAVING?
HERA HAS SWORN TO KILL US ALL. SO WE SEEK THE ONLY ONE WITH THE POWER TO COUNTER HERS:
HER HUSBAND AND OUR FATHER, ZEUS HIMSELF...
R-REALLY...?
...WHO ABIDES HERE IN HADES SINCE HIS DISPATCH AT THE HANDS OF ACCURSED MIKABOSHI.
THAT'S HELL?
A CASINO?
ONE OF ITS ENTRANCES.
AS THE MASTER OF ALL THINGS SUBTERRANEAN, PLUTO HAS ALWAYS COVETED GEMS AND GOLD. HIS NAME MEANS "RICH ONE," AFTER ALL.
WHAT BETTER WAY TO AUGMENT HIS HOARD?
casino
AND YOU WERE GOING TO TELL ME YOUR "SECRET WEAPON" AGAINST HERA WAS OUR FATHER... WHEN?
WHAT ARE YOU TALKING ABOUT? I JUST DID.
I AM YOUR BROTHER, ATHENA PARTHENOS.
NOT YOUR PUPPET.
DO NOT THINK THAT MY LOVE FOR YOU WILL PREVENT YOUR SCHEMES FROM ONE DAY PUSHING ME TOO FAR.
WHAT'S HIS PROBLEM?
AMADEUS, FOCUS NOW. THOUGH YOU FIGHT AT THE SIDE OF GODS, YOU REMAIN MERELY MORTAL. THIS WILL BE YOUR MOST DANGEROUS VENTURE YET.
YEAH, YEAH. I KNOW THE MYTHS. DON' EAT ANYTHING DON'T LOOK BACK...
WELL, DON'T.

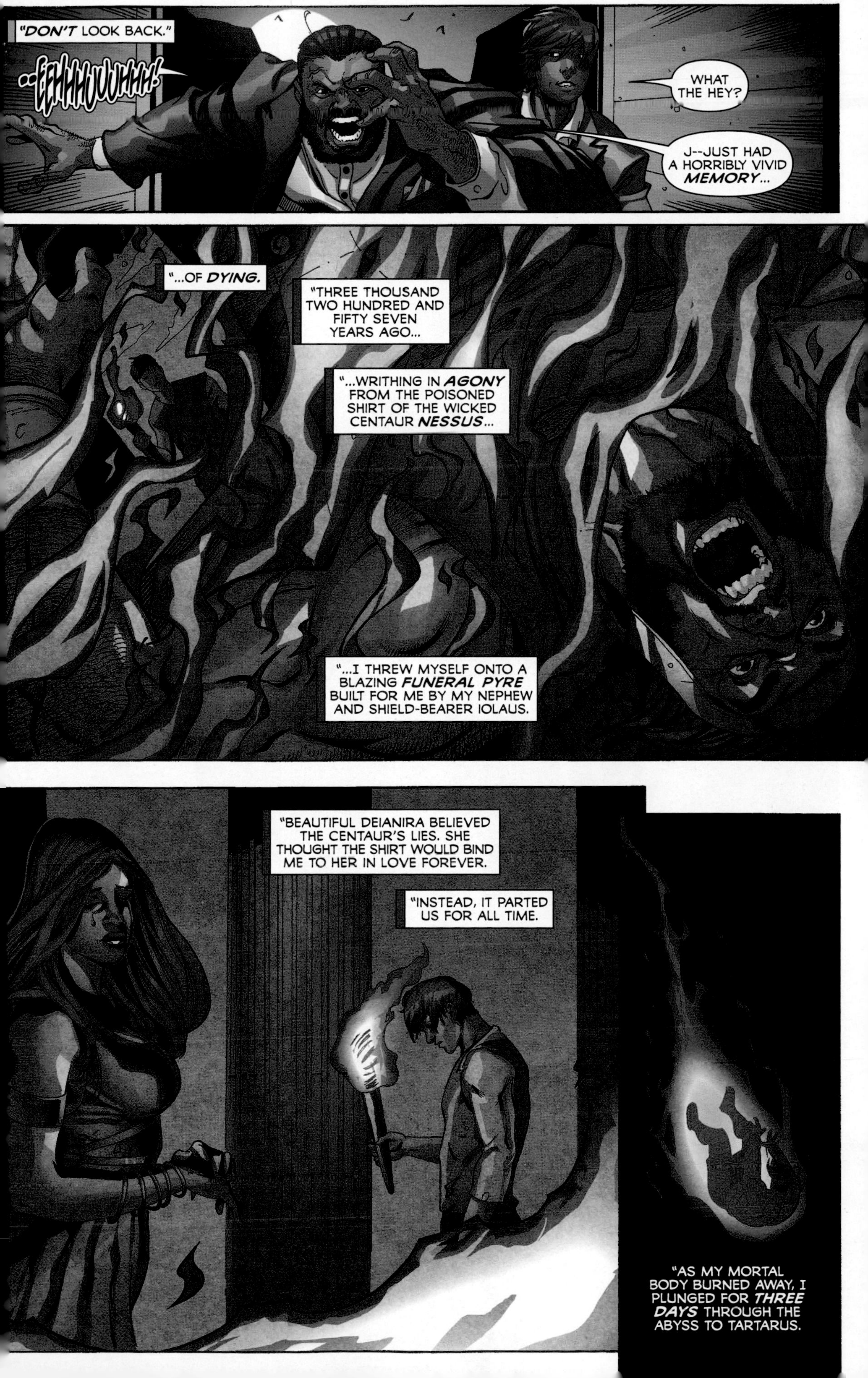
"DON'T LOOK BACK."
--EEHHHOUUHHH!
WHAT THE HEY?
J--JUST HAD A HORRIBLY VIVID MEMORY...
"...OF DYING.
"THREE THOUSAND TWO HUNDRED AND FIFTY SEVEN YEARS AGO...
"...WRITHING IN AGONY FROM THE POISONED SHIRT OF THE WICKED CENTAUR NESSUS...
"...I THREW MYSELF ONTO A BLAZING FUNERAL PYRE BUILT FOR ME BY MY NEPHEW AND SHIELD-BEARER IOLAUS.
"BEAUTIFUL DEIANIRA BELIEVED THE CENTAUR'S LIES. SHE THOUGHT THE SHIRT WOULD BIND ME TO HER IN LOVE FOREVER.
"INSTEAD, IT PARTED US FOR ALL TIME.
"AS MY MORTAL BODY BURNED AWAY, I PLUNGED FOR THREE DAYS THROUGH THE ABYSS TO TARTARUS.

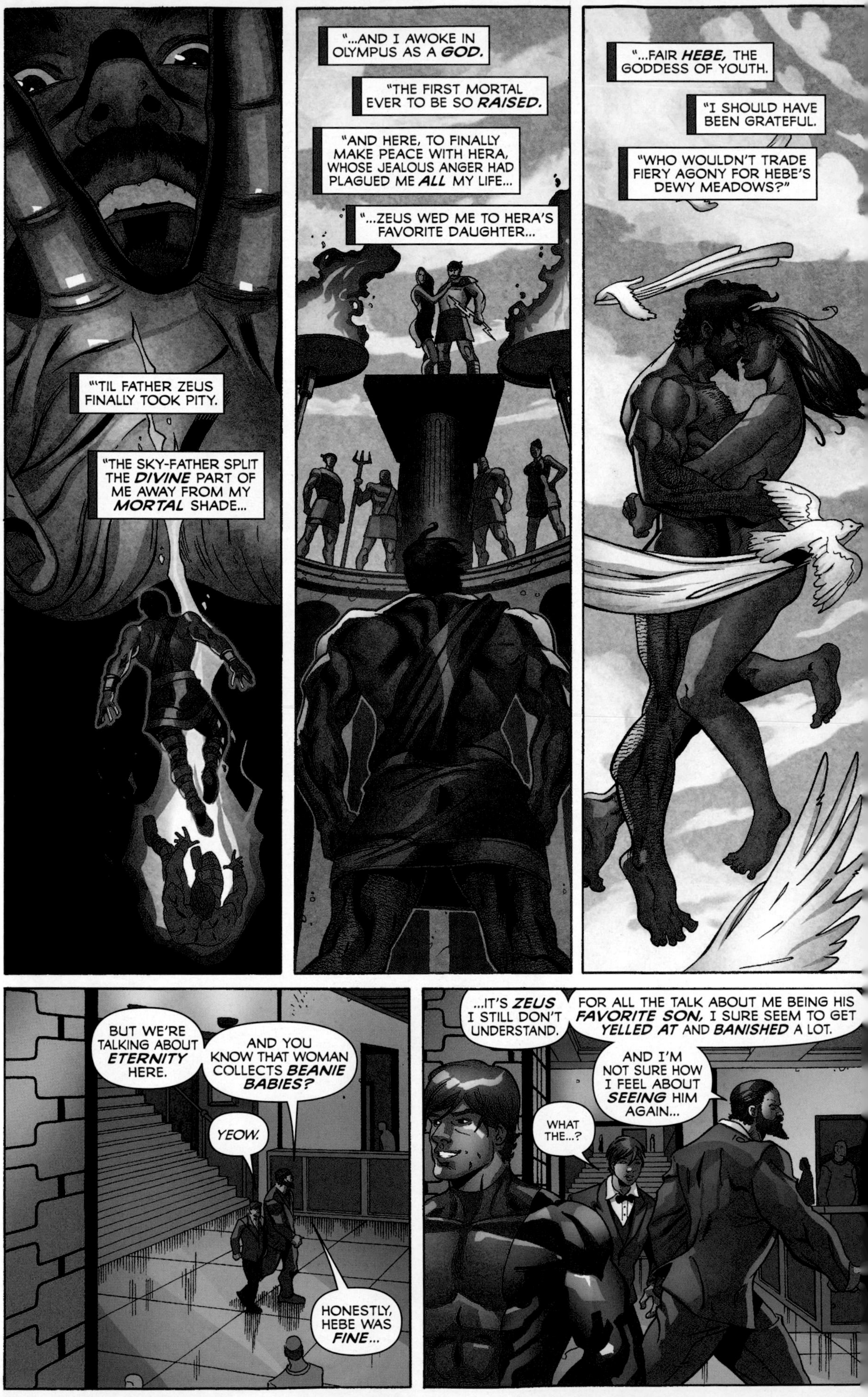
"'TIL FATHER ZEUS FINALLY TOOK PITY.
"THE SKY-FATHER SPLIT THE DIVINE PART OF ME AWAY FROM MY MORTAL SHADE...
"...AND I AWOKE IN OLYMPUS AS A GOD.
"THE FIRST MORTAL EVER TO BE SO RAISED.
"AND HERE, TO FINALLY MAKE PEACE WITH HERA, WHOSE JEALOUS ANGER HAD PLAGUED ME ALL MY LIFE...
"...ZEUS WED ME TO HERA'S FAVORITE DAUGHTER...
"...FAIR HEBE, THE GODDESS OF YOUTH.
"I SHOULD HAVE BEEN GRATEFUL.
"WHO WOULDN'T TRADE FIERY AGONY FOR HEBE'S DEWY MEADOWS?"
BUT WE'RE TALKING ABOUT ETERNITY HERE.
AND YOU KNOW THAT WOMAN COLLECTS BEANIE BABIES?
YEOW.
HONESTLY, HEBE WAS FINE...
...IT'S ZEUS I STILL DON'T UNDERSTAND.
FOR ALL THE TALK ABOUT ME BEING HIS FAVORITE SON, I SURE SEEM TO GET YELLED AT AND BANISHED A LOT.
AND I'M NOT SURE HOW I FEEL ABOUT SEEING HIM AGAIN...
WHAT THE...?

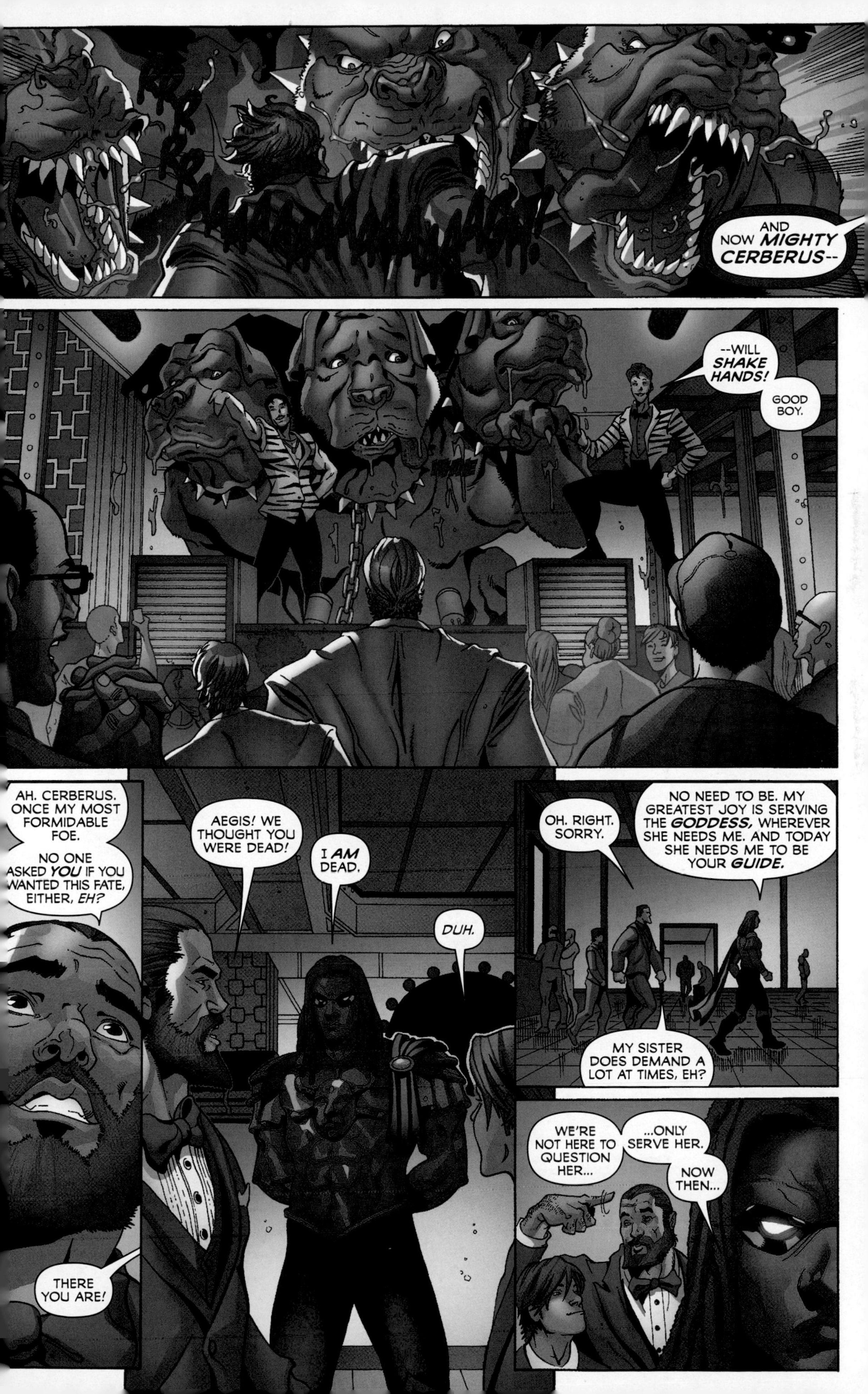
RRRRAAAAAAAAAAAAAGH!
AND NOW MIGHTY CERBERUS--
--WILL SHAKE HANDS!
GOOD BOY.
AH. CERBERUS. ONCE MY MOST FORMIDABLE FOE.
NO ONE ASKED YOU IF YOU WANTED THIS FATE, EITHER, EH?
AEGIS! WE THOUGHT YOU WERE DEAD!
I AM DEAD.
DUH.
THERE YOU ARE!
OH. RIGHT. SORRY.
NO NEED TO BE. MY GREATEST JOY IS SERVING THE GODDESS, WHEREVER SHE NEEDS ME. AND TODAY SHE NEEDS ME TO BE YOUR GUIDE.
MY SISTER DOES DEMAND A LOT AT TIMES, EH?
WE'RE NOT HERE TO QUESTION HER...
...ONLY SERVE HER.
NOW THEN...

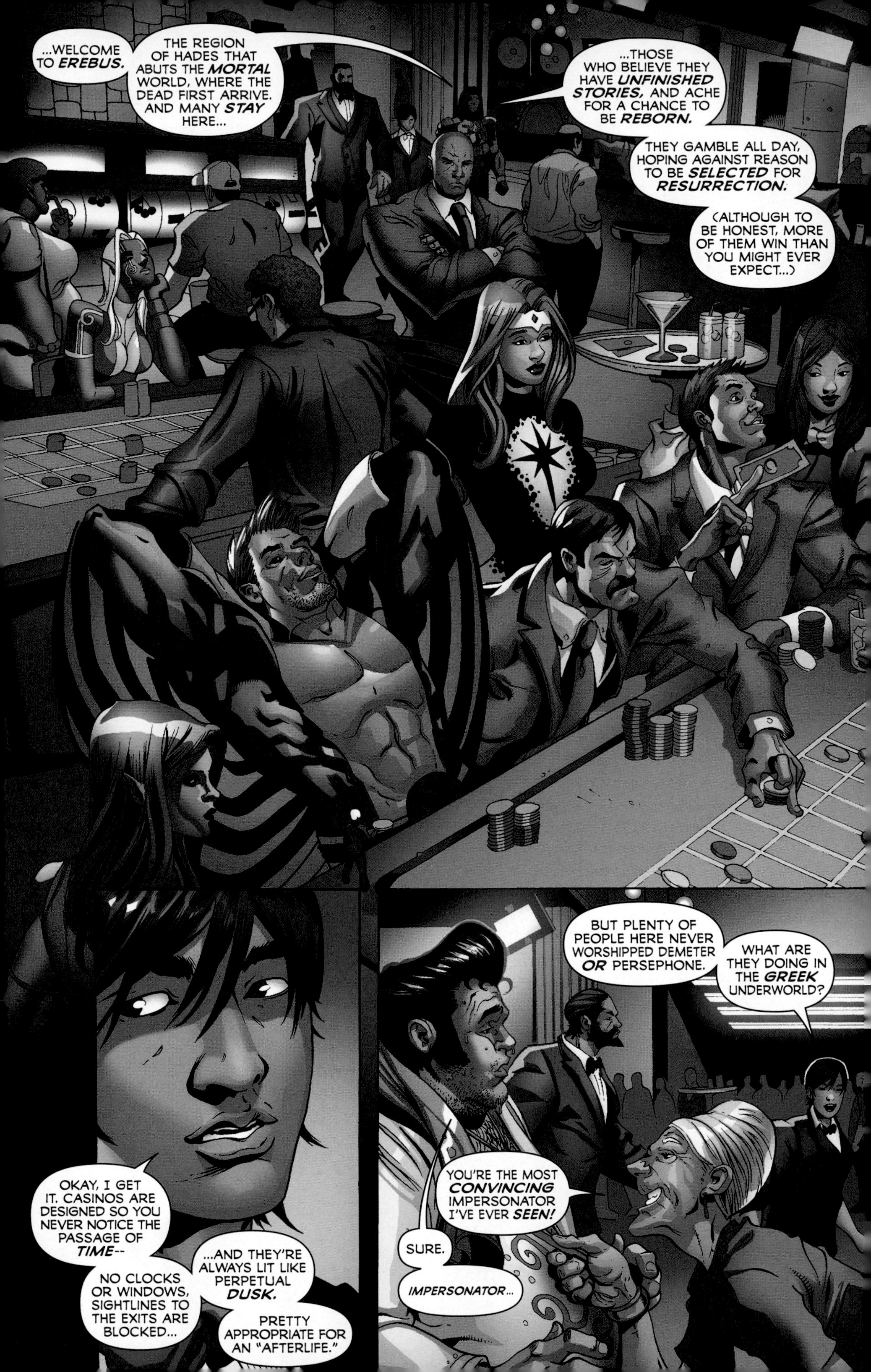

...WELCOME TO EREBUS.
THE REGION OF HADES THAT ABUTS THE MORTAL WORLD, WHERE THE DEAD FIRST ARRIVE. AND MANY STAY HERE...
...THOSE WHO BELIEVE THEY HAVE UNFINISHED STORIES, AND ACHE FOR A CHANCE TO BE REBORN.
THEY GAMBLE ALL DAY, HOPING AGAINST REASON TO BE SELECTED FOR RESURRECTION.
(ALTHOUGH TO BE HONEST, MORE OF THEM WIN THAN YOU MIGHT EVER EXPECT...)
OKAY, I GET IT. CASINOS ARE DESIGNED SO YOU NEVER NOTICE THE PASSAGE OF TIME--
NO CLOCKS OR WINDOWS, SIGHTLINES TO THE EXITS ARE BLOCKED...
...AND THEY'RE ALWAYS LIT LIKE PERPETUAL DUSK.
PRETTY APPROPRIATE FOR AN "AFTERLIFE."
BUT PLENTY OF PEOPLE HERE NEVER WORSHIPPED DEMETER OR PERSEPHONE.
WHAT ARE THEY DOING IN THE GREEK UNDERWORLD?
YOU'RE THE MOST CONVINCING IMPERSONATOR I'VE EVER SEEN!
SURE.
IMPERSONATOR...

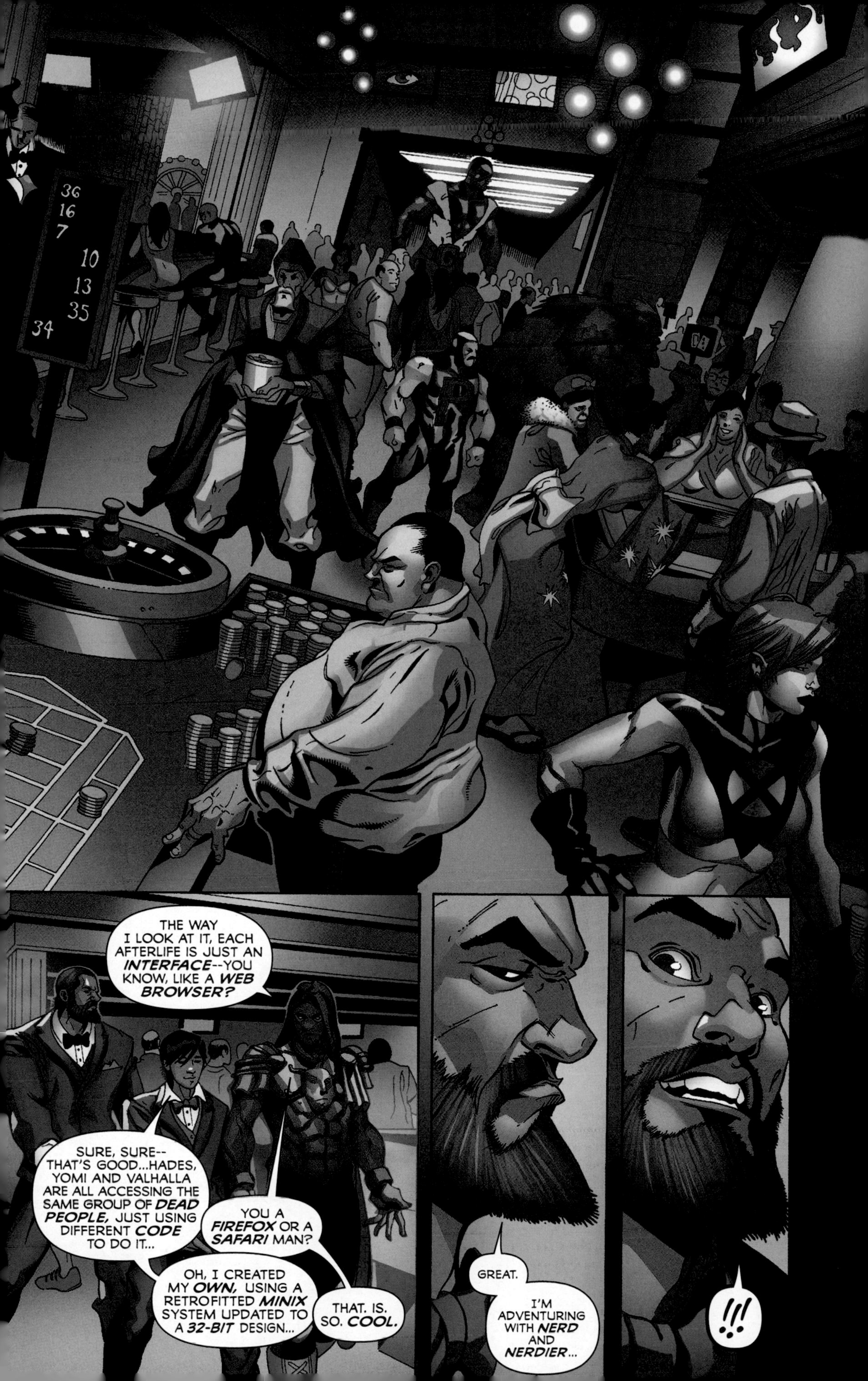
36
16
7
10
13
35
34
THE WAY I LOOK AT IT, EACH AFTERLIFE IS JUST AN INTERFACE--YOU KNOW, LIKE A WEB BROWSER?
SURE, SURE-- THAT'S GOOD...HADES, YOMI AND VALHALLA ARE ALL ACCESSING THE SAME GROUP OF DEAD PEOPLE, JUST USING DIFFERENT CODE TO DO IT...
YOU A FIREFOX OR A SAFARI MAN?
OH, I CREATED MY OWN, USING A RETROFITTED MINIX SYSTEM UPDATED TO A 32-BIT DESIGN...
THAT. IS. SO. COOL.
GREAT.
I'M ADVENTURING WITH NERD AND NERDIER...
!!!

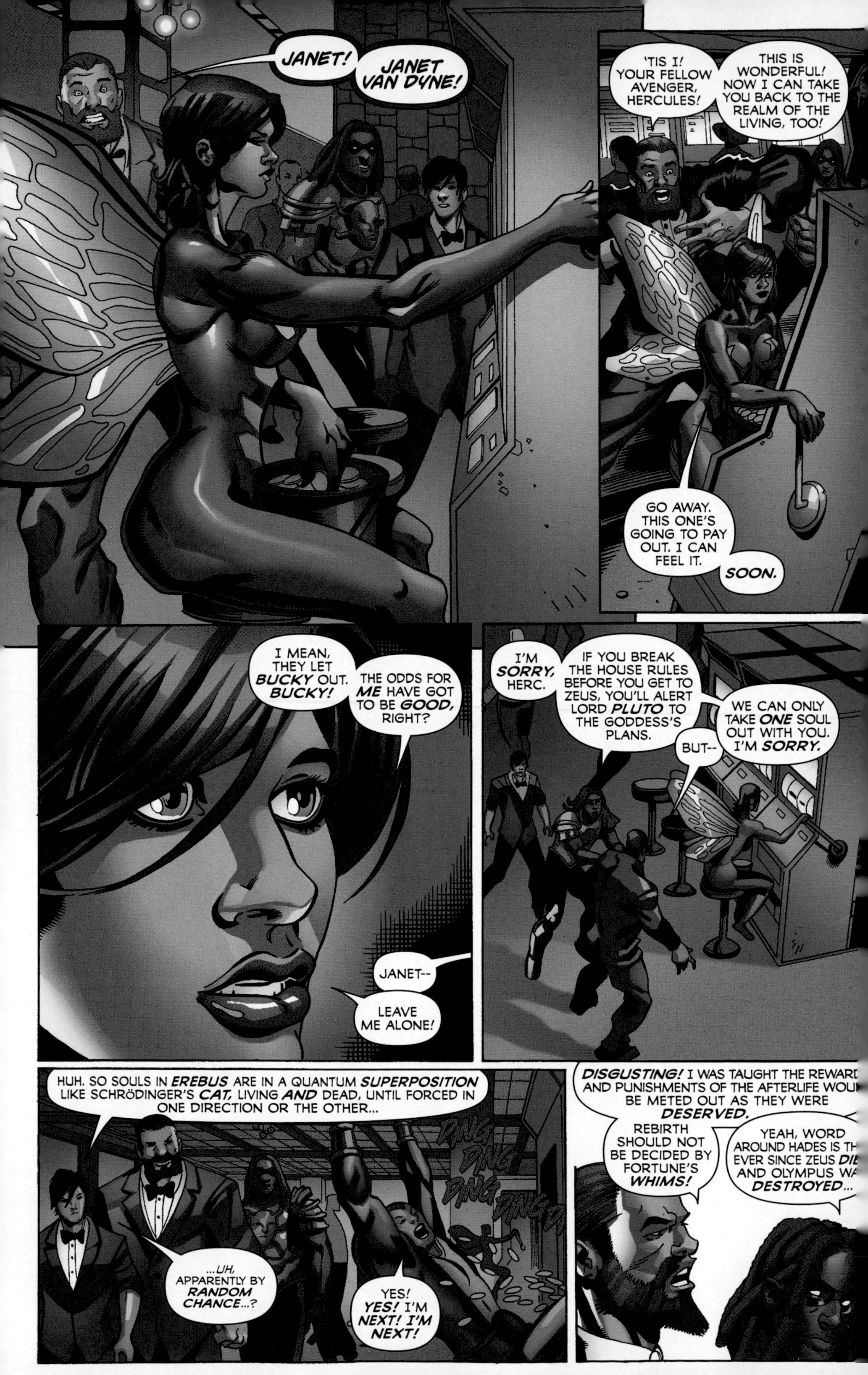
JANET!
JANET VAN DYNE!
'TIS I! YOUR FELLOW AVENGER, HERCULES!
THIS IS WONDERFUL! NOW I CAN TAKE YOU BACK TO THE REALM OF THE LIVING, TOO!
GO AWAY. THIS ONE'S GOING TO PAY OUT. I CAN FEEL IT.
SOON.
I MEAN, THEY LET BUCKY OUT. BUCKY!
THE ODDS FOR ME HAVE GOT TO BE GOOD, RIGHT?
JANET--
LEAVE ME ALONE!
I'M SORRY, HERC.
IF YOU BREAK THE HOUSE RULES BEFORE YOU GET TO ZEUS, YOU'LL ALERT LORD PLUTO TO THE GODDESS'S PLANS.
WE CAN ONLY TAKE ONE SOUL OUT WITH YOU. I'M SORRY.
BUT--
HUH. SO SOULS IN EREBUS ARE IN A QUANTUM SUPERPOSITION LIKE SCHRÖDINGER'S CAT, LIVING AND DEAD, UNTIL FORCED IN ONE DIRECTION OR THE OTHER...
...UH, APPARENTLY BY RANDOM CHANCE...?
DING DING DING DING
YES! YES! I'M NEXT! I'M NEXT!
DISGUSTING! I WAS TAUGHT THE REWARD AND PUNISHMENTS OF THE AFTERLIFE WOU BE METED OUT AS THEY WERE DESERVED.
REBIRTH SHOULD NOT BE DECIDED BY FORTUNE'S WHIMS!
YEAH, WORD AROUND HADES IS TH EVER SINCE ZEUS DI AND OLYMPUS WA DESTROYED...

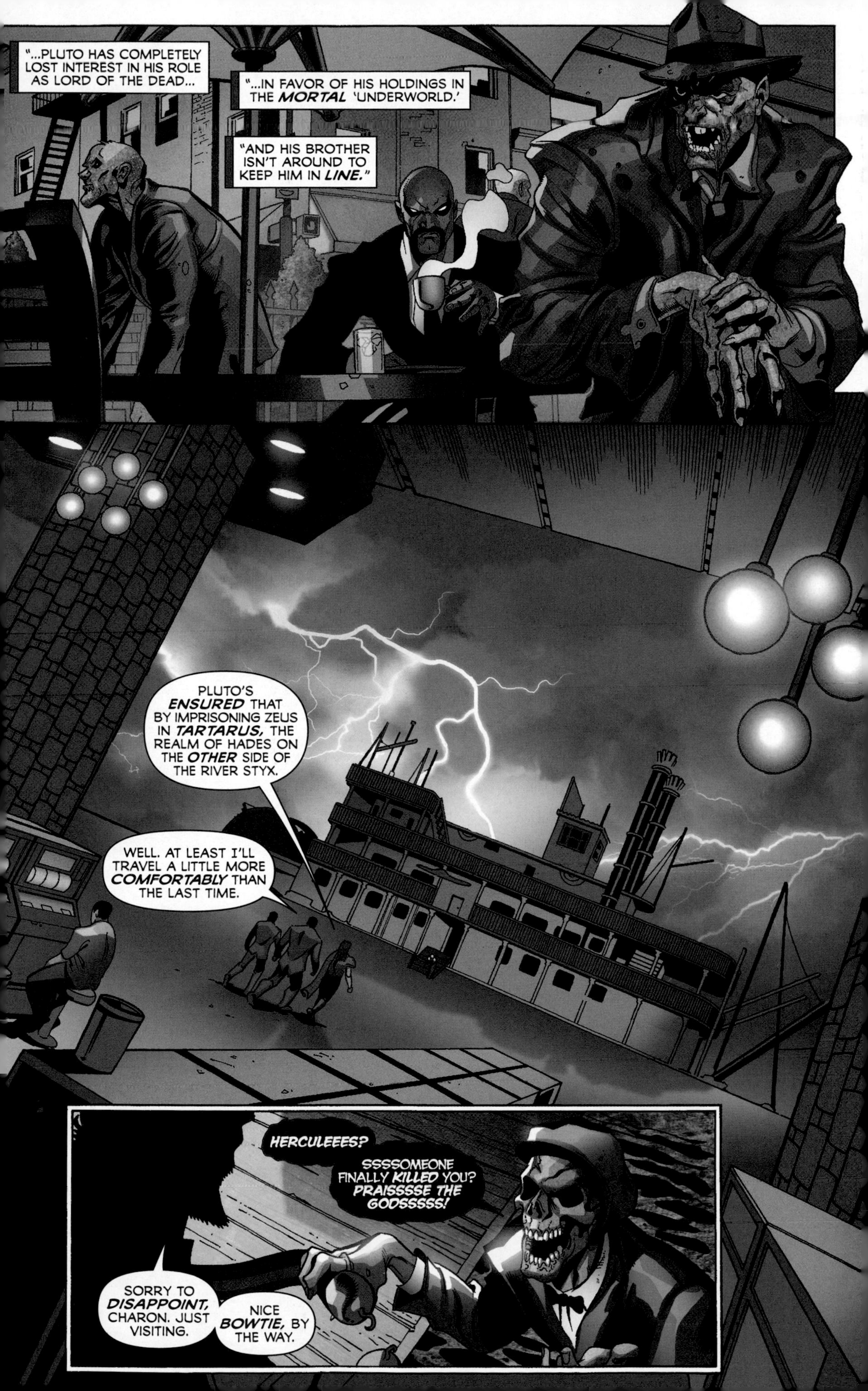
"...PLUTO HAS COMPLETELY LOST INTEREST IN HIS ROLE AS LORD OF THE DEAD...
"...IN FAVOR OF HIS HOLDINGS IN THE MORTAL 'UNDERWORLD.'
"AND HIS BROTHER ISN'T AROUND TO KEEP HIM IN LINE."
PLUTO'S ENSURED THAT BY IMPRISONING ZEUS IN TARTARUS, THE REALM OF HADES ON THE OTHER SIDE OF THE RIVER STYX.
WELL. AT LEAST I'LL TRAVEL A LITTLE MORE COMFORTABLY THAN THE LAST TIME.
HERCULEEEES?
SSSSOMEONE FINALLY KILLED YOU? PRAISSSSE THE GODSSSSS!
SORRY TO DISAPPOINT, CHARON. JUST VISITING.
NICE BOWTIE, BY THE WAY.

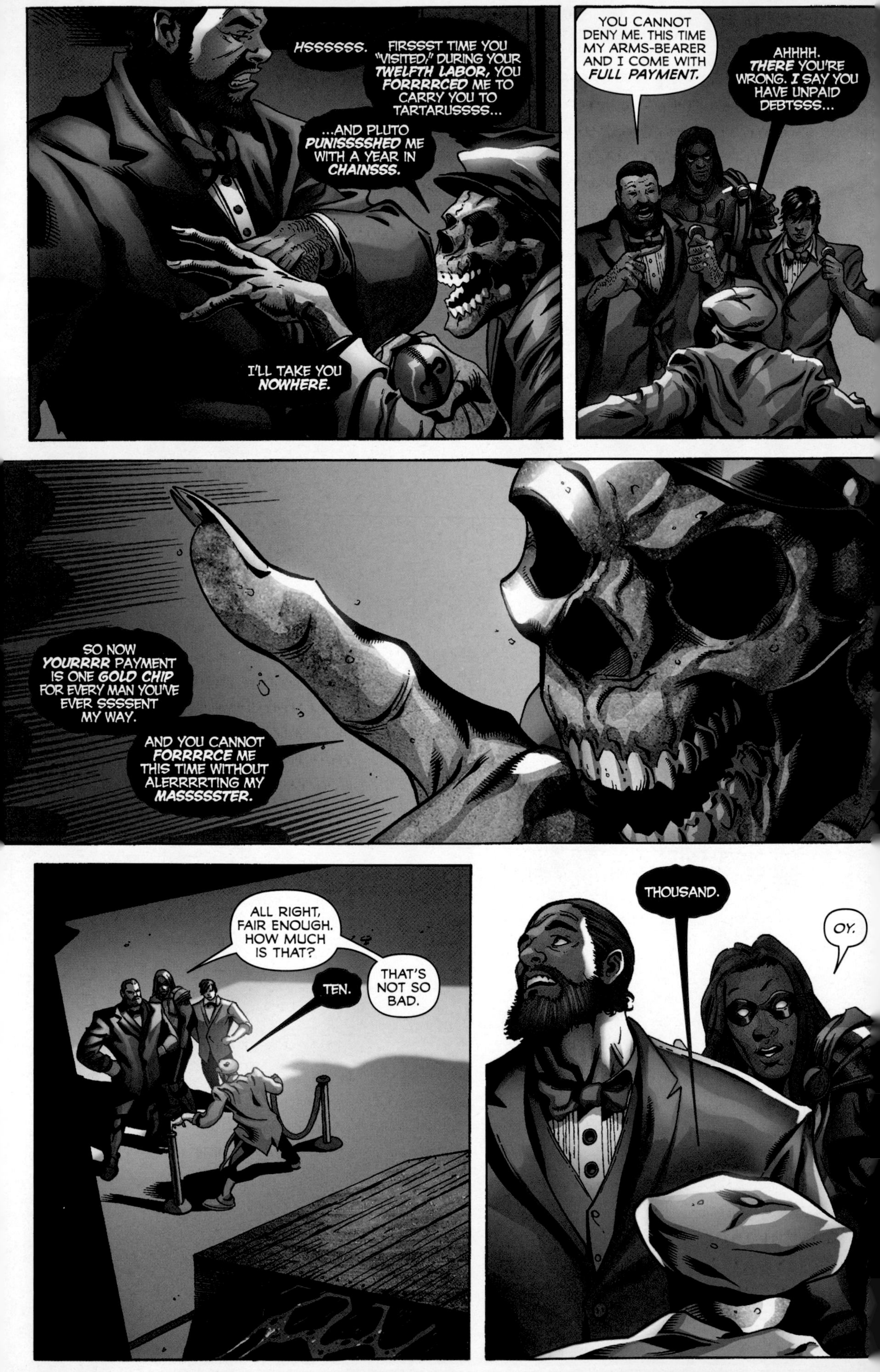
HSSSSSS.
FIRSSST TIME YOU "VISITED," DURING YOUR TWELFTH LABOR, YOU FORRRRCED ME TO CARRY YOU TO TARTARUSSSS...
...AND PLUTO PUNISSSSHED ME WITH A YEAR IN CHAINSSS.
I'LL TAKE YOU NOWHERE.
YOU CANNOT DENY ME. THIS TIME MY ARMS-BEARER AND I COME WITH FULL PAYMENT.
AHHHH. THERE YOU'RE WRONG. I SAY YOU HAVE UNPAID DEBTSSS...
SO NOW YOURRRR PAYMENT IS ONE GOLD CHIP FOR EVERY MAN YOU'VE EVER SSSSENT MY WAY.
AND YOU CANNOT FORRRRCE ME THIS TIME WITHOUT ALERRRRTING MY MASSSSSTER.
ALL RIGHT, FAIR ENOUGH. HOW MUCH IS THAT?
TEN.
THAT'S NOT SO BAD.
THOUSAND.
OY.

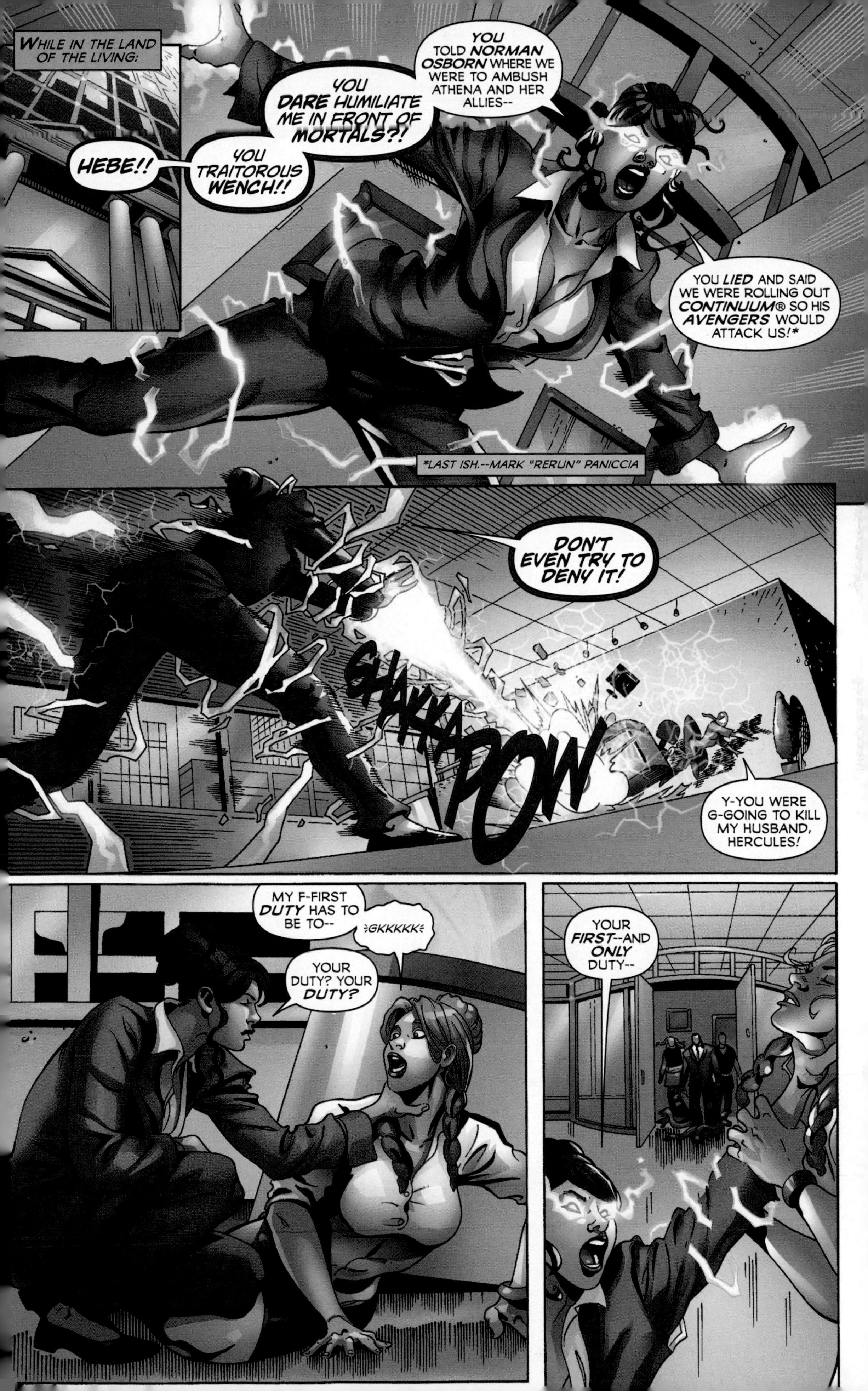
WHILE IN THE LAND OF THE LIVING:
HEBE!!
YOU TRAITOROUS WENCH!!
YOU DARE HUMILIATE ME IN FRONT OF MORTALS?!
YOU TOLD NORMAN OSBORN WHERE WE WERE TO AMBUSH ATHENA AND HER ALLIES--
YOU LIED AND SAID WE WERE ROLLING OUT CONTINUUM® SO HIS AVENGERS WOULD ATTACK US!*
*LAST ISH.--MARK "RERUN" PANICCIA
DON'T EVEN TRY TO DENY IT!
CHAKKAPOW
Y-YOU WERE G-GOING TO KILL MY HUSBAND, HERCULES!
MY F-FIRST DUTY HAS TO BE TO--
GKKKKK
YOUR DUTY? YOUR DUTY?
YOUR FIRST--AND ONLY DUTY--

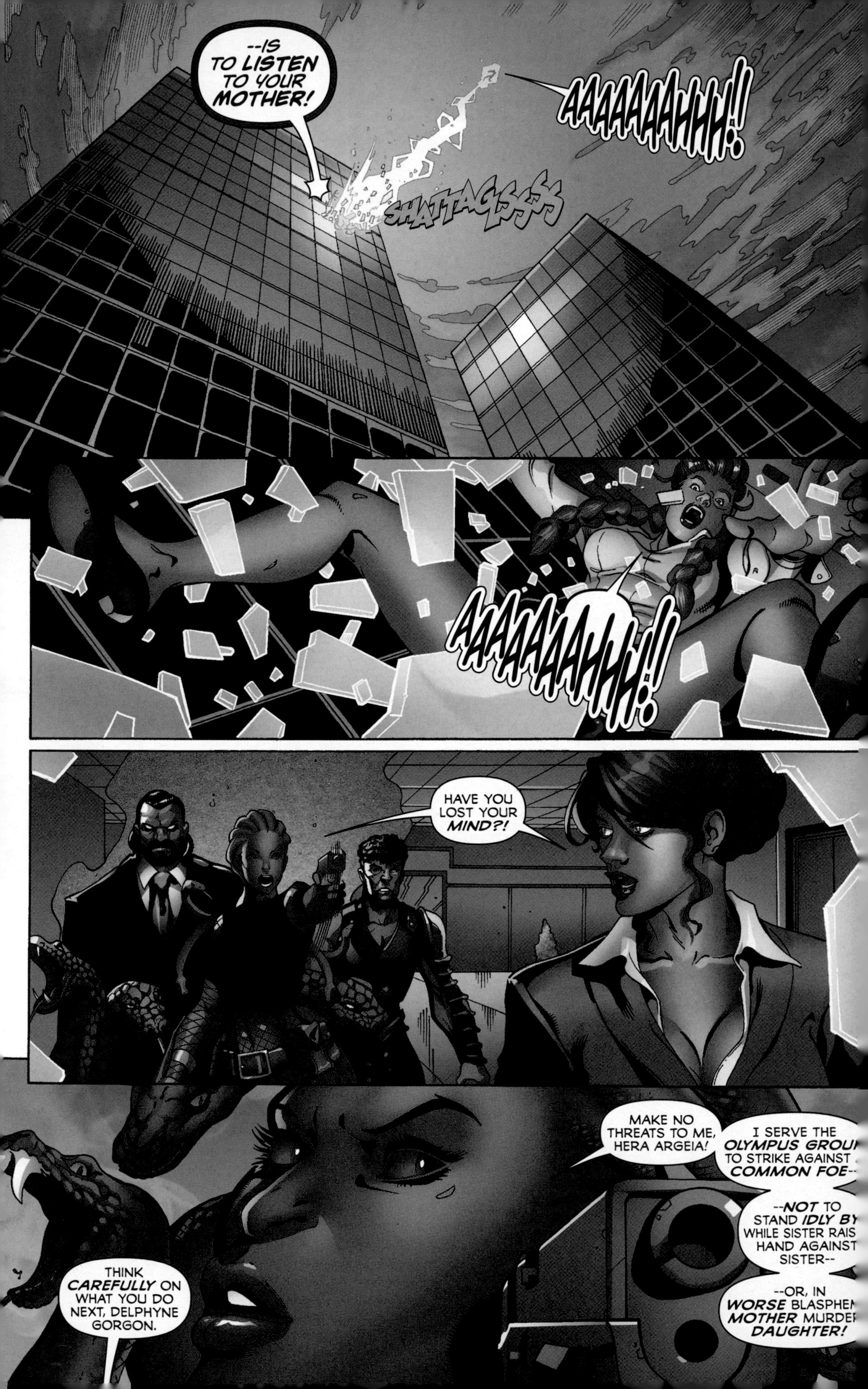
--IS TO LISTEN TO YOUR MOTHER!
AAAAAAAHHH!!
SHATTAGSSSS
AAAAAAAAHHH!!
HAVE YOU LOST YOUR MIND?!
MAKE NO THREATS TO ME, HERA ARGEIA!
I SERVE THE OLYMPUS GROU TO STRIKE AGAINST COMMON FOE--
--NOT TO STAND IDLY BY WHILE SISTER RAIS HAND AGAINST SISTER--
--OR, IN WORSE BLASPHEM MOTHER MURDER DAUGHTER!
THINK CAREFULLY ON WHAT YOU DO NEXT, DELPHYNE GORGON.

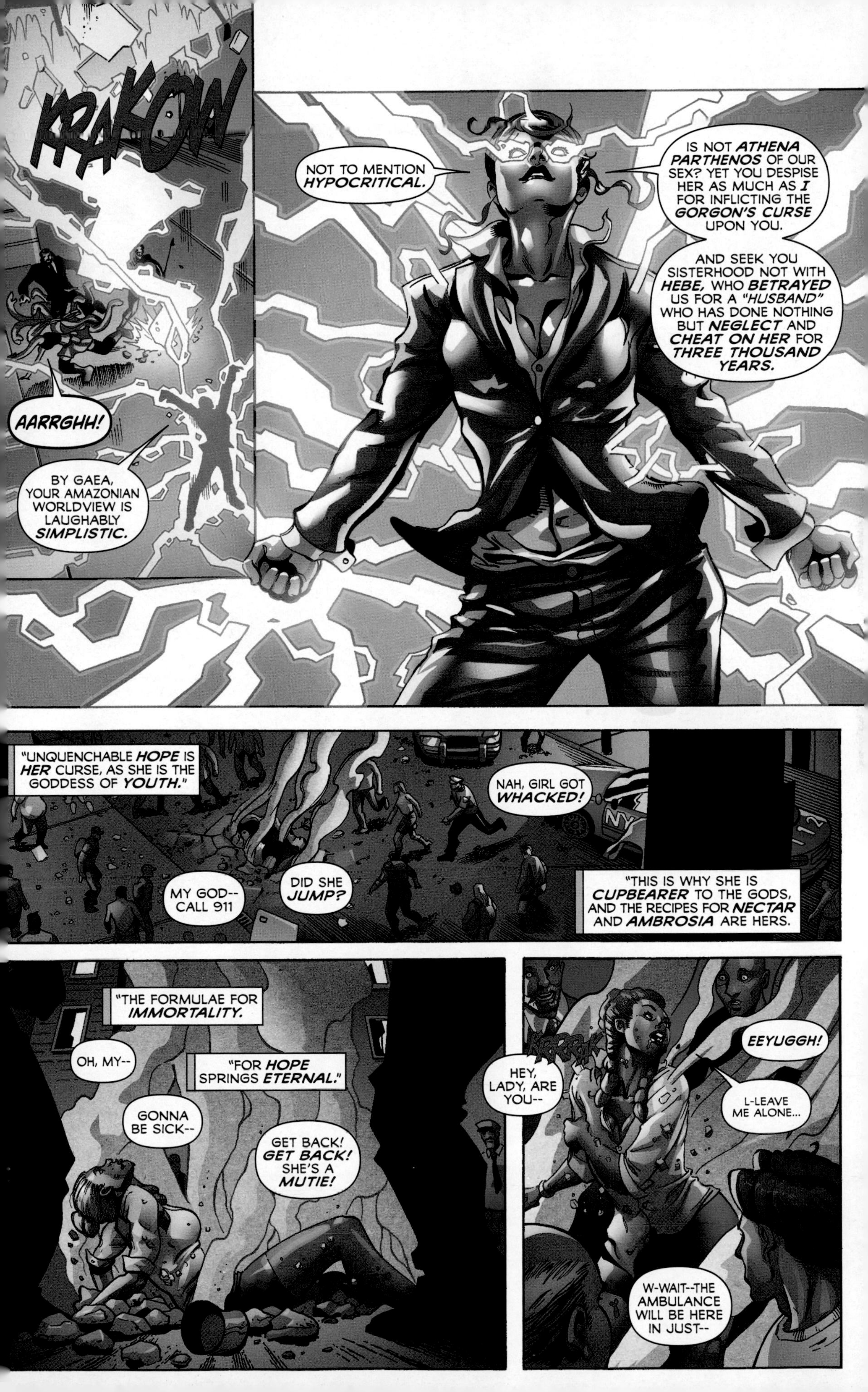
KRAKOW
AARRGHH!
BY GAEA, YOUR AMAZONIAN WORLDVIEW IS LAUGHABLY SIMPLISTIC.
NOT TO MENTION HYPOCRITICAL.
IS NOT ATHENA PARTHENOS OF OUR SEX? YET YOU DESPISE HER AS MUCH AS I FOR INFLICTING THE GORGON'S CURSE UPON YOU.
AND SEEK YOU SISTERHOOD NOT WITH HEBE, WHO BETRAYED US FOR A "HUSBAND" WHO HAS DONE NOTHING BUT NEGLECT AND CHEAT ON HER FOR THREE THOUSAND YEARS.
"UNQUENCHABLE HOPE IS HER CURSE, AS SHE IS THE GODDESS OF YOUTH."
NAH, GIRL GOT WHACKED!
MY GOD-- CALL 911
DID SHE JUMP?
"THIS IS WHY SHE IS CUPBEARER TO THE GODS, AND THE RECIPES FOR NECTAR AND AMBROSIA ARE HERS.
"THE FORMULAE FOR IMMORTALITY.
OH, MY--
"FOR HOPE SPRINGS ETERNAL."
GONNA BE SICK--
GET BACK! GET BACK! SHE'S A MUTIE!
KRRRAK
HEY, LADY, ARE YOU--
EEYUGGH!
L-LEAVE ME ALONE...
W-WAIT--THE AMBULANCE WILL BE HERE IN JUST--

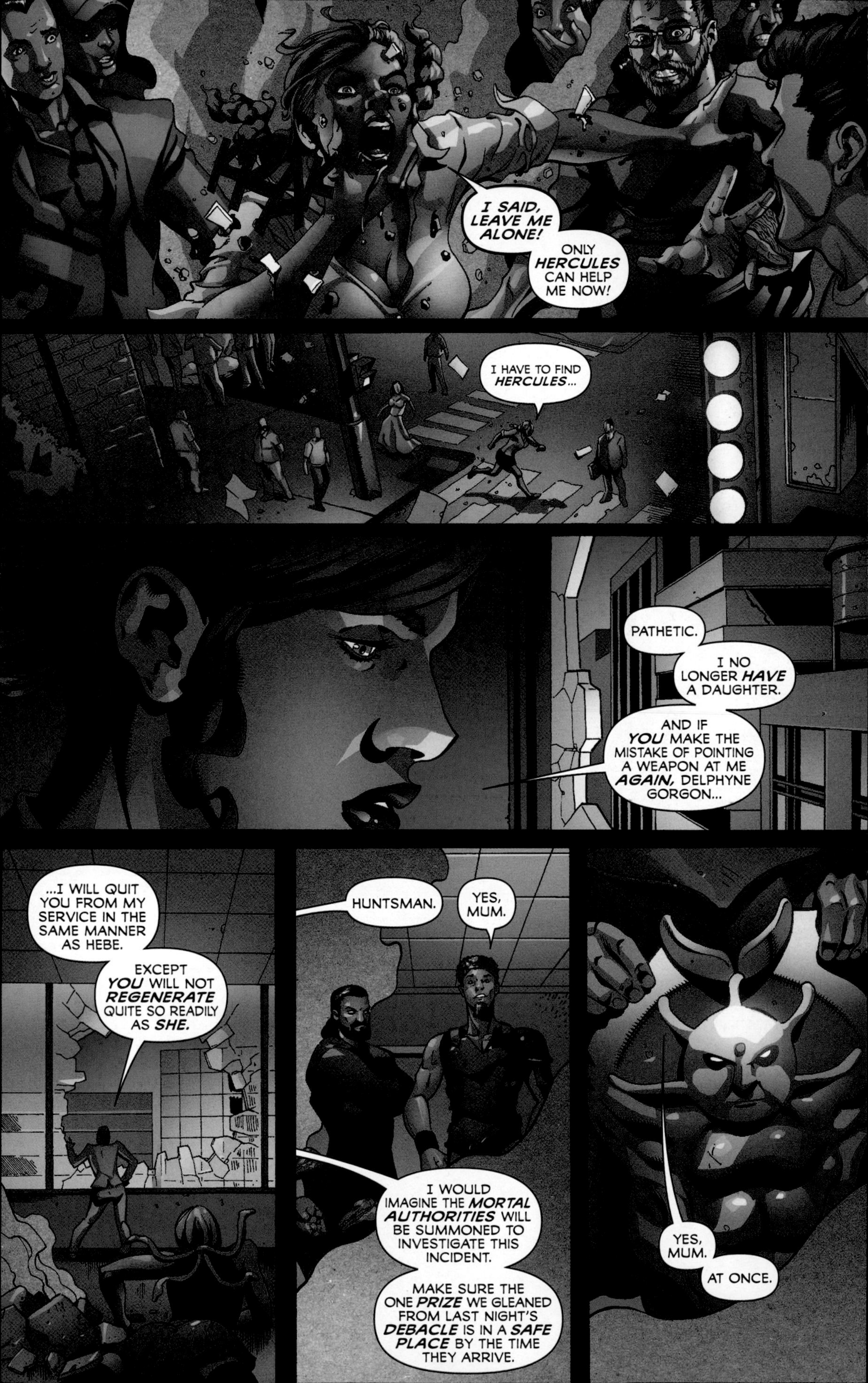
I SAID, LEAVE ME ALONE!
ONLY HERCULES CAN HELP ME NOW!
I HAVE TO FIND HERCULES...
PATHETIC.
I NO LONGER HAVE A DAUGHTER.
AND IF YOU MAKE THE MISTAKE OF POINTING A WEAPON AT ME AGAIN, DELPHYNE GORGON...
...I WILL QUIT YOU FROM MY SERVICE IN THE SAME MANNER AS HEBE.
EXCEPT YOU WILL NOT REGENERATE QUITE SO READILY AS SHE.
HUNTSMAN.
YES, MUM.
I WOULD IMAGINE THE MORTAL AUTHORITIES WILL BE SUMMONED TO INVESTIGATE THIS INCIDENT.
MAKE SURE THE ONE PRIZE WE GLEANED FROM LAST NIGHT'S DEBACLE IS IN A SAFE PLACE BY THE TIME THEY ARRIVE.
YES, MUM.
AT ONCE.

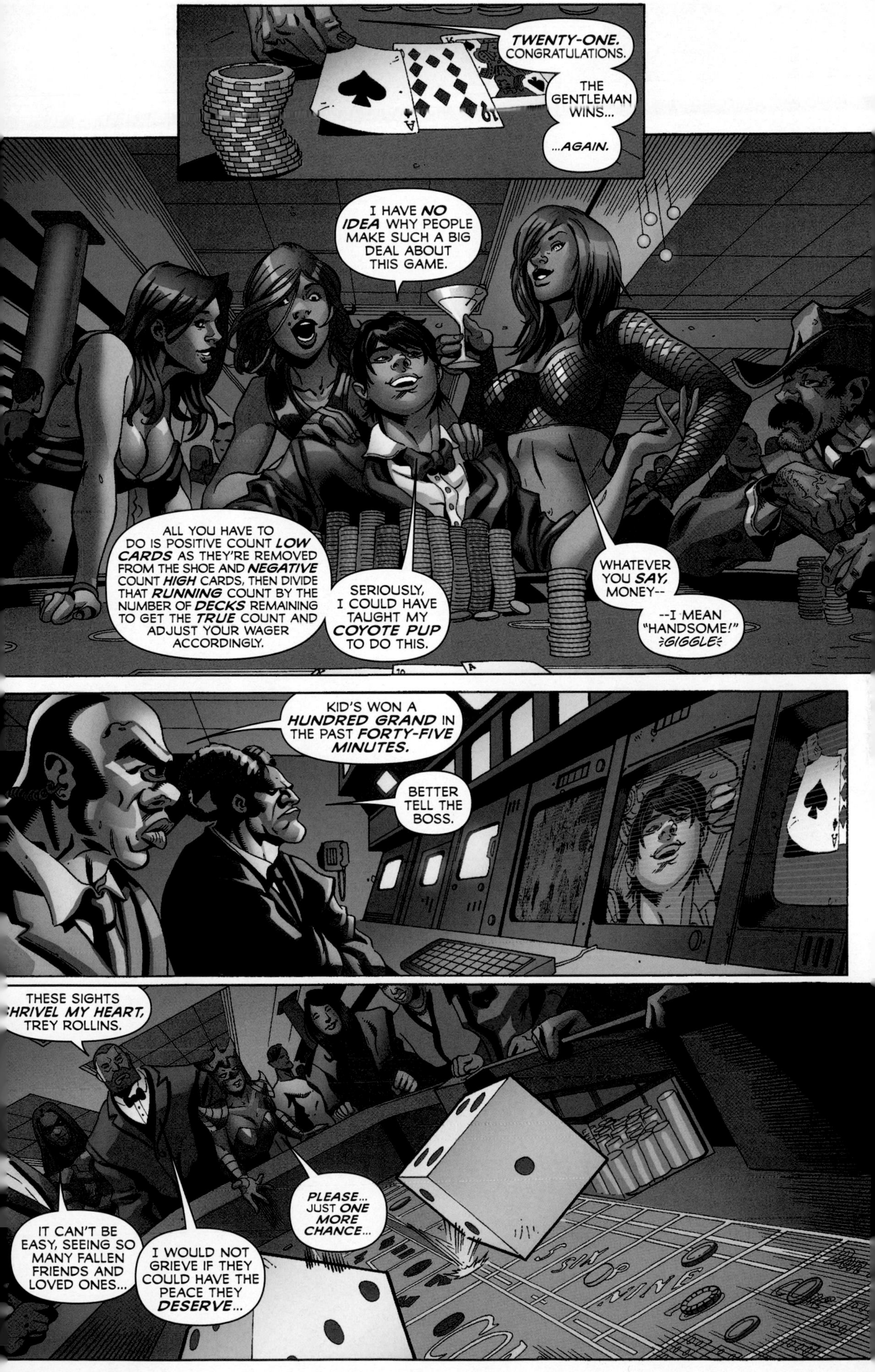
TWENTY-ONE. CONGRATULATIONS.
THE GENTLEMAN WINS...
...AGAIN.
I HAVE NO IDEA WHY PEOPLE MAKE SUCH A BIG DEAL ABOUT THIS GAME.
ALL YOU HAVE TO DO IS POSITIVE COUNT LOW CARDS AS THEY'RE REMOVED FROM THE SHOE AND NEGATIVE COUNT HIGH CARDS, THEN DIVIDE THAT RUNNING COUNT BY THE NUMBER OF DECKS REMAINING TO GET THE TRUE COUNT AND ADJUST YOUR WAGER ACCORDINGLY.
SERIOUSLY, I COULD HAVE TAUGHT MY COYOTE PUP TO DO THIS.
WHATEVER YOU SAY, MONEY--
--I MEAN "HANDSOME!" GIGGLE
KID'S WON A HUNDRED GRAND IN THE PAST FORTY-FIVE MINUTES.
BETTER TELL THE BOSS.
THESE SIGHTS SHRIVEL MY HEART, TREY ROLLINS.
IT CAN'T BE EASY, SEEING SO MANY FALLEN FRIENDS AND LOVED ONES...
I WOULD NOT GRIEVE IF THEY COULD HAVE THE PEACE THEY DESERVE...
PLEASE... JUST ONE MORE CHANCE...

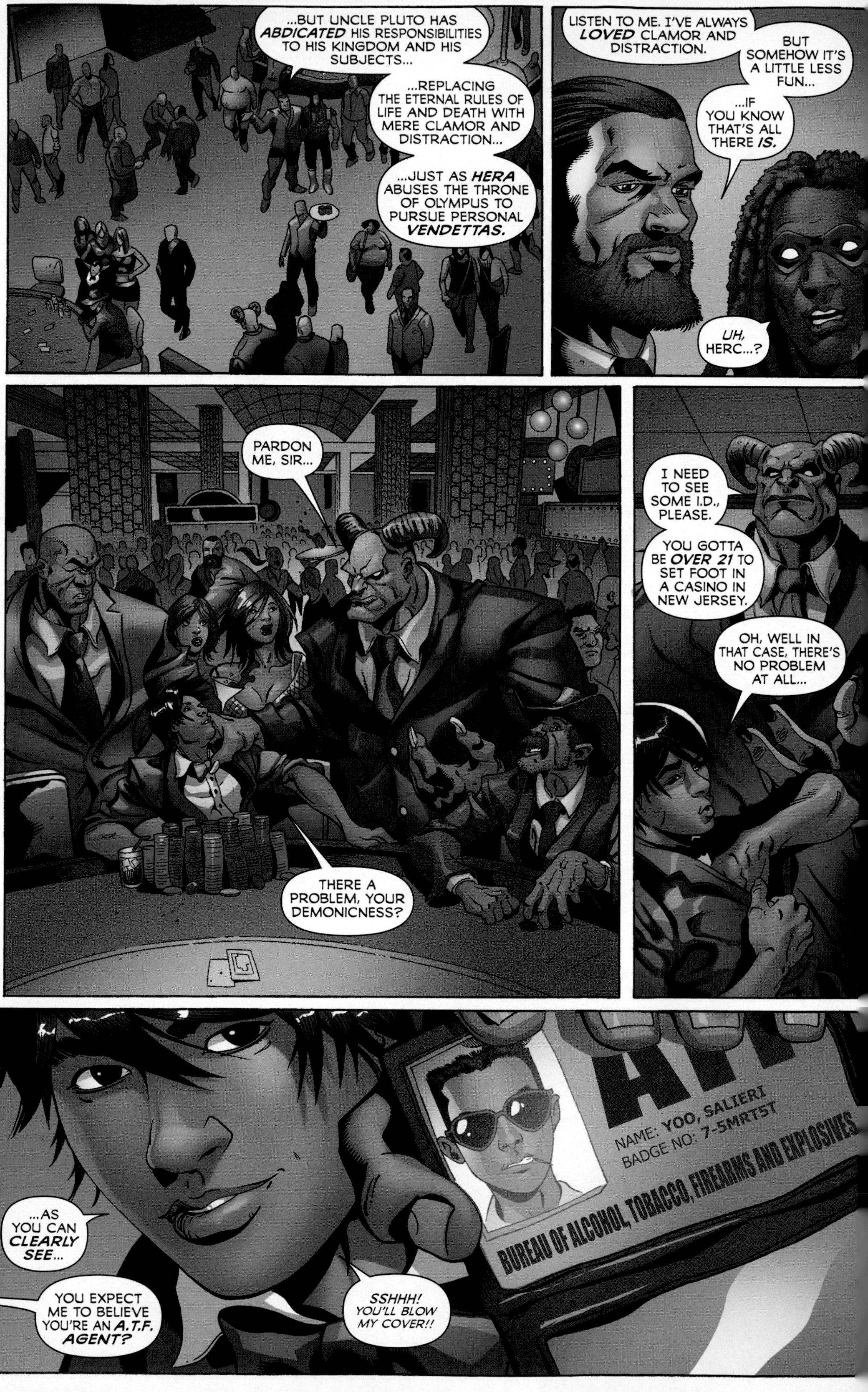
...BUT UNCLE PLUTO HAS ABDICATED HIS RESPONSIBILITIES TO HIS KINGDOM AND HIS SUBJECTS...
...REPLACING THE ETERNAL RULES OF LIFE AND DEATH WITH MERE CLAMOR AND DISTRACTION...
...JUST AS HERA ABUSES THE THRONE OF OLYMPUS TO PURSUE PERSONAL VENDETTAS.
LISTEN TO ME. I'VE ALWAYS LOVED CLAMOR AND DISTRACTION.
BUT SOMEHOW IT'S A LITTLE LESS FUN...
...IF YOU KNOW THAT'S ALL THERE IS.
UH, HERC...?
PARDON ME, SIR...
THERE A PROBLEM, YOUR DEMONICNESS?
I NEED TO SEE SOME I.D., PLEASE.
YOU GOTTA BE OVER 21 TO SET FOOT IN A CASINO IN NEW JERSEY.
OH, WELL IN THAT CASE, THERE'S NO PROBLEM AT ALL...
NAME: YOO, SALIERI
BADGE NO: 7-5MRT5T
BUREAU OF ALCOHOL, TOBACCO, FIREARMS AND EXPLOSIVES
...AS YOU CAN CLEARLY SEE...
YOU EXPECT ME TO BELIEVE YOU'RE AN A.T.F. AGENT?
SSHHH! YOU'LL BLOW MY COVER!!

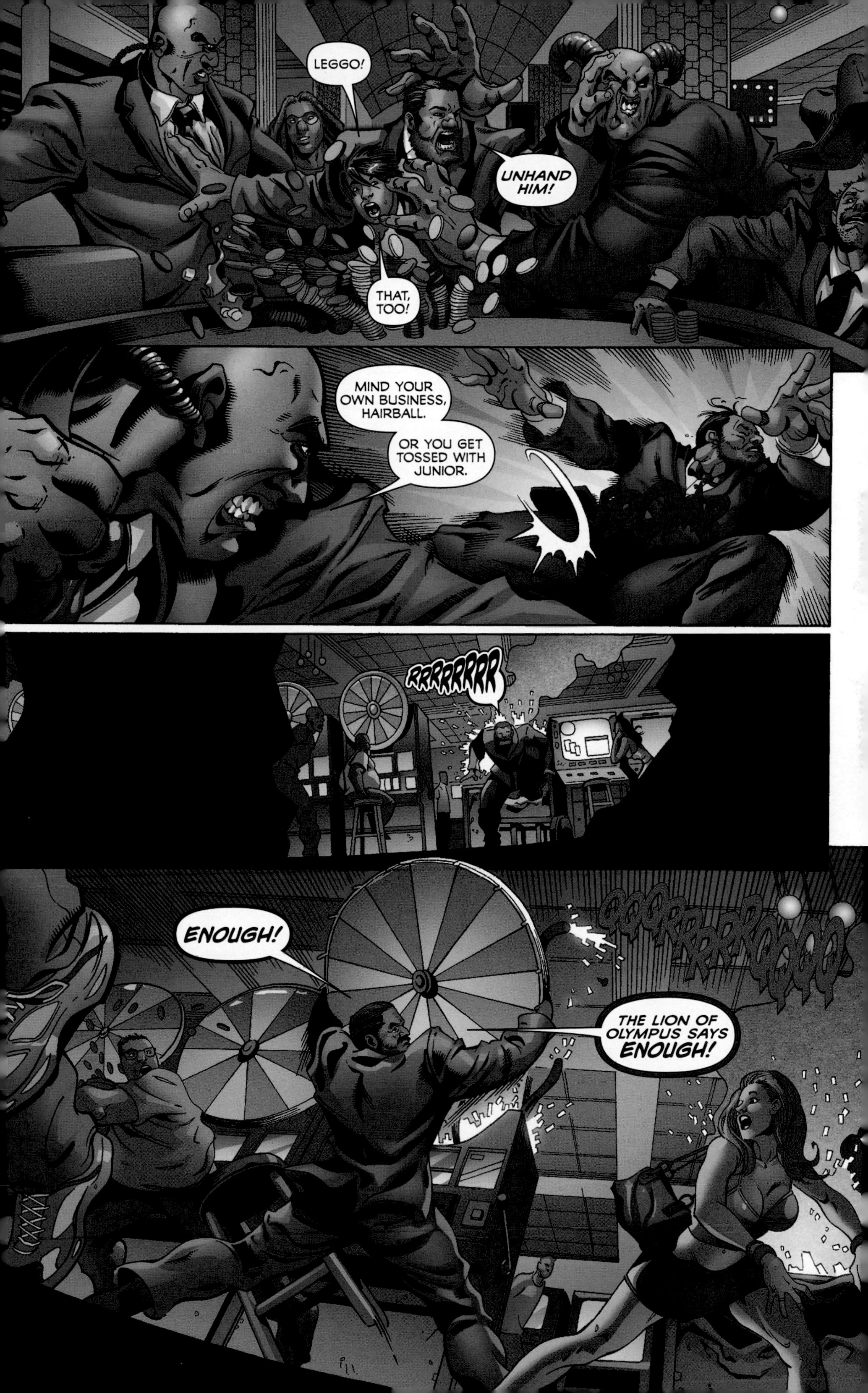
LEGGO!
UNHAND HIM!
THAT, TOO!
MIND YOUR OWN BUSINESS, HAIRBALL.
OR YOU GET TOSSED WITH JUNIOR.
RRRRRRRR
ENOUGH!
GGGRRRRRROOOO
THE LION OF OLYMPUS SAYS ENOUGH!

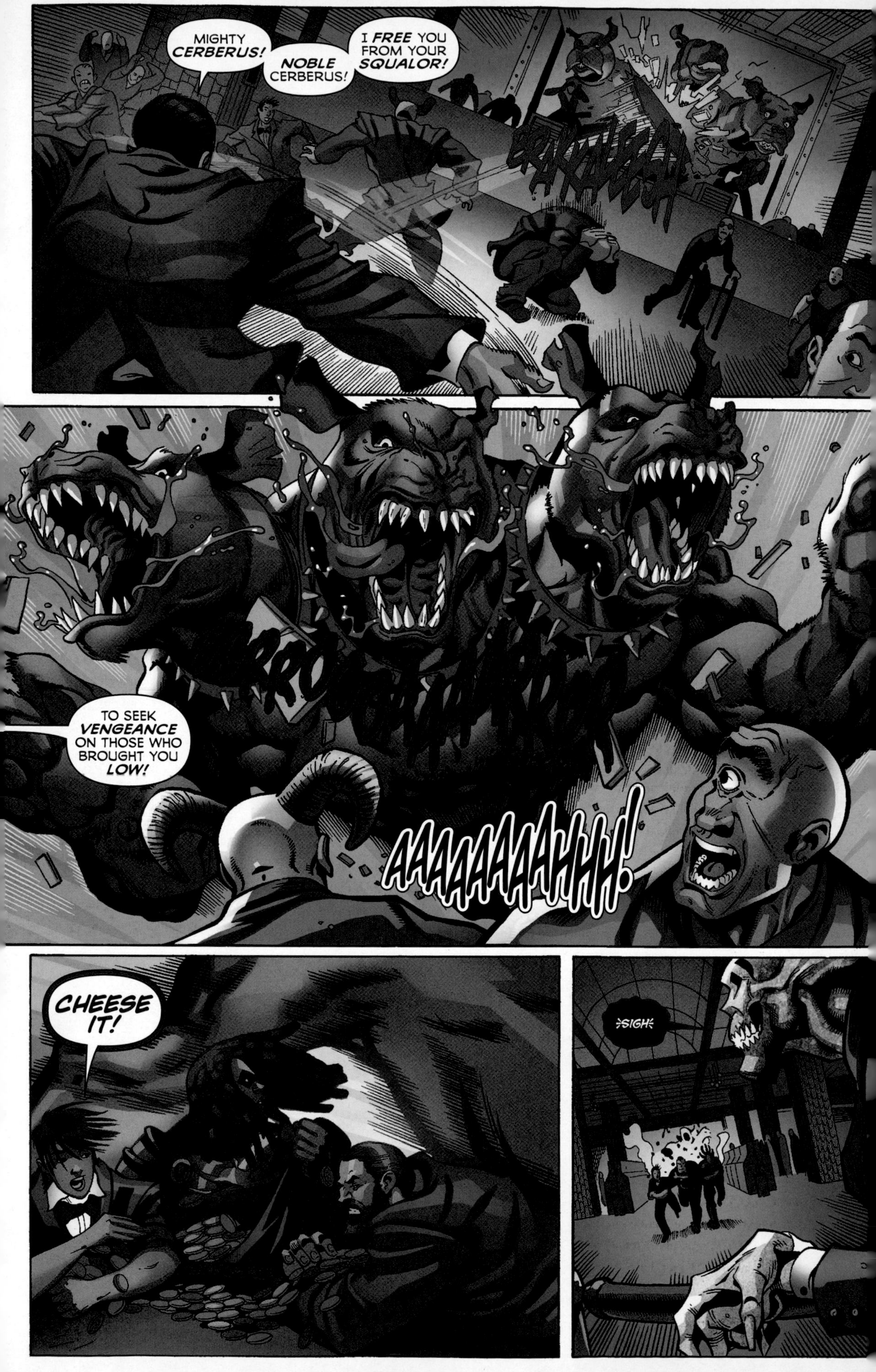
MIGHTY CERBERUS!
NOBLE CERBERUS!
I FREE YOU FROM YOUR SQUALOR!
BRAKABOOM
RRROWRRRR
TO SEEK VENGEANCE ON THOSE WHO BROUGHT YOU LOW!
AAAAAAAAHHH!
CHEESE IT!
SIGH

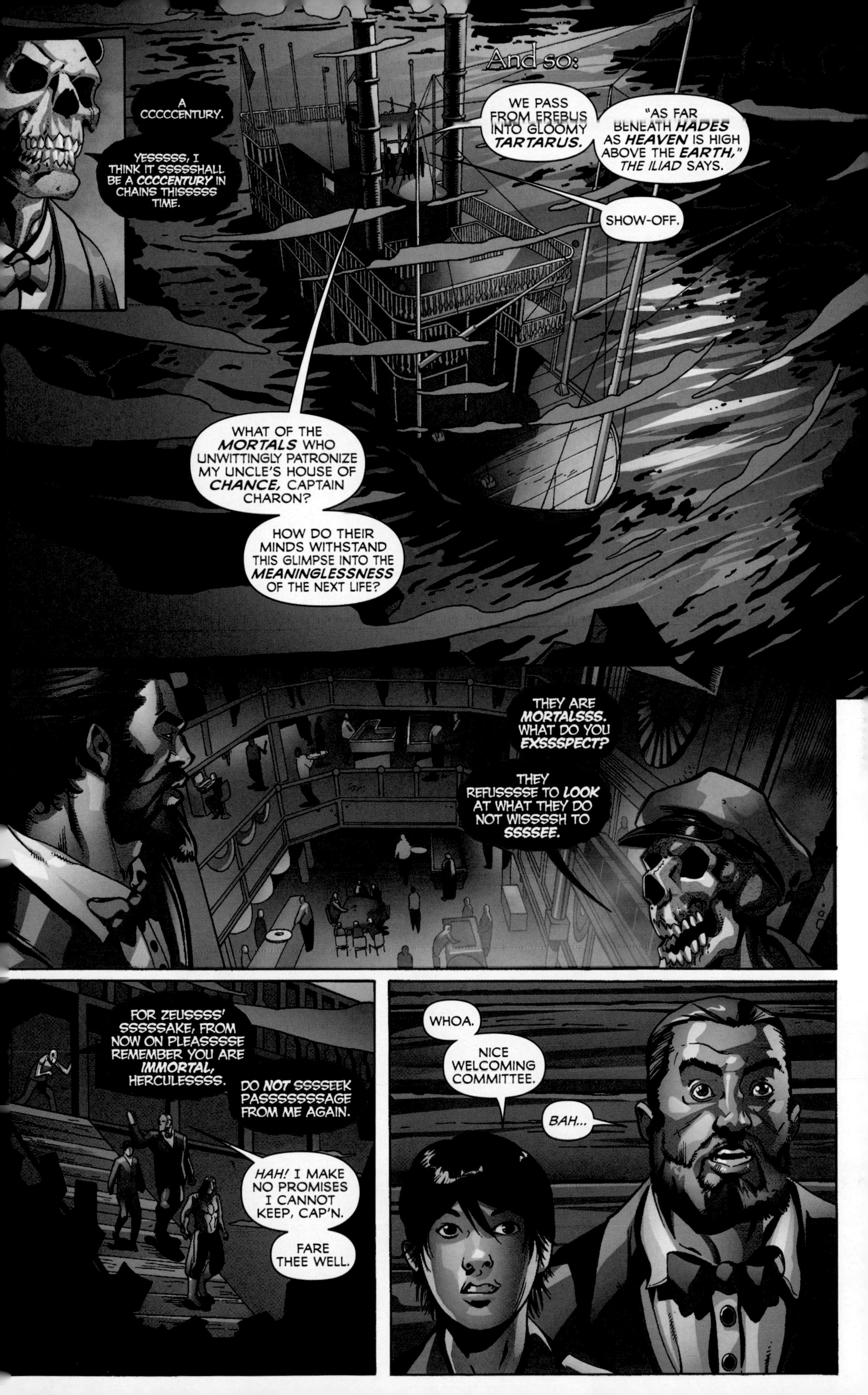
And so:
A CCCCCENTURY.
YESSSSS, I THINK IT SSSSSHALL BE A CCCCENTURY IN CHAINS THISSSSS TIME.
WE PASS FROM EREBUS INTO GLOOMY TARTARUS.
"AS FAR BENEATH HADES AS HEAVEN IS HIGH ABOVE THE EARTH," THE ILIAD SAYS.
SHOW-OFF.
WHAT OF THE MORTALS WHO UNWITTINGLY PATRONIZE MY UNCLE'S HOUSE OF CHANCE, CAPTAIN CHARON?
HOW DO THEIR MINDS WITHSTAND THIS GLIMPSE INTO THE MEANINGLESSNESS OF THE NEXT LIFE?
THEY ARE MORTALSSS. WHAT DO YOU EXSSSPECT?
THEY REFUSSSSE TO LOOK AT WHAT THEY DO NOT WISSSSH TO SSSSEE.
FOR ZEUSSSS' SSSSSAKE, FROM NOW ON PLEASSSSE REMEMBER YOU ARE IMMORTAL, HERCULESSSS.
DO NOT SSSSEEK PASSSSSSSAGE FROM ME AGAIN.
HAH! I MAKE NO PROMISES I CANNOT KEEP, CAP'N.
FARE THEE WELL.
WHOA.
NICE WELCOMING COMMITTEE.
BAH...

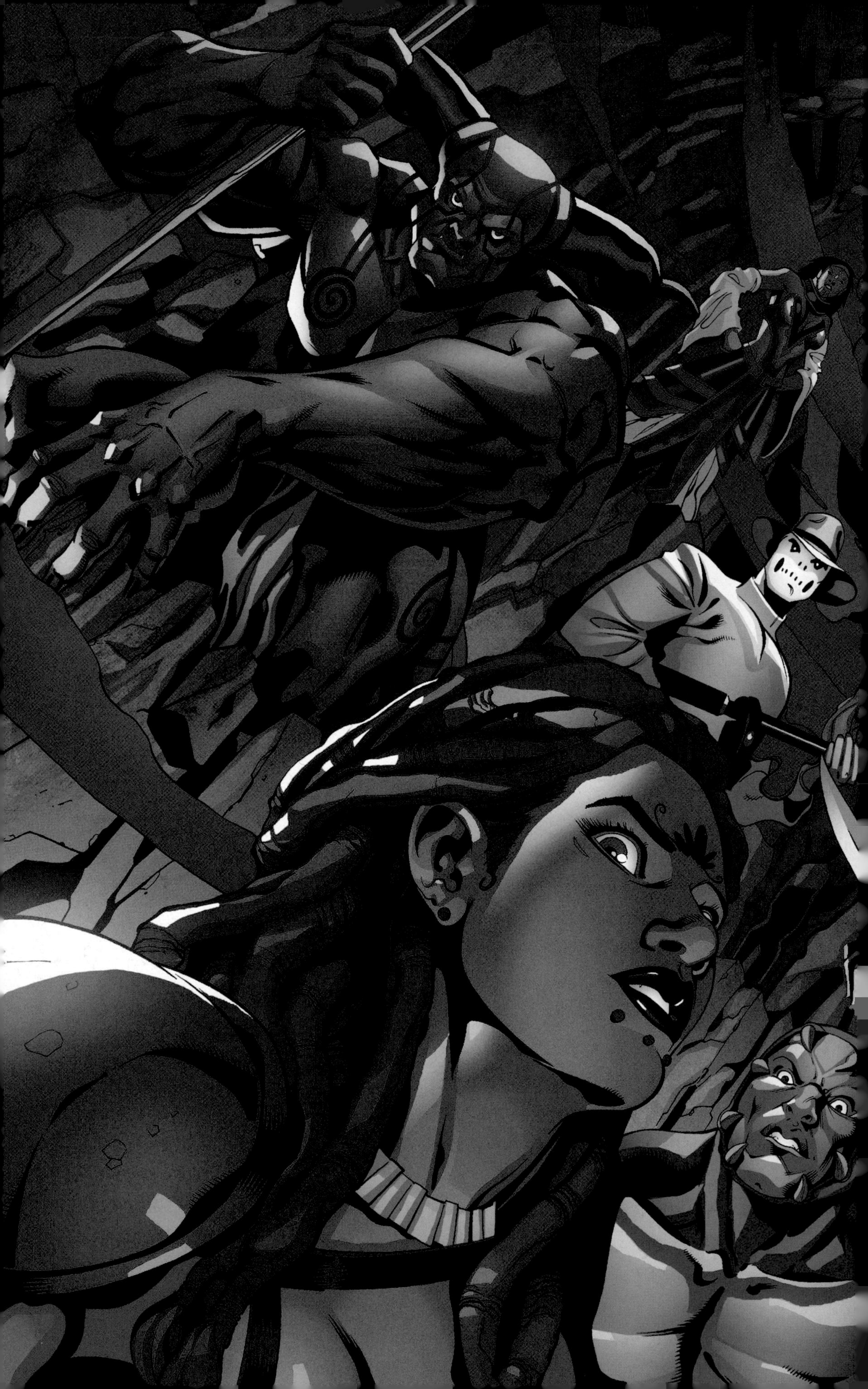

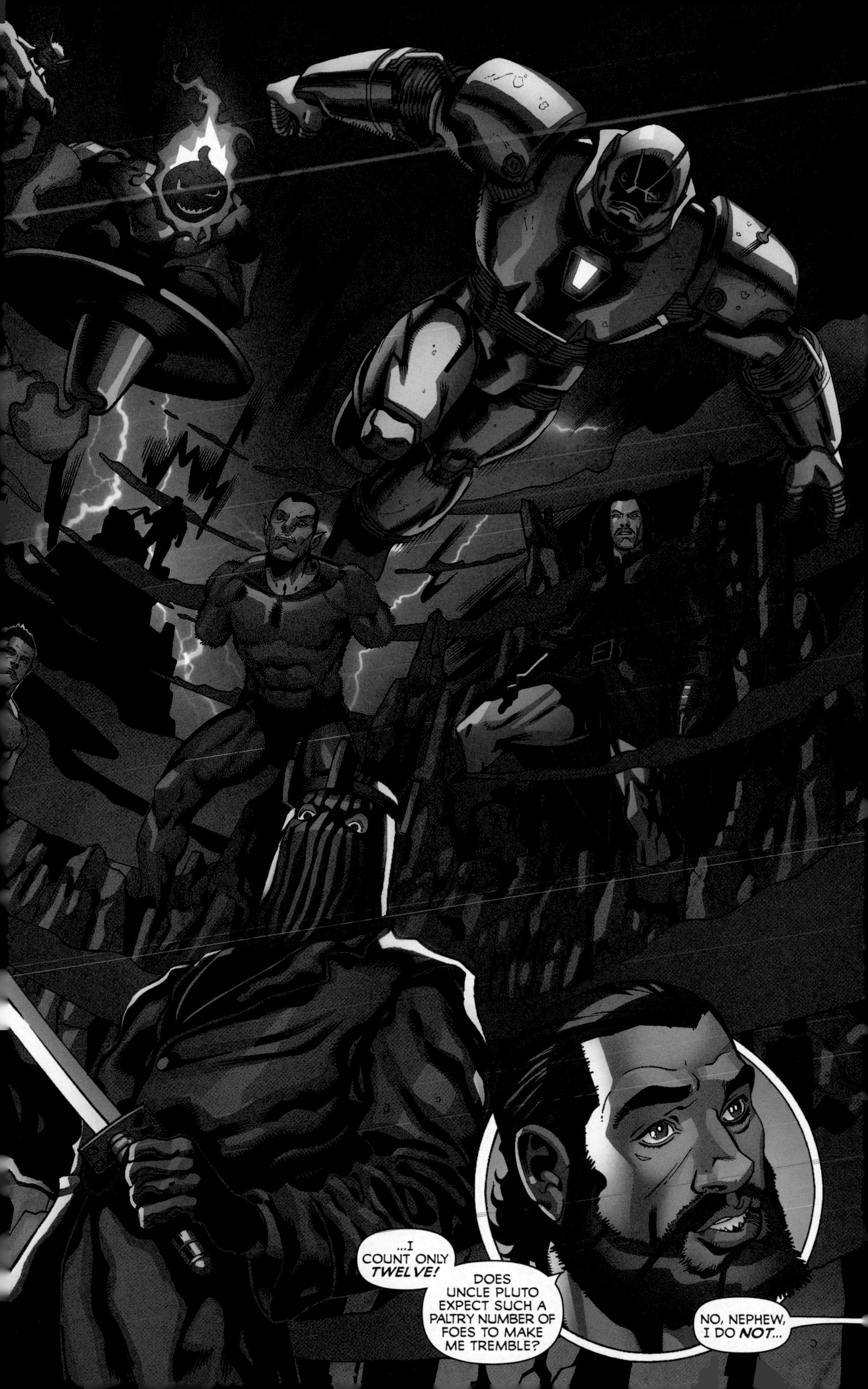
...I COUNT ONLY *TWELVE!*
DOES UNCLE PLUTO EXPECT SUCH A PALTRY NUMBER OF FOES TO MAKE ME TREMBLE?
NO, NEPHEW, I DO *NOT*...

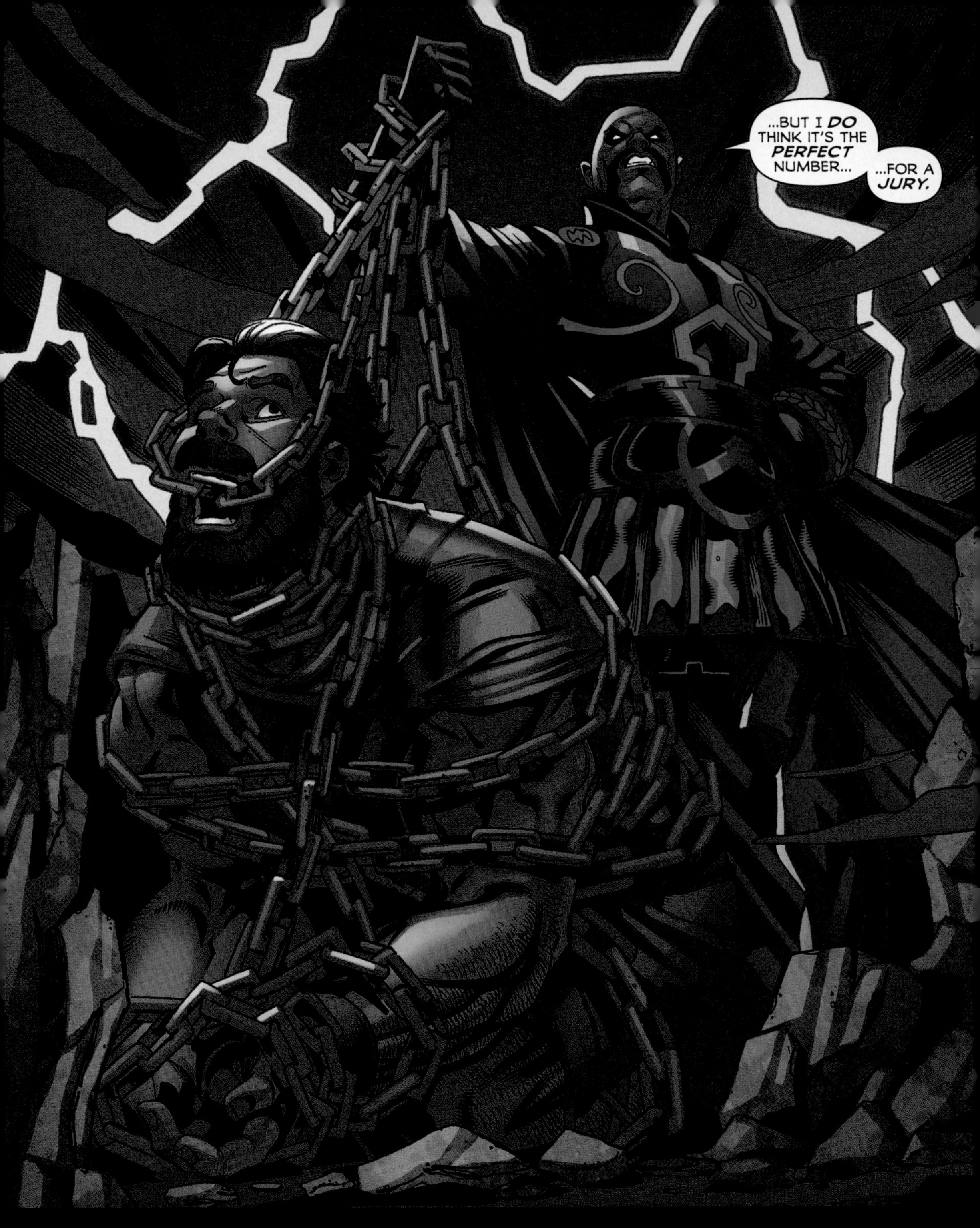
...BUT I DO THINK IT'S THE PERFECT NUMBER...
...FOR A JURY.

THE DESCENT

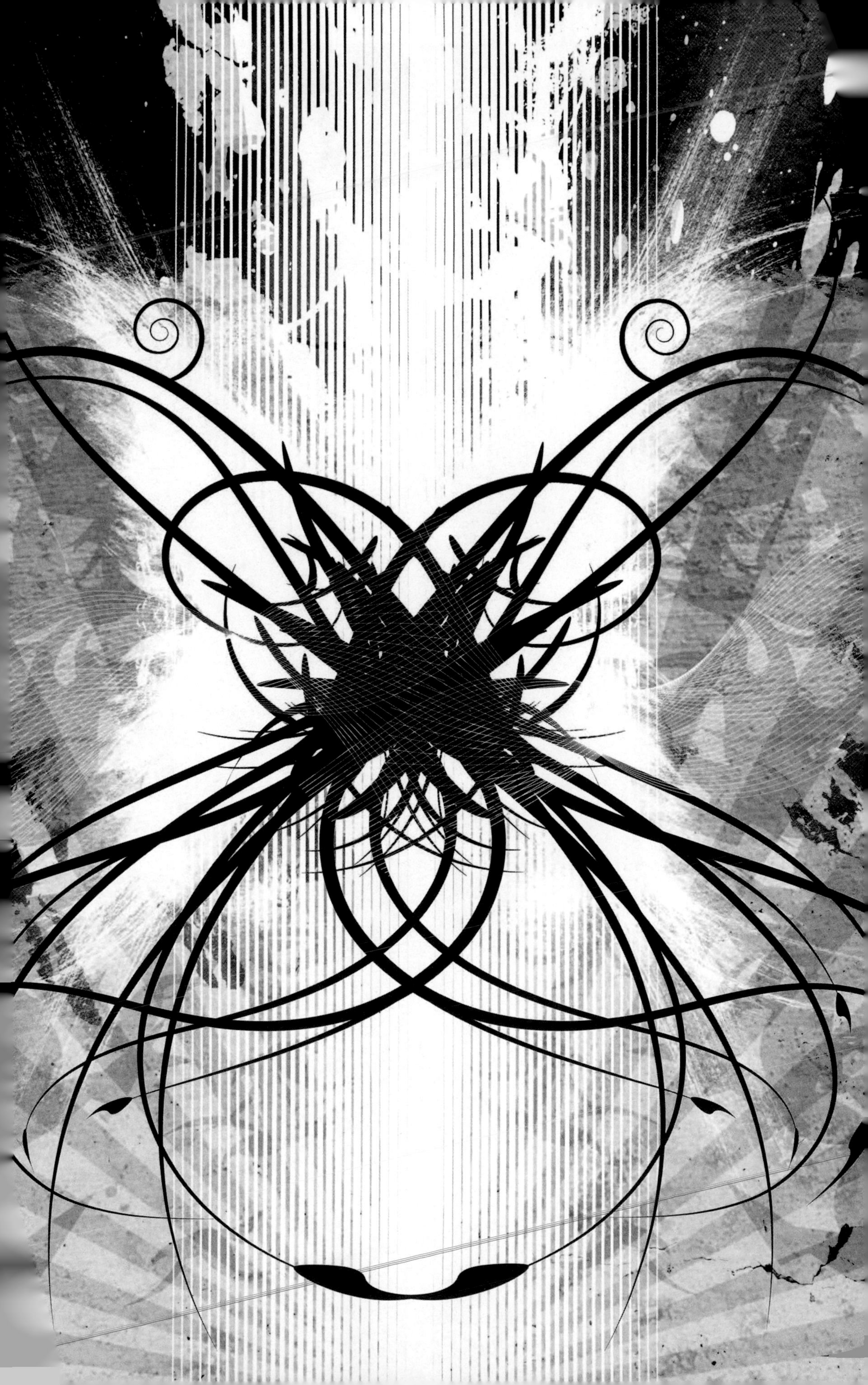

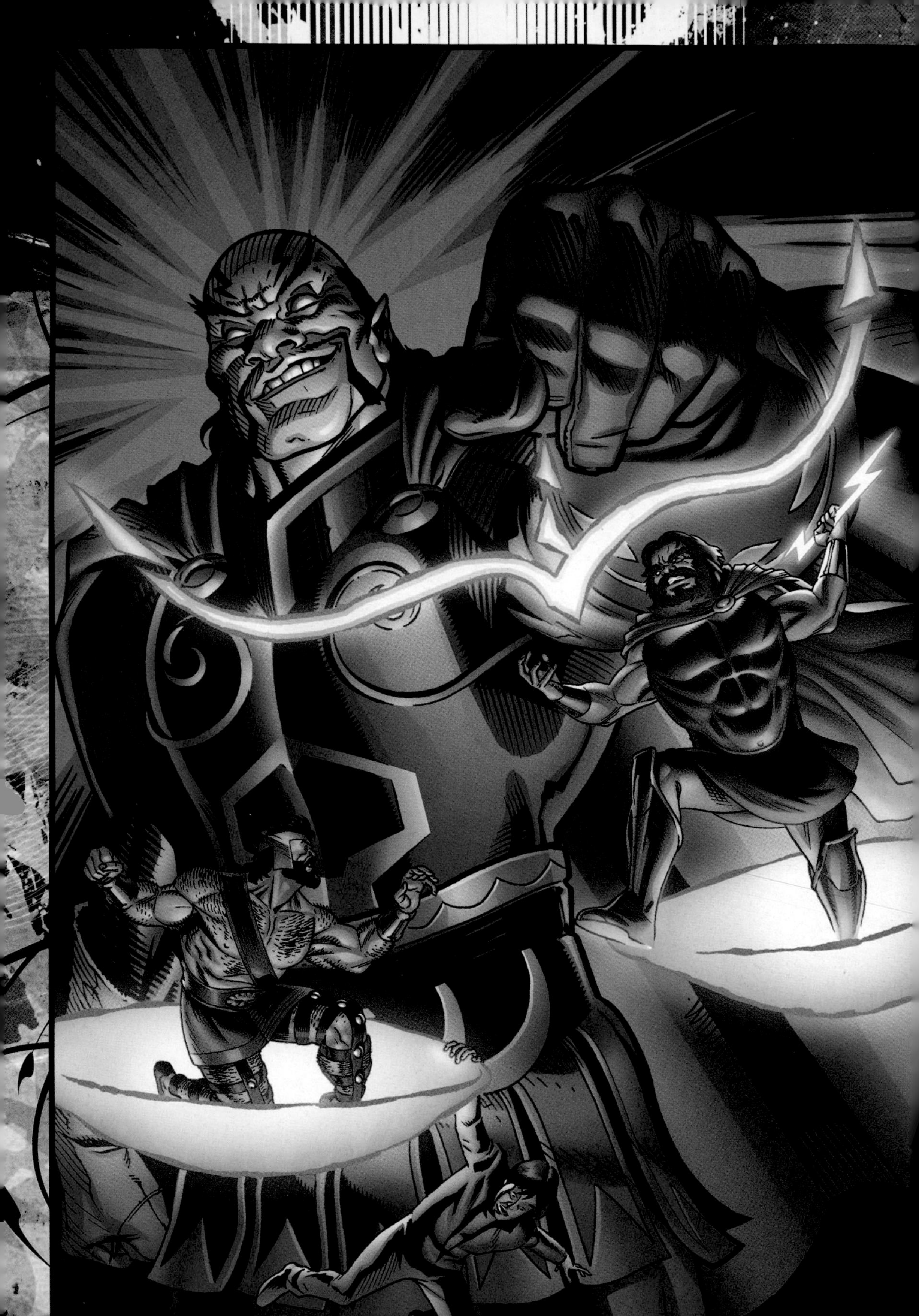

INCREDIBLE HERCULES #130

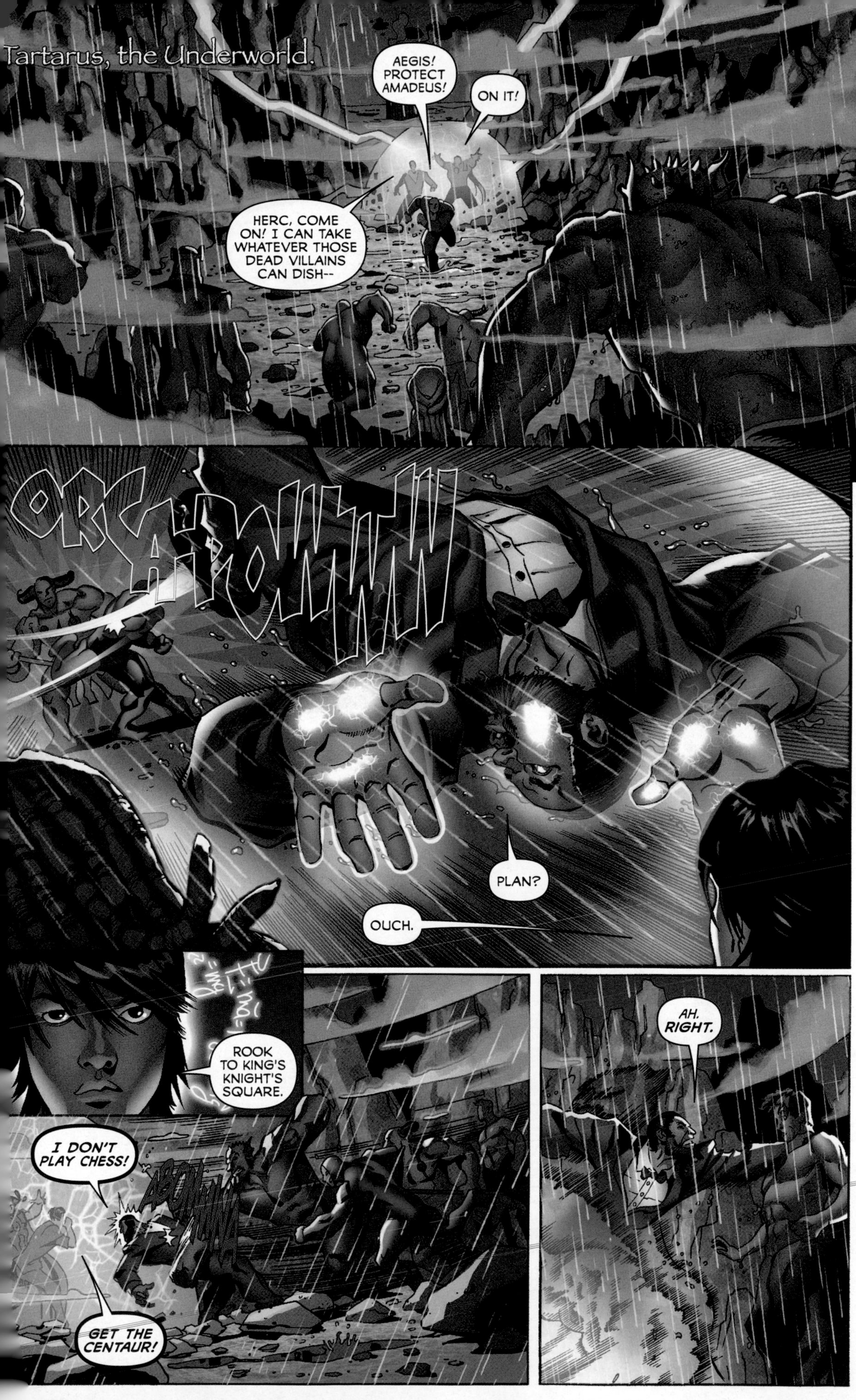
Tartarus, the Underworld.
AEGIS! PROTECT AMADEUS!
ON IT!
HERC, COME ON! I CAN TAKE WHATEVER THOSE DEAD VILLAINS CAN DISH--
PLAN?
OUCH.
ROOK TO KING'S KNIGHT'S SQUARE.
I DON'T PLAY CHESS!
GET THE CENTAUR!
AH. RIGHT.

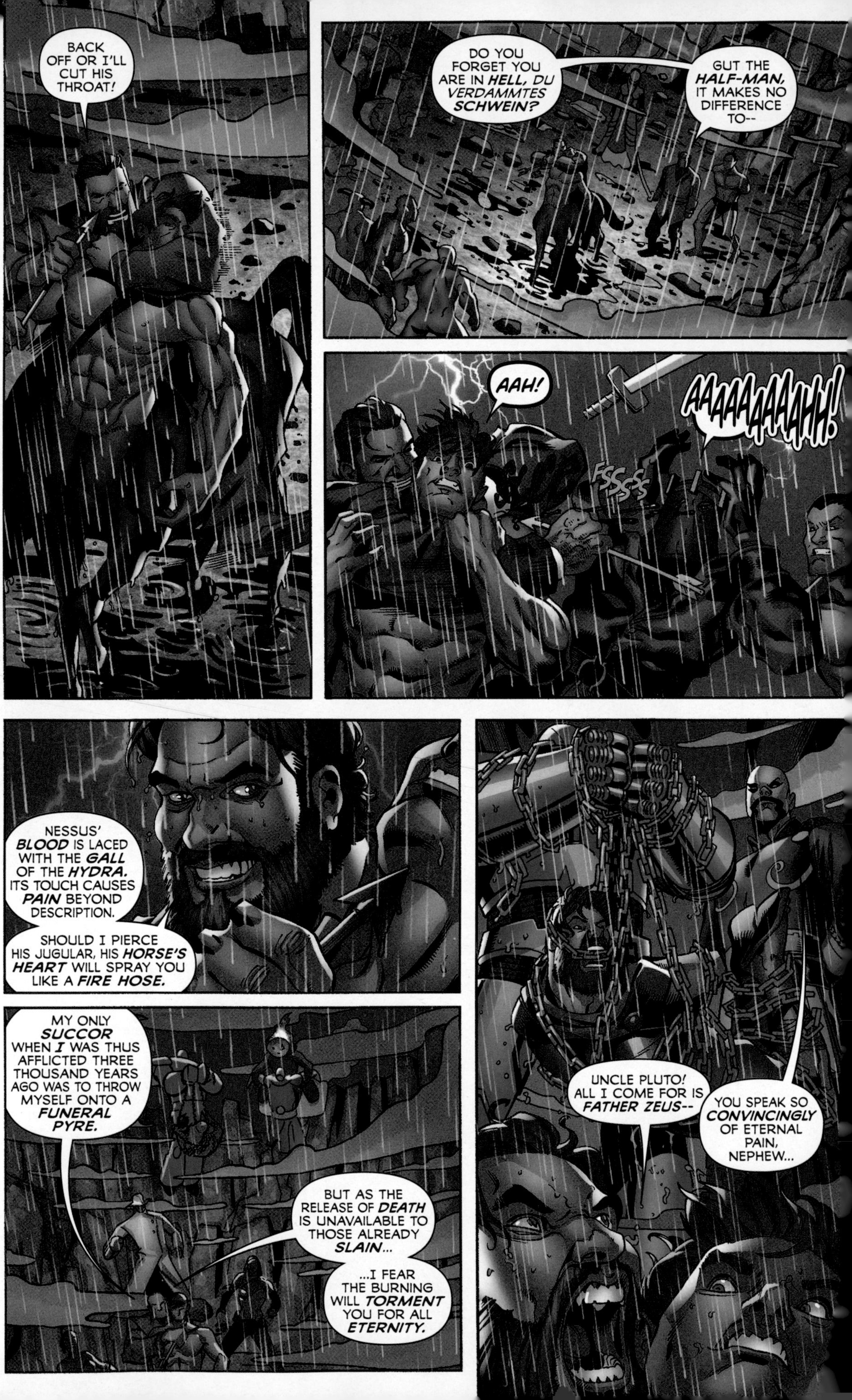
BACK OFF OR I'LL CUT HIS THROAT!
DO YOU FORGET YOU ARE IN HELL, DU VERDAMMTES SCHWEIN?
GUT THE HALF-MAN, IT MAKES NO DIFFERENCE TO--
AAH!
AAAAAAAAAHH!
FSSSSS
NESSUS' BLOOD IS LACED WITH THE GALL OF THE HYDRA. ITS TOUCH CAUSES PAIN BEYOND DESCRIPTION.
SHOULD I PIERCE HIS JUGULAR, HIS HORSE'S HEART WILL SPRAY YOU LIKE A FIRE HOSE.
MY ONLY SUCCOR WHEN I WAS THUS AFFLICTED THREE THOUSAND YEARS AGO WAS TO THROW MYSELF ONTO A FUNERAL PYRE.
BUT AS THE RELEASE OF DEATH IS UNAVAILABLE TO THOSE ALREADY SLAIN...
...I FEAR THE BURNING WILL TORMENT YOU FOR ALL ETERNITY.
UNCLE PLUTO! ALL I COME FOR IS FATHER ZEUS--
YOU SPEAK SO CONVINCINGLY OF ETERNAL PAIN, NEPHEW...

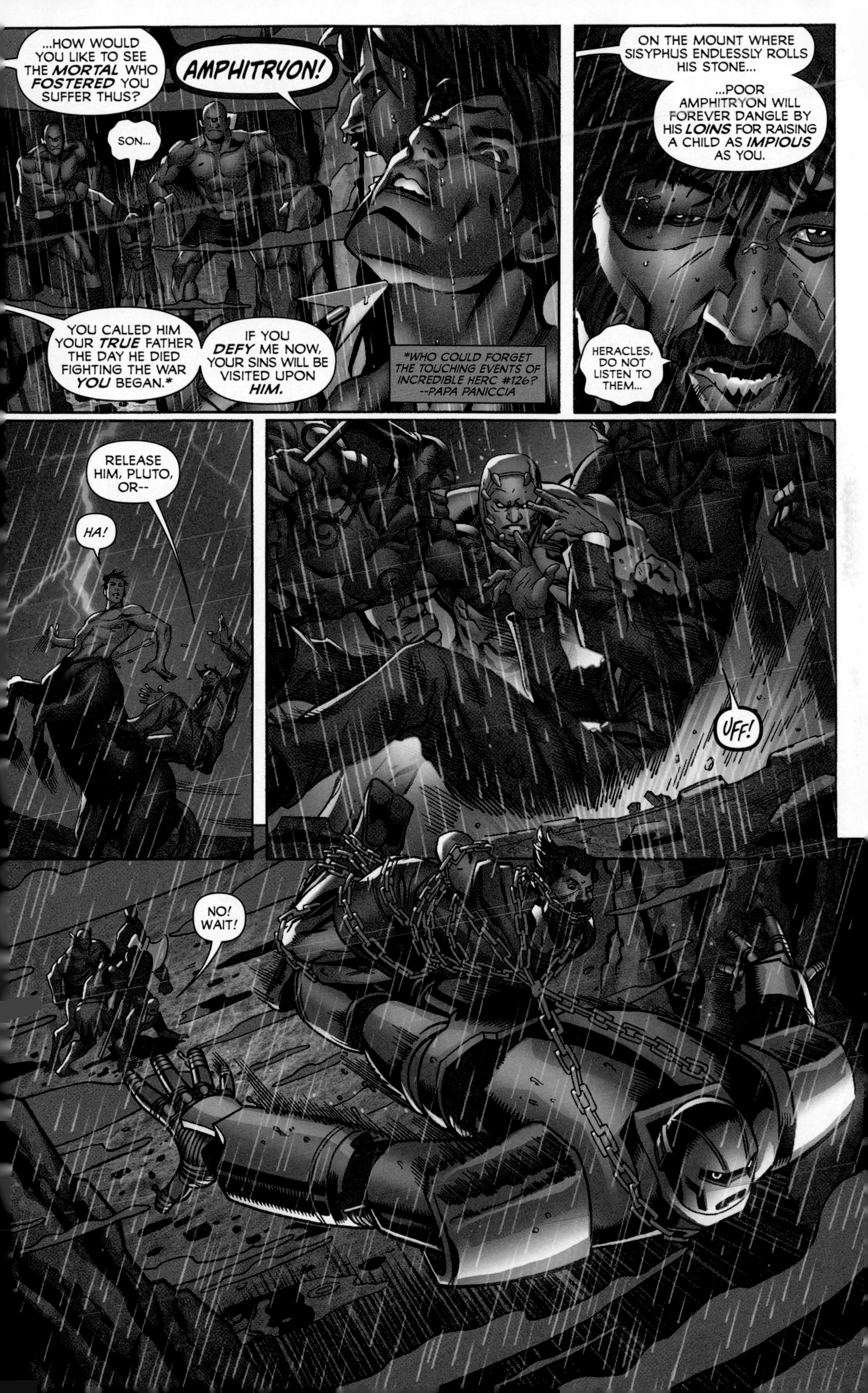
...HOW WOULD YOU LIKE TO SEE THE MORTAL WHO FOSTERED YOU SUFFER THUS?
AMPHITRYON!
SON...
YOU CALLED HIM YOUR TRUE FATHER THE DAY HE DIED FIGHTING THE WAR YOU BEGAN.*
IF YOU DEFY ME NOW, YOUR SINS WILL BE VISITED UPON HIM.
*WHO COULD FORGET THE TOUCHING EVENTS OF INCREDIBLE HERC #126? --PAPA PANICCIA
ON THE MOUNT WHERE SISYPHUS ENDLESSLY ROLLS HIS STONE...
...POOR AMPHITRYON WILL FOREVER DANGLE BY HIS LOINS FOR RAISING A CHILD AS IMPIOUS AS YOU.
HERACLES, DO NOT LISTEN TO THEM...
RELEASE HIM, PLUTO, OR--
HA!
UFF!
NO! WAIT!

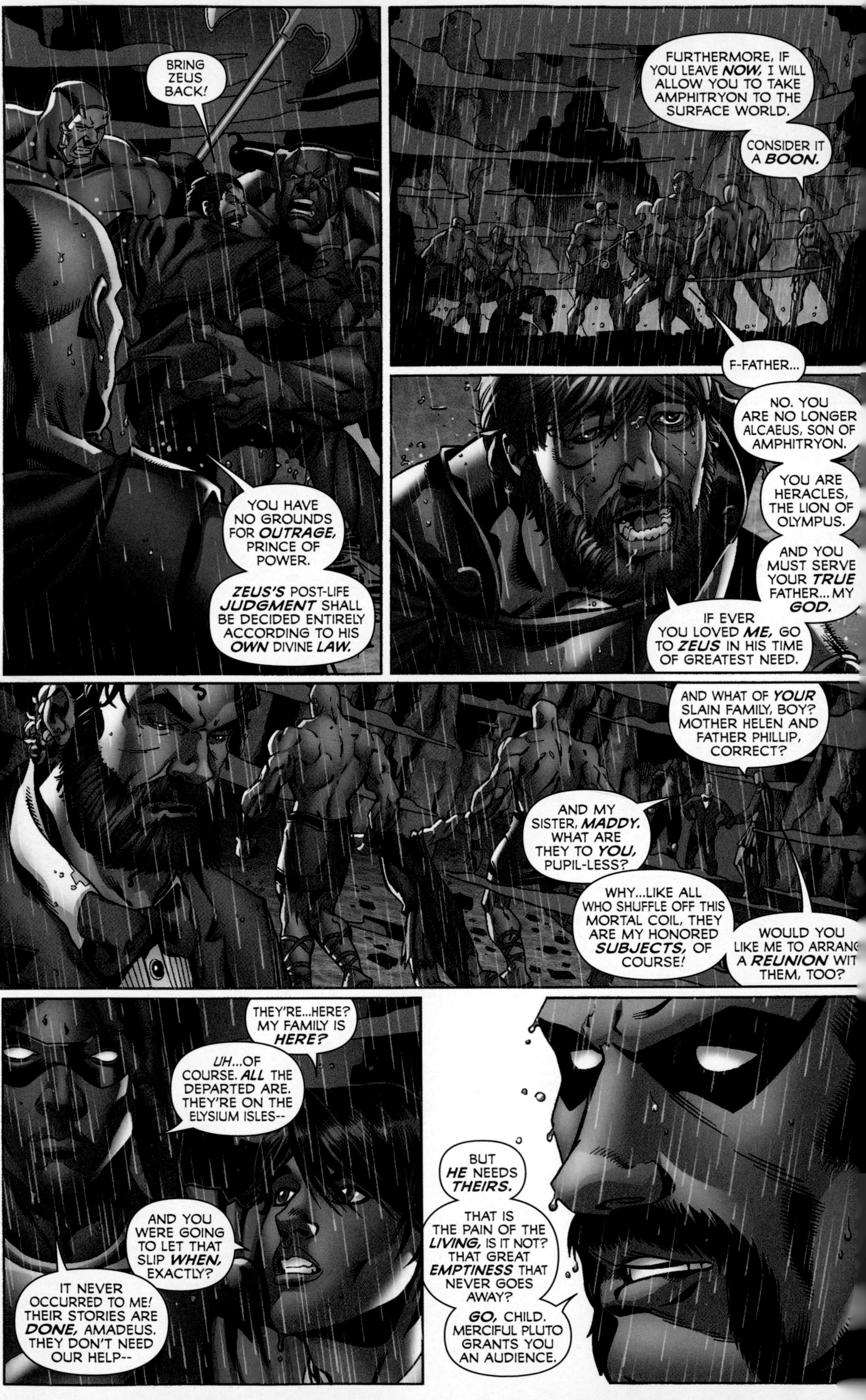
BRING ZEUS BACK!
YOU HAVE NO GROUNDS FOR OUTRAGE, PRINCE OF POWER.
ZEUS'S POST-LIFE JUDGMENT SHALL BE DECIDED ENTIRELY ACCORDING TO HIS OWN DIVINE LAW.
FURTHERMORE, IF YOU LEAVE NOW, I WILL ALLOW YOU TO TAKE AMPHITRYON TO THE SURFACE WORLD.
CONSIDER IT A BOON.
F-FATHER...
NO. YOU ARE NO LONGER ALCAEUS, SON OF AMPHITRYON.
YOU ARE HERACLES, THE LION OF OLYMPUS.
AND YOU MUST SERVE YOUR TRUE FATHER... MY GOD.
IF EVER YOU LOVED ME, GO TO ZEUS IN HIS TIME OF GREATEST NEED.
AND WHAT OF YOUR SLAIN FAMILY, BOY? MOTHER HELEN AND FATHER PHILLIP, CORRECT?
AND MY SISTER, MADDY. WHAT ARE THEY TO YOU, PUPIL-LESS?
WHY...LIKE ALL WHO SHUFFLE OFF THIS MORTAL COIL, THEY ARE MY HONORED SUBJECTS, OF COURSE!
WOULD YOU LIKE ME TO ARRANG A REUNION WIT THEM, TOO?
THEY'RE...HERE? MY FAMILY IS HERE?
UH...OF COURSE. ALL THE DEPARTED ARE. THEY'RE ON THE ELYSIUM ISLES--
AND YOU WERE GOING TO LET THAT SLIP WHEN, EXACTLY?
IT NEVER OCCURRED TO ME! THEIR STORIES ARE DONE, AMADEUS. THEY DON'T NEED OUR HELP--
BUT HE NEEDS THEIRS.
THAT IS THE PAIN OF THE LIVING, IS IT NOT? THAT GREAT EMPTINESS THAT NEVER GOES AWAY?
GO, CHILD. MERCIFUL PLUTO GRANTS YOU AN AUDIENCE.

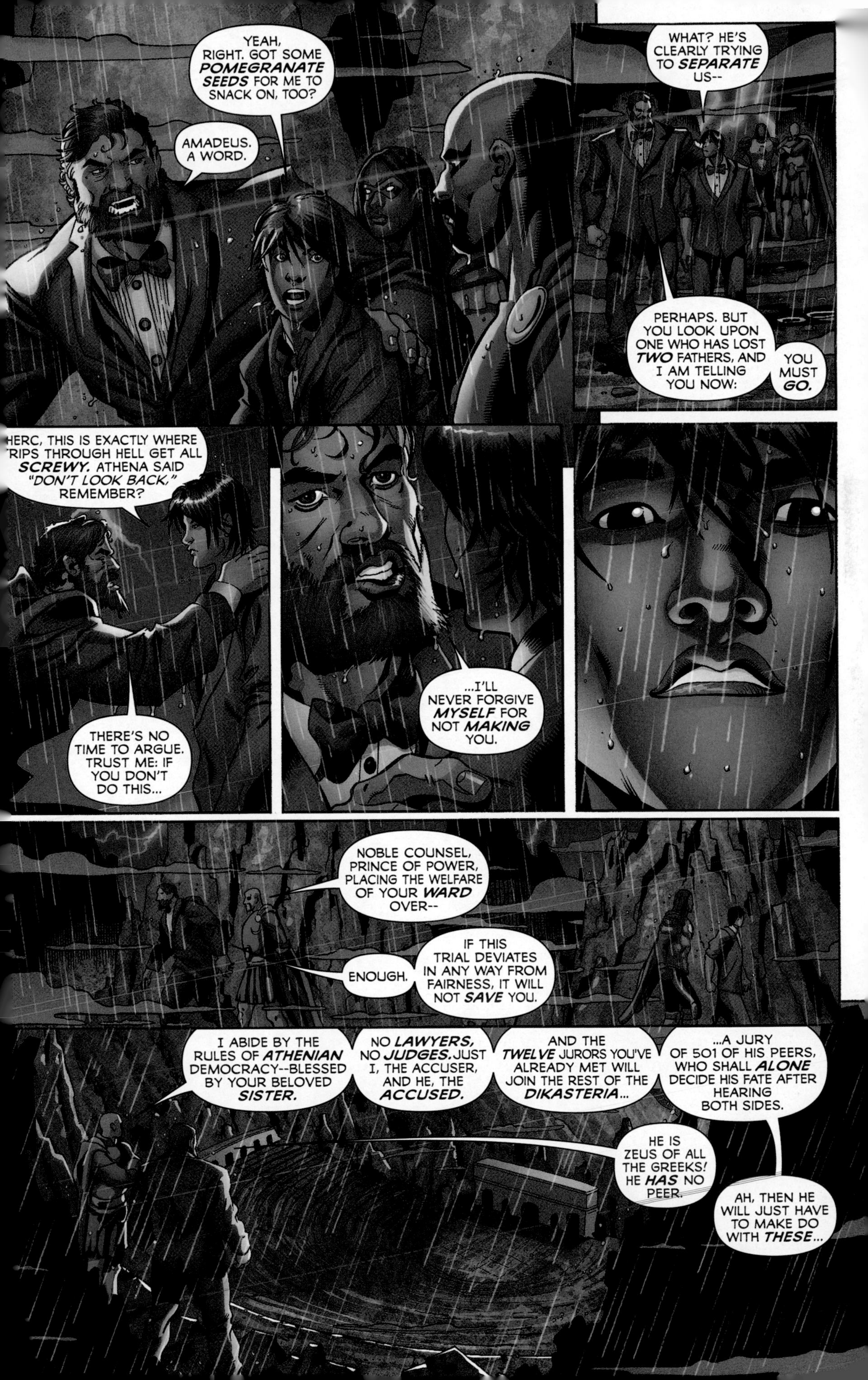
YEAH, RIGHT. GOT SOME POMEGRANATE SEEDS FOR ME TO SNACK ON, TOO?
AMADEUS. A WORD.
WHAT? HE'S CLEARLY TRYING TO SEPARATE US--
PERHAPS. BUT YOU LOOK UPON ONE WHO HAS LOST TWO FATHERS, AND I AM TELLING YOU NOW:
YOU MUST GO.
HERC, THIS IS EXACTLY WHERE TRIPS THROUGH HELL GET ALL SCREWY. ATHENA SAID "DON'T LOOK BACK," REMEMBER?
THERE'S NO TIME TO ARGUE. TRUST ME: IF YOU DON'T DO THIS...
...I'LL NEVER FORGIVE MYSELF FOR NOT MAKING YOU.
NOBLE COUNSEL, PRINCE OF POWER, PLACING THE WELFARE OF YOUR WARD OVER--
ENOUGH.
IF THIS TRIAL DEVIATES IN ANY WAY FROM FAIRNESS, IT WILL NOT SAVE YOU.
I ABIDE BY THE RULES OF ATHENIAN DEMOCRACY--BLESSED BY YOUR BELOVED SISTER.
NO LAWYERS, NO JUDGES. JUST I, THE ACCUSER, AND HE, THE ACCUSED.
AND THE TWELVE JURORS YOU'VE ALREADY MET WILL JOIN THE REST OF THE DIKASTERIA...
...A JURY OF 501 OF HIS PEERS, WHO SHALL ALONE DECIDE HIS FATE AFTER HEARING BOTH SIDES.
HE IS ZEUS OF ALL THE GREEKS! HE HAS NO PEER.
AH, THEN HE WILL JUST HAVE TO MAKE DO WITH THESE...

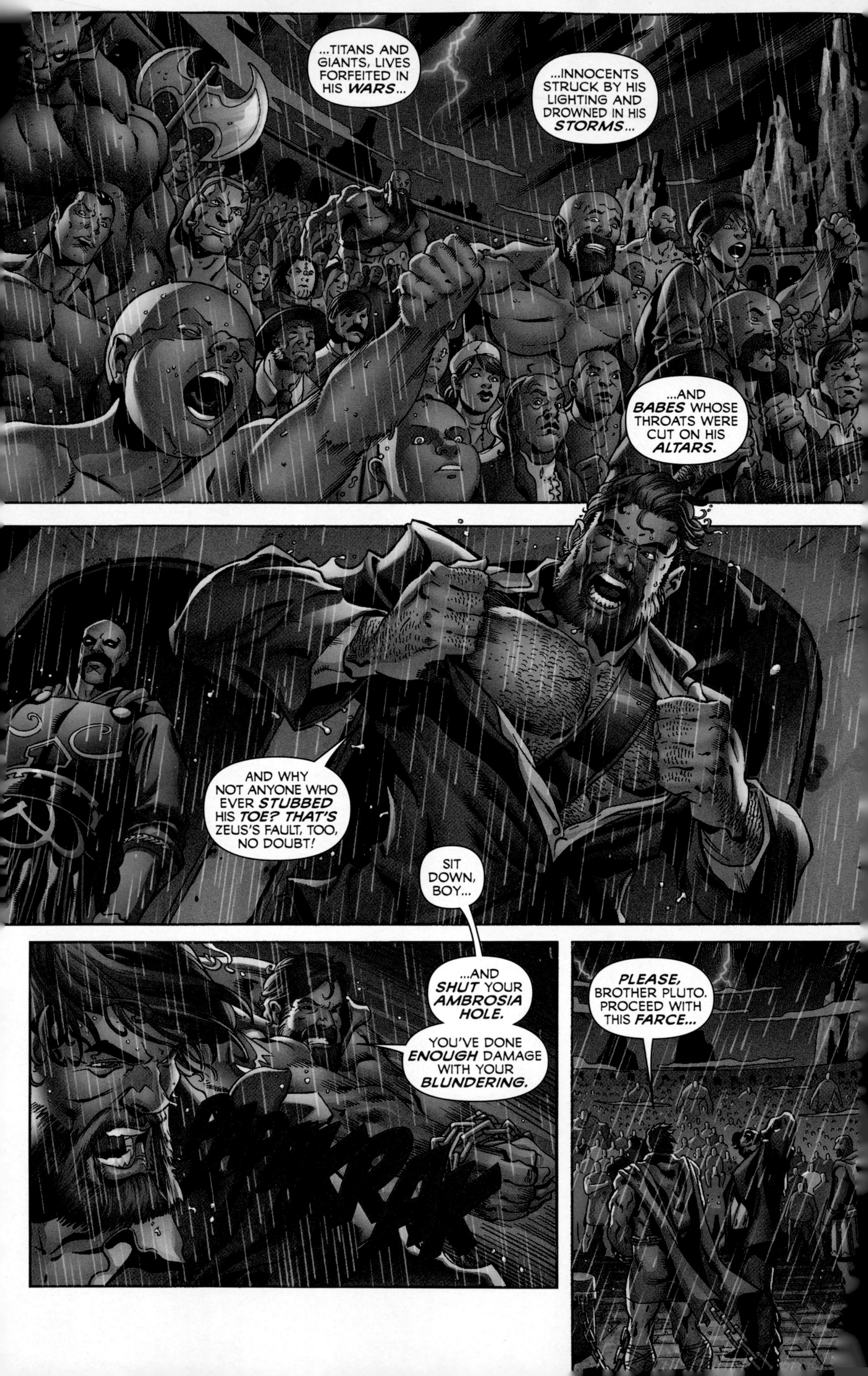
...TITANS AND GIANTS, LIVES FORFEITED IN HIS WARS...
...INNOCENTS STRUCK BY HIS LIGHTING AND DROWNED IN HIS STORMS...
...AND BABES WHOSE THROATS WERE CUT ON HIS ALTARS.
AND WHY NOT ANYONE WHO EVER STUBBED HIS TOE? THAT'S ZEUS'S FAULT, TOO, NO DOUBT!
SIT DOWN, BOY...
...AND SHUT YOUR AMBROSIA HOLE.
YOU'VE DONE ENOUGH DAMAGE WITH YOUR BLUNDERING.
PLEASE, BROTHER PLUTO. PROCEED WITH THIS FARCE...

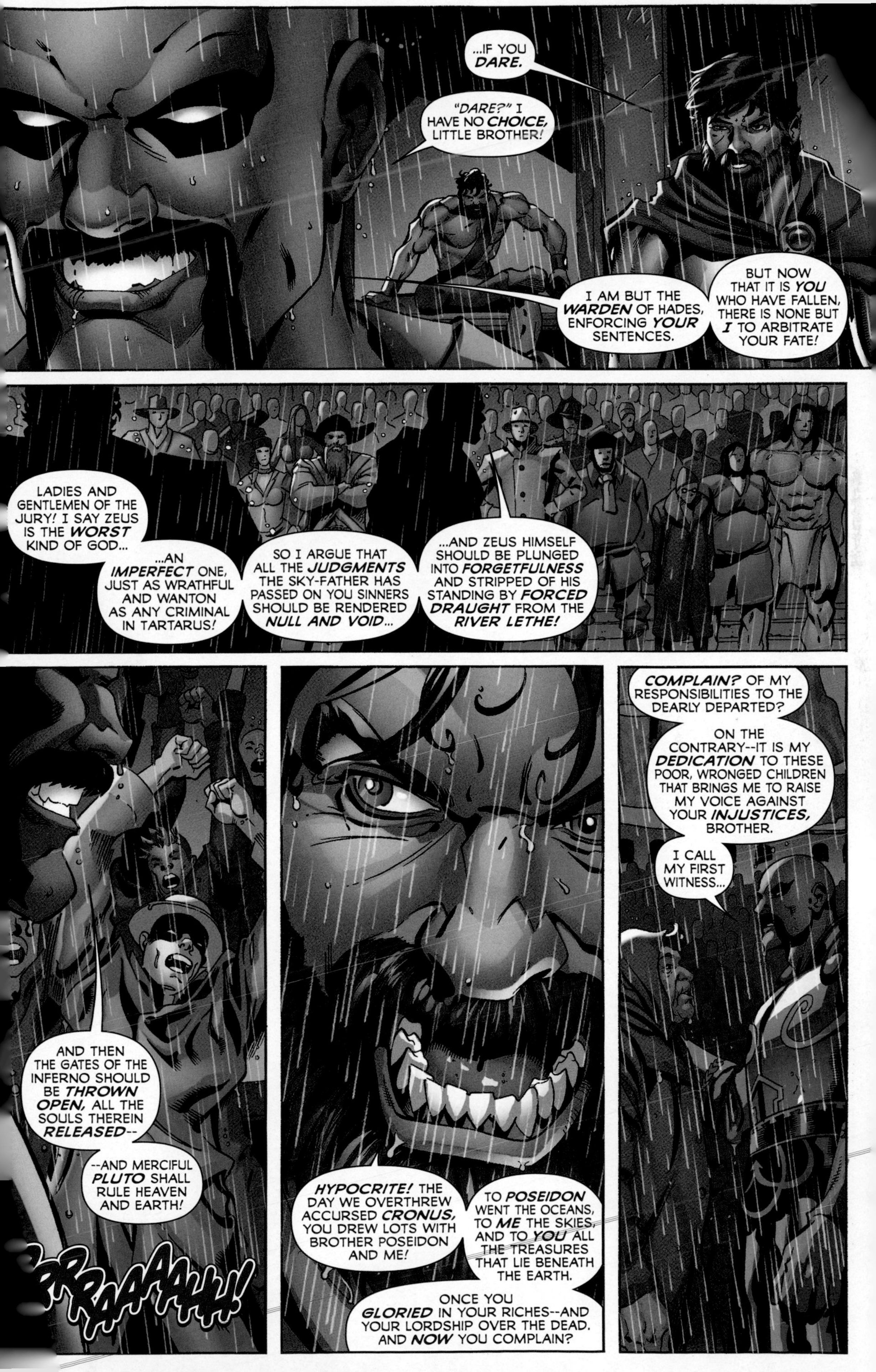
...IF YOU DARE.
"DARE?" I HAVE NO CHOICE, LITTLE BROTHER!
I AM BUT THE WARDEN OF HADES, ENFORCING YOUR SENTENCES.
BUT NOW THAT IT IS YOU WHO HAVE FALLEN, THERE IS NONE BUT I TO ARBITRATE YOUR FATE!
LADIES AND GENTLEMEN OF THE JURY! I SAY ZEUS IS THE WORST KIND OF GOD...
...AN IMPERFECT ONE, JUST AS WRATHFUL AND WANTON AS ANY CRIMINAL IN TARTARUS!
SO I ARGUE THAT ALL THE JUDGMENTS THE SKY-FATHER HAS PASSED ON YOU SINNERS SHOULD BE RENDERED NULL AND VOID...
...AND ZEUS HIMSELF SHOULD BE PLUNGED INTO FORGETFULNESS AND STRIPPED OF HIS STANDING BY FORCED DRAUGHT FROM THE RIVER LETHE!
AND THEN THE GATES OF THE INFERNO SHOULD BE THROWN OPEN, ALL THE SOULS THEREIN RELEASED--
--AND MERCIFUL PLUTO SHALL RULE HEAVEN AND EARTH!
RRAAAAHH!
HYPOCRITE! THE DAY WE OVERTHREW ACCURSED CRONUS, YOU DREW LOTS WITH BROTHER POSEIDON AND ME!
TO POSEIDON WENT THE OCEANS, TO ME THE SKIES, AND TO YOU ALL THE TREASURES THAT LIE BENEATH THE EARTH.
ONCE YOU GLORIED IN YOUR RICHES--AND YOUR LORDSHIP OVER THE DEAD. AND NOW YOU COMPLAIN?
COMPLAIN? OF MY RESPONSIBILITIES TO THE DEARLY DEPARTED?
ON THE CONTRARY--IT IS MY DEDICATION TO THESE POOR, WRONGED CHILDREN THAT BRINGS ME TO RAISE MY VOICE AGAINST YOUR INJUSTICES, BROTHER.
I CALL MY FIRST WITNESS...

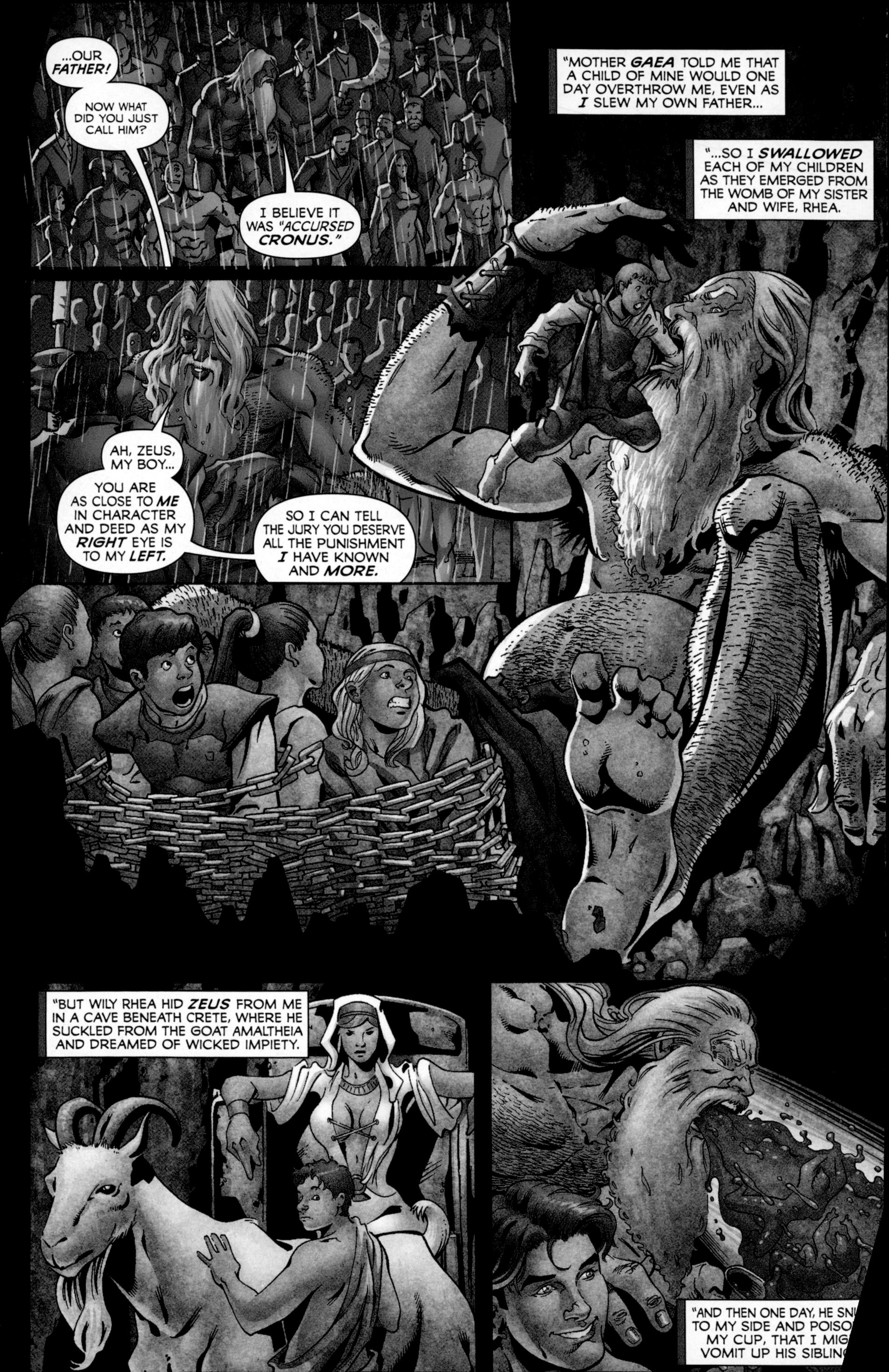

...OUR FATHER!
NOW WHAT DID YOU JUST CALL HIM?
I BELIEVE IT WAS "ACCURSED CRONUS."
"MOTHER GAEA TOLD ME THAT A CHILD OF MINE WOULD ONE DAY OVERTHROW ME, EVEN AS I SLEW MY OWN FATHER...
"...SO I SWALLOWED EACH OF MY CHILDREN AS THEY EMERGED FROM THE WOMB OF MY SISTER AND WIFE, RHEA.
AH, ZEUS, MY BOY...
YOU ARE AS CLOSE TO ME IN CHARACTER AND DEED AS MY RIGHT EYE IS TO MY LEFT.
SO I CAN TELL THE JURY YOU DESERVE ALL THE PUNISHMENT I HAVE KNOWN AND MORE.
"BUT WILY RHEA HID ZEUS FROM ME IN A CAVE BENEATH CRETE, WHERE HE SUCKLED FROM THE GOAT AMALTHEIA AND DREAMED OF WICKED IMPIETY.
"AND THEN ONE DAY, HE SN TO MY SIDE AND POISO MY CUP, THAT I MIG VOMIT UP HIS SIBLIN

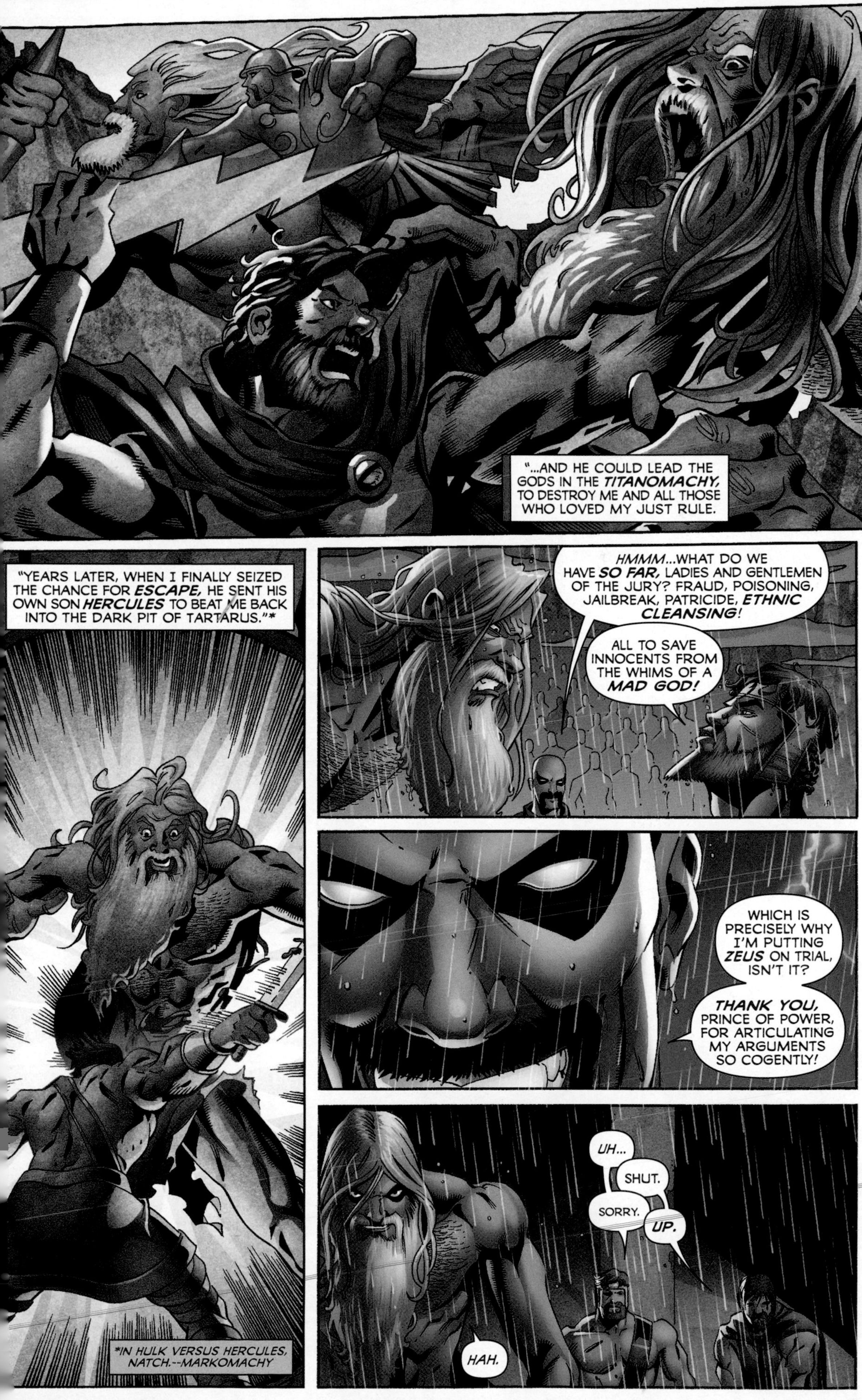
"...AND HE COULD LEAD THE GODS IN THE *TITANOMACHY,* TO DESTROY ME AND ALL THOSE WHO LOVED MY JUST RULE.
"YEARS LATER, WHEN I FINALLY SEIZED THE CHANCE FOR *ESCAPE,* HE SENT HIS OWN SON *HERCULES* TO BEAT ME BACK INTO THE DARK PIT OF TARTARUS."*
*IN HULK VERSUS HERCULES, NATCH.--MARKOMACHY
HMMM...WHAT DO WE HAVE *SO FAR,* LADIES AND GENTLEMEN OF THE JURY? FRAUD, POISONING, JAILBREAK, PATRICIDE, *ETHNIC CLEANSING*!
ALL TO SAVE INNOCENTS FROM THE WHIMS OF A *MAD GOD!*
WHICH IS PRECISELY WHY I'M PUTTING *ZEUS* ON TRIAL, ISN'T IT?
THANK YOU, PRINCE OF POWER, FOR ARTICULATING MY ARGUMENTS SO COGENTLY!
UH...
SHUT.
SORRY.
UP.
HAH.

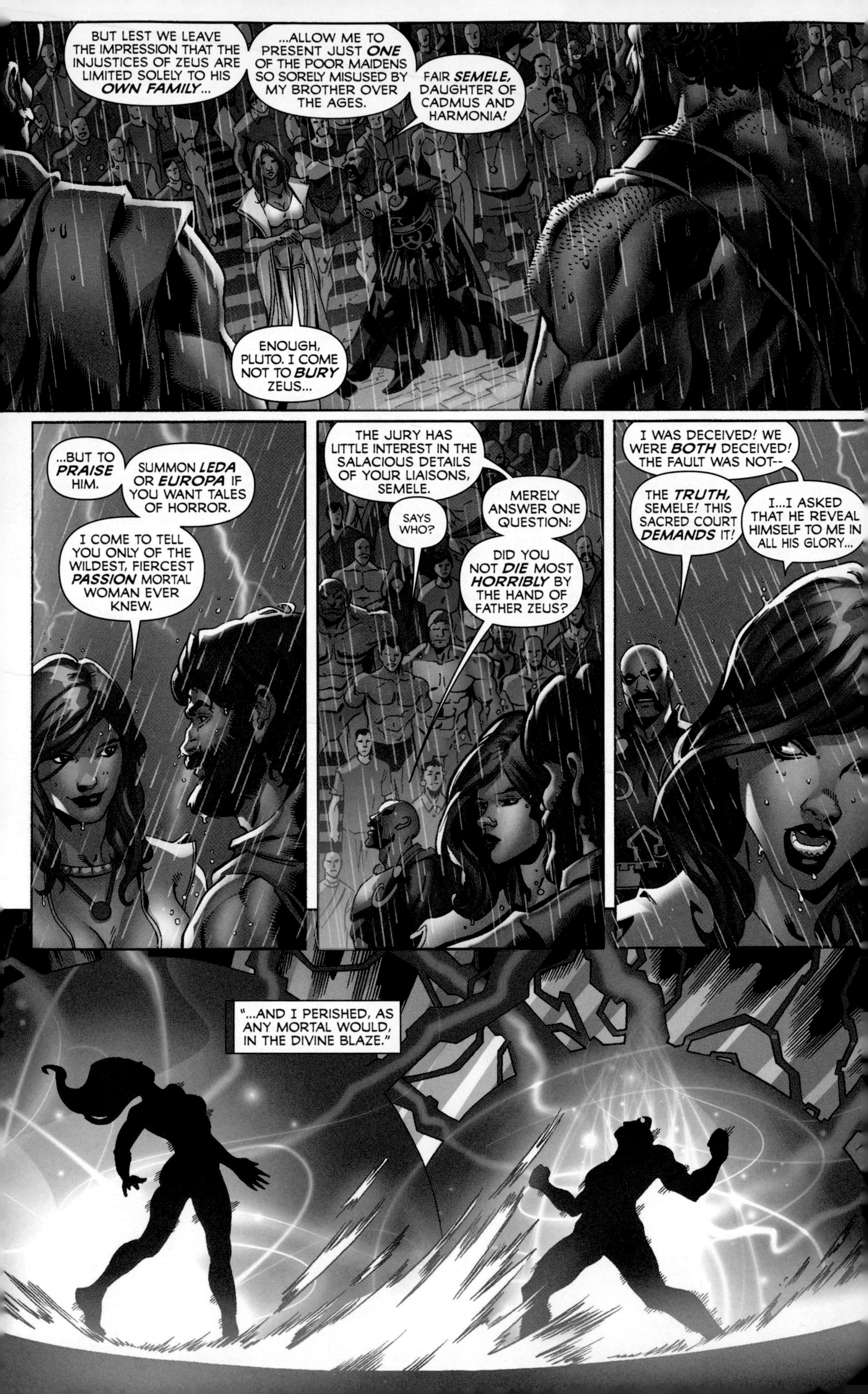
BUT LEST WE LEAVE THE IMPRESSION THAT THE INJUSTICES OF ZEUS ARE LIMITED SOLELY TO HIS OWN FAMILY...
...ALLOW ME TO PRESENT JUST ONE OF THE POOR MAIDENS SO SORELY MISUSED BY MY BROTHER OVER THE AGES.
FAIR SEMELE, DAUGHTER OF CADMUS AND HARMONIA!
ENOUGH, PLUTO. I COME NOT TO BURY ZEUS...
...BUT TO PRAISE HIM.
SUMMON LEDA OR EUROPA IF YOU WANT TALES OF HORROR.
I COME TO TELL YOU ONLY OF THE WILDEST, FIERCEST PASSION MORTAL WOMAN EVER KNEW.
THE JURY HAS LITTLE INTEREST IN THE SALACIOUS DETAILS OF YOUR LIAISONS, SEMELE.
SAYS WHO?
MERELY ANSWER ONE QUESTION:
DID YOU NOT DIE MOST HORRIBLY BY THE HAND OF FATHER ZEUS?
I WAS DECEIVED! WE WERE BOTH DECEIVED! THE FAULT WAS NOT--
THE TRUTH, SEMELE! THIS SACRED COURT DEMANDS IT!
I...I ASKED THAT HE REVEAL HIMSELF TO ME IN ALL HIS GLORY...
"...AND I PERISHED, AS ANY MORTAL WOULD, IN THE DIVINE BLAZE."

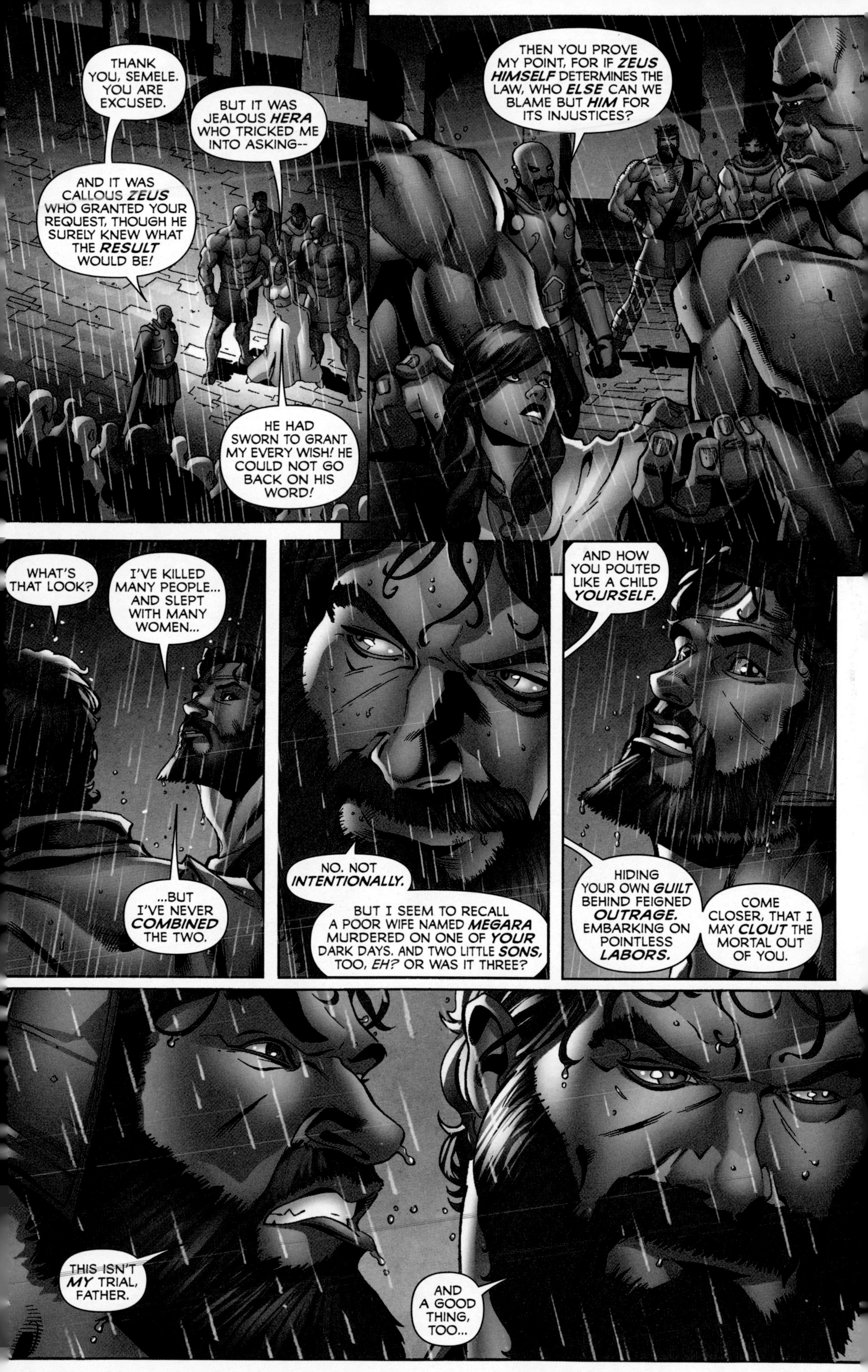
THANK YOU, SEMELE. YOU ARE EXCUSED.
BUT IT WAS JEALOUS HERA WHO TRICKED ME INTO ASKING--
AND IT WAS CALLOUS ZEUS WHO GRANTED YOUR REQUEST, THOUGH HE SURELY KNEW WHAT THE RESULT WOULD BE!
HE HAD SWORN TO GRANT MY EVERY WISH! HE COULD NOT GO BACK ON HIS WORD!
THEN YOU PROVE MY POINT, FOR IF ZEUS HIMSELF DETERMINES THE LAW, WHO ELSE CAN WE BLAME BUT HIM FOR ITS INJUSTICES?
WHAT'S THAT LOOK?
I'VE KILLED MANY PEOPLE... AND SLEPT WITH MANY WOMEN...
...BUT I'VE NEVER COMBINED THE TWO.
NO. NOT INTENTIONALLY.
BUT I SEEM TO RECALL A POOR WIFE NAMED MEGARA MURDERED ON ONE OF YOUR DARK DAYS. AND TWO LITTLE SONS, TOO, EH? OR WAS IT THREE?
AND HOW YOU POUTED LIKE A CHILD YOURSELF.
HIDING YOUR OWN GUILT BEHIND FEIGNED OUTRAGE. EMBARKING ON POINTLESS LABORS.
COME CLOSER, THAT I MAY CLOUT THE MORTAL OUT OF YOU.
THIS ISN'T MY TRIAL, FATHER.
AND A GOOD THING, TOO...

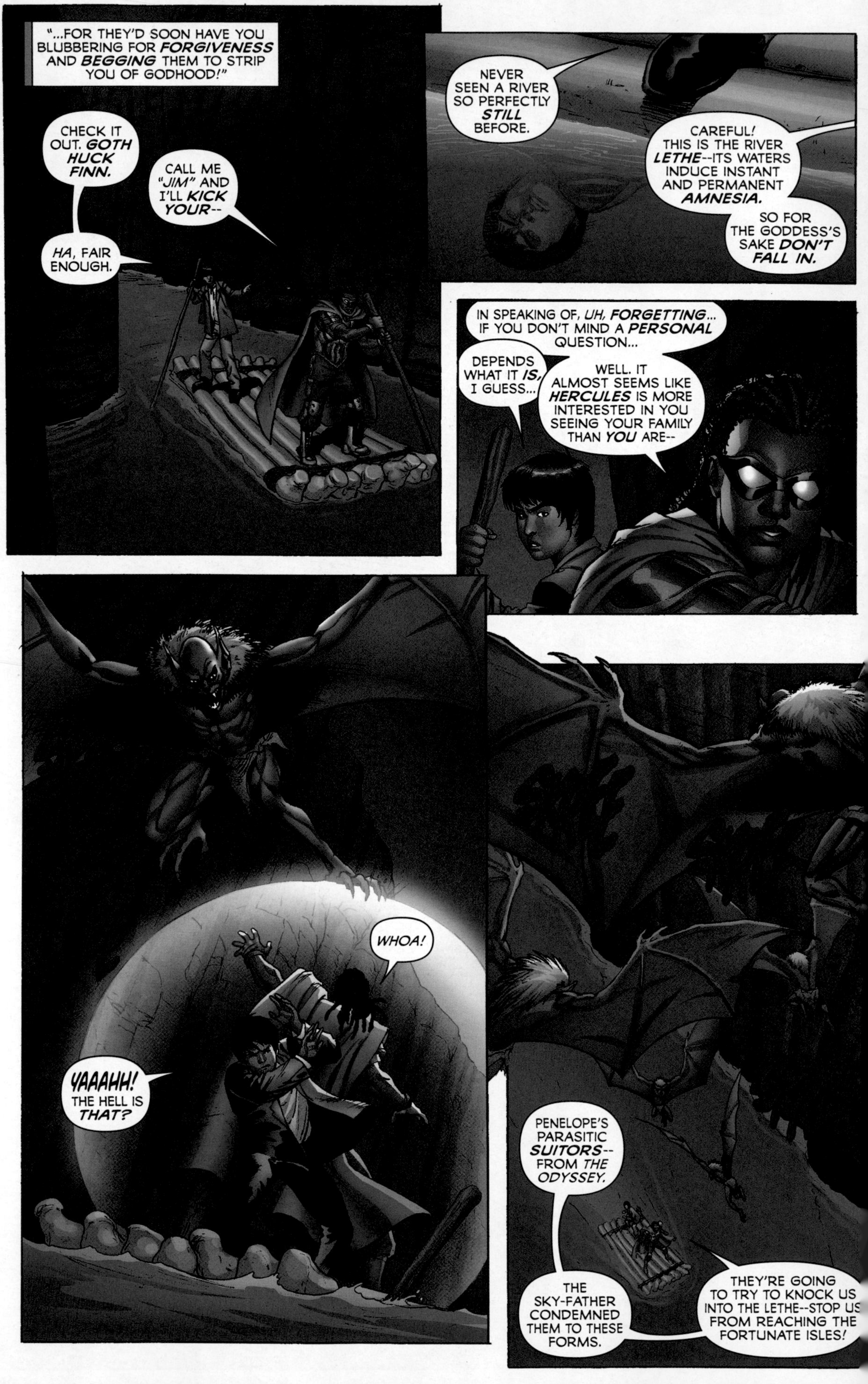
"...FOR THEY'D SOON HAVE YOU BLUBBERING FOR *FORGIVENESS* AND *BEGGING* THEM TO STRIP YOU OF GODHOOD!"
CHECK IT OUT. *GOTH HUCK FINN.*
CALL ME *"JIM"* AND I'LL *KICK YOUR*--
HA, FAIR ENOUGH.
NEVER SEEN A RIVER SO PERFECTLY *STILL* BEFORE.
CAREFUL! THIS IS THE RIVER *LETHE*--ITS WATERS INDUCE INSTANT AND PERMANENT *AMNESIA.*
SO FOR THE GODDESS'S SAKE *DON'T FALL IN.*
IN SPEAKING OF, *UH, FORGETTING*... IF YOU DON'T MIND A *PERSONAL* QUESTION...
DEPENDS WHAT IT *IS,* I GUESS...
WELL. IT ALMOST SEEMS LIKE *HERCULES* IS MORE INTERESTED IN YOU SEEING YOUR FAMILY THAN *YOU* ARE--
WHOA!
YAAAHH! THE HELL IS *THAT?*
PENELOPE'S PARASITIC *SUITORS*-- FROM *THE ODYSSEY.*
THE SKY-FATHER CONDEMNED THEM TO THESE FORMS.
THEY'RE GOING TO TRY TO KNOCK US INTO THE LETHE--STOP US FROM REACHING THE FORTUNATE ISLES!

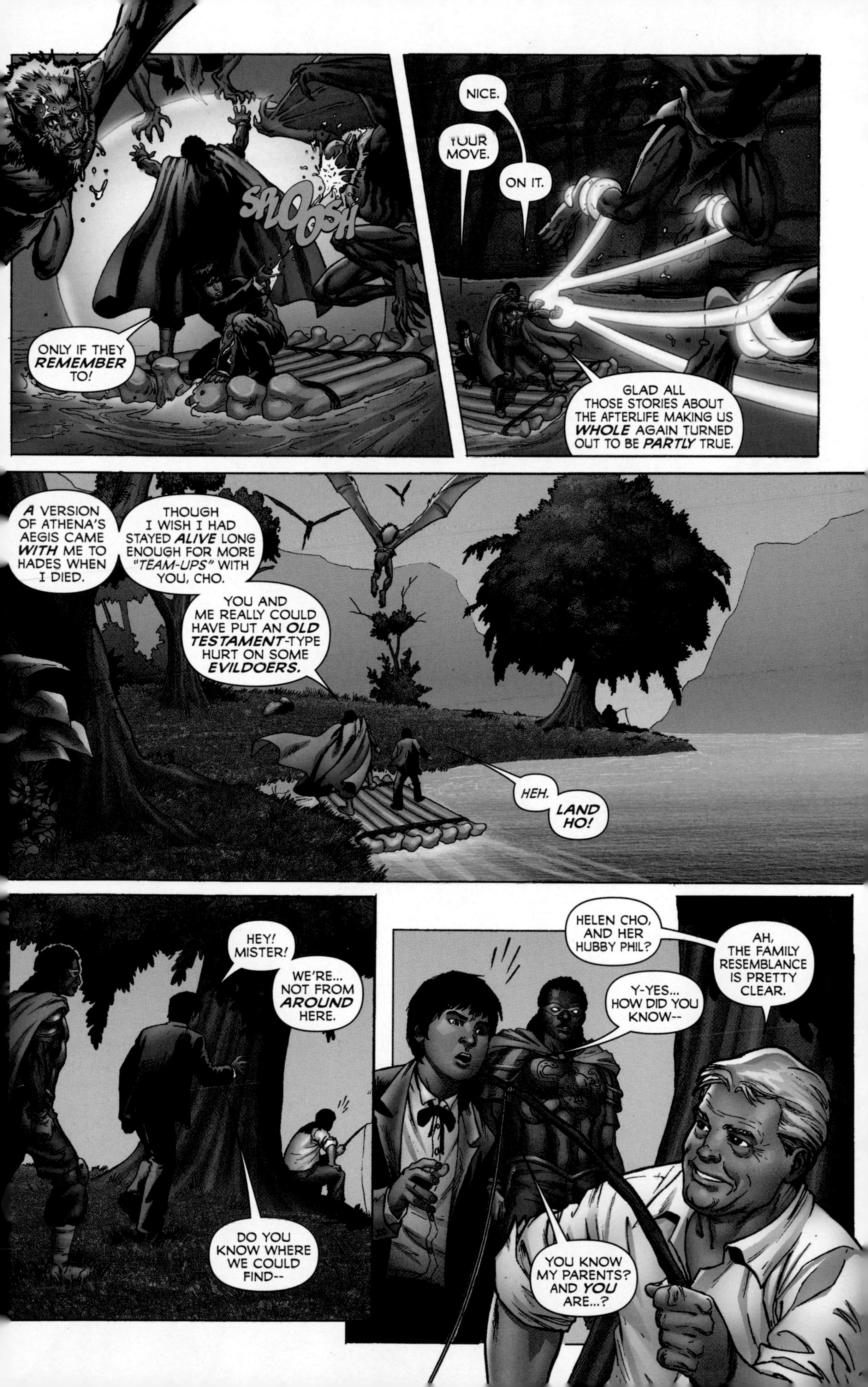
SPLOOSH
ONLY IF THEY *REMEMBER* TO!
NICE.
YOUR MOVE.
ON IT.
GLAD ALL THOSE STORIES ABOUT THE AFTERLIFE MAKING US *WHOLE* AGAIN TURNED OUT TO BE *PARTLY* TRUE.
A VERSION OF ATHENA'S AEGIS CAME *WITH* ME TO HADES WHEN I DIED.
THOUGH I WISH I HAD STAYED *ALIVE* LONG ENOUGH FOR MORE *"TEAM-UPS"* WITH YOU, CHO.
YOU AND ME REALLY COULD HAVE PUT AN *OLD TESTAMENT*-TYPE HURT ON SOME *EVILDOERS.*
HEH.
LAND HO!
HEY! *MISTER!*
WE'RE... NOT FROM *AROUND* HERE.
DO YOU KNOW WHERE WE COULD FIND--
HELEN CHO, AND HER HUBBY PHIL?
AH, THE FAMILY RESEMBLANCE IS PRETTY CLEAR.
Y-YES... HOW DID YOU KNOW--
YOU KNOW MY PARENTS? AND *YOU* ARE...?

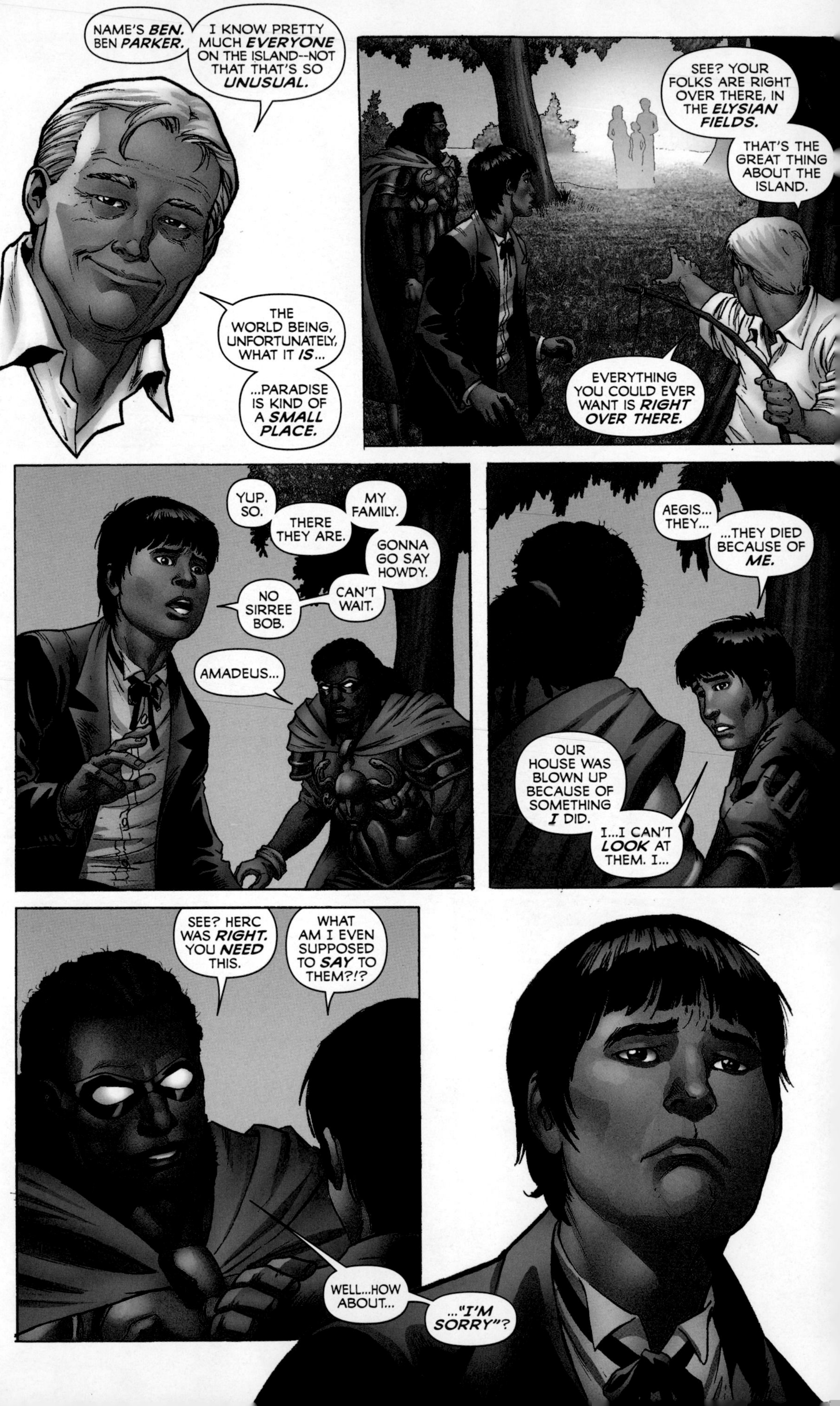
NAME'S BEN. BEN PARKER.
I KNOW PRETTY MUCH EVERYONE ON THE ISLAND--NOT THAT THAT'S SO UNUSUAL.
THE WORLD BEING, UNFORTUNATELY, WHAT IT IS...
...PARADISE IS KIND OF A SMALL PLACE.
SEE? YOUR FOLKS ARE RIGHT OVER THERE, IN THE ELYSIAN FIELDS.
THAT'S THE GREAT THING ABOUT THE ISLAND.
EVERYTHING YOU COULD EVER WANT IS RIGHT OVER THERE.
YUP. SO.
THERE THEY ARE.
MY FAMILY.
GONNA GO SAY HOWDY.
CAN'T WAIT.
NO SIRREE BOB.
AMADEUS...
AEGIS... THEY...
...THEY DIED BECAUSE OF ME.
OUR HOUSE WAS BLOWN UP BECAUSE OF SOMETHING I DID.
I...I CAN'T LOOK AT THEM. I...
SEE? HERC WAS RIGHT. YOU NEED THIS.
WHAT AM I EVEN SUPPOSED TO SAY TO THEM?!?
WELL...HOW ABOUT...
..."I'M SORRY"?

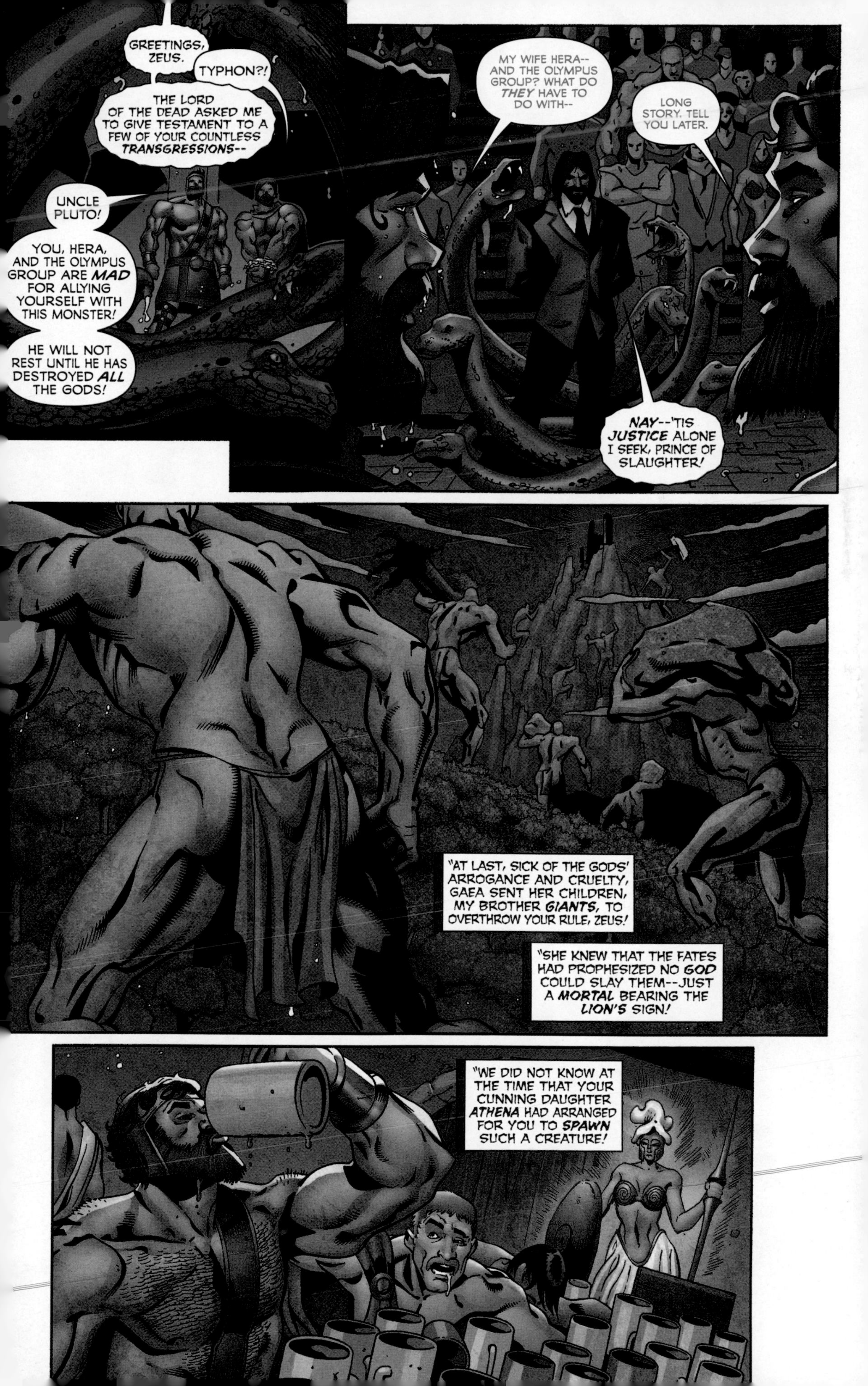
GREETINGS, ZEUS.
TYPHON?!
THE LORD OF THE DEAD ASKED ME TO GIVE TESTAMENT TO A FEW OF YOUR COUNTLESS TRANSGRESSIONS--
UNCLE PLUTO!
YOU, HERA, AND THE OLYMPUS GROUP ARE MAD FOR ALLYING YOURSELF WITH THIS MONSTER!
HE WILL NOT REST UNTIL HE HAS DESTROYED ALL THE GODS!
MY WIFE HERA-- AND THE OLYMPUS GROUP? WHAT DO THEY HAVE TO DO WITH--
LONG STORY. TELL YOU LATER.
NAY--'TIS JUSTICE ALONE I SEEK, PRINCE OF SLAUGHTER!
"AT LAST, SICK OF THE GODS' ARROGANCE AND CRUELTY, GAEA SENT HER CHILDREN, MY BROTHER GIANTS, TO OVERTHROW YOUR RULE, ZEUS!
"SHE KNEW THAT THE FATES HAD PROPHESIZED NO GOD COULD SLAY THEM--JUST A MORTAL BEARING THE LION'S SIGN!
"WE DID NOT KNOW AT THE TIME THAT YOUR CUNNING DAUGHTER ATHENA HAD ARRANGED FOR YOU TO SPAWN SUCH A CREATURE!

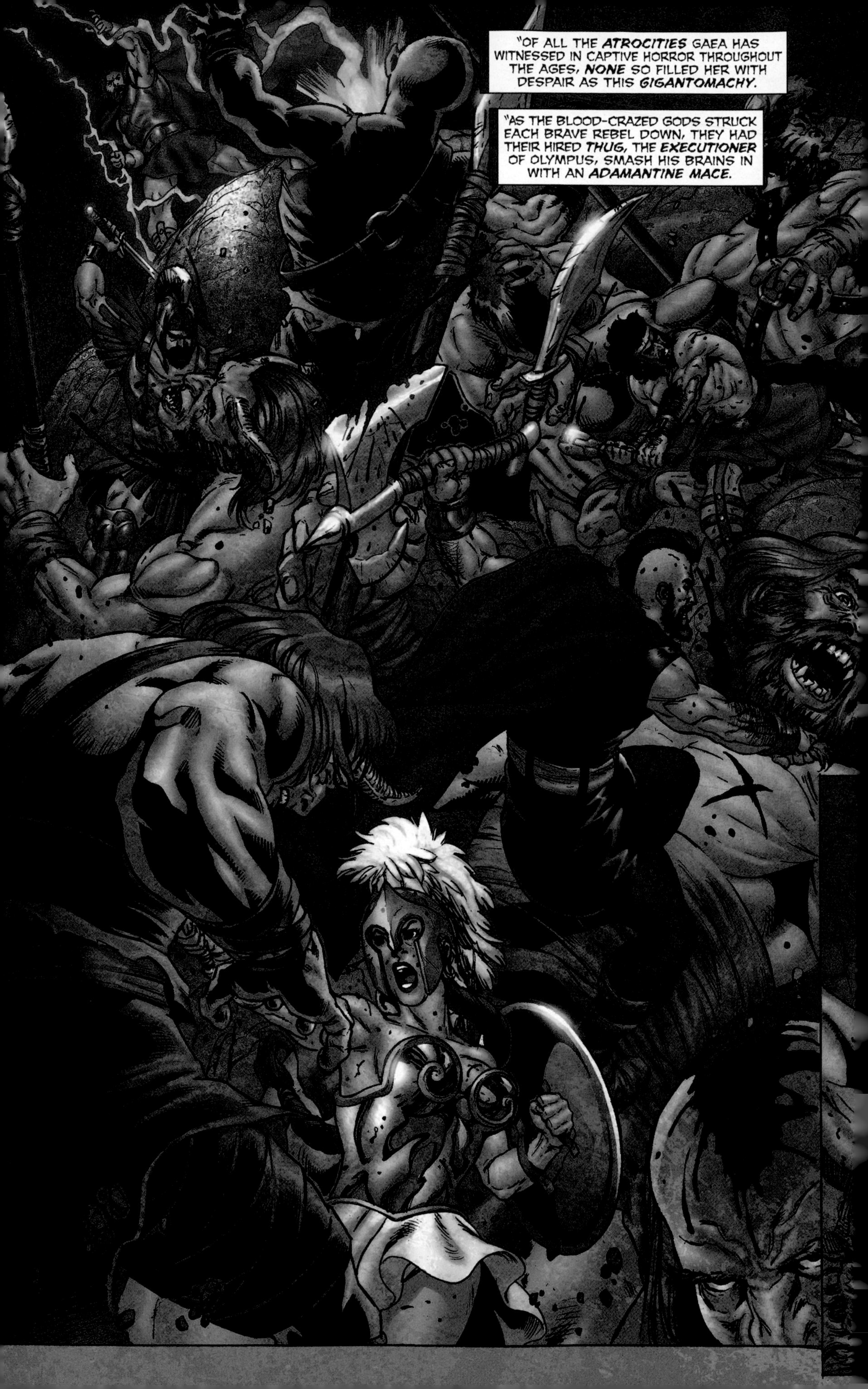
"OF ALL THE ATROCITIES GAEA HAS WITNESSED IN CAPTIVE HORROR THROUGHOUT THE AGES, NONE SO FILLED HER WITH DESPAIR AS THIS GIGANTOMACHY.
"AS THE BLOOD-CRAZED GODS STRUCK EACH BRAVE REBEL DOWN, THEY HAD THEIR HIRED THUG, THE EXECUTIONER OF OLYMPUS, SMASH HIS BRAINS IN WITH AN ADAMANTINE MACE.

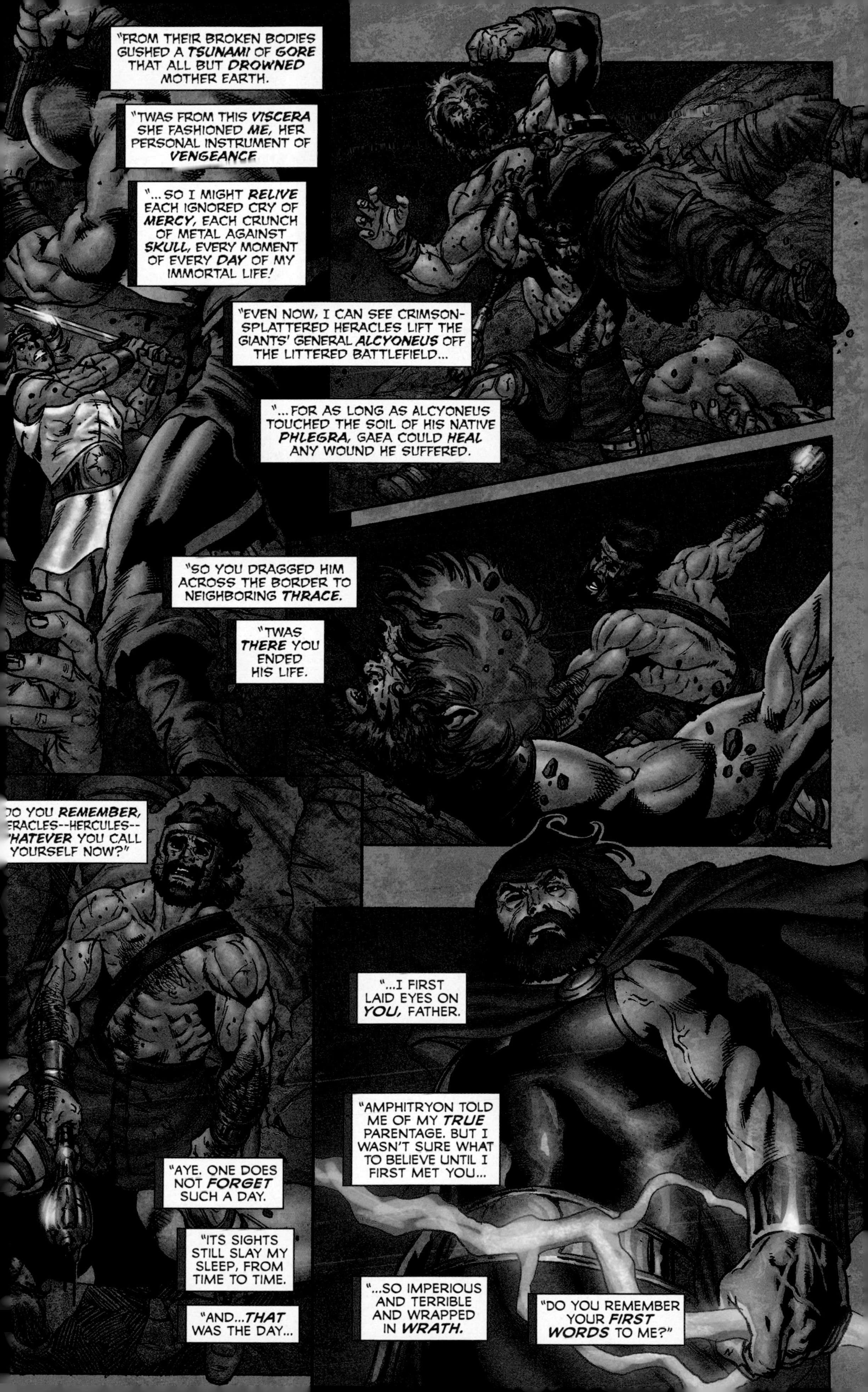
"FROM THEIR BROKEN BODIES GUSHED A TSUNAMI OF GORE THAT ALL BUT DROWNED MOTHER EARTH.
"TWAS FROM THIS VISCERA SHE FASHIONED ME, HER PERSONAL INSTRUMENT OF VENGEANCE
"...SO I MIGHT RELIVE EACH IGNORED CRY OF MERCY, EACH CRUNCH OF METAL AGAINST SKULL, EVERY MOMENT OF EVERY DAY OF MY IMMORTAL LIFE!
"EVEN NOW, I CAN SEE CRIMSON-SPLATTERED HERACLES LIFT THE GIANTS' GENERAL ALCYONEUS OFF THE LITTERED BATTLEFIELD...
"...FOR AS LONG AS ALCYONEUS TOUCHED THE SOIL OF HIS NATIVE PHLEGRA, GAEA COULD HEAL ANY WOUND HE SUFFERED.
"SO YOU DRAGGED HIM ACROSS THE BORDER TO NEIGHBORING THRACE.
"TWAS THERE YOU ENDED HIS LIFE.
DO YOU REMEMBER, ERACLES--HERCULES--HATEVER YOU CALL YOURSELF NOW?"
"AYE. ONE DOES NOT FORGET SUCH A DAY.
"ITS SIGHTS STILL SLAY MY SLEEP, FROM TIME TO TIME.
"AND...THAT WAS THE DAY...
"...I FIRST LAID EYES ON YOU, FATHER.
"AMPHITRYON TOLD ME OF MY TRUE PARENTAGE. BUT I WASN'T SURE WHAT TO BELIEVE UNTIL I FIRST MET YOU...
"...SO IMPERIOUS AND TERRIBLE AND WRAPPED IN WRATH.
"DO YOU REMEMBER YOUR FIRST WORDS TO ME?"

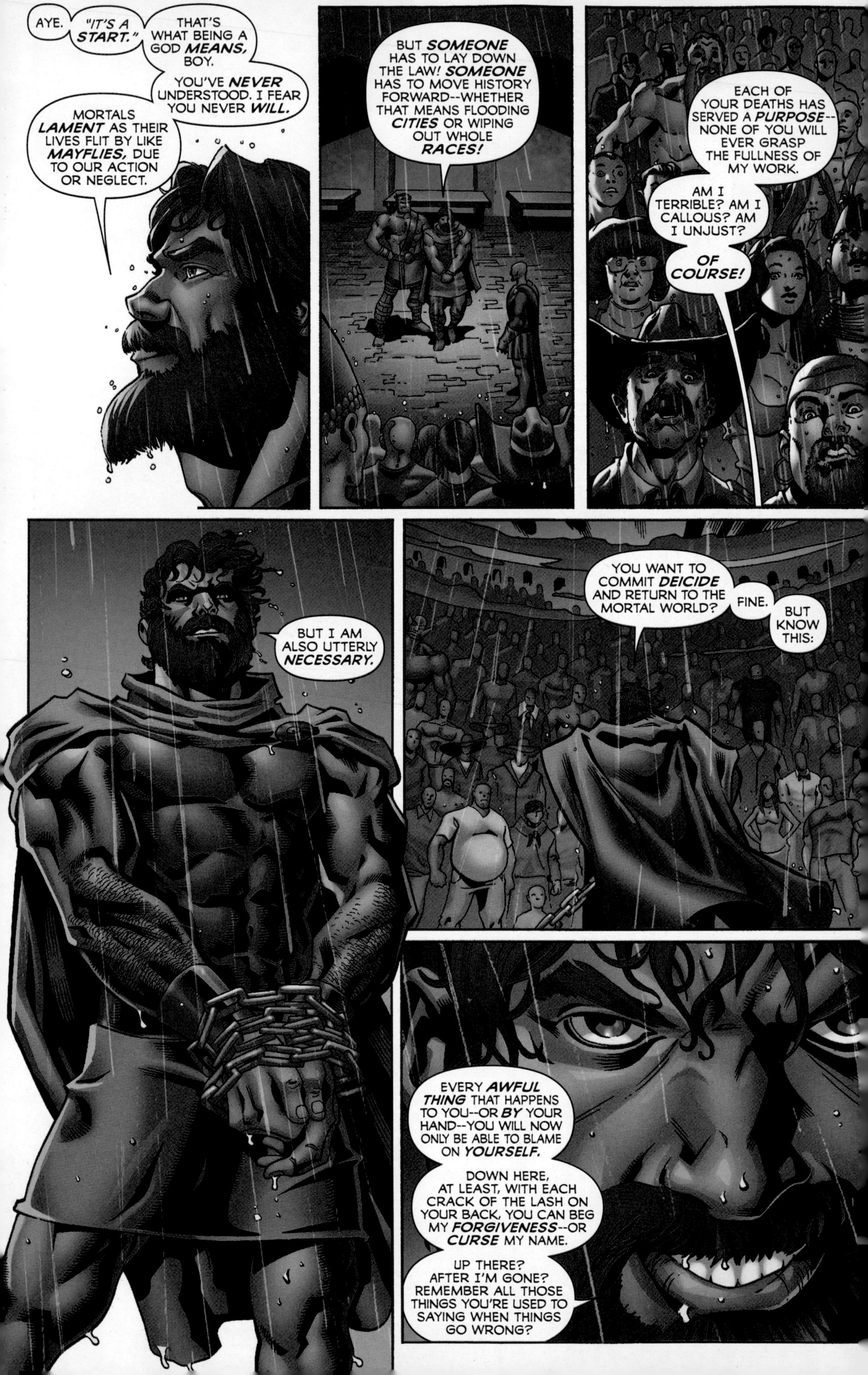
AYE.
"IT'S A START."
THAT'S WHAT BEING A GOD MEANS, BOY.
YOU'VE NEVER UNDERSTOOD. I FEAR YOU NEVER WILL.
MORTALS LAMENT AS THEIR LIVES FLIT BY LIKE MAYFLIES, DUE TO OUR ACTION OR NEGLECT.
BUT SOMEONE HAS TO LAY DOWN THE LAW! SOMEONE HAS TO MOVE HISTORY FORWARD--WHETHER THAT MEANS FLOODING CITIES OR WIPING OUT WHOLE RACES!
EACH OF YOUR DEATHS HAS SERVED A PURPOSE--NONE OF YOU WILL EVER GRASP THE FULLNESS OF MY WORK.
AM I TERRIBLE? AM I CALLOUS? AM I UNJUST?
OF COURSE!
BUT I AM ALSO UTTERLY NECESSARY.
YOU WANT TO COMMIT DEICIDE AND RETURN TO THE MORTAL WORLD?
FINE.
BUT KNOW THIS:
EVERY AWFUL THING THAT HAPPENS TO YOU--OR BY YOUR HAND--YOU WILL NOW ONLY BE ABLE TO BLAME ON YOURSELF.
DOWN HERE, AT LEAST, WITH EACH CRACK OF THE LASH ON YOUR BACK, YOU CAN BEG MY FORGIVENESS--OR CURSE MY NAME.
UP THERE? AFTER I'M GONE? REMEMBER ALL THOSE THINGS YOU'RE USED TO SAYING WHEN THINGS GO WRONG?

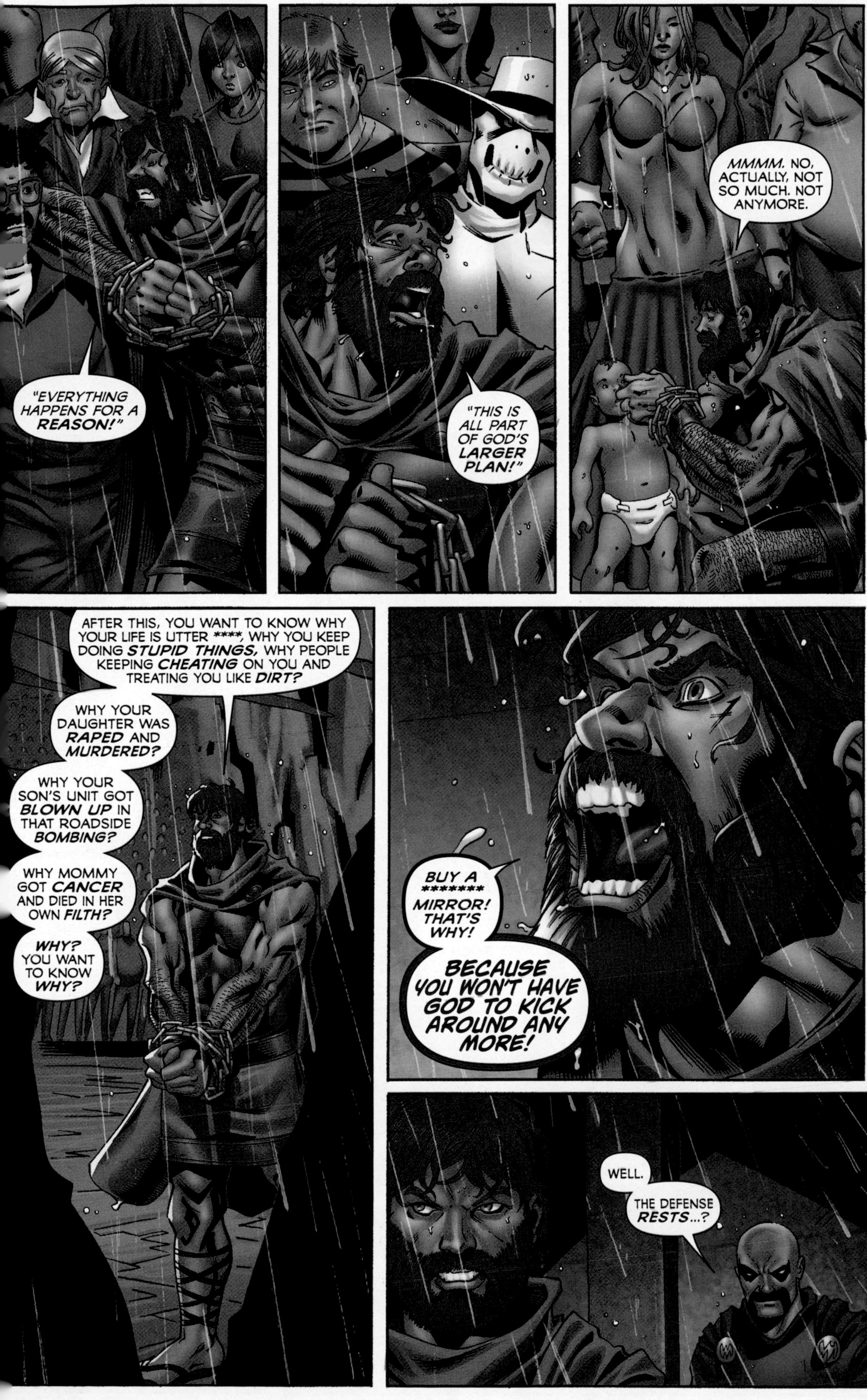
"EVERYTHING HAPPENS FOR A REASON!"
"THIS IS ALL PART OF GOD'S LARGER PLAN!"
MMMM. NO, ACTUALLY, NOT SO MUCH. NOT ANYMORE.
AFTER THIS, YOU WANT TO KNOW WHY YOUR LIFE IS UTTER ****, WHY YOU KEEP DOING STUPID THINGS, WHY PEOPLE KEEPING CHEATING ON YOU AND TREATING YOU LIKE DIRT?
WHY YOUR DAUGHTER WAS RAPED AND MURDERED?
WHY YOUR SON'S UNIT GOT BLOWN UP IN THAT ROADSIDE BOMBING?
WHY MOMMY GOT CANCER AND DIED IN HER OWN FILTH?
WHY? YOU WANT TO KNOW WHY?
BUY A ******* MIRROR! THAT'S WHY!
BECAUSE YOU WON'T HAVE GOD TO KICK AROUND ANY MORE!
WELL.
THE DEFENSE RESTS...?

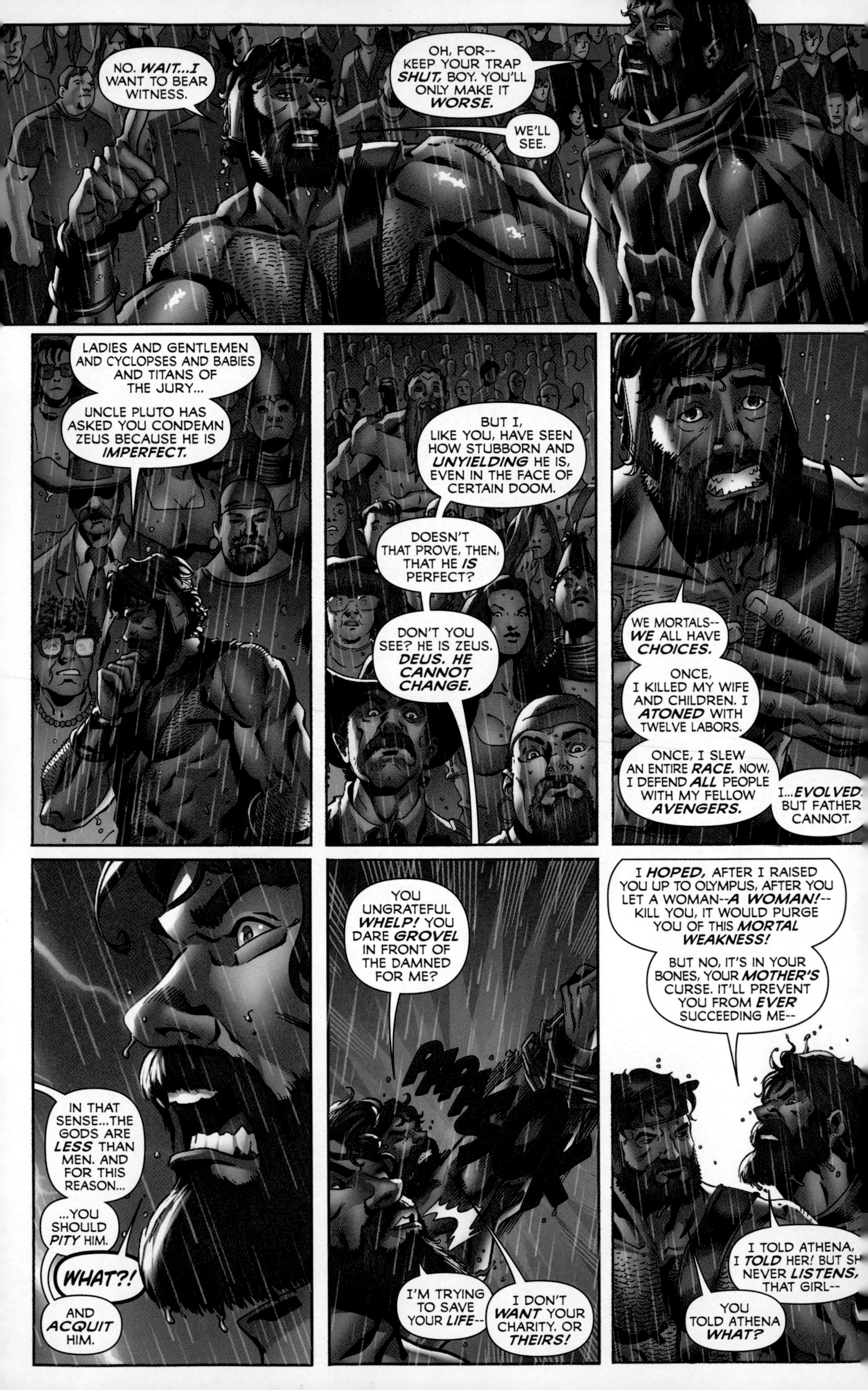

NO. WAIT...I WANT TO BEAR WITNESS.
OH, FOR-- KEEP YOUR TRAP SHUT, BOY. YOU'LL ONLY MAKE IT WORSE.
WE'LL SEE.
LADIES AND GENTLEMEN AND CYCLOPSES AND BABIES AND TITANS OF THE JURY...
UNCLE PLUTO HAS ASKED YOU CONDEMN ZEUS BECAUSE HE IS IMPERFECT.
BUT I, LIKE YOU, HAVE SEEN HOW STUBBORN AND UNYIELDING HE IS, EVEN IN THE FACE OF CERTAIN DOOM.
DOESN'T THAT PROVE, THEN, THAT HE IS PERFECT?
DON'T YOU SEE? HE IS ZEUS. DEUS. HE CANNOT CHANGE.
WE MORTALS-- WE ALL HAVE CHOICES.
ONCE, I KILLED MY WIFE AND CHILDREN. I ATONED WITH TWELVE LABORS.
ONCE, I SLEW AN ENTIRE RACE. NOW, I DEFEND ALL PEOPLE WITH MY FELLOW AVENGERS.
I...EVOLVED. BUT FATHER CANNOT.
IN THAT SENSE...THE GODS ARE LESS THAN MEN. AND FOR THIS REASON...
...YOU SHOULD PITY HIM.
WHAT?!
AND ACQUIT HIM.
YOU UNGRATEFUL WHELP! YOU DARE GROVEL IN FRONT OF THE DAMNED FOR ME?
PAPAKOOM
I'M TRYING TO SAVE YOUR LIFE--
I DON'T WANT YOUR CHARITY. OR THEIRS!
I HOPED, AFTER I RAISED YOU UP TO OLYMPUS, AFTER YOU LET A WOMAN--A WOMAN!-- KILL YOU, IT WOULD PURGE YOU OF THIS MORTAL WEAKNESS!
BUT NO, IT'S IN YOUR BONES, YOUR MOTHER'S CURSE. IT'LL PREVENT YOU FROM EVER SUCCEEDING ME--
I TOLD ATHENA, I TOLD HER! BUT SH NEVER LISTENS, THAT GIRL--
YOU TOLD ATHENA WHAT?

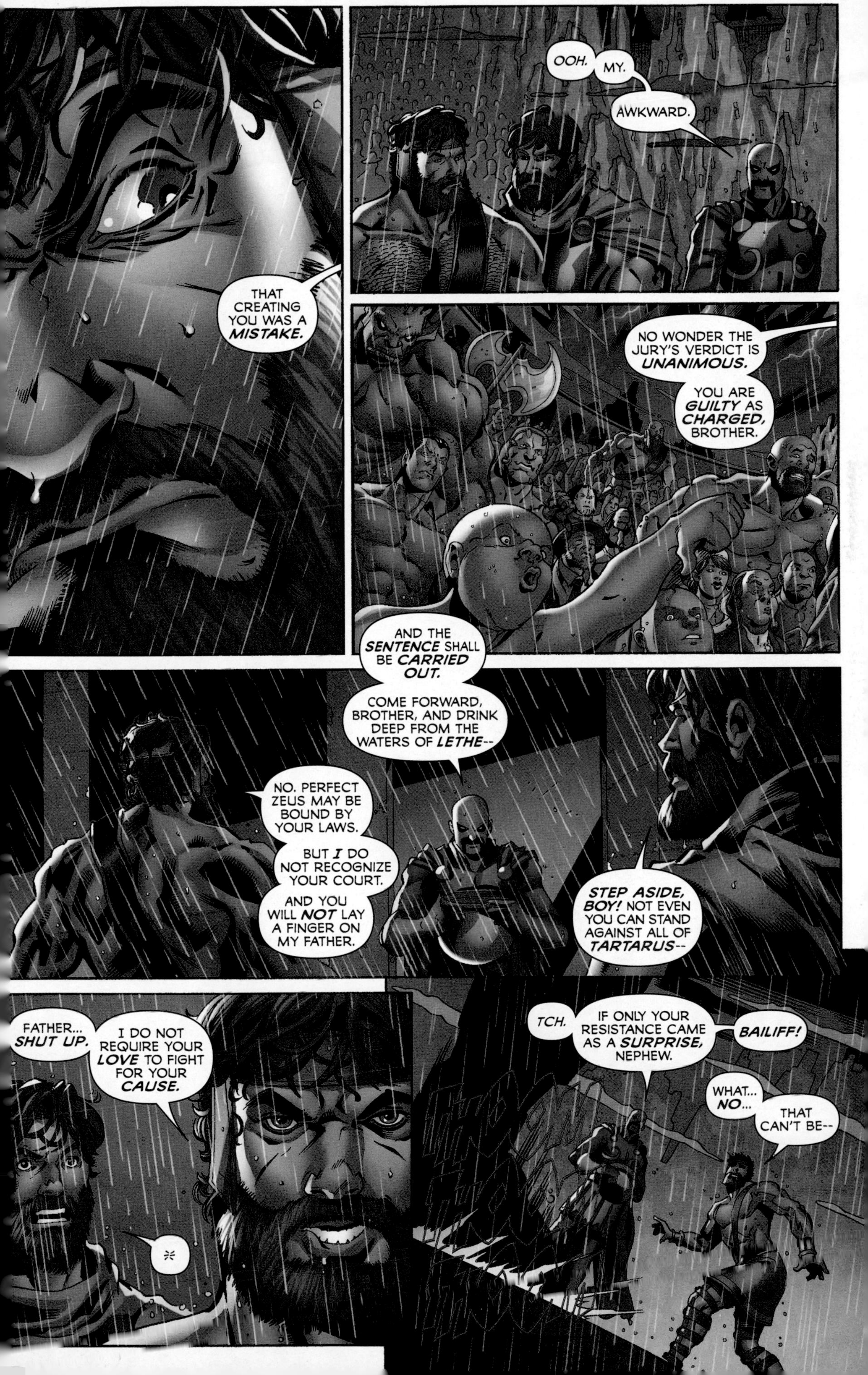
THAT CREATING YOU WAS A MISTAKE.
OOH.
MY.
AWKWARD.
NO WONDER THE JURY'S VERDICT IS UNANIMOUS.
YOU ARE GUILTY AS CHARGED, BROTHER.
AND THE SENTENCE SHALL BE CARRIED OUT.
COME FORWARD, BROTHER, AND DRINK DEEP FROM THE WATERS OF LETHE--
NO. PERFECT ZEUS MAY BE BOUND BY YOUR LAWS.
BUT I DO NOT RECOGNIZE YOUR COURT.
AND YOU WILL NOT LAY A FINGER ON MY FATHER.
STEP ASIDE, BOY! NOT EVEN YOU CAN STAND AGAINST ALL OF TARTARUS--
FATHER... SHUT UP.
I DO NOT REQUIRE YOUR LOVE TO FIGHT FOR YOUR CAUSE.
TCH.
IF ONLY YOUR RESISTANCE CAME AS A SURPRISE, NEPHEW.
BAILIFF!
WHAT... NO...
THAT CAN'T BE--

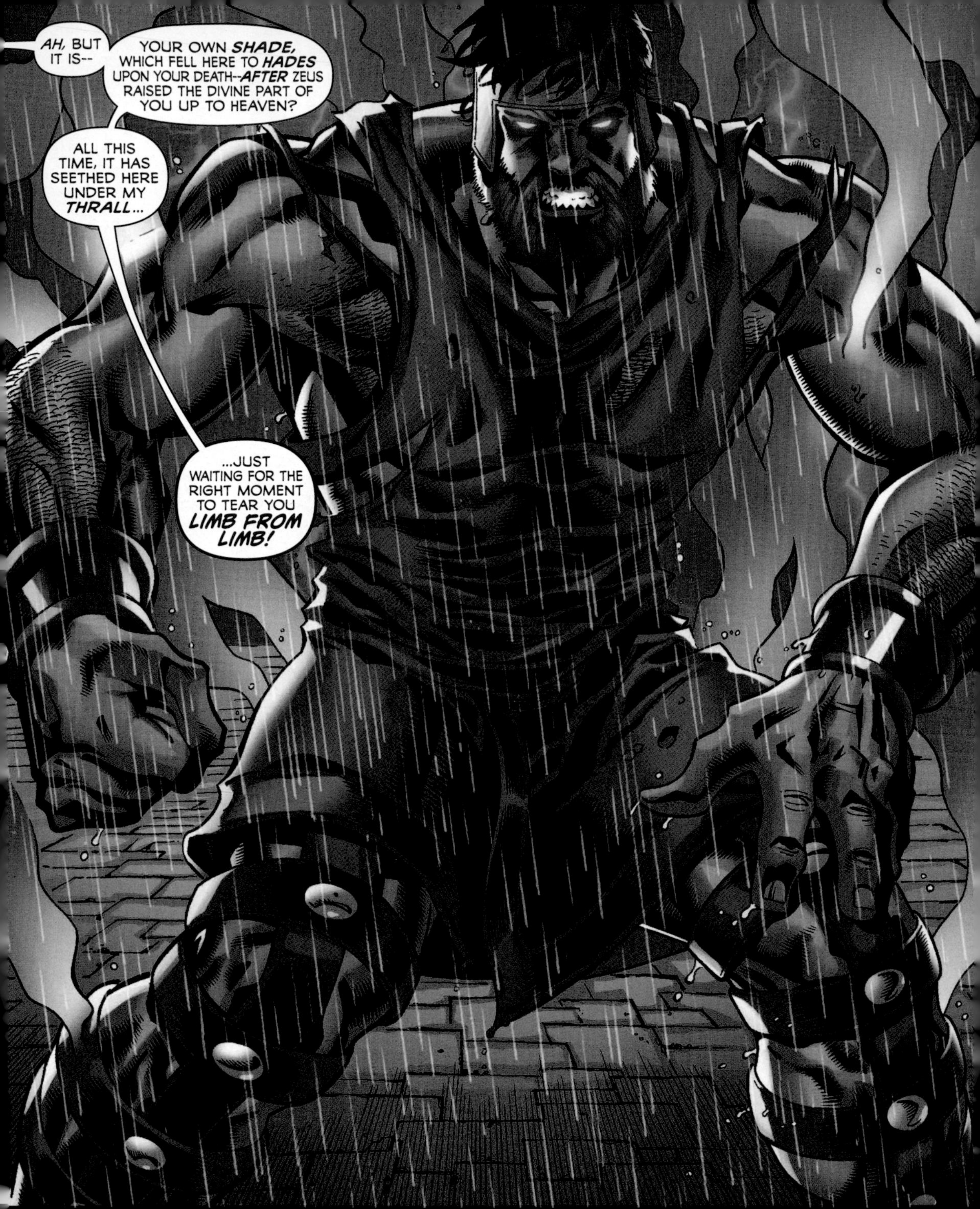
AH, BUT IT IS--
YOUR OWN SHADE, WHICH FELL HERE TO HADES UPON YOUR DEATH--AFTER ZEUS RAISED THE DIVINE PART OF YOU UP TO HEAVEN?
ALL THIS TIME, IT HAS SEETHED HERE UNDER MY THRALL...
...JUST WAITING FOR THE RIGHT MOMENT TO TEAR YOU LIMB FROM LIMB!

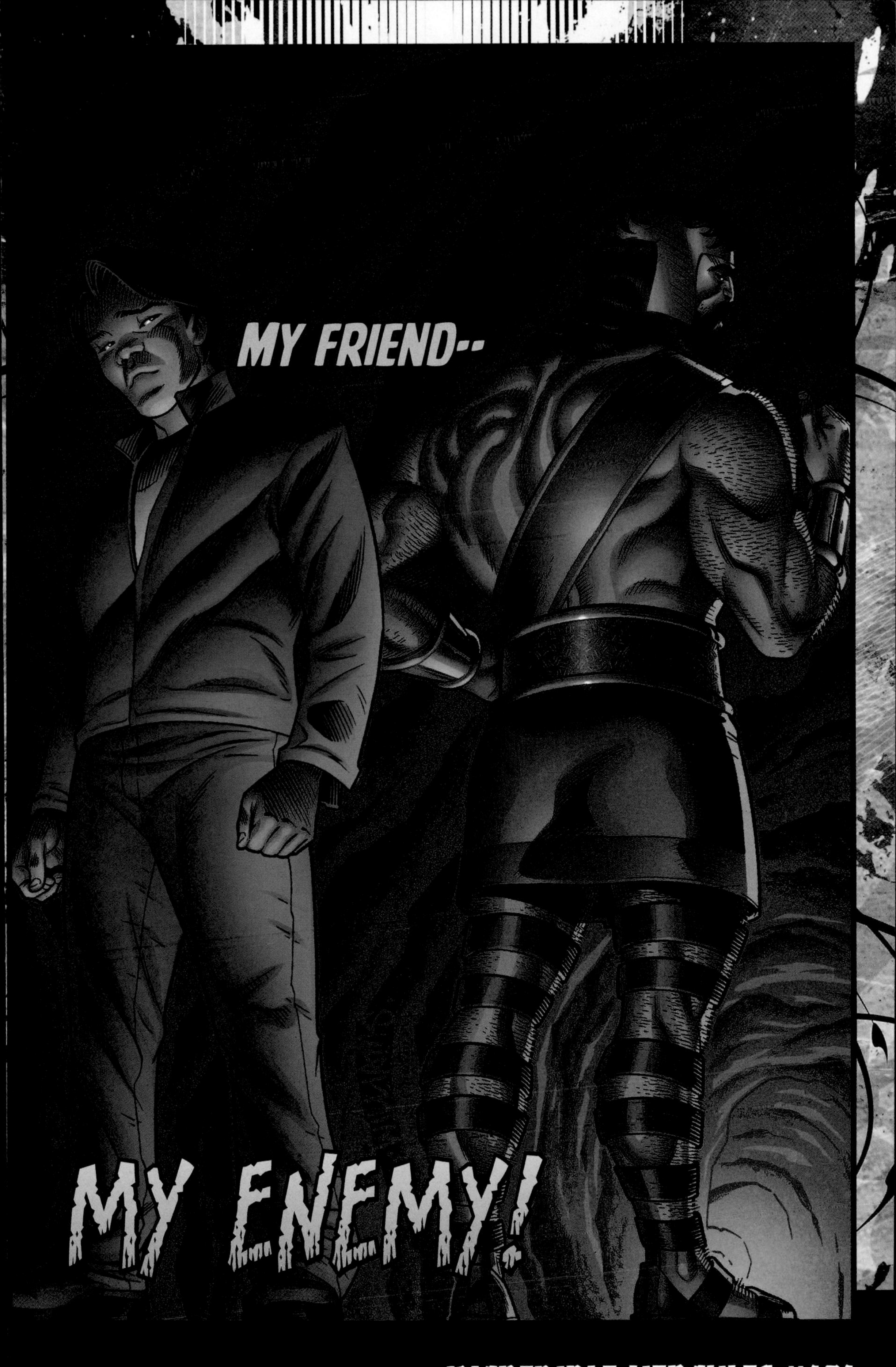
MY FRIEND--
MY ENEMY!

INCREDIBLE HERCULES #131

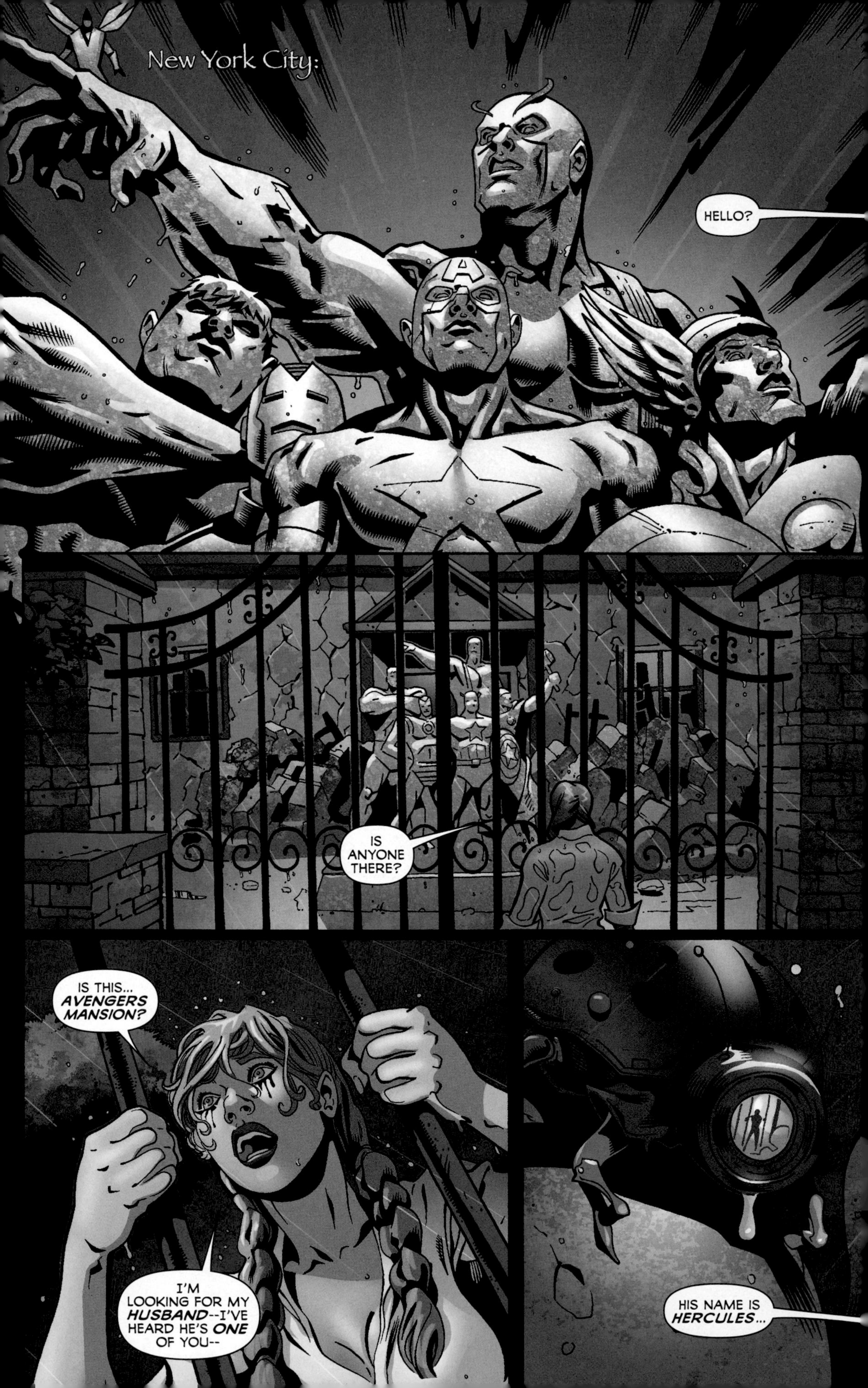
New York City:
HELLO?
IS ANYONE THERE?
IS THIS... AVENGERS MANSION?
I'M LOOKING FOR MY HUSBAND--I'VE HEARD HE'S ONE OF YOU--
HIS NAME IS HERCULES...

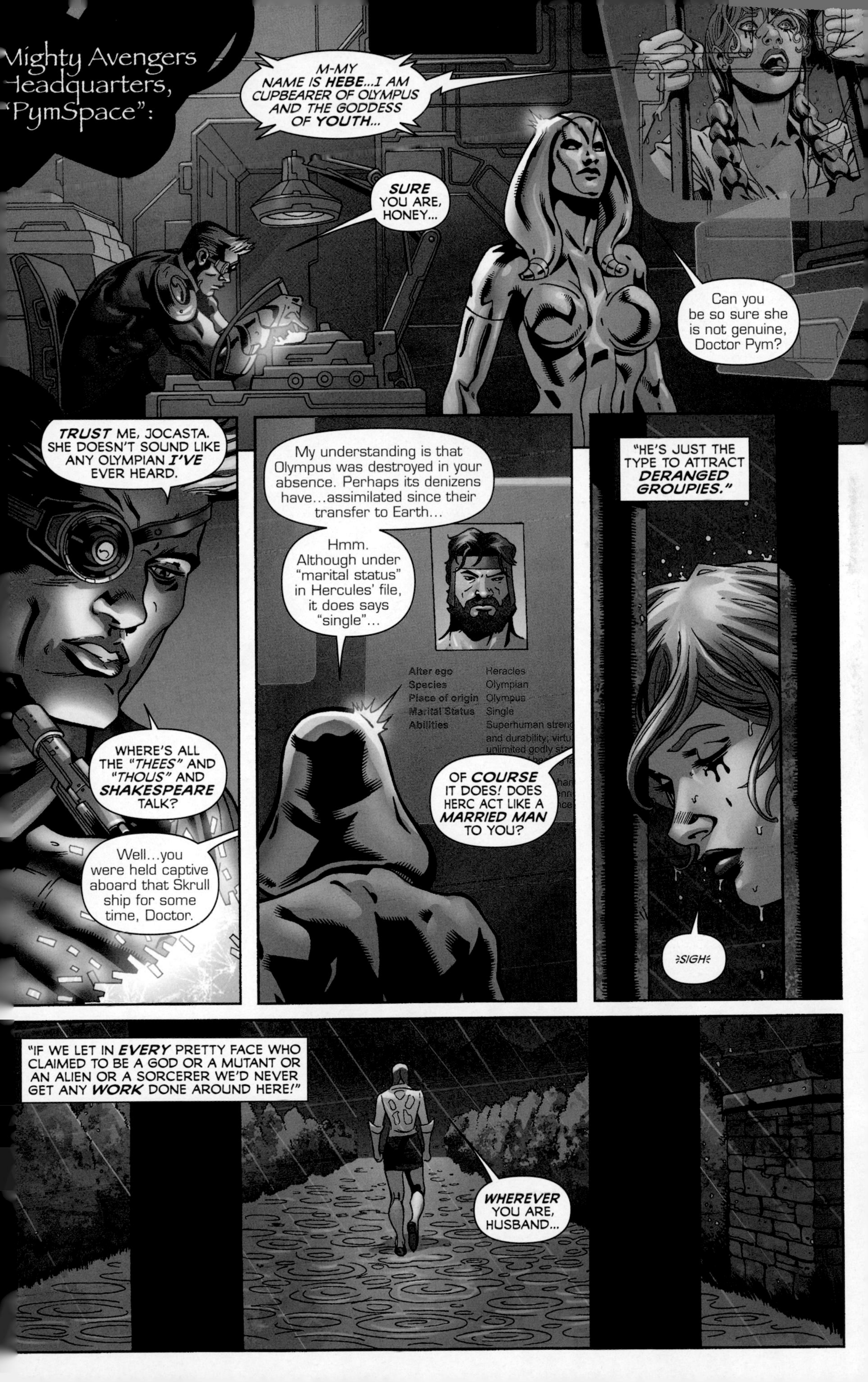
Mighty Avengers Headquarters, "PymSpace":
M-MY NAME IS HEBE...I AM CUPBEARER OF OLYMPUS AND THE GODDESS OF YOUTH...
SURE YOU ARE, HONEY...
Can you be so sure she is not genuine, Doctor Pym?
TRUST ME, JOCASTA. SHE DOESN'T SOUND LIKE ANY OLYMPIAN I'VE EVER HEARD.
WHERE'S ALL THE "THEES" AND "THOUS" AND SHAKESPEARE TALK?
Well...you were held captive aboard that Skrull ship for some time, Doctor.
My understanding is that Olympus was destroyed in your absence. Perhaps its denizens have...assimilated since their transfer to Earth...
Hmm. Although under "marital status" in Hercules' file, it does says "single"...
Alter ego Heracles
Species Olympian
Place of origin Olympus
Marital Status Single
Abilities Superhuman streng
OF COURSE IT DOES! DOES HERC ACT LIKE A MARRIED MAN TO YOU?
"HE'S JUST THE TYPE TO ATTRACT DERANGED GROUPIES."
SIGH
"IF WE LET IN EVERY PRETTY FACE WHO CLAIMED TO BE A GOD OR A MUTANT OR AN ALIEN OR A SORCERER WE'D NEVER GET ANY WORK DONE AROUND HERE!"
WHEREVER YOU ARE, HUSBAND...

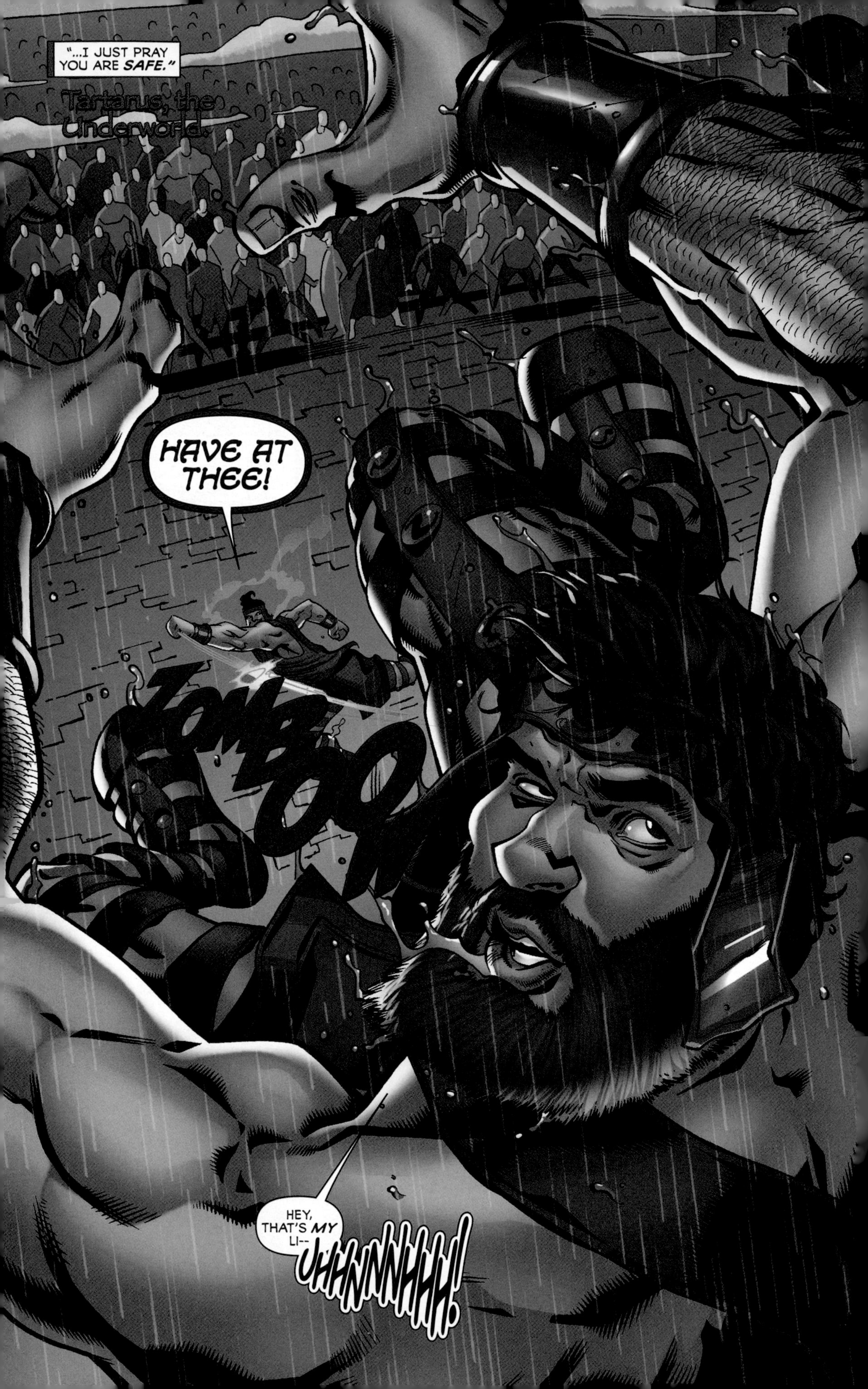
"...I JUST PRAY YOU ARE SAFE."
Tartarus, the Underworld.
HAVE AT THEE!
ZOWOOM
HEY, THAT'S MY LI--
UHHNNHHH!

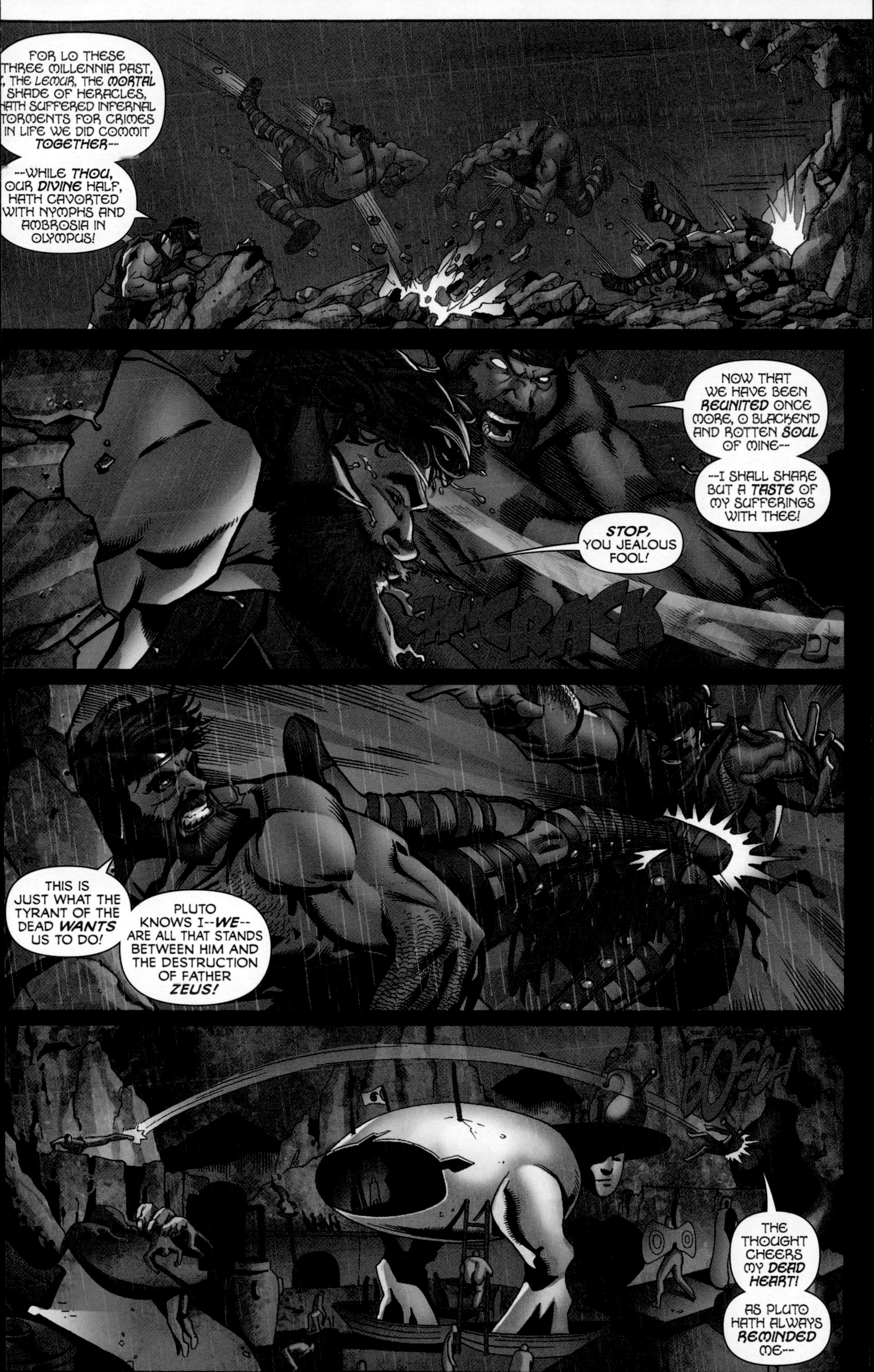
FOR LO THESE THREE MILLENNIA PAST, I, THE LEMUR, THE MORTAL SHADE OF HERACLES, HATH SUFFERED INFERNAL TORMENTS FOR CRIMES IN LIFE WE DID COMMIT TOGETHER--
--WHILE THOU, OUR DIVINE HALF, HATH CAVORTED WITH NYMPHS AND AMBROSIA IN OLYMPUS!
NOW THAT WE HAVE BEEN REUNITED ONCE MORE, O BLACKEN'D AND ROTTEN SOUL OF MINE--
--I SHALL SHARE BUT A TASTE OF MY SUFFERINGS WITH THEE!
STOP, YOU JEALOUS FOOL!
THIS IS JUST WHAT THE TYRANT OF THE DEAD WANTS US TO DO!
PLUTO KNOWS I--WE--ARE ALL THAT STANDS BETWEEN HIM AND THE DESTRUCTION OF FATHER ZEUS!
BOOSH
THE THOUGHT CHEERS MY DEAD HEART!
AS PLUTO HATH ALWAYS REMINDED ME--

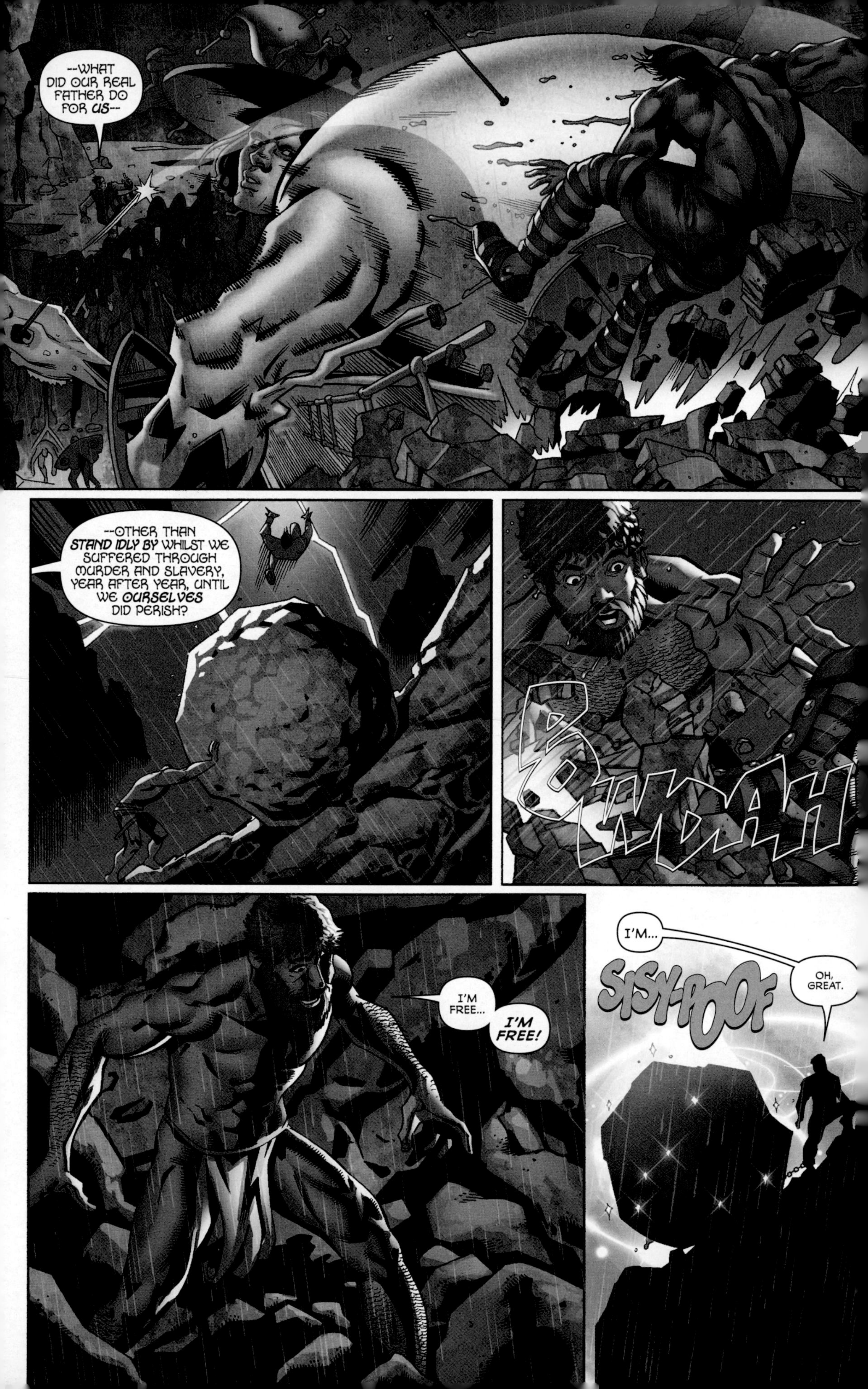
--WHAT DID OUR REAL FATHER DO FOR US--
--OTHER THAN STAND IDLY BY WHILST WE SUFFERED THROUGH MURDER AND SLAVERY, YEAR AFTER YEAR, UNTIL WE OURSELVES DID PERISH?
BWDAH
I'M FREE...
I'M FREE!
I'M...
SISY-POOF
OH, GREAT.

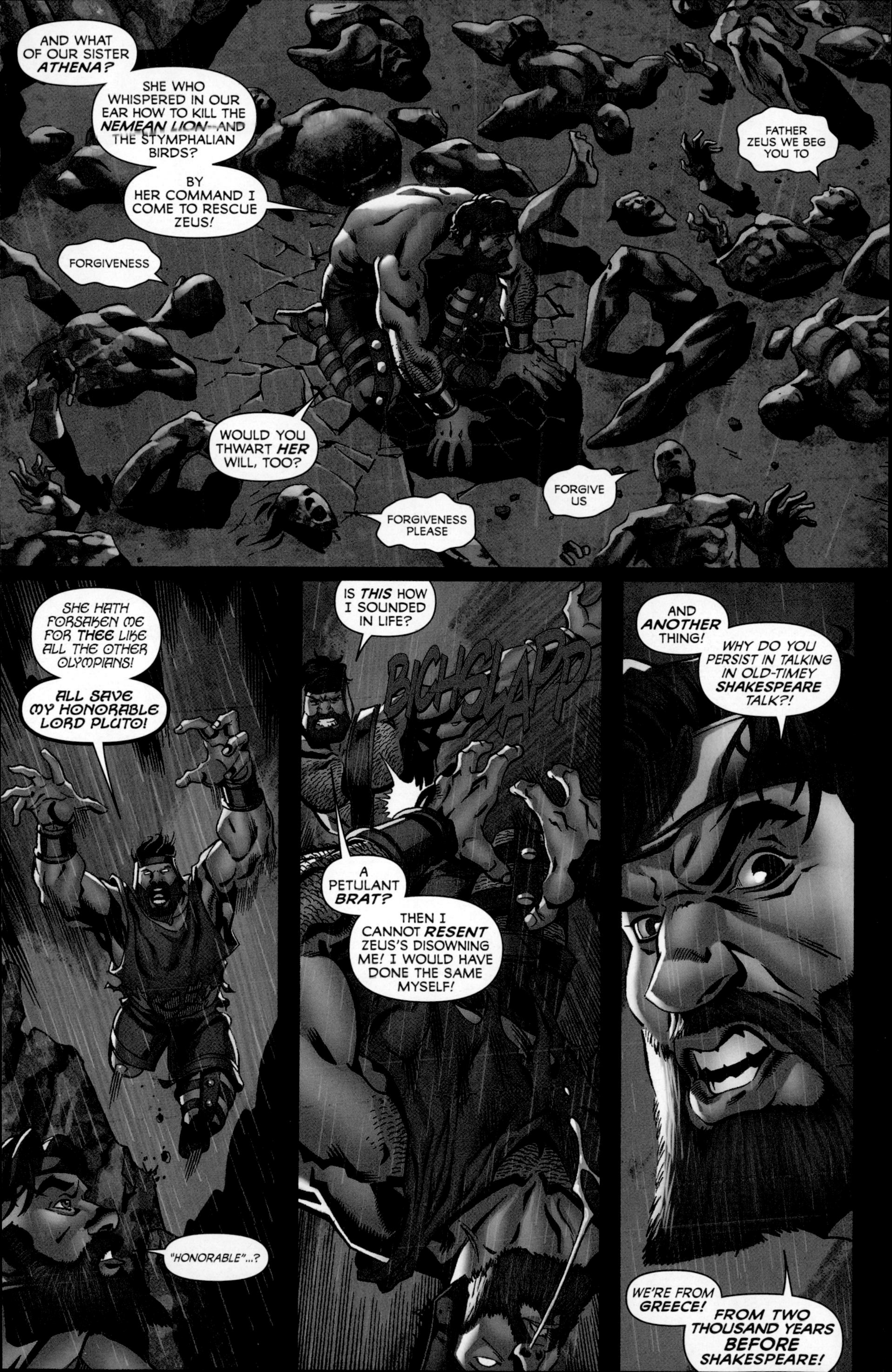
AND WHAT OF OUR SISTER ATHENA?
SHE WHO WHISPERED IN OUR EAR HOW TO KILL THE NEMEAN LION--AND THE STYMPHALIAN BIRDS?
BY HER COMMAND I COME TO RESCUE ZEUS!
FATHER ZEUS WE BEG YOU TO
FORGIVENESS
WOULD YOU THWART HER WILL, TOO?
FORGIVE US
FORGIVENESS PLEASE
SHE HATH FORSAKEN ME FOR THEE LIKE ALL THE OTHER OLYMPIANS!
ALL SAVE MY HONORABLE LORD PLUTO!
"HONORABLE"...?
IS THIS HOW I SOUNDED IN LIFE?
BICHSLAPP
A PETULANT BRAT?
THEN I CANNOT RESENT ZEUS'S DISOWNING ME! I WOULD HAVE DONE THE SAME MYSELF!
AND ANOTHER THING!
WHY DO YOU PERSIST IN TALKING IN OLD-TIMEY SHAKESPEARE TALK?!
WE'RE FROM GREECE!
FROM TWO THOUSAND YEARS BEFORE SHAKESPEARE!

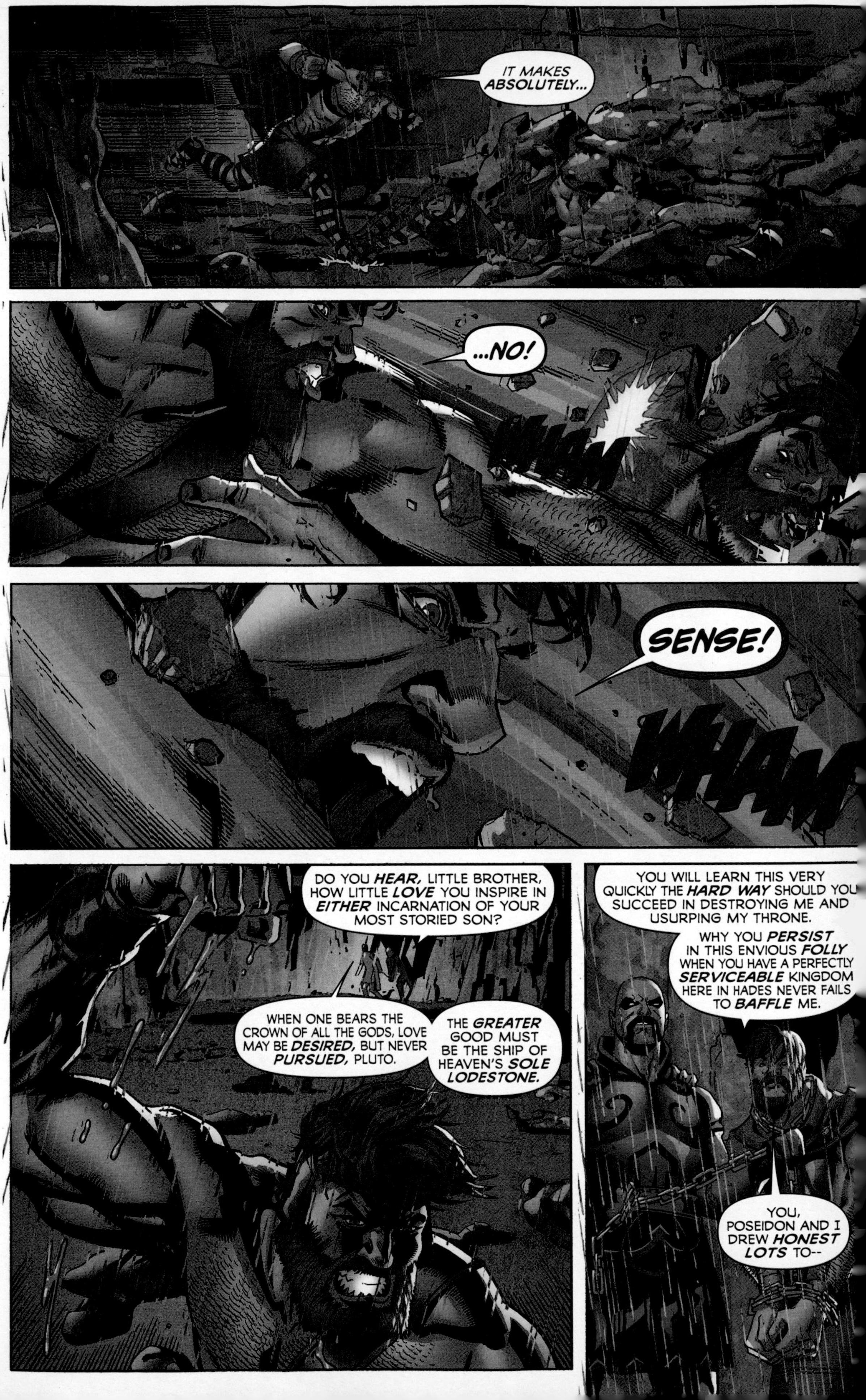
IT MAKES ABSOLUTELY...
...NO!
WHAM
SENSE!
WHAM
DO YOU HEAR, LITTLE BROTHER, HOW LITTLE LOVE YOU INSPIRE IN EITHER INCARNATION OF YOUR MOST STORIED SON?
WHEN ONE BEARS THE CROWN OF ALL THE GODS, LOVE MAY BE DESIRED, BUT NEVER PURSUED, PLUTO.
THE GREATER GOOD MUST BE THE SHIP OF HEAVEN'S SOLE LODESTONE.
YOU WILL LEARN THIS VERY QUICKLY THE HARD WAY SHOULD YOU SUCCEED IN DESTROYING ME AND USURPING MY THRONE.
WHY YOU PERSIST IN THIS ENVIOUS FOLLY WHEN YOU HAVE A PERFECTLY SERVICEABLE KINGDOM HERE IN HADES NEVER FAILS TO BAFFLE ME.
YOU, POSEIDON AND I DREW HONEST LOTS TO--

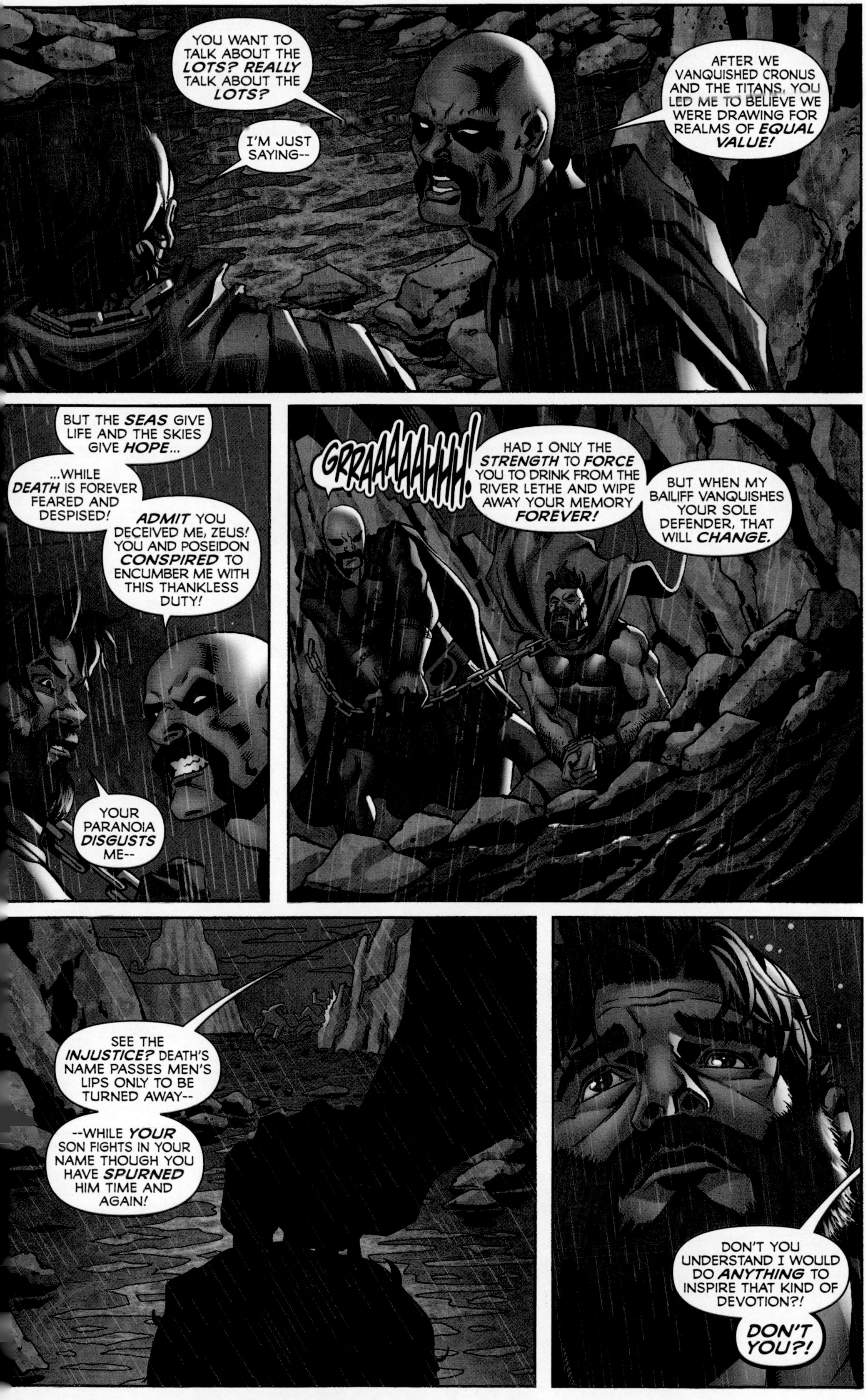
YOU WANT TO TALK ABOUT THE LOTS? REALLY TALK ABOUT THE LOTS?
I'M JUST SAYING--
AFTER WE VANQUISHED CRONUS AND THE TITANS, YOU LED ME TO BELIEVE WE WERE DRAWING FOR REALMS OF EQUAL VALUE!
BUT THE SEAS GIVE LIFE AND THE SKIES GIVE HOPE...
...WHILE DEATH IS FOREVER FEARED AND DESPISED!
ADMIT YOU DECEIVED ME, ZEUS! YOU AND POSEIDON CONSPIRED TO ENCUMBER ME WITH THIS THANKLESS DUTY!
YOUR PARANOIA DISGUSTS ME--
GRRAAAAAHHH!
HAD I ONLY THE STRENGTH TO FORCE YOU TO DRINK FROM THE RIVER LETHE AND WIPE AWAY YOUR MEMORY FOREVER!
BUT WHEN MY BAILIFF VANQUISHES YOUR SOLE DEFENDER, THAT WILL CHANGE.
SEE THE INJUSTICE? DEATH'S NAME PASSES MEN'S LIPS ONLY TO BE TURNED AWAY--
--WHILE YOUR SON FIGHTS IN YOUR NAME THOUGH YOU HAVE SPURNED HIM TIME AND AGAIN!
DON'T YOU UNDERSTAND I WOULD DO ANYTHING TO INSPIRE THAT KIND OF DEVOTION?!
DON'T YOU?!

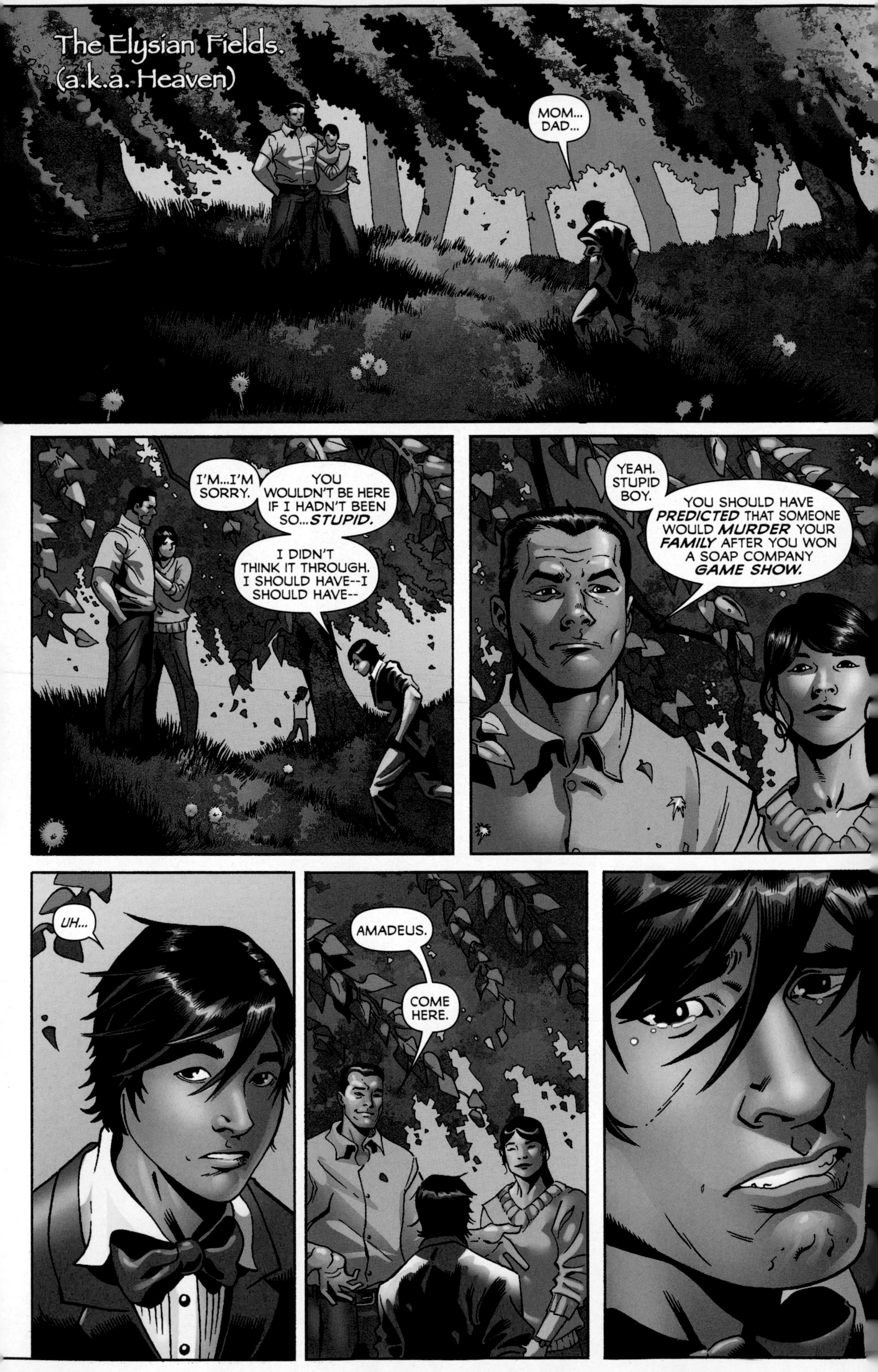
The Elysian Fields.
(a.k.a. Heaven)
MOM... DAD...
I'M...I'M SORRY.
YOU WOULDN'T BE HERE IF I HADN'T BEEN SO...STUPID.
I DIDN'T THINK IT THROUGH. I SHOULD HAVE--I SHOULD HAVE--
YEAH. STUPID BOY.
YOU SHOULD HAVE PREDICTED THAT SOMEONE WOULD MURDER YOUR FAMILY AFTER YOU WON A SOAP COMPANY GAME SHOW.
UH...
AMADEUS.
COME HERE.

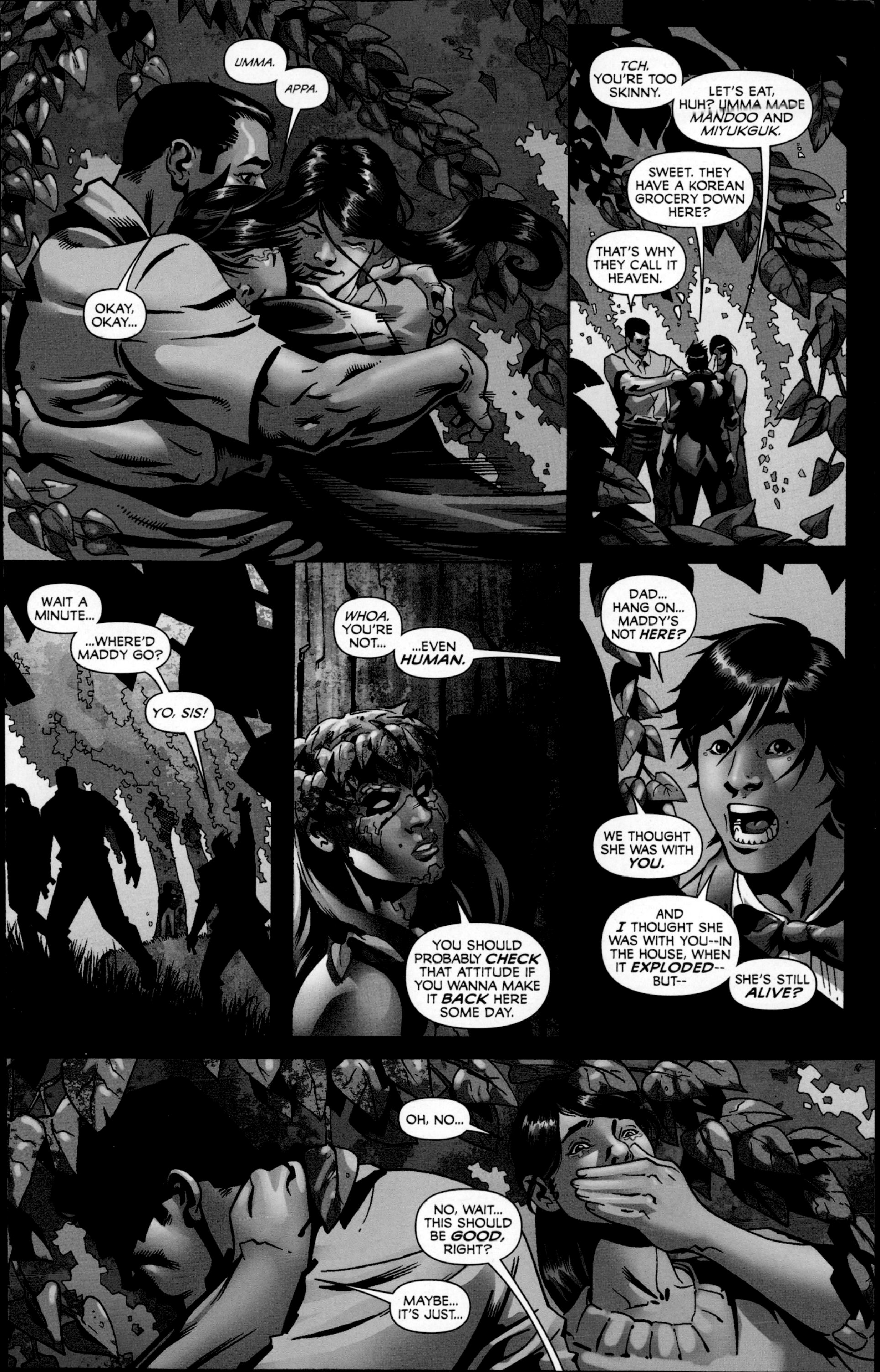
UMMA.
APPA.
OKAY, OKAY...
TCH. YOU'RE TOO SKINNY.
LET'S EAT, HUH? UMMA MADE MANDOO AND MIYUKGUK.
SWEET. THEY HAVE A KOREAN GROCERY DOWN HERE?
THAT'S WHY THEY CALL IT HEAVEN.
WAIT A MINUTE...
...WHERE'D MADDY GO?
YO, SIS!
WHOA. YOU'RE NOT...
...EVEN HUMAN.
YOU SHOULD PROBABLY CHECK THAT ATTITUDE IF YOU WANNA MAKE IT BACK HERE SOME DAY.
DAD... HANG ON... MADDY'S NOT HERE?
WE THOUGHT SHE WAS WITH YOU.
AND I THOUGHT SHE WAS WITH YOU--IN THE HOUSE, WHEN IT EXPLODED-- BUT--
SHE'S STILL ALIVE?
OH, NO...
NO, WAIT... THIS SHOULD BE GOOD, RIGHT?
MAYBE... IT'S JUST...

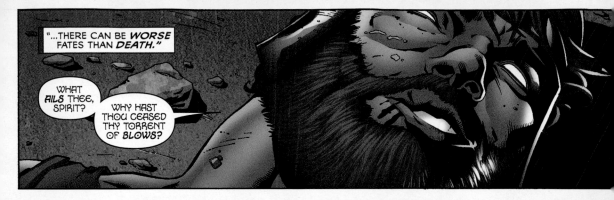

"...THERE CAN BE *WORSE* FATES THAN *DEATH.*"

WHAT *AILS* THEE, SPIRIT?

WHY HAST THOU CEASED THY TORRENT OF *BLOWS?*

JUST... CATCHING MY BREATH...

DOST THOU *TIRE?* GOD THOUGH THOU MAYEST *BE,* FATIGUE STILL *BEDEVILS* THEE.

WHILE A *DEAD MAN* SUCH AS I IS *BEYOND* SUCH BURDENS!

I HAVE ABSORBED *PUNISHMENT* FOR EVERY WAKING MOMENT FOR *MILLENNIA*--

--NOT *WASTED* MY IMMORTAL LIFE IN DIVINE *BACCHANALS!*

IXION

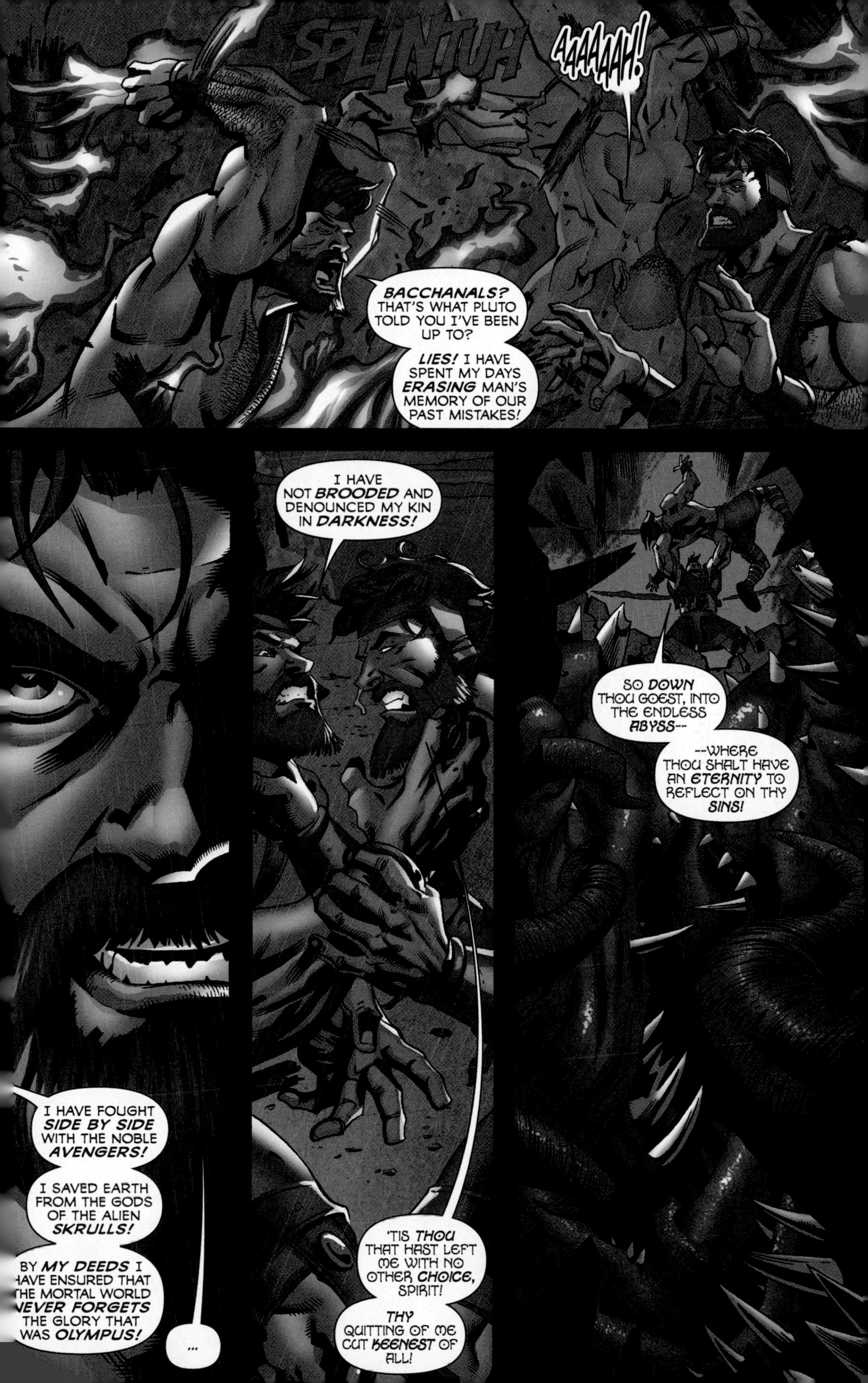
SPLINTUH
AAAAAAH!
BACCHANALS? THAT'S WHAT PLUTO TOLD YOU I'VE BEEN UP TO?
LIES! I HAVE SPENT MY DAYS ERASING MAN'S MEMORY OF OUR PAST MISTAKES!
I HAVE FOUGHT SIDE BY SIDE WITH THE NOBLE AVENGERS!
I SAVED EARTH FROM THE GODS OF THE ALIEN SKRULLS!
BY MY DEEDS I HAVE ENSURED THAT THE MORTAL WORLD NEVER FORGETS THE GLORY THAT WAS OLYMPUS!
...
I HAVE NOT BROODED AND DENOUNCED MY KIN IN DARKNESS!
'TIS THOU THAT HAST LEFT ME WITH NO OTHER CHOICE, SPIRIT!
THY QUITTING OF ME CUT KEENEST OF ALL!
SO DOWN THOU GOEST, INTO THE ENDLESS ABYSS--
--WHERE THOU SHALT HAVE AN ETERNITY TO REFLECT ON THY SINS!

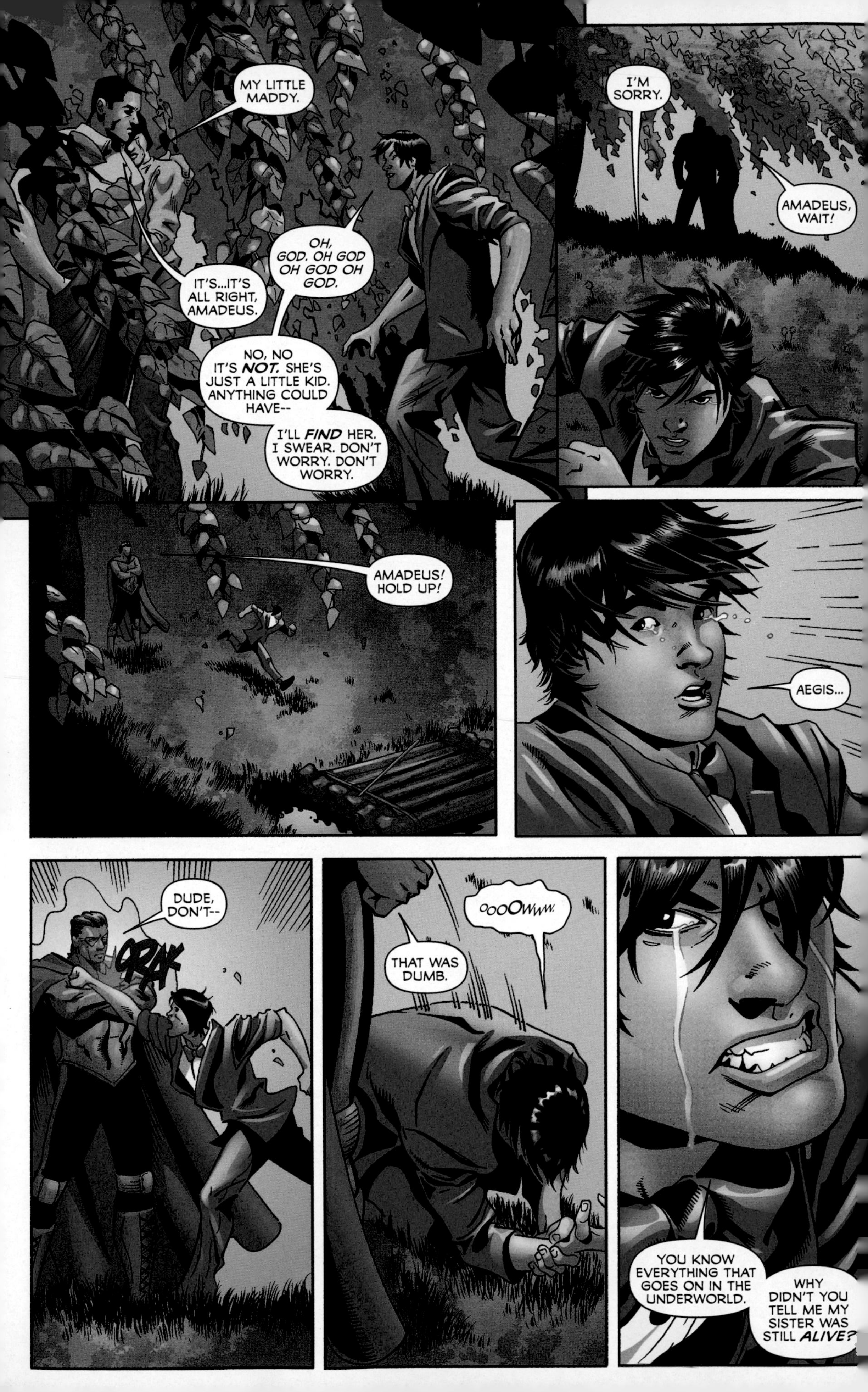
MY LITTLE MADDY.
OH, GOD. OH GOD OH GOD OH GOD.
IT'S...IT'S ALL RIGHT, AMADEUS.
NO, NO IT'S NOT. SHE'S JUST A LITTLE KID. ANYTHING COULD HAVE--
I'LL FIND HER. I SWEAR. DON'T WORRY. DON'T WORRY.
I'M SORRY.
AMADEUS, WAIT!
AMADEUS! HOLD UP!
AEGIS...
DUDE, DON'T--
KRAK
OOOOWWW.
THAT WAS DUMB.
YOU KNOW EVERYTHING THAT GOES ON IN THE UNDERWORLD.
WHY DIDN'T YOU TELL ME MY SISTER WAS STILL ALIVE?

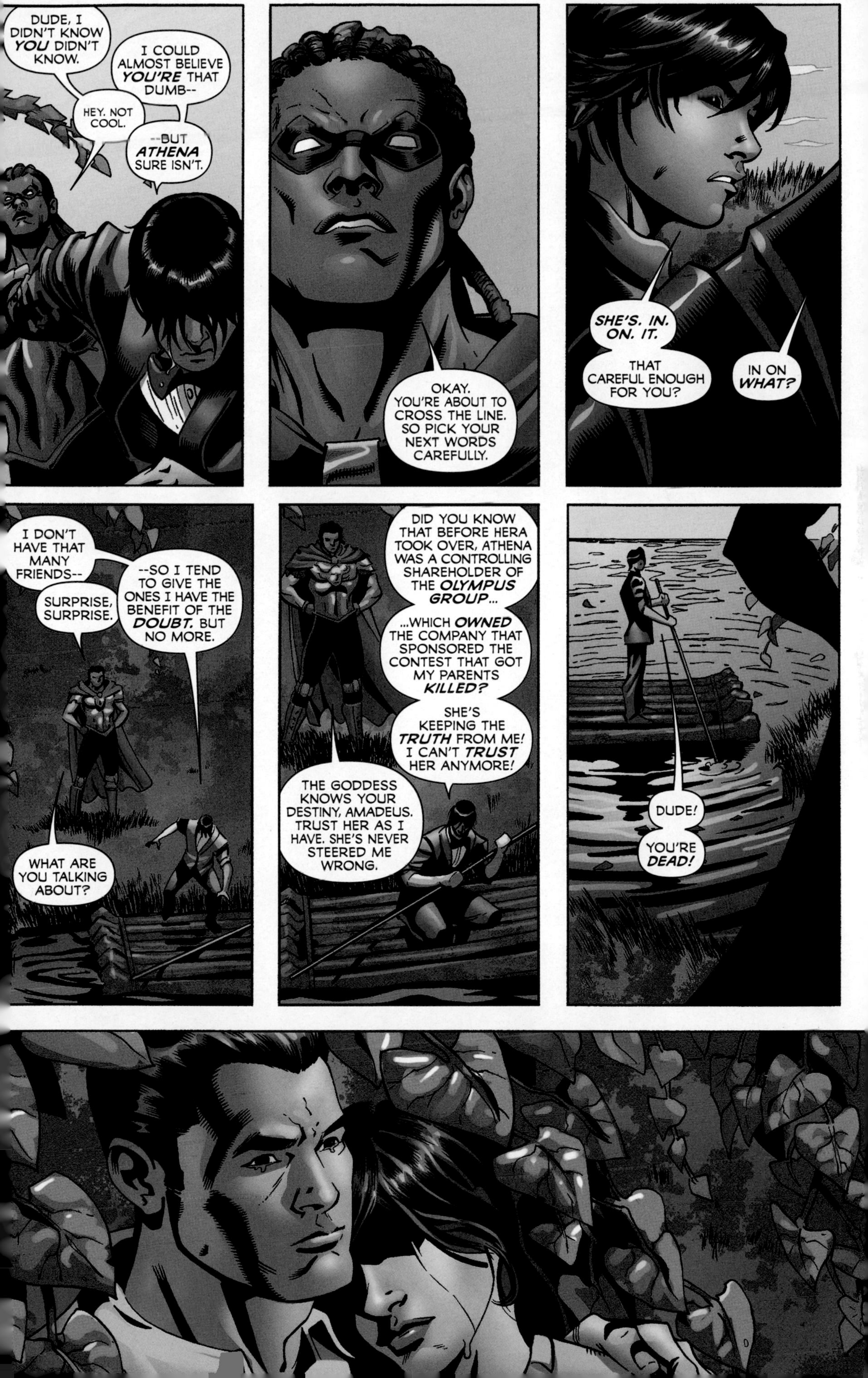
DUDE, I DIDN'T KNOW *YOU* DIDN'T KNOW.
I COULD ALMOST BELIEVE *YOU'RE* THAT DUMB--
HEY. NOT COOL.
--BUT *ATHENA* SURE ISN'T.
OKAY. YOU'RE ABOUT TO CROSS THE LINE. SO PICK YOUR NEXT WORDS CAREFULLY.
SHE'S. IN. ON. IT.
THAT CAREFUL ENOUGH FOR YOU?
IN ON *WHAT?*
I DON'T HAVE THAT MANY FRIENDS--
SURPRISE, SURPRISE.
--SO I TEND TO GIVE THE ONES I HAVE THE BENEFIT OF THE *DOUBT.* BUT NO MORE.
WHAT ARE YOU TALKING ABOUT?
DID YOU KNOW THAT BEFORE HERA TOOK OVER, ATHENA WAS A CONTROLLING SHAREHOLDER OF THE *OLYMPUS GROUP*...
...WHICH *OWNED* THE COMPANY THAT SPONSORED THE CONTEST THAT GOT MY PARENTS *KILLED?*
SHE'S KEEPING THE *TRUTH* FROM ME! I CAN'T *TRUST* HER ANYMORE!
THE GODDESS KNOWS YOUR DESTINY, AMADEUS. TRUST HER AS I HAVE. SHE'S NEVER STEERED ME WRONG.
DUDE!
YOU'RE *DEAD!*

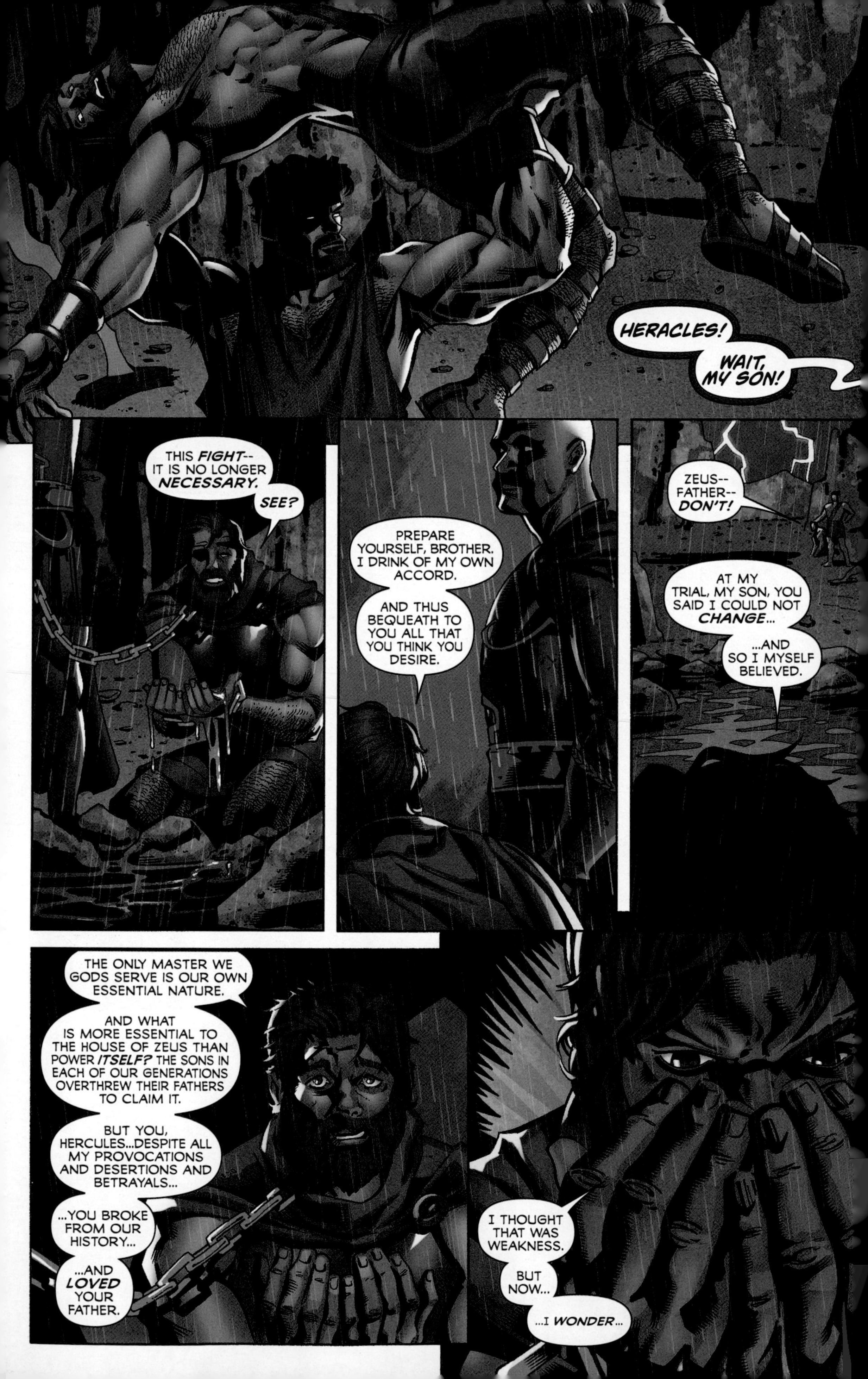
HERACLES!
WAIT, MY SON!
THIS FIGHT-- IT IS NO LONGER NECESSARY.
SEE?
PREPARE YOURSELF, BROTHER. I DRINK OF MY OWN ACCORD.
AND THUS BEQUEATH TO YOU ALL THAT YOU THINK YOU DESIRE.
ZEUS-- FATHER-- DON'T!
AT MY TRIAL, MY SON, YOU SAID I COULD NOT CHANGE...
...AND SO I MYSELF BELIEVED.
THE ONLY MASTER WE GODS SERVE IS OUR OWN ESSENTIAL NATURE.
AND WHAT IS MORE ESSENTIAL TO THE HOUSE OF ZEUS THAN POWER ITSELF? THE SONS IN EACH OF OUR GENERATIONS OVERTHREW THEIR FATHERS TO CLAIM IT.
BUT YOU, HERCULES...DESPITE ALL MY PROVOCATIONS AND DESERTIONS AND BETRAYALS...
...YOU BROKE FROM OUR HISTORY...
...AND LOVED YOUR FATHER.
I THOUGHT THAT WAS WEAKNESS.
BUT NOW...
...I WONDER...

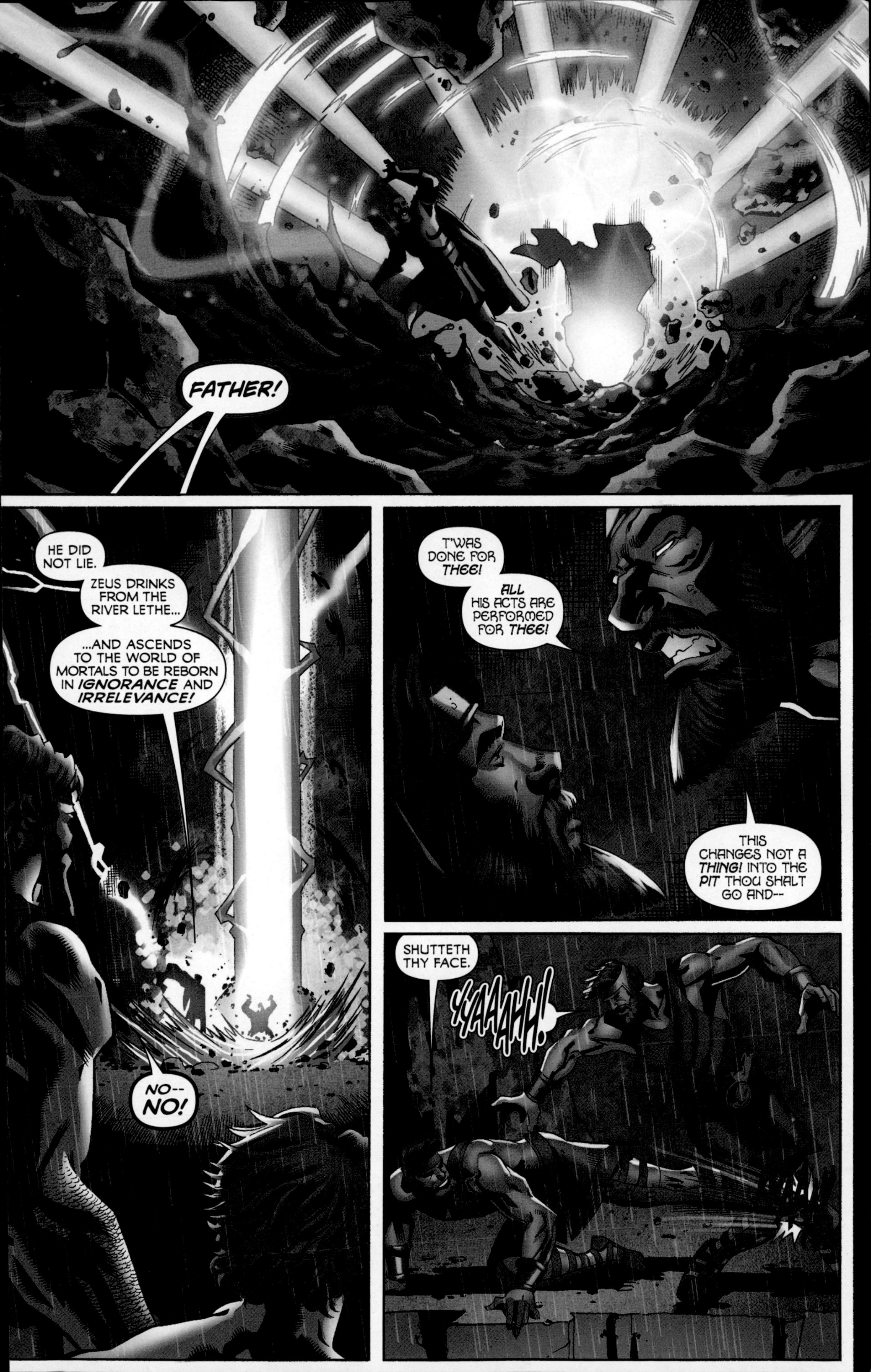
FATHER!
HE DID NOT LIE.
ZEUS DRINKS FROM THE RIVER LETHE...
...AND ASCENDS TO THE WORLD OF MORTALS TO BE REBORN IN IGNORANCE AND IRRELEVANCE!
NO-- NO!
T'WAS DONE FOR THEE!
ALL HIS ACTS ARE PERFORMED FOR THEE!
THIS CHANGES NOT A THING! INTO THE PIT THOU SHALT GO AND--
SHUTTETH THY FACE.
YAAAHH!

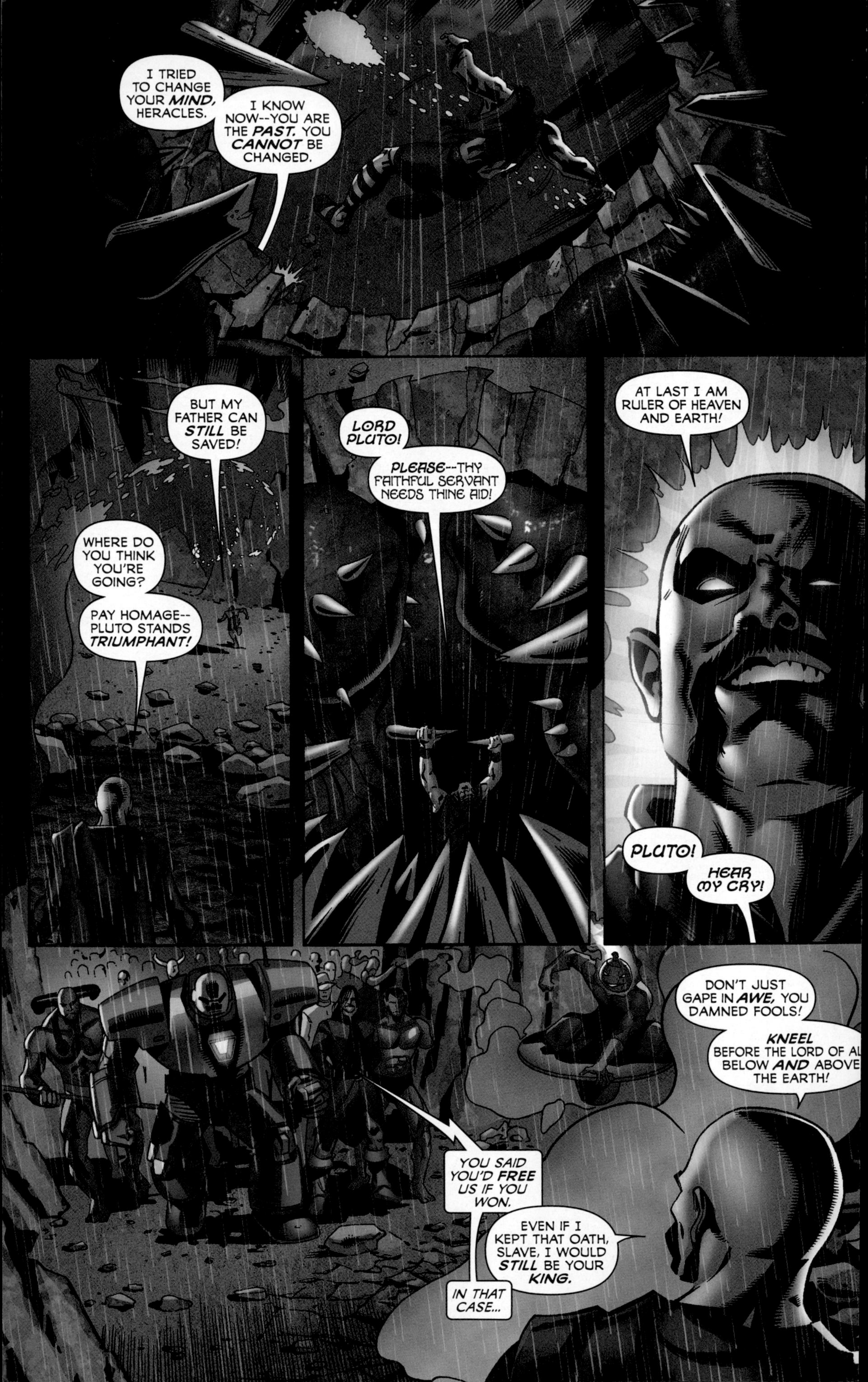
I TRIED TO CHANGE YOUR MIND, HERACLES.
I KNOW NOW--YOU ARE THE PAST. YOU CANNOT BE CHANGED.
BUT MY FATHER CAN STILL BE SAVED!
WHERE DO YOU THINK YOU'RE GOING?
PAY HOMAGE--PLUTO STANDS TRIUMPHANT!
LORD PLUTO!
PLEASE--THY FAITHFUL SERVANT NEEDS THINE AID!
AT LAST I AM RULER OF HEAVEN AND EARTH!
PLUTO!
HEAR MY CRY!
DON'T JUST GAPE IN AWE, YOU DAMNED FOOLS!
KNEEL BEFORE THE LORD OF AL BELOW AND ABOVE THE EARTH!
YOU SAID YOU'D FREE US IF YOU WON.
EVEN IF I KEPT THAT OATH, SLAVE, I WOULD STILL BE YOUR KING.
IN THAT CASE...

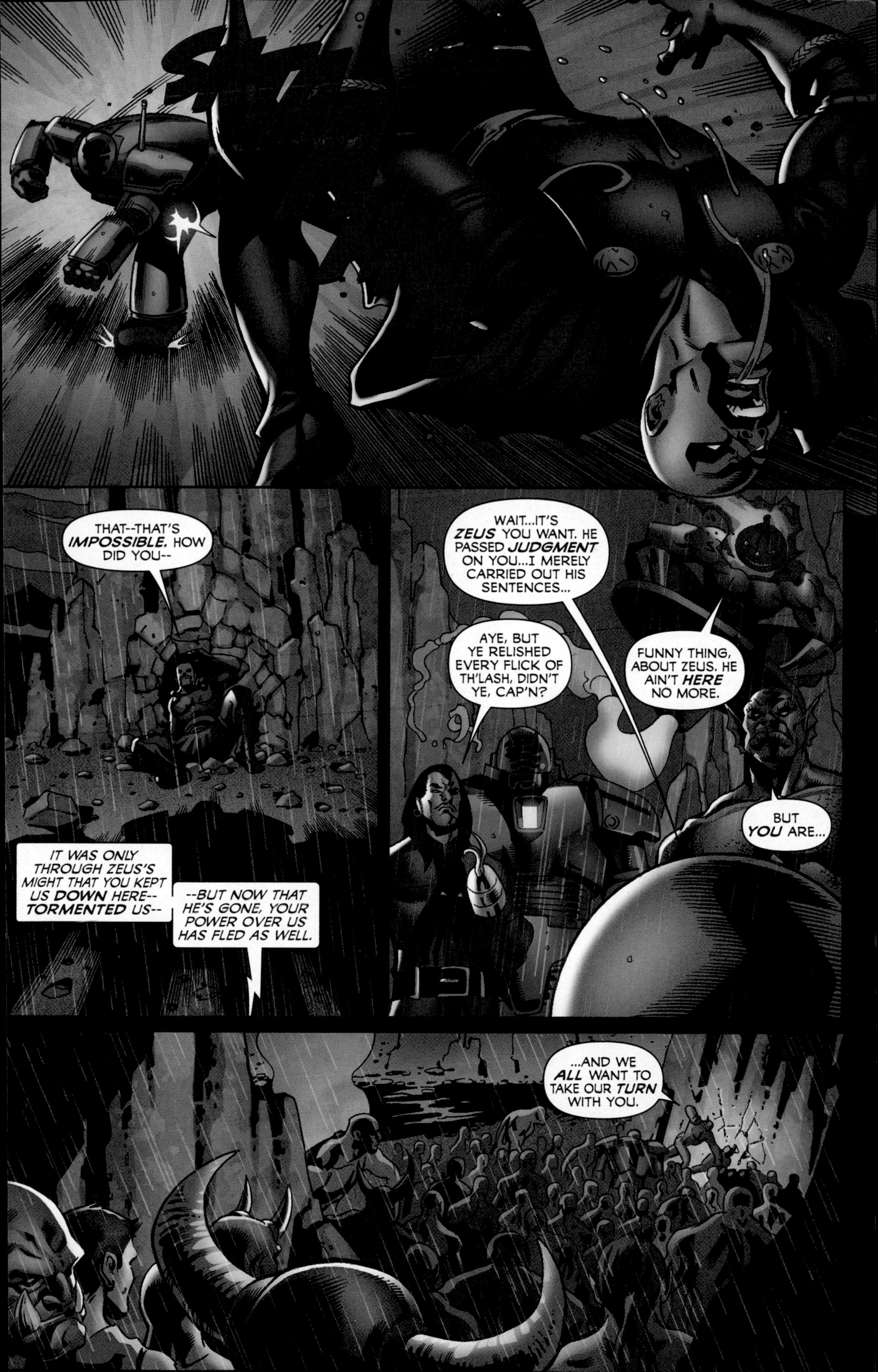

THAT--THAT'S *IMPOSSIBLE.* HOW DID YOU--
*IT WAS ONLY THROUGH ZEUS'S MIGHT THAT YOU KEPT US **DOWN** HERE-- **TORMENTED** US--*
--BUT NOW THAT HE'S GONE, YOUR POWER OVER US HAS FLED AS WELL.
WAIT...IT'S ***ZEUS*** YOU WANT. HE PASSED ***JUDGMENT*** ON YOU...I MERELY CARRIED OUT HIS SENTENCES...
AYE, BUT YE RELISHED EVERY FLICK OF TH'LASH, DIDN'T YE, CAP'N?
FUNNY THING, ABOUT ZEUS. HE AIN'T ***HERE*** NO MORE.
BUT ***YOU*** ARE...
...AND WE ***ALL*** WANT TO TAKE OUR ***TURN*** WITH YOU.

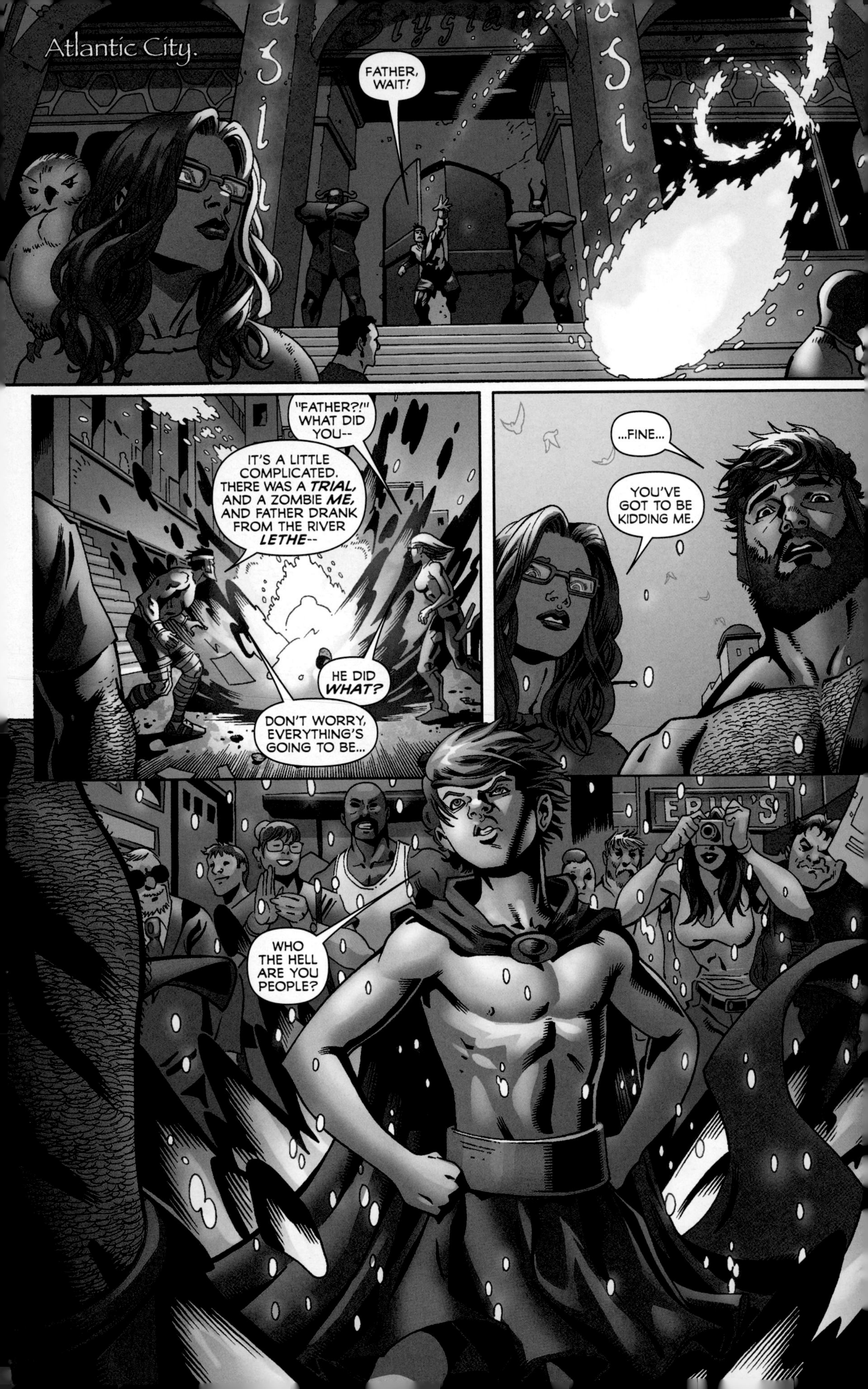
Atlantic City.
FATHER, WAIT!
"FATHER?!" WHAT DID YOU--
IT'S A LITTLE COMPLICATED. THERE WAS A TRIAL, AND A ZOMBIE ME, AND FATHER DRANK FROM THE RIVER LETHE--
HE DID WHAT?
DON'T WORRY, EVERYTHING'S GOING TO BE...
...FINE...
YOU'VE GOT TO BE KIDDING ME.
ERIN'S
WHO THE HELL ARE YOU PEOPLE?

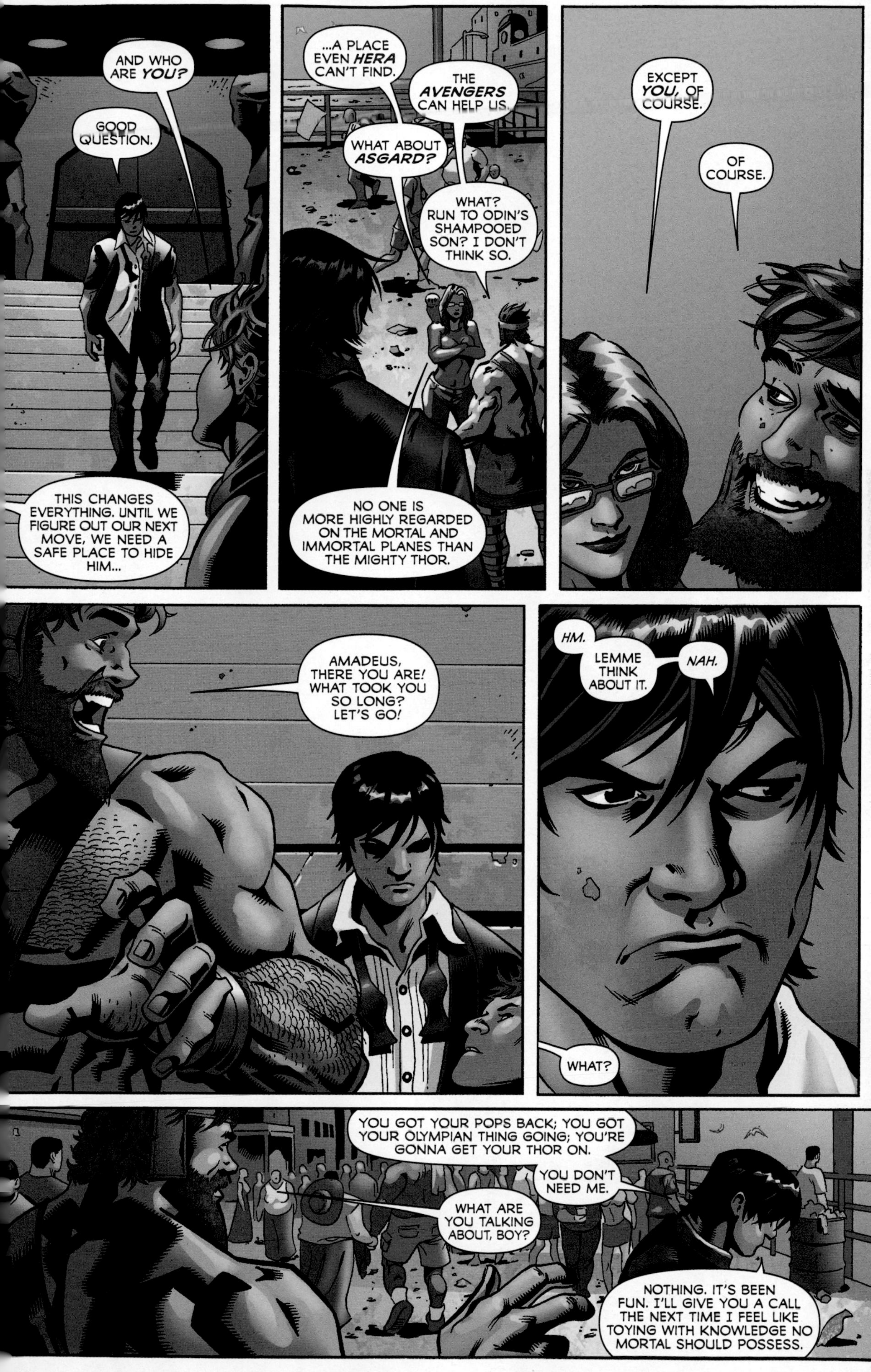
AND WHO ARE YOU?
GOOD QUESTION.
THIS CHANGES EVERYTHING. UNTIL WE FIGURE OUT OUR NEXT MOVE, WE NEED A SAFE PLACE TO HIDE HIM...
...A PLACE EVEN HERA CAN'T FIND.
THE AVENGERS CAN HELP US.
WHAT ABOUT ASGARD?
WHAT? RUN TO ODIN'S SHAMPOOED SON? I DON'T THINK SO.
NO ONE IS MORE HIGHLY REGARDED ON THE MORTAL AND IMMORTAL PLANES THAN THE MIGHTY THOR.
EXCEPT YOU, OF COURSE.
OF COURSE.
AMADEUS, THERE YOU ARE! WHAT TOOK YOU SO LONG? LET'S GO!
HM.
LEMME THINK ABOUT IT.
NAH.
WHAT?
YOU GOT YOUR POPS BACK; YOU GOT YOUR OLYMPIAN THING GOING; YOU'RE GONNA GET YOUR THOR ON.
YOU DON'T NEED ME.
WHAT ARE YOU TALKING ABOUT, BOY?
NOTHING. IT'S BEEN FUN. I'LL GIVE YOU A CALL THE NEXT TIME I FEEL LIKE TOYING WITH KNOWLEDGE NO MORTAL SHOULD POSSESS.

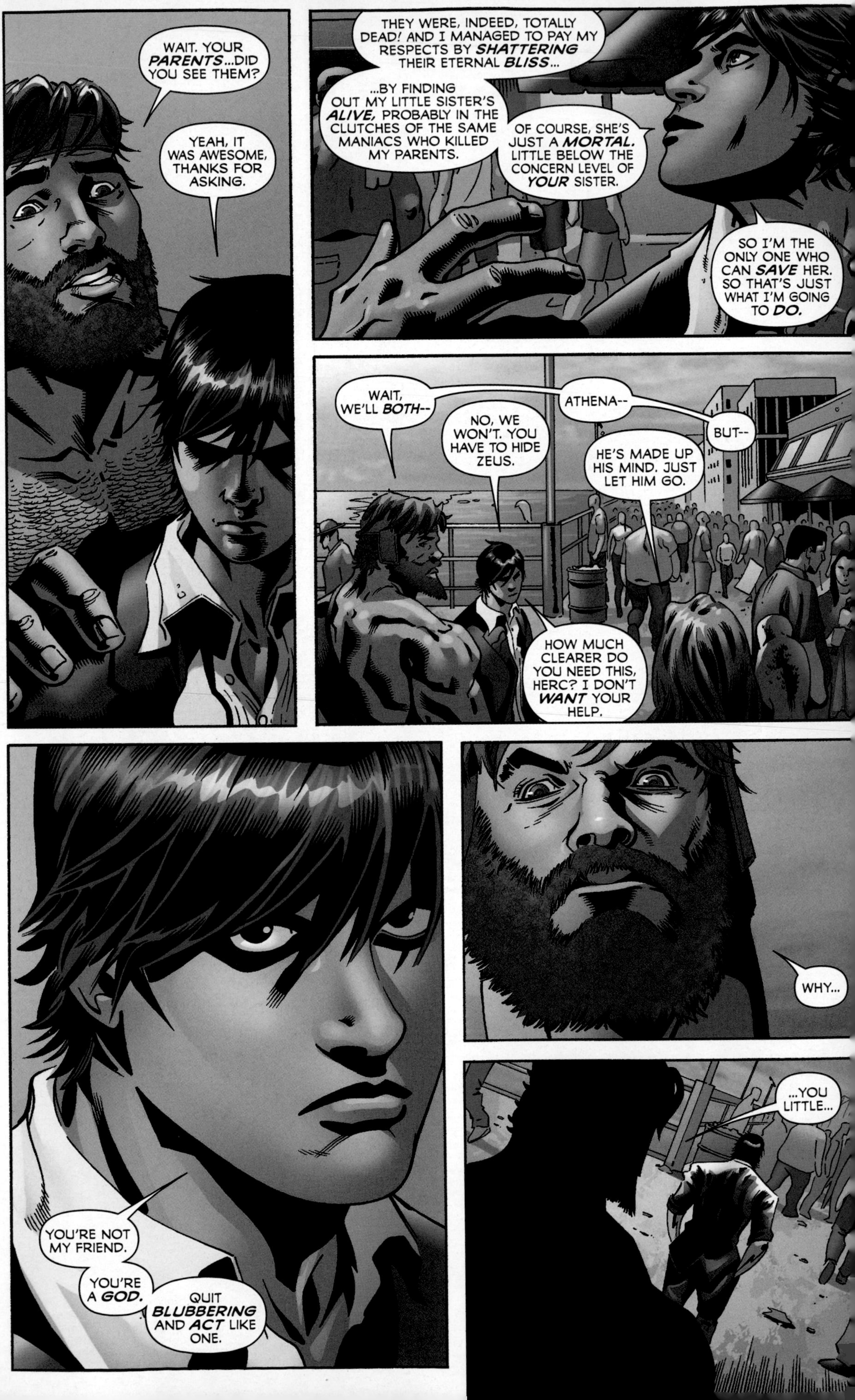
WAIT. YOUR PARENTS...DID YOU SEE THEM?
YEAH, IT WAS AWESOME, THANKS FOR ASKING.
THEY WERE, INDEED, TOTALLY DEAD! AND I MANAGED TO PAY MY RESPECTS BY SHATTERING THEIR ETERNAL BLISS...
...BY FINDING OUT MY LITTLE SISTER'S ALIVE, PROBABLY IN THE CLUTCHES OF THE SAME MANIACS WHO KILLED MY PARENTS.
OF COURSE, SHE'S JUST A MORTAL. LITTLE BELOW THE CONCERN LEVEL OF YOUR SISTER.
SO I'M THE ONLY ONE WHO CAN SAVE HER. SO THAT'S JUST WHAT I'M GOING TO DO.
WAIT, WE'LL BOTH--
NO, WE WON'T. YOU HAVE TO HIDE ZEUS.
ATHENA--
BUT--
HE'S MADE UP HIS MIND. JUST LET HIM GO.
HOW MUCH CLEARER DO YOU NEED THIS, HERC? I DON'T WANT YOUR HELP.
YOU'RE NOT MY FRIEND.
YOU'RE A GOD.
QUIT BLUBBERING AND ACT LIKE ONE.
WHY...
...YOU LITTLE...

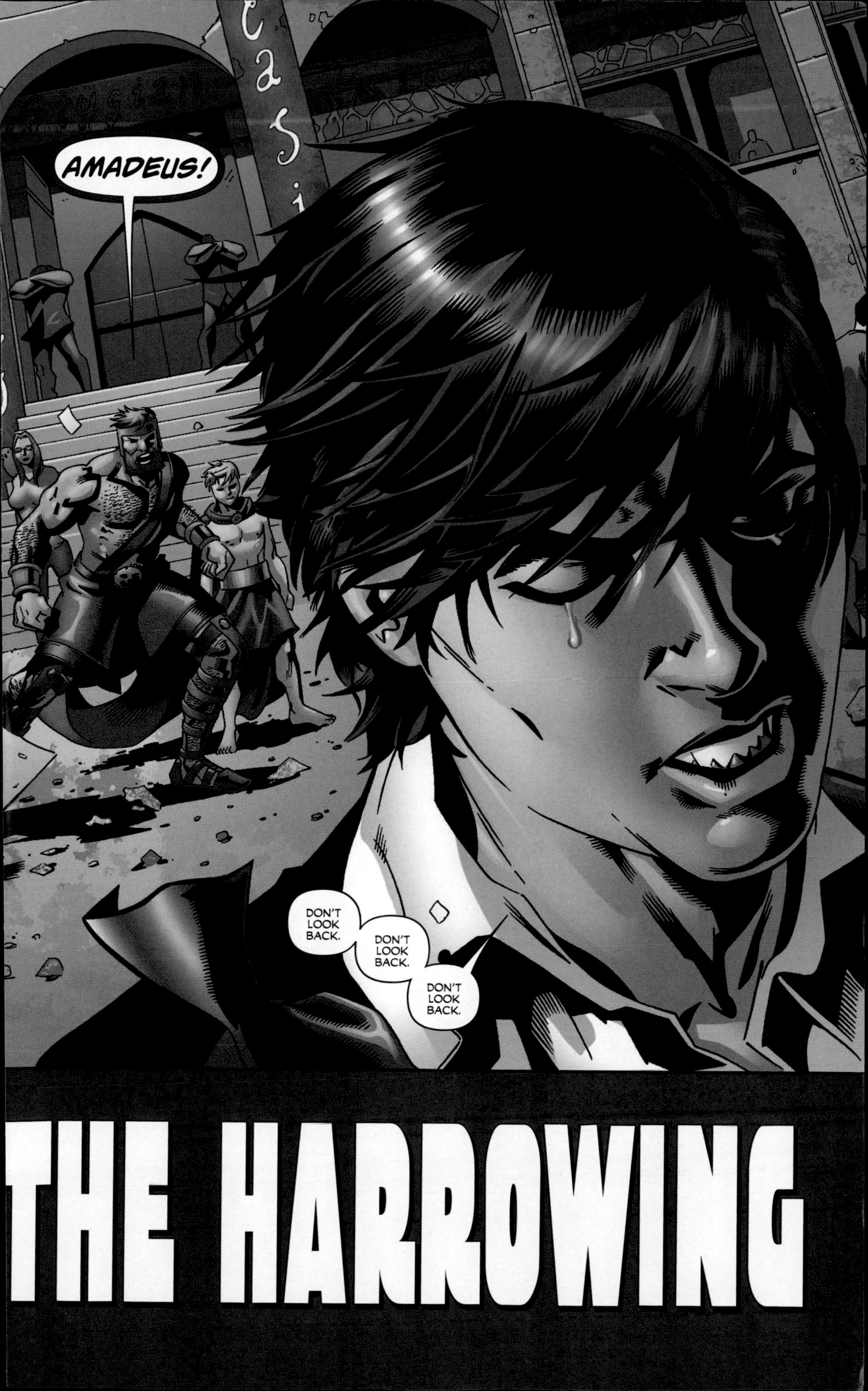
AMADEUS!
DON'T LOOK BACK.
DON'T LOOK BACK.
DON'T LOOK BACK.
THE HARROWING

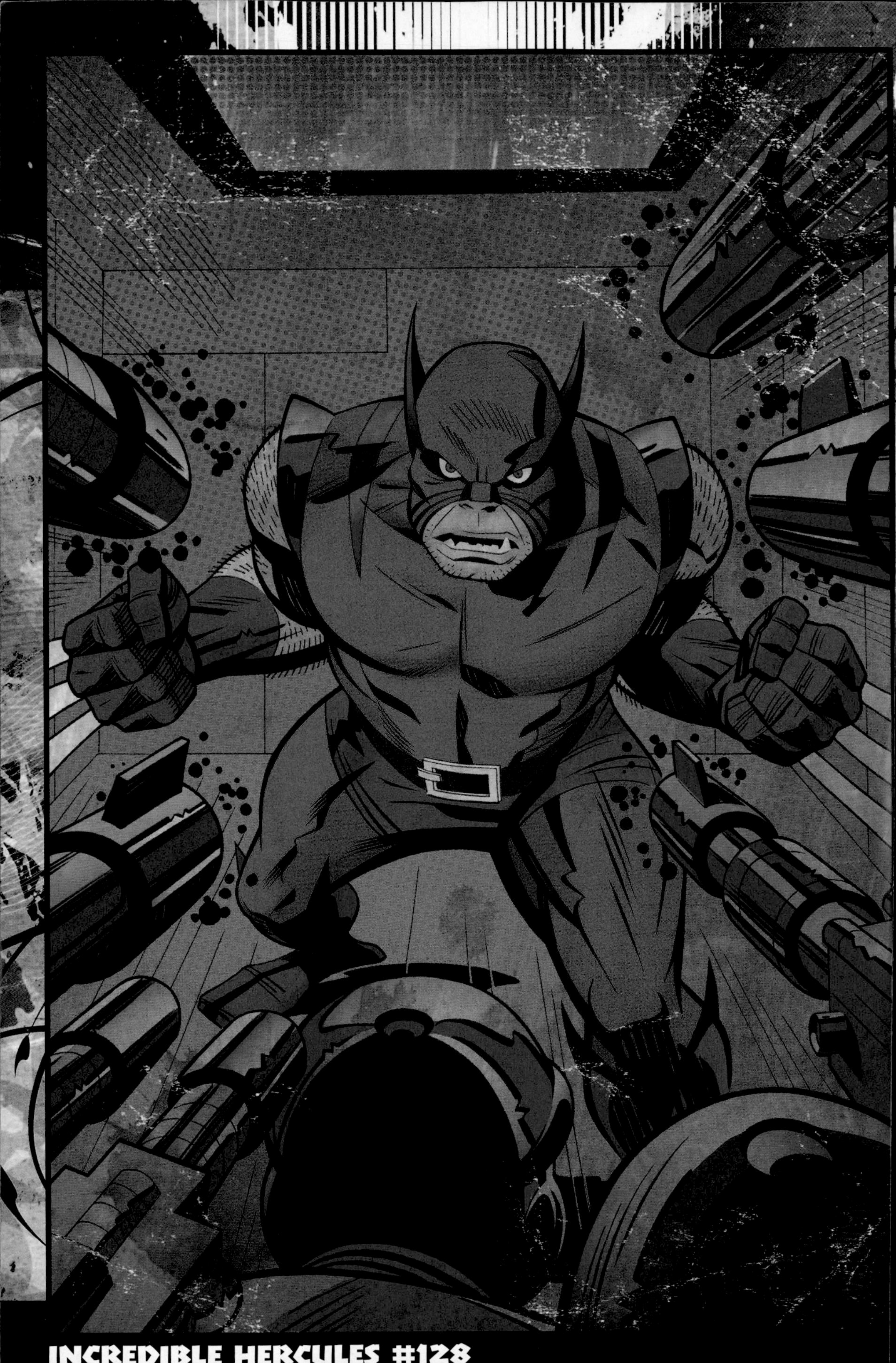

INCREDIBLE HERCULES #128

WOLVERINE ART APPRECIATION VARIANT BY DAVID WILLIAMS

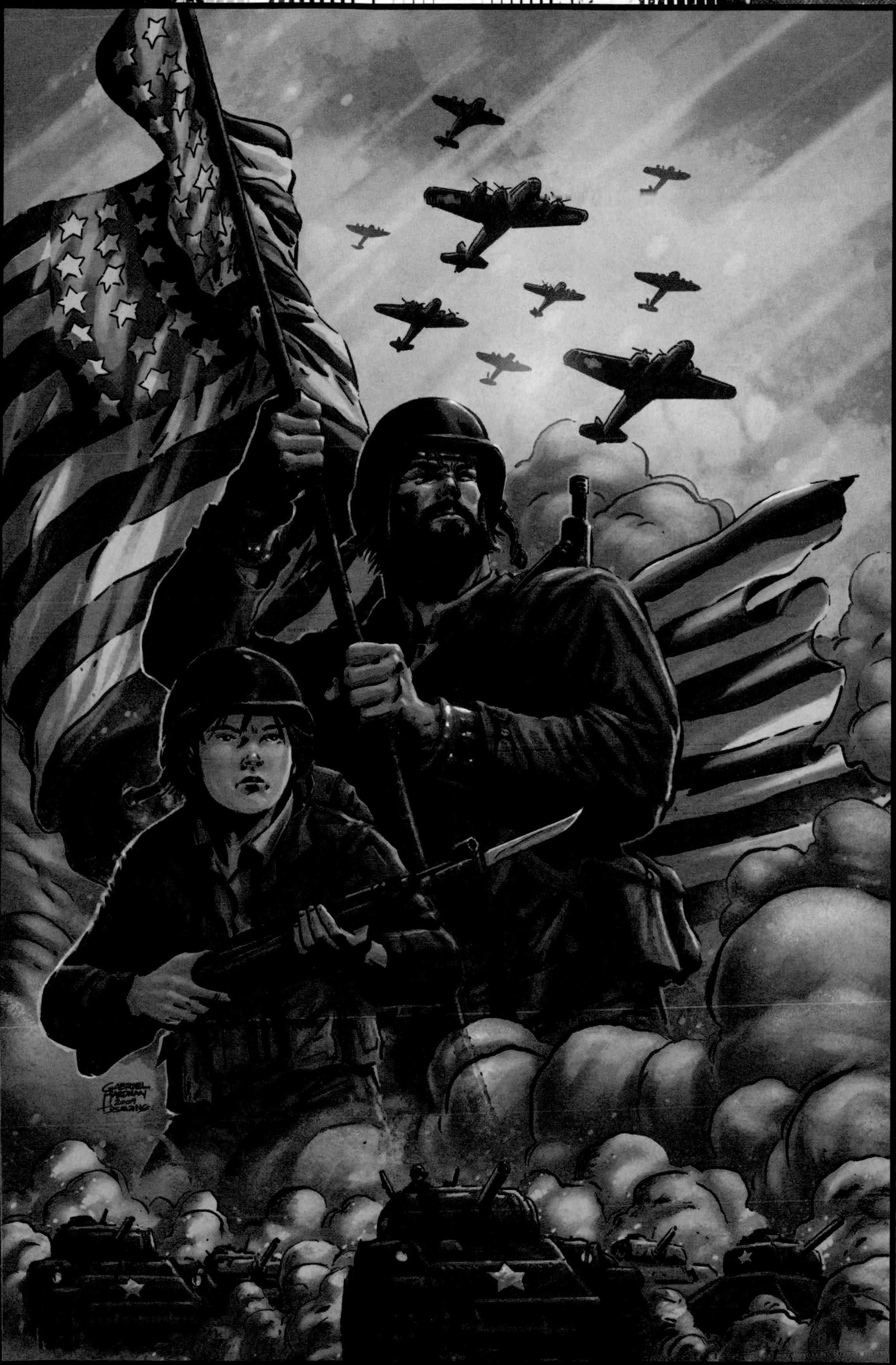

INCREDIBLE HERCULES #131
'40S DECADE VARIANT BY GABRIEL HARDMAN

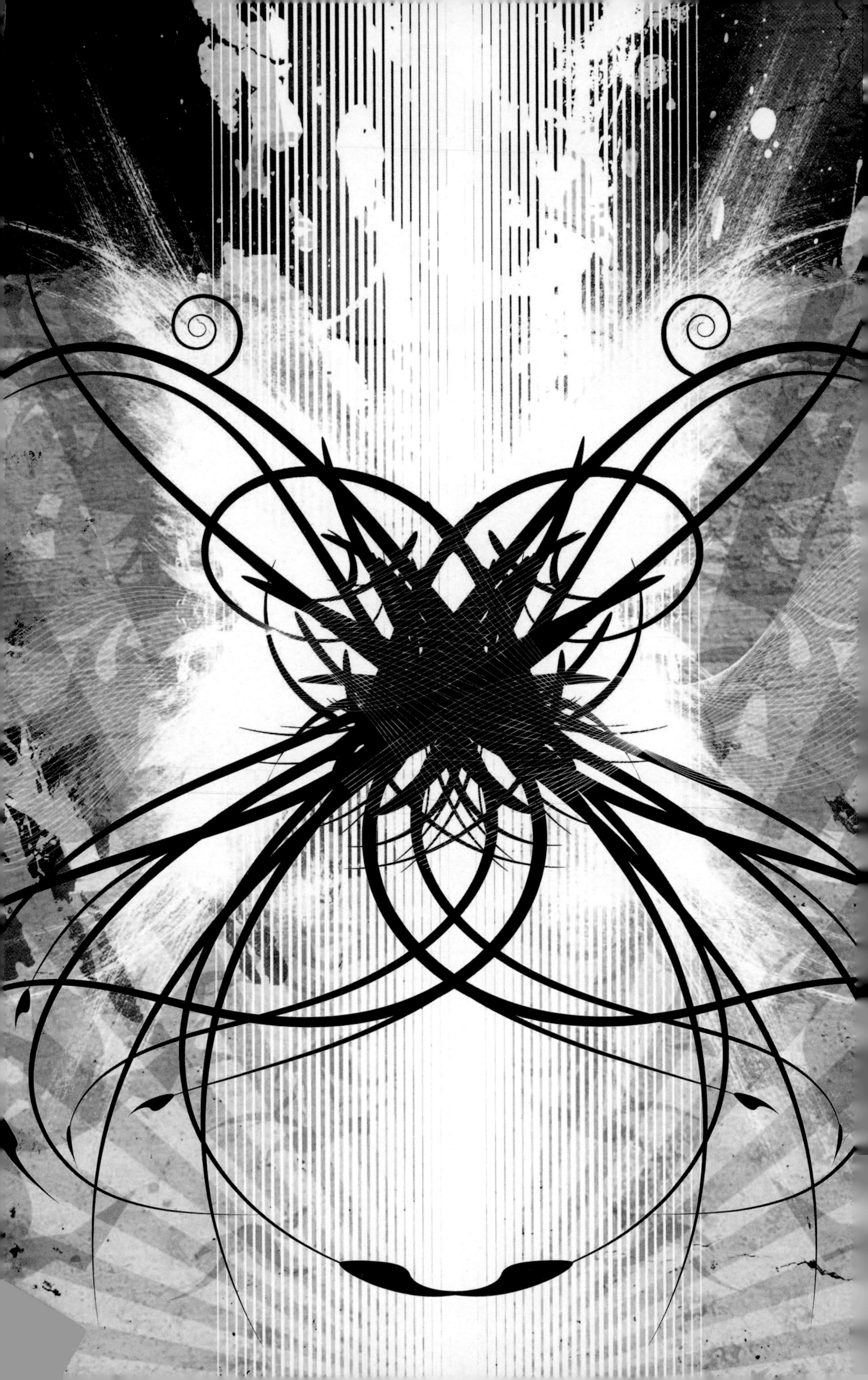